CASES IN ETHICS
AND THE CONDUCT
OF BUSINESS

JOHN R. BOATRIGHT

LOYOLA UNIVERSITY
OF CHICAGO

Prentice Hall
Englewood Cliffs, New Jersey 07632

Library of Congress Cataloging-in-Publication Data

Cases in ethics and the conduct of business / John R. Boatright.
    p. cm.
    "A companion volume to Ethics and the conduct of business"—Pref.
    ISBN 0-13-120601-X
    1. Business ethics.   2. Social responsibility of business.
I. Boatright, John Raymond, 1941– . II. Boatright, John Raymond,
1941–   Ethics and the conduct of business.
HF5387.C363   1994
174'.4—dc20
                                        94-379
                                         CIP

Acquisitions editor: Ted Bolen
Editorial/production supervision, interior design,
   and electronic page makeup: Mary Araneo
Production Coordinator: Peter Havens
Editorial assistant: Nicole Gray
Cover designer: Bruce Kenselaar

© 1995 by Prentice-Hall, Inc.
A Simon & Schuster Company
Englewood Cliffs, New Jersey 07632

All rights reserved. No part of this book may be
reproduced, in any form or by any means,
without permission in writing from the publisher.

Printed in the United States of America
10 9 8 7 6 5 4 3 2 1

ISBN 0-13-120601-X

Prentice-Hall International (UK) Limited, *London*
Prentice-Hall of Australia Pty. Limited, *Sydney*
Prentice-Hall Canada Inc., *Toronto*
Prentice-Hall Hispanoamericana, S.A., *Mexico*
Prentice-Hall of India Private Limited, *New Delhi*
Prentice-Hall of Japan, Inc., *Tokyo*
Simon & Schuster Asia Pte. Ltd., *Singapore*
Editora Prentice-Hall do Brasil, Ltda., *Rio de Janeiro*

CONTENTS

4   ETHICS IN MARKETING AND PRODUCT SAFETY 160

5   THE CORPORATION AND SOCIETY   263

PREFACE

This collection of cases is intended to be a companion volume to *Ethics and the Conduct of Business*. That book provides many examples and incidents for discussion but does not include full cases that lend themselves to the case study method. Although a certain amount of information is essential for understanding ethical problems in business, the experience of analyzing and discussing cases is also important—especially in the education of students who will assume decision-making positions in business. Either book can be used alone, but combining text and cases together is especially effective for a course in business ethics.

The cases in this book have been selected to illustrate the range of ethical issues in a standard business ethics course. Some are well-known cases that have become classics, whereas others are published here for the first time. The emphasis is on cases that pose difficult decision-making situations for members of business organizations at all levels—from personal dilemmas that might face employees in entry-level positions to issues of corporate policy that would be made on the highest levels.

A few of the cases are short, but the majority are fairly lengthy and detailed. One reason for this preference is that many brief ethical scenarios are readily available, whereas longer, "business-school type" cases are more difficult and costly to collect for student use. Another reason, however, is the need to include cases that reveal the complexity of decision making in a modern corporate setting. It is only by contact with realistic business situations that students can develop an ability to make ethical decisions, which is—or certainly ought to be—one goal of a course in business ethics.

The cases are both real and fictional. The former have the ring of authenticity, but the latter type of case is often based on actual people and events that must be disguised. Real-life case studies have the added benefit of providing useful information, but both types of cases are equally suitable for classroom discussion. In selecting cases, I have attempted to identify the best ones available, without regard for whether they are real or fictional.

In preparing this casebook, I am indebted to all of the authors of the cases used, some of whom I have worked with closely, whereas others are unknown to me. I also want to express my deep appreciation to the many authors who submitted cases for possible inclusion. Only a few of these could be accepted, but the quality of this collection was improved by the opportunity to consider a broad range of cases.

In addition, helpful assistance has been provided by G. Robert Baechle, Arthur Andersen & Co.; Jeffrey A. Barach, Tulane University; Thomas Donaldson, Georgetown University; Thomas W. Dunfee, Wharton School, University of Pennsylvania; Ronald Duska, Rosemont College; R. Edward Freeman, Darden School, University of Virginia; Al Gini, Loyola University of Chicago; Kirk O. Hanson, Stanford University and the Business Enterprise Trust; James W. Kuhn, Columbia University; John Seeger of Bentley College, editor of *Case Research Journal*; Lynn Sharp Paine, Harvard Business School; and Patricia H. Werhane, Darden School, University of Virginia. For the help of all of these, I am deeply grateful.

I would like to express my appreciation for the assistance of Ted Bolen and Nicole Gray at Prentice Hall. Finally, to Eileen Colan at John Carroll University I owe a special debt of gratitude for her invaluable service.

ETHICS IN THE WORLD OF BUSINESS

INTRODUCTION

Most of the cases in this book describe business situations in which conflicting, evenly balanced ethical considerations can lead even reasonable and well-meaning people to different conclusions about what is right or what ought to be done in particular business circumstances. Another kind of ethical dilemma occurs, however, when we attempt to act on our ethical convictions in the face of strong opposing forces, which seem, on occasion, to place limits on what morality can require of us.

In some instances, the ethical course of action involves great personal risk, including the loss of a job or damage to a career. Both Kate Simpson and Dave Stewart, in the fictional cases that bear their names, are confronted with choices that must be carefully thought through, since their futures may ride on the outcome. These cases also raise the question: Is personal interest a consideration separate from morality, or do Kate Simpson and Dave Stewart have a right to consider their own well-being—and the well-being of their families—in making a decision?

In addition, Kate Simpson and Dave Stewart must consider their role as employees in a business organization and the need to get the job done. Some contend that strict adherence to personal standards of ethics is not always possible in business and that compromises are sometimes necessary to achieve a more important good. Others hold that moral rules are different in business, so that what might be unethical in our personal lives is not always so at work. Even if this is true, Kate Simpson and Dave Stewart would still have to decide whether their own situations were exceptions in some way.

Another opposing force is the profit-making objective of a firm. Profit is not the only objective, of course; corporations exist to provide goods and services, to create jobs, and, in general, to benefit the communities where they are located. Dilemmas arise for corporate managers, however, from disagreements about the relative importance of these diverse objectives— especially in difficult times when it is not possible to achieve them all. Decision making in business is also highly formalized, primarily with a view to profitability, so that individual managers are often left wondering about how to integrate these other objectives and, indeed, whether these are legitimate objectives for the organization.

The case study titled "ABC Corporation and Employment Stabilization" describes the uncertainty of a manager who believes that stable employment is important for employee morale and ultimately for the profitability of the company. His superior, however, emphasizes financial performance alone, despite corporate documents that list benefits for employees as a major objective. A new decentralized structure gives the manager considerable leeway to interpret corporate objectives in his own way, but his job and those of an entire division depend on the success of his plan to cut costs while stabilizing employment. Afterward, the manager asks whether his concern for the "people" aspect of business is appropriate and whether it can be reconciled with other corporate objectives.

A similar situation was faced in real life by Walter Shipley, who was chairman of Chemical Bank during a critical period. The second case study in this section describes how corporate giving had long been an important part of Chemical's dedication to public service. However, competitive pressures in the banking industry now required cost-cutting across the board. Should the contributions budget be spared? Some reductions would increase the profitability of the bank in the short run, but giving had been started in the belief that the bank's long-term survival depended on a favorable community image. A recent act of Congress (the Community Reinvestment Act of 1978) created additional pressure on banks to meet community needs, so that Chemical's ability to grow also depended on favorable evaluations by government regulators. The decision that Walter Shipley had to make required him to balance a range of corporate objectives. Even if financial performance is the overriding objective, other objectives, such as service to the community, are integral to the bank's profitability.

Personal Ethical Dilemmas

Kate Simpson

Cara F. Jonassen

Kate had joined the investment banking firm of Lawton Medical Financing, Inc., just four days earlier and was in the process of adjusting to her new working pace. Although the subsidiary of a larger firm, Lawton was still quite small, numbering only 60 people nationwide. The Atlanta branch, where Kate was working, consisted of three professionals and two secretaries. It was a young and rapidly growing enterprise that had an "all hands on deck" sort of atmosphere that Kate found both exhilarating and exhausting.

The senior vice president, David Moore, was intelligent, affable, and possessed of an almost obnoxious amount of energy. He seemed to have entered the field in part because of rather altruistic feelings; the idea of financing not-for-profit hospitals appealed to him. On the other hand, he was clearly a very savvy businessman whose relationships with his lenders were the envy of all his competitors. Having spoken with him several times before she even applied for a job, Kate had the impression that David had a very strong moral sense, yet he also had the pragmatic streak necessary for success. She wondered whether there were times when that pragmatism crossed the line to expediency.

Bill Hillman, the company's vice president, was only a few years younger than David, although his boyish appearance and rather brash manner made him seem quite a bit younger. He had joined the firm some 18 months earlier and had been transferred from New York to Atlanta about four months ago. He made it clear that he had no intention of moving back to New York and seemed to spend a lot of time on contingency plans to be implemented should the firm try to transfer him from Atlanta.

While David could analyze the numbers involved in a deal very quickly, he really enjoyed coming out with new approaches to financing and actually getting people to sit down and agree to his plans. Bill did not have the same diplomatic abilities, but he liked to make the numbers work and was actively involved in the solicitation of new business.

Kate, as the new associate, had ostensibly been assigned to do a massive spreadsheet on the details of all the deals done in hospital financing over the past two years. It was already becoming apparent, however, that she was really supposed to be available to help out in whatever capacity

This case was prepared by Cara F. Jonassen, M.B.A. candidate, Graduate School of Business, Stanford University, as a basis for class discussion rather than to illustrate either effective or ineffective handling of an administrative situation. Copyright © 1979 by Cara F. Jonassen.

was needed. At one moment she might be researching some legislation for David, at the next she could be running an amortization schedule for Bill. Both of the men were anxious to teach her, and she was looking forward to learning as much as possible before returning to graduate business school in six months.

This morning had provided a new source of excitement. She would be making her first business trip the next day. As David had explained it, they were to help a hospital client in Nashville choose a consultant to do the feasibility study for the planned takeover of another facility. There were to be four consultants presenting proposals; she and David were to hear the presentations and summarize the differences among the proposals to the hospital's board of directors.

She had spent all morning poring over the three proposals they had received thus far. Of those three, the one by Roberts and Company had emerged as the best study for the least amount of money. She supposed that part of their job would be to help the administrator of the hospital keep the board of directors from automatically choosing the least expensive study; each of the three fees quoted probably far exceeded the annual salary of any of the board members. It was obvious that a study would never have been approved had it not been required for the official Certificate of Need, which itself was required for the acquisition.

Kate was annoyed when she glanced up and realized that it was already 3 P.M. Rice, Mitchell & Co., the fourth consulting firm, had promised her a copy of its proposal by 2:30 that afternoon. David would be back in the office at 4:30, expecting her to have finished her part of the assessment. When she called her secretary to see whether the proposal had arrived, she discovered that Bill, who she thought was not involved in this project, was on the phone with Bob Smythe, his counterpart at Rice, Mitchell, at that very moment. As she wandered over to Bill's office to find out what was going on, she felt a little annoyed since Smythe knew perfectly well from their conversation that morning that the preliminary work on this project was her responsibility.

Bill was about to hang up the phone as she entered. "Fine, Bob. You owe me one, but don't worry about it. Good luck getting the thing cranked out by morning."

She watched Bill slide the Roberts and Company proposal into a crisp envelope with Lawton Medical Financing emblazoned across the flap. "Those guys at Rice really like to run it down to the wire," he said. "Bob's just starting on the Nashville proposal. I told him we'd let him glance at Roberts's version of the thing. Why don't you run it upstairs for him? You can wait and make sure we get it back."

As she headed for the elevator, Kate was furious with Bill for having placed her in this situation. She had only a few moments to decide what she should do.

DAVE STEWART

Stephen B. Cook

On a Sunday in mid-April 1983, Dave Stewart, a second-year leasing agent for Holmes Company, was jogging along the tree-lined suburban streets of Washington, D.C. The large houses with well-landscaped yards that he passed reminded him of how much might be at stake when he met with his boss, Tom Kane, the next day: his two years' progress with the company, his reputation, his family, his financial solvency, his future.

Before obtaining an M.B.A., Dave had received a B.S. in mechanical engineering from a midwestern university, as well as several awards for his academic and service records. In addition to his job, Dave was involved in many extracurricular activities, from athletics to business and social clubs.

When Dave joined Holmes Company at age 26 in July 1981 after graduate business school, he had visions of a glamorous job in real estate and a position as partner with the firm within three years. Changes in company policy, conflicts in the office, and several incidents of questionable business ethics had left him disillusioned. Tomorrow's luncheon with Tom Kane had been arranged by Dave to discuss conflicts in the office. Dave thought it might turn into more than that, and he had only a few hours to make some important decisions, not only about what he would say to Tom the next day, but also what action he should take regarding his career with Holmes.

HOLMES COMPANY

Holmes Company, a commercial real estate development and investment firm, was involved in financing, marketing, and managing office buildings, industrial buildings, and shopping centers, as well as commercial land development and construction. Founded in 1948, it presently boasted 45 offices and 550 employees in several countries, which placed it among the largest real estate firms in the world.

Holmes's success could be partially attributed to its "bottom-up" organizational structure, which emphasized local office autonomy with decentralized responsibility and profit motivation. Company growth followed a common principle of duplication, whereby a given founding office would establish one or more satellite offices, each of which would forfeit a

This case was prepared by Stephen B. Cook, Research Assistant, under the supervision of Lynn Sharp Paine, Visiting Assistant Professor, and Henry W. Tulloch, Executive Director, Olsson Center for Applied Ethics. Copyright ©1984 by University of Virginia, Darden Graduate Business School Foundation, Charlottesville, VA. All rights reserved.

percentage of its profit to the founding office but otherwise remain autonomous. These satellite offices, in turn, could become founding offices from which other satellite offices were spawned. Ultimately, any given office would pass on to its founding office a percentage of its own profits as well as a percentage of profits it received from its satellite offices. For example, an office might end up with 50 percent of its own profits, 25 percent of total profits from its satellite offices, 12 1/2 percent of total profits from its satellites' satellites, and so forth. Communication between offices and the policy-making ten-member managing board in Boston was largely of a financial nature.

The career path for a Holmes employee between the entry-level position of leasing agent and the top position of managing partner was remarkably short; in fact, only two positions—project manager and partner in the firm— separated the two. Advancement in a given office was largely controlled by the managing partner, with little influence from Boston headquarters.

During the time that Dave had been employed at Holmes, the company had made three changes in its policy on promotion. Ten months after Dave joined the company, it had instituted a mandatory three-year employment period before partnership. Two or three months later, the company decided that a new partner's equity was to be vested at a rate of 20 percent per year for five years, rather than 100 percent vested at once. This second policy change was in response to several occasions on which recently appointed partners had cashed in their equity immediately after receiving it and left the company. Eighteen months into Dave's tenure with Holmes, the company added a mandatory two-year position—project manager— between leasing agent and partner on the career path. These policy changes were not written down and circulated among Holmes employees, but were transmitted verbally.

The last two policy changes had angered company leasing agents, particularly those on the verge of becoming partners, who suddenly found themselves effectively pushed back two years on the promotional ladder. A fair number of top-quality leasing agents had left the company out of disgust. Still, 80 percent of the M.B.A.s that had been recruited over the period 1973–1983 were still with the company.

THE WASHINGTON OFFICE

Among those working with Dave in the Washington office were leasing agent Greg Bailey, a 1980 M.B.A. from the same school as Dave, and Kane, the managing partner. Since Dave had joined the company, two employees had come and gone—one secretary and one leasing agent. Dave suspected that two other secretaries were interviewing seriously for other jobs.

Dave's boss Tom had graduated from a mid-Atlantic technical school with a B.S. in industrial engineering and from a well-known Eastern graduate business school with Highest Distinction. Tom was one of the most profitable of the Holmes partners; as a partner in every building he constructed in Washington, he received additional income based on the profit and loss of those buildings. Tom had been with Holmes since 1973; he had moved to Washington to open an office in 1979 following six years in the western United States.

Dave viewed Tom as a very intelligent manager from a financial perspective but a poor manager in his dealings with employees and clients. Tom usually took his desire for profit to extremes; he never left a penny on the table for the sake of goodwill. Dave recalled one time around Labor Day 1982, when one of Tom's leased buildings was flooded. Some of the basement tenants thought that the landlord should pay for the installation of new carpet, because the floor drains had become clogged and prevented the water from escaping. It wouldn't have cost the office much to replace the water-drenched carpet, but Tom haggled with the tenants for weeks and never budged on the issue.

Dave shared the responsibility for construction, leasing, and management of 12 new buildings and 20 older buildings with Greg. He was the same age as Dave and had been a leasing agent with Holmes a full year before Dave arrived. Prior to his employment at Holmes, Greg's experience had been limited to a summer of waitering and a little over a year in banking. Dave had had two years' experience as a professional fund-raiser, in addition to experience as financial analyst for a private real estate development firm prior to joining the Washington office.

When Dave arrived at Holmes, Tom had told him that teamwork and trust were important parts of his job. In response, Dave had made several attempts to establish a trusting, congenial relationship with Greg. He met Greg's clients on numerous occasions when Greg was unable to make an appointment; he even made an effort to get to know Greg socially, inviting him and his girlfriend over for dinner. Greg's reactions ranged from unresponsive to outwardly aggressive. Dave was particularly surprised because he had been informed through a mutual acquaintance at business school that Greg had a good deal of respect for him. Dave guessed that Greg was irked at having to share business with him and that he viewed Dave as a threat, because Dave had shown promise as a leasing agent quite early. (Dave had signed his first lease after only six weeks on the job.)

As Dave's relationship with Greg deteriorated, so did the general atmosphere in the office. There was no straightforward communication. No directions were set forth by Tom; no lines were drawn. Dave felt he was constantly "walking on eggshells" around fellow workers. He took every opportunity to get out of the office. When he left, he always locked his desk drawers for fear of losing good leads to another leasing agent. An atmosphere of distrust and competition prevailed, in which one used anything one could to accomplish what one wanted to accomplish. Dave felt sorry for the secretaries, whom he viewed as "the real victims of the intensity." The secretaries often got caught in the middle between two leasing agents, each trying quietly to withhold information from the other for the sake of self-protection or self-advancement.

DAVE'S JOB AT THE WASHINGTON OFFICE

Dave's gradual disillusionment with the situation at Holmes began quite early. In the job interview, Tom had emphasized the partnership aspect of the job. They never really talked about what Dave would actually be doing. Dave didn't ask; it seemed to him to be one of those things you just don't do (for fear of hurting your chances of getting the job). The job turned out to be a lot less glamorous than Dave had expected. On a typical day, he would drive to the warehousing district and park in the safest spot he could find. Then he'd walk from company to company, asking each if it needed leasing space and if anyone knew other companies needing space. Dave followed up every lead; there was tremendous pressure to sell space. Maybe one in ten needed space; one in 20 needed a new building. Dave changed his dress slightly to accommodate different situations, but he always tried to appear serious and professional.

To Dave, leasing was a "negative-input" job. He had discovered that "when everything is going right, you never hear anything from your tenants; when something goes wrong, they start bitching." Nonetheless, he was more upset with the lack of warning about the nature of the job than he was about the job itself. Dave felt that the key ingredient for a successful leasing agent was tenacity more than anything else. A good agent would keep coming back even when someone else might have given up. Reputation was also important; so much of the real estate business was done verbally on a handshake. Lots of money could pass hands and yet nothing was written down.

During Dave's first year at Holmes, he was asked by Tom on several occasions to respond to clients in ways that made Dave feel very uncomfortable. He remembered a typical example when Tom instructed him to tell a client (a small branch of a $200 million company) as late as May 15 that construction of a building it was supposed to move into was on schedule for a July 1 occupancy. Construction had not even begun, and delay was inevitable. Dave reluctantly complied with Tom's wishes.

THE D.B. SNOW SITUATION

Dave's problems had only recently been compounded by a particularly troublesome situation involving a major international corporation—D.B. Snow—relocating its North American engineering division to the Washington, D.C. area. Three disturbing events related to this relocation had occurred within the last two weeks, and Dave had been the leasing agent and primary contact with the company in the negotiations.

The first problem arose in connection with the lease agreement between Holmes and D.B. Snow. At the time that Snow first accepted a location offered by the Washington office, one of the buildings it hoped to occupy was nothing but a shell. Under the agreement, Holmes was to have the insides of the building—including interior walls, carpeting, plumbing, and lighting—completed according to Snow's specifications. In addition, Holmes was to finance the construction and amortize this considerable expense over a ten-year period. In return, Snow agreed to lease the building for a period of ten years at a rate of $600,000 per year, with the option to buy out Holmes at the end of five years.

Snow and Dave agreed that the buy-out would equal the construction expenses incurred by Holmes that had not been amortized at the end of the five-year period. Dave was in charge of presenting the buy-out amount to Snow. According to real estate custom, this amount would most likely be undocumented and unquestioned, as a matter of trust.

Tom calculated that the actual amount of unamortized expenses would be $600,000, assuming a 16 percent annual rate on the bank loan to be taken out by Holmes for construction. He was not pleased, however, with the idea that Snow might buy out of the $600,000 annual lease after five years. As a gamble for greater profit under the buy-out option, Tom told Dave to present $900,000 as the actual unamortized expense figure to Snow. Dave knew that even Tom's $600,000 calculation was high, because it assumed a 16 percent interest rate at a time when money was readily available at 12 percent. If, however, he had been told to describe the $900,000 as the unamortized expenses plus an additional penalty for taking the buy-out option, he wouldn't have been bothered; that at least would have been an honest statement, even if the penalty itself was too high. Only with great reluctance, therefore, did Dave give Snow the $900,000 buy-out price as Holmes's actual unamortized expenses. It was never questioned.

The second problem with the Snow relocation involved a separate signed agreement between the two parties—an agreement that required a piece of land adjacent to the property leased by Snow to be reserved for a period of three years. Snow hoped to build an administration building on this adjacent land in the near future and had chosen the Holmes location over alternatives partly because of this land's future availability. At the time this agreement was signed, both Dave and D.B. Snow believed that enough land was available for the administrative building. As Dave was in the early stages of designing an engineering building for Snow on the land next to that which had been reserved for the administrative building, however, he discovered that the combination of a sewer easement, a floodplain, and the size of the building he was designing severely limited the amount of land that would be available for the future administration building. When Dave informed Tom about the problem he had discovered, Tom told him to keep quiet about it and act as though nothing were wrong. Dave reluctantly acquiesced and prepared drawings for Snow which included the administration building that could never be built.

A third problem arose in connection with the commission due Smithson-Palmer, Inc., broker for Snow in its relocation to Washington. Smithson-Palmer's standard commission on a leasing deal was 4 percent of the amount specified in the lease agreement for the full term of the lease. Under the Snow agreement, Holmes, the lessor, would receive $600,000 annually for ten years, or a total of $6,000,000, of which Smithson-Palmer would be due 4 percent, or $240,000. The amount due Smithson-Palmer was standard unless otherwise agreed in writing before the deal was signed. Smithson-Palmer made it clear to Dave verbally that it expected 4 percent on the ten-year lease term. Dave relayed this message to Tom before the lease was signed. Several weeks after the lease was signed, Tom told Dave to go back to Smithson-Palmer with the news that Holmes would pay Smithson-Palmer only half its expected commission, or $120,000, because Snow had the option to buy out after the fifth year of the lease term. Tom's motive was simply to save Holmes $120,000. Dave told Tom that his proposal contradicted the deal with Smithson-Palmer; Tom replied that he was doing it for "the betterment of the company."

Dave was particularly concerned about the commission problem because, should he carry out Tom's instructions, he risked the possibility of doing damage to his reputation as an individual within the brokerage community, and with Smithson-Palmer in particular. When Dave finally brought up the question of ethics with Tom apropos the Snow situation, Tom told him that, if he didn't want to follow the instructions, Greg would. Dave was really beginning to wonder whether he was naive to think that business should be conducted on a totally open, ethical basis. He viewed himself as almost compulsively honest, often to his own detriment. If he had to absorb a personal financial setback in the interest of sticking to the letter of a bargain with a client, he thought he would do so without hesitation. He also believed that the short-run loss would be returned fivefold in the long run on the basis of his reputation for fair business conduct.

Dave wasn't sure whether conduct in Tom's office was typical of real estate in general or of Holmes or just the Washington office. He spoke with two people connected with Holmes outside his immediate office in an effort to discover what their experience had been. A friend and fellow leasing agent in another Holmes office said that his situation was vastly different; business was conducted in an honest manner, and communication in the office was open and relaxed. The friend also felt that his own situation was far more common than Dave's. This feeling was confirmed by Dave's second contact—a friend who worked as an auditor within the Holmes organization and had occasion to visit many company offices around the country. He had visited Dave's office and felt that the uncomfortably tense atmosphere created there by both the personal conflicts and the questionable business activity was unusual.

THE DECISION

Three weeks had passed since the D.B. Snow problems had arisen. Dave had presented the inflated $900,000 unamortized expense figure to Snow, and thus far had remained quiet on the issue of the adjacent land requirement—both requests of Tom. He had not yet approached Smithson-Palmer with the change in the commission amount.

His personal situation complicated matters: He still had school debts to pay off; his savings account held the equivalent of a month's salary; his wife had just had their first child. When he arrived in Washington, he had had $50.00 in his pocket and was driving a $200.00 car; now, 21 months later, he was earning close to $50,000 in salary and commission and just beginning to turn the corner financially.

Many thoughts raced through Dave's mind as he contemplated his luncheon with Tom the following day. Those episodes related to D.B. Snow really bothered him; he hadn't slept well lately. Should he tell Snow the whole story? That might satisfy his own personal sense of right and wrong, but it would ruin his career with Holmes. Maybe he should get out of real estate or just leave Holmes quietly, with no big uproar over the ethics business. Was he blowing the whole thing way out of proportion? He had grown up on a farm where everyone left keys in the car overnight; maybe his personal code of ethics was totally abnormal. In New York no one would think twice about business ethics, he thought; it was all "buyer beware." He had $5,000 in commissions to gain from this latest deal. Could he afford to sacrifice that money? Wasn't company loyalty an admirable trait? Greg was certainly a company man. But Dave's conflict with Greg was worse than ever. Maybe if his problems with Greg were resolved somehow, he could deal with everything else. Maybe he should stand up to Tom—tell him everything on his mind. Tom might respect him for that. Things might work out. Why take a defeatist's attitude?

ETHICS AND CORPORATE OBJECTIVES

ABC Corporation and Employment Stabilization

Henry W. Tulloch

In 1978 the Special Products Division (SPD) of a Fortune 500 manufacturer, ABC Corporation, was faced with a rapidly declining sales volume that was substantially below budget. Pressure by top management to meet the bud-

This case was prepared by Henry W. Tulloch in connection with Professor Louis T. Rader for the Olsson Center for Applied Ethics. Copyright © 1981 by University of Virginia, Darden Graduate Business School Foundation, Charlottesville, VA. All rights reserved.

geted profit goal was growing very intense. Ray Lewis, general manager of SPD, a newly established division in a new plant, strongly believed that providing "steady work" for employees, however, should be a major goal of any business executive.

NATURE OF SPD

SPD contained 12 product groups in industrial electronics, no one of which represented over 18% of the total division's volume. Products of SPD did not stay fixed in design for any significant length of time. Bringing out new products was required so often and so rapidly that planned costs were rarely attained on the first few orders. New circuits and techniques had heavy starting costs that were barely overcome before new specifications in the rapidly changing electronics field were being demanded by customers.

These types of problems, inherent in the product lines of the division, had not been acute when sales volume was rapidly increasing. In fact, the wide differences in market applications of the many lines, both military and commercial, had resulted in an employment situation where dips in any one or a few lines had usually been offset by increases in others. A wage structure with broad job classifications made it possible to move factory operators from one job to another without much dissatisfaction or delay. The knowledge by operators that every effort was being made to keep them working removed any incentive on their part to slow down when they saw that work in their product areas was declining.

The wide diversity of SPD's products and the need for plans to concentrate on profitable items had concerned Mr. Lewis for some time. At one point he had received a memo from his manager of Marketing Planning, Charley Haney, as follows:

> I believe we should concentrate on our business as of today, the short range, to the point of establishing a good, firm foundation of products, policies, methods, and profits. We may be doing too much thinking of the long range and the bright future of some of our more sensational product lines. We need to decide what business we want now, and go after it, declining the marginal and novel. We need to standardize our products, our marketing policies and customers, our engineering designs and processes, and our manufacturing methods and functions.

In a follow-up meeting with his functional managers in December, Mr. Lewis said:

> If you make money in this company, you're a hero. If not, you're a bum. This is the first objective. The word from on top is that we must double our volume in 5 years, make 7% profit, and 15% return on investment. We expect our people to work hard, but I also want them to have steady jobs. And what about Haney's memo on planning this business?

COMPANY DECENTRALIZATION

While Mr. Lewis and his staff at SPD were wrestling with these problems of declining sales volume, business planning, and employment stability, the ABC Corporation was feeling its way to decentralizing the organization and management of the company. The new management philosophy was being implemented through a Statement of Objectives (Exhibit 1) and the introduction of a concept of key results to be the basis for measurement of each decentralized division's performance. Most germane to Mr. Lewis's immediate problems was the statement that a company objective was "to provide good jobs, wages, working conditions, opportunities for advancement, and the stablest possible employment." Among the measurements of division performance were profitability, productivity, and employee attitudes. Mr. Lewis believed that success in these measurements depended heavily on stable employment, a thought not especially exciting to either those on his staff such as Charley Haney nor to his boss, George Brandon, in New York.

During the next several weeks, in his regular staff meetings to forecast orders, shipments, and income for the next quarter and the total year, Mr. Lewis focused attention on the "people" aspect of the business as well as the financial picture. He was not at all sure that this would be considered the proper focus by Mr. Brandon, who went strictly by "the numbers" regardless of the "fancy talk" in company pamphlets. Mr. Lewis believed, however, that if he could hold his organization together while taking the heat himself for any temporary decline in net income, it would be in the best long-range interest of both the company and the division. He also thought that the new decentralization philosophy of the company left him some freedom to set his own course of how to operate—as long as he could "sell" Mr. Brandon that any deviation from the budgeted goal of net income was "temporary."

THE 1979 DECLINE

Ray Lewis's strategy became more and more difficult to maintain. Sales volume continued to decline each month below the budgeted level as substantial cancellations occurred in both government and commercial orders. Also, more complex engineering requirements increased engineering costs per dollar of sales to a higher level than had previously been considered normal for the business. The nature of design and manufacturing work was characterized by even greater variety of products, low quantities per order, and intermittent runs, resulting in unstable labor requirements in several areas of the shop. Customers were demanding shorter delivery times, and competitors were not only meeting those demands but also outbidding SPD on price. Daily telephone calls by Mr. Brandon were becoming more and more heated. Mr. Brandon was threatening to "come down to the plant and run the business myself." Mr. Lewis was getting the message loud and clear that, regardless of employment, profitability was the only thing that mattered to his boss.

Nevertheless, he kept his tensions to himself while he directed his staff to increase the cost-reduction goal, have a plantwide campaign to eliminate waste, eliminate all "dead wood," and still maintain employment as steady as possible.

The stabilization program devised by his staff took the following directions:

1. With each forecasted reduction in direct-labor requirements in a particular product line, manufacturing supervision evaluated with marketing the extent of the dip before making plans for adjustments in hours of work.
2. "Short time" was instituted before reducing forces, after discussion with the affected employees.
3. First the third shift, and then the second shift, were reduced wherever possible by moving employees to the first shift.
4. Employees were used for factory maintenance such as painting and window washing.
5. Some parts were built ahead of need.
6. Farmed-out parts were brought back for manufacture in the plant.
7. A few loss orders were taken.
8. Information to employees about the business situation was increased.

In the office area, the Marketing, Engineering, and Manufacturing personnel addressed the problems in Mr. Haney's memo by preparing a product listing of more standardized, pre-engineered, well-defined product applications for volume and profit. As a result of this planning, the division was poised to increase volume while reducing novel propositions, custom engineering, nonrepetitive orders, special pricing, and long manufacturing cycles. Also, the added attention to product cost reduction paid off, and the booking of some loss orders led to technical breakthroughs.

THE TURNAROUND IN 1980

By early 1980, incoming orders had begun to move upward, and the telephone calls from Mr. Brandon not only declined but even became pleasant. As Ray Lewis pondered over the recent experience, however, he asked a lot of questions:

- Is there really a place in ABC for a division manager who believes that maintenance of steady employment in its work force should have a very high priority?
- How can the goal of steady work for employees be reconciled with the economics of business?
- What else could have been done to "weather the storm"? Was I just lucky that business got better? What did I learn from this experience?

EXHIBIT 1

ABC CORPORATION

STATEMENT OF OBJECTIVES

- Carry on a profitable business in the field of electronics.
- Lead in research in fields of science relating to the electronics business.
- Operate each business venture through decentralized operating management.
- Provide products and services with good quality and at fair prices for such quality.
- Build public confidence and goodwill through sound customer service.
- Provide good jobs, wages, working conditions, opportunities for advancement, and the stablest possible employment.
- Manage the human and material resources of the company wisely and well.
- Attract and retain investor capital adequate to finance the enterprise.
- Cooperate fully with all suppliers and distributors as a public service.
- Act as a good corporate citizen in meeting social, civic, and economic responsibilities.

CHEMICAL BANK: CORPORATE CONTRIBUTIONS

Susan E. Woodward

In January 1984, Mr. Walter Shipley, chairman of the board of Chemical Bank, faced a difficult decision. The increasingly competitive banking environment had mandated strenuous efforts to reduce costs; Chemical Bank was responding by trimming expenditures in all departments and calling for savings and increased productivity. In light of these cost-cutting efforts, consensus had been achieved in November 1983 by the three Chemical Bank presidents that reductions should be sought in the 1984 contributions budget.

Chemical's long history of giving, which many regarded as a critical component of successful banking, complicated Mr. Shipley's decision. Moreover, the bank's extensive involvement in corporate philanthropy and community service had been developed under the guidance of Mr.

This case was prepared by Susan E. Woodward, Research Assistant, under the supervision of Lynn Sharp Paine, Visiting Assistant Professor, and Henry W. Tulloch, Executive Director, Olsson Center for Applied Ethics. Copyright © 1984 by University of Virginia, Darden Graduate Business School Foundation, Charlottesville, VA. All rights reserved.

Shipley's predecessor, Mr. Donald Platten, who had retired three months earlier. Mr. Platten's approach to corporate support of local and regional nonprofit and community groups reflected his belief that "it would be wrong for the private sector to turn its back on the public. [Giving] is the right thing to do, and it is easy to face yourself if you are doing the right thing."

CHEMICAL BANK

With $51.2 billion in assets and approximately 19,400 employees, Chemical operated nationally and internationally through 400 domestic offices in New York and 10 other states, as well as a network of overseas branches, representative offices, and subsidiaries. In terms of total deposits, Chemical Bank was the fifth largest commercial bank in New York and the sixth largest in the United States. Financial information is presented in Exhibit 1.

Domestically, Chemical's financial services included personal and commercial checking accounts, loans, consumer financing, leasing, real estate financing, individual credit cards, money transfer, cash management, safe-deposit facilities, payroll management, factoring, correspondent banking, trust administration, full investment services, U.S. government and federal agency securities dealership, and state and municipal government securities underwriting. Internationally, services included banking, business and government loans, leasing, correspondent banking arrangements, letters of credit, acceptances, collections, merchant banking, foreign-exchange activities, and cash management.

LEGAL ASPECTS OF CORPORATE PHILANTHROPY

In 1935, Congress amended the Internal Revenue Code to allow corporations to deduct charitable contributions from their taxable income. This deduction was limited to 5% of the company's net income before taxes.[1] In passing this amendment, Congress gave national approval and encouragement to a practice that had been growing slowly since pre–Civil War days, when railroads contributed to the construction of YMCA buildings around the country, and more rapidly since World War I, when corporations contributed heavily to local War Chests and Red Cross campaigns.

Although this tax law established the tax deductibility of corporate gifts, it did not settle the question of whether gifts that did not directly increase stockholders' profits were within the power of the corporation. These lingering doubts were laid to rest by the landmark case of *A.P. Smith Manufacturing Co. vs. Barlow* in 1952, when a stockholder of A.P. Smith challenged a company gift of $1,500 to Princeton University by claiming that the gift produced no direct benefit for the company. The New Jersey Supreme Court decided in favor of A.P. Smith's management on the grounds that such gifts were "essential to public welfare, and therefore, of necessity to corporate welfare." The justification lay not just in what philanthropy achieved for the community, but in what it did to protect the wider corporate environment that sustained shareholders' profitable investment.[2]

CHEMICAL BANK'S CONTRIBUTIONS PROGRAM

Contributions at Chemical were divided into four distinct efforts: Banking Units; Urban Services; Corporate Social Policy, which included Matching Gifts; and the Officer-Directors Fund, a discretionary fund for the chairman and presidents. This fund was used to contribute to organizations and fund-raising causes outside the bank's contributions guidelines but of special interest to senior management and important to business relationships at the senior level.

BANKING UNITS

The first divisional area, Banking Units, consisted of World Banking, Domestic Banking, and Metropolitan. World Banking's international contributions were negligible, and the small amount channeled through Domestic Banking represented various donations given in U.S. cities other than New York. Most of the giving was done through Metropolitan, which encompassed the bank's branch operations. Giving through the branches played an especially important role at Chemical, since each manager was encouraged to view his or her branch as his or her own business operating within a unique community. Because of this philosophy, managers such as Mr. Matthew McPartland, vice-president and divisional manager of Chemical's Upper Manhattan/Bronx division, worked constantly to discover the individual financial and management needs of their communities and how Chemical could best meet those needs.

Before coming to Chemical, Mr. McPartland's experience included marketing, personnel, operations, and 20 years of service on the New York City police force. In his opinion, this diverse background contributed to his ability to "size up people in a hurry." As of 1983, Mr. McPartland had been with Chemical for 8 years and was responsible for 26 branches, most of which operated in economically deprived residential areas. The nature of these communities meant that nonprofit organizations, especially those involved with health, housing, or social welfare, played an important role. Mr. McPartland encouraged his branch managers to volunteer their own time to these organizations as well as to provide any unique banking services that may have been needed. Examples of these "unique" services included loans at lower-than-market rates, printing services for an organization's special events, and what Mr. McPartland described as "reverse factoring" for Montefiore Hospital: Mr. McPartland explained that payments to the hospital's vendors were often due before the hospital received its government funding. Chemical would pay off the vendors and allow the hospital to repay the bank when it was able.

The branches' principal method of contributing, however, was to give cash grants. Mr. McPartland's division alone donated $70–$80 thousand per year, through a selection process that began with a written proposal submitted by the potential recipient explaining how the proposed grant would be spent. A recipient organization was expected to follow through with its proposed action plan and submit monthly progress reports to the bank. He stated that giving the money away was just one step in Chemical's contributions process and that he and his branch managers often visited recipient organizations. Mr. McPartland explained:

> Not only how you spend but how you communicate what you spend is important. We believe in following through. For example, most companies might buy tickets to a fund-raising dinner but not bother to show up. If Chemical Bank can't get people to go, I'll give back the extra tickets so the sponsor can give them to friends.

Even when Chemical Bank had pre-existing business relationships with recipient organizations, Mr. McPartland believed that donations of time and money were valuable "business tools" and added, "When I contribute, I feel free to talk about banking services." In Mr. McPartland's division alone, deposits had grown from $433 million in 1982 to their present level of $700 million. Many of these new deposits came from local nonprofits.[3] On a larger scale, Chemical claimed more than half of all the nonprofit and cultural business in the entire New York City area, and the bank's responsiveness to these organizations had successfully eliminated any major competitive threat within the nonprofit market. Mr. McPartland saw his biggest competition coming from minority and community banks such as New York National or Community National, both of which were also actively involved in community development. He recognized the necessity of their place in the market, however, and often worked with them on loan packages and community projects.

Not all of Mr. McPartland's contributions were made in anticipation of future profits. Chemical often donated funds to organizations such as The Mid-Bronx Desperados, a local housing development group, even though there would probably never be "strong business ties" between the organization and the bank. He admitted, however, that giving to local "unknowns" stimulated good relationships with local government officials. Although Chemical's policy prevented him from supporting individual politicians, Mr. McPartland knew that giving to certain groups could win support from the city that would be helpful when the bank wanted to open, close, or move a branch.[4]

Mr. McPartland believed that, by helping to improve the community, Chemical would improve its own chances for survival in an uncertain future. He compared his "business tool" approach to corporate giving with the more traditional philanthropic one by saying:

> I see a place for both, especially due to the size, nature, and reputation of the large banks. Even if there is no business relationship to be developed, it is good public relations. By impacting the community's perception of large banks, we can provide a safety net for bad times.

Not all units in the Metropolitan Division made their contributions based on the criteria used by Mr. McPartland. Another division of the bank made grants based solely on account relationships and made no effort to measure the impact of the recipient organization on the overall community. Gifts were made largely to civic/fraternal organizations, athletic clubs, and special events. The policy of this division was that "the only reason to make a contribution was to satisfy a customer." The other divisions in Metro fell into the vast middle ground between these two approaches.

URBAN SERVICES

Although Urban Services was not part of Banking Units, it maintained close contact with the branches, as they performed similar functions and often worked with the same recipient organizations. Urban Services served as a channel through which the bank tried to match its resources with individual community needs. Mr. Michael Schochat, vice-president of Urban Services, had worked for the City of New York, participating as a Chemical Bank "officer on loan" during the New York financial crisis of 1975. In response to the New York mayor's request for management assistance from large New York corporations, Mr. Schochat had served as a deputy commissioner for two years.

Urban Services consisted of three functional areas: Urban Affairs, Urban Finance, and the Community Reinvestment Act (CRA) Group.

Urban Affairs, which was founded in the late 1960s in the wake of urban unrest, provided financial aid and management services to small, grass-roots organizations involved with local programs in the areas of housing development, senior citizens, drug rehabilitation, the community, health, etc. The staff of Urban Affairs were called Streetbankers, meaning that these individuals conducted their banking business on the streets of New York almost exclusively in the most depressed and blighted neighborhoods. Streetbankers were trained to provide community-based organizations with a variety of services: contributions, technical assistance, and bridge loans. The technical assistance covered a broad range—from helping with financial management to serving as advocates to city funding sources. The bridge loans were made against executed government contracts to help with cash-flow problems and, depending on the market, were never more than two points above prime. The cash grants given through Urban Affairs were relatively small, averaging $2,500; only 20 groups had received grants over $5,000. These grants were often the first corporate gifts received by these groups, however, and were therefore invaluable in leveraging additional support. Often the recipient groups were unsophisticated in the art of fund raising.

In response to some of the needs identified by the Streetbankers, Chemical's management had created two new departments to focus on solutions to the problems of disadvantaged communities, the Urban Lending Unit and the Urban Housing Unit. They were later combined into the Urban Finance Unit. In 1971, the Urban Lending Unit was set up to give special assistance to small enterprises, especially those owned and operated by minorities. Chemical did not require loans made to those enterprises to have a minimum amount or be guaranteed by the U.S. Small Business Association; thus the bank channelled them through Urban Lending instead of the normal branch route, so that branches would not be penalized in special credit situations.

The Urban Housing Unit was created in 1974 and operated in conjunction with the Urban Lending Unit by developing lending strategies to facilitate new housing construction or neighborhood rehabilitation: "[Urban Housing] developed a coherent housing rehabilitation policy that emphasized the use of funds to leverage government and private resources and also emphasized cooperation with community groups to explore new ways of meeting loan needs."[5] Examples cited by Mr. Schochat included financing the construction of modular housing in the troubled Brownsville area of Brooklyn and facilitating the sale of low-income co-ops for as little as $25,000 each. Although Mr. Schochat said that he found satisfaction in seeing people live in houses that Chemical Bank helped to provide, the CRA provided additional motivation for bankers to become involved with community development.

Congress passed the Community Reinvestment Act in November 1978 in response to the many charges of "redlining" brought against banks.[6] In doing so, Congress created a mechanism to encourage financial institutions to meet the credit needs of their neighborhoods. Under the CRA, certain government agencies were empowered to consider a bank's record of meeting community needs when reviewing the bank's application for a new deposit facility. The act's basic premise was that institutions that had not done enough for their communities should be enjoined from future growth.[7] The CRA department of Chemical Bank monitored the bank's branches, measured their impact on the community, and submitted reports to management and regulatory agencies every six months that updated branch activity. Recently the CRA department had reversed a Chemical decision to close a branch in the Bushwick area of Brooklyn after it had researched the potential reactions and consequences of such a move.

Although the branch had been unprofitable and was located in a high-crime neighborhood, the CRA group discovered that every other bank was preparing to leave the area as well and saw an opportunity for Chemical to serve an untapped market. Chemical Bank took the CRA very seriously and, consequently, had seldom encountered a CRA challenge. Mr. Schochat summarized the functions of Urban Services as follows: "Besides the bottom line, the 'soft side' of business is important, especially in a large, service-driven industry. Giving is an expense which has many dividends."

CORPORATE SOCIAL POLICY

The major portion of Chemical's monetary contributions was distributed through the Corporate Social Policy Department, which originated in 1978 when the bank's board of directors formed its Public Policy Committee to oversee the bank's public and social policy concerns. Prior to that time, contributions were distributed by the Corporate Contributions Department, which was later subsumed under Corporate Social Policy. It was not until 1980, however, that Corporate Social Policy adopted its present structure and responsibilities.

Corporate Social Policy consisted of two groups: Social Risk Analysis and Community Programming. Social Risk Analysis involved everything from community concerns to the human rights policies of foreign loan applicants. Ms. Marie Lee, the director of Corporate Social Policy, explained, "Basically, this division is responsible for analyzing the 'human issues' which are affected by banking decisions." Community Programming comprised several separate areas: Corporate Contributions, Volunteer Center, Public Education, and Matching Gifts. Prior to 1980, these areas were not combined; thus the bank's giving-related activities were disjointed and, according to Executive Vice-President for Human Resources Patrick Scollard, "eclectic." Under Ms. Lee, the bank's contribution program became more cohesive and responsive to community needs.

Community Programming was responsible for reviewing and analyzing all contribution requests from the large, traditional agencies as well as any agency, regardless of size, that had a citywide constituency and impact. The giving was divided into four categories: arts and culture, community improvement and social issues, education, and health and human services. Health and human services received the bulk of Corporate Social Policy's contributions budget (49%) with education second at 31%, arts and culture third, and community improvement last. Recipients in each of these categories included such large and traditional organizations as the United Way, major universities, and Lincoln Center for the Performing Arts as well as small women's groups that provide employment training. Community Programming was also responsible for developing major giving programs and, under the direction of senior management and the Public Policy Committee, setting bankwide contributions policy and philosophy.

This latter was done in conjunction with the Social Risk staff so that, according to Ms. Lee, "we would be sure that our money was allocated to help solve urban problems, but that these were the problems that it was most logical for the bank to tackle." For example, in 1982, a Special Projects Fund of $250,000 was established to allow the bank to make two or three significant gifts in specific target areas. These areas were determined to be public schools, economic development, and senior citizens. As a result, a gift of $100,000 was given to the New York Urban Coalition for its work in the New York City schools; $75,000 was given to the Local Initiative Support Corporation for local economic development activities in the South Bronx and Brooklyn; and a Request for Proposal was issued to all of the city's senior-citizen centers to assist them with their recreational and educational programming.

Donald Platten had a major impact on the development of contributions policy, particularly as it was implemented by Corporate Social Policy/Community Programming. Under his leadership, Chemical always had subscribed to the philosophy that the bank's gifts should be unrestricted, and that the bank should support a wide range, in terms of size and discipline, of institutions that had a positive impact on New York City. Mr. Platten believed that if the bank, as a financial institution, were to provide support to the voluntary sector, it was obligated to help nonprofits effectively manage their resources.

This philosophy resulted in two major giving programs: the Basic Grant program and Higher Education Grant program. These programs, which provided unrestricted cash grants to chosen organizations for a period of three years, were developed to give the nonprofits flexibility in the use of funds and to allow nonprofits to project income, which would make it easier for them to conduct short-term financial planning. As Mr. Platten said in a letter to all trustees of the 51 schools in the Higher Education Grant program and 28 Basic Grant recipients,

> Our principles behind these two programs were simple. We did not earmark our gifts. Facing up to institutions' need for unrestricted support and our belief that university management is more able to determine the best use of this income, and as a result of observing the difficulty not-for-profits have in financial planning, we made the commitment of funds. If replicated by other funders, this will allow schools to begin projecting revenues and plan more realistically for the future.

In recognition of the bank's obligation to help nonprofits manage better, two other areas were formed within Community Programming. The Volunteer Center matched Chemical Bank employees with nonprofit agencies that could benefit from their expertise and experience. The Public Education Office offered, free of charge, about 30 technical-assistance workshops each year on such topics as fiscal management, public relations, and fund raising.

In 1982, Mr. Platten discussed with the board and staff the fact that the future of nonprofits rested not just on their own management skills and corporate and foundation support, but also on the largesse of individuals. Therefore, the bank expanded its program to match employee gifts to virtually all tax-exempt institutions in the United States up to $1,000/donor and to schools up to $5,000/donor. Another option made available was the two-for-one match, where the bank contributed $2 for every $1 up to $200 per donor per year. This step made the Chemical Bank Matching Gift program one of the most liberal in the country and radically increased employee participation. In 1981, the bank matched just under $300,000; in 1983, it matched close to $700,000.

During this time, all changes in contributions were reviewed by a Contributions Committee composed of senior management. In 1982, the name of the committee was changed to Corporate Responsibility Committee to reflect the broad range of issues it discussed.

THE CONTRIBUTIONS BUDGET

Of the $63 billion contributed to U.S. nonprofit organizations in 1983, corporate gifts made up $3.5 billion, and this amount was expected to grow at an inflation-adjusted rate of 4.6% through 1988.[8] When determining the amount of their annual contributions, most large companies first looked at the amount they gave the year before and then compared that amount with a goal based on their predicted pre-tax net income for the upcoming year. In addition, many corporations, including Chemical, often compared their own goals with those of competitors. Mr. Platten commented:

> Chemical ranks second, behind Chase Manhattan, for contributions as a percent of net income after taxes [referring to New York banks only]. Right now we give about 1.5%, but I would like to see it go up to 2%. The generally accepted guideline for U.S. corporations is 1% after taxes, but we also like to see what other banks are doing.

Ms. Marian Stern, assistant vice-president for Community Planning, explained that, for the most part, the New York banks cooperated with one another:

> Corporate Social Policy maintains contact with our counterparts in other New York banks so we can get information as to what percentage they will be giving as well as how fast their budgets are growing. We have a tacit agreement of confidentiality.

Chemical Bank's budgeting process for contributions began with the Corporate Social Policy staff, but because the department had been in existence for only a few years, a set process had not yet been developed, and according to Ms. Stern, the staff often resorted to a "seat of the pants" method. Once Corporate Social Policy obtained the bank's projected earnings for 1984, a contributions percentage was applied to get a rough dollar amount, which was then distributed among the major contributions channels of the bank. (See Exhibit 2 for a copy of the 1984 contributions budget.) The majority of funds went to Corporate Social Policy and were subsequently divided into a "committed" portion and a "discretionary" portion.

The committed funds covered gifts to United Way, payments on multiyear pledges, including the Basic Grant and Higher Education grants programs, and Matching Gifts (a projection). Monies were also committed to the Officer-Directors Fund, Urban Services, and Banking Units, although most of these funds were for the discretionary use of these groups. Within Community Programming's budget, staff set aside funds for anticipated gifts to agencies that they were supporting and planned to continue to support. Discretionary monies were used to cover unanticipated requests as well as donations to struggling, young organizations.

When the proposed budget was complete, Corporate Social Policy submitted it to the Corporate Responsibility and Public Policy committees for discussion and approval. From there, it would go to the chairman for final approval.

CHEMICAL'S PHILOSOPHY OF CONTRIBUTING

Chemical's contributions efforts reflected its concern for corporate responsibility. Mr. Platten had believed that "corporations must relate to the rest of the world in all its aspects. They are responsible as an independent entity and as an agent holding stockholders' money. The obligation is there."

Chemical's contributions programs were not without their critics, however. Some feared that the long-term nature of the Basic Grant and Higher Education Grant made recipients dependent on the bank or susceptible to its control. Mr. Platten rejected this argument and said that the individual grants were not large enough to promote dependence or control. Other opposition came from stockholders, who at times expressed concern that too much—or too little—was being given. Even recipient organizations had complained about other recipients of Chemical support. The Knights of Columbus, for example, had threatened to picket Chemical's Park Avenue offices to protest the bank's grant to Planned Parenthood. Nevertheless, most of Chemical's management believed that the bank's contributions were investments that paid off, not only through improved public relations, but by an increased deposit base. Mr. Platten believed "that Chemical Bank benefited from its giving. There is no question that Chemical is known as a responsive bank." This was particularly true in the early 1980s when the federal government cut back on its support of nonprofits and corporations helped to fill the gap.

BUDGET CUTS

Because of the increasingly competitive banking environment and resultant expense-control environment, Chemical Bank began to cut back on staffing, call for savings, and increase productivity. Despite these efforts, the contributions budget had grown rapidly from 1979 until November 1983, when the recommendation was made that the 1984 budget be reduced from its proposed amount of $4.9 million to $4.5 million (see Exhibits 3 and 4). The Corporate Social Policy staff had met immediately to review the areas where cutbacks were possible and to determine how it could effectively deal with a budget reduction after several years of increases. The uncommitted portion of the budget would have to be reduced the most, which would affect the small, grass-roots organizations. Financially, these groups did not represent important business ties for the bank, but many of them formed the foundation for the bank's good reputation with the surrounding communities and CRA officials. The Corporate Responsibility Committee had begun making its own "arbitrary" reductions to the budget when Chairman Shipley was made aware of the situation and intervened. In light of the significance of corporate philanthropy to Chemical Bank's philosophy, as well as the sacrifices being made in the cost-reduction program, should Mr. Shipley cut the budget or not? If so, what areas should he reduce?

NOTES

1. The Economic Recovery Act of 1981 raised the deduction limit from 5% to 10% [The Conference Board's Annual Survey of Corporate Contributions (New York: 1984), p. 6].
2. Carl Bakal, *Charity U.S.A.* (New York: Time, Inc., 1979), p. 65.
3. This growth in retail business was especially vital to Chemical Bank, as 20–30% of the bank's earnings came from its retail operations.
4. See section on Community Reinvestment Act under Urban Services section that follows.
5. *Banking on New York* (New York: Chemical Bank, 1983), p. 8.
6. "Redlining" refers to the practice of drawing boundaries on a map in red ink to delineate areas in which mortgage loans were not to be considered.
7. Eric Compton, *Inside Commercial Banking* (New York: John Wiley & Sons, 1983), p. 36.
8. *Giving and Getting: A Chemical Bank Study of Charitable Contributions, 1983 through 1988* (New York: Chemical Bank, 1982), p. 5.

Exhibit 1

Chemical Bank

Consolidated Statement of Income

CHEMICAL NEW YORK CORPORATION & SUBSIDIARIES
Year Ended December 31 (in thousands)

	1981	1982	1983
Interest Income			
Interest & Fees on Loans	$4,160,668	$4,227,548	$3,662,967
Interest on Investment Securities:			
Taxable	230,394	192,147	284,898
Exempt from Federal Income Tax	85,448	106,274	80,648
Interest on Trading Account Assets	89,881	67,577	75,525
Interest on Federal Funds Sold & Securities			
Purchased Under Agreements to Resell	165,427	124,247	82,170
Interest on Deposits in Other Banks	666,141	460,850	264,825
	$5,397,959	$5,178,643	$4,451,033
Interest Expense			
Deposits	$3,056,397	$2,687,196	$2,029,547
Short-Term Borrowings	1,275,965	1,184,202	1,003,397
Long-Term Debt	51,410	56,158	64,264
	$4,383,772	$3,927,556	$3,097,208
Net Interest Income	$1,014,187	$1,251,087	$1,353,825
Provision for Loan Losses	97,415	117,143	166,340
Net Interest Income After Provision for Loan Losses	$ 916,772	$1,133,944	$1,187,485
Noninterest Income			
Trust Fees & Commissions	$ 65,072	$ 67,334	$ 75,251
Fees for Other Services	176,222	213,283	257,401
Trading Account Profits & Commissions	19,338	33,600	20,507
Foreign Exchange Trading Profits	39,490	55,513	40,357
Investment Securities Gains (Losses)	(21,147)	(70,082)	12,652
Other Income	32,735	19,779	46,044
	$ 311,710	$ 319,427	$ 452,212
Noninterest Expense			
Salaries	$ 403,587	464,445	$ 502,082
Employee Benefits	115,893	139,073	149,327
Occupancy Expense	103,396	130,333	149,942
Equipment Expense	48,544	68,883	83,290
Other Expense	268,750	329,090	363,289
	$ 940,170	$1,131,824	$1,247,930
Income Before Income Tax Expense & Extraordinary Gain	$ 288,312	321,547	391,767
Income Tax Expense	83,146	80,987	86,204
	208,166	240,560	305,563
Income Before Extraordinary Gain			
Extraordinary Gain (Tax Free, $.42 per Share; Fully Diluted, $.36)	9,873	-	-
Net Income	$ 215,039	$ 240,560	$ 305,563

EXHIBIT 1 CONTINUED

Earnings per Share
Primary:

Income Before Extraordinary Gain	$8.28	$8.41	$9.50
Net Income	8.70	8.41	9.50

Fully Diluted:

Income Before Extraordinary Gain	7.31	7.68	9.03
Net Income	7.67	7.68	9.03
Cash Dividends Declared	$2.56	$2.88	$3.24

EXHIBIT 2

CHEMICAL BANK

TOTAL 1984 CONTRIBUTIONS BUDGET

$4,993,000

Total Breakdown as Follows:
Total Corporate Social Policy/PCC $2,742,450

Committed

Higher Education Grant	$ 660,000
Basic Grant	320,000
Volunteer Center	11,000
Pledges	48,500
Special Projects	250,000
United Way	730,000
Urban Services	150,000
Subtotal	2,169,500

Discretionary

Education	$ 48,000
Community Improvement	109,000
Arts & Culture	188,500
Health & Human Services	197,500
Subtotal	543,000

(+ $30,000 absorption of gifts of Urban Services, Upstate, Long Island, and Westchester)

(Total Discretionary)

Officer-Directors	590,500
Urban Services	460,000
Matching Gifts	850,000
Metropolitan	200,000
Domestic	100,000
Overseas	50,000

EXHIBIT 3

CHEMICAL BANK

CONTRIBUTIONS BUDGET (1979–83)

	1979	1980	1981	1982	1983
Chemical ($)	1.675	1.973	2.550	4.1	4.893
% Increase		18	29	61	19
% of After Tax	1.22	1.12	1.18	1.5	NA

(Does not include giving abroad, estimated in 1982 at $70,000, or Met in the Park at $200,000.)

AS COMPARED WITH OTHER MAJOR NEW YORK CITY BANKS

	1979	1980	1981	1982	1983
Bankers ($)	1.200	1.663	2.211	2.520	3.000
% Increase		39	33	14	19
% of AT	1.04	.78	1.2	1.03	NA
Chase ($)	3.153	5.285	6.559	8.880	6.500
% Increase		68	24	35	(27)
% of AT	1.01	1.5	1.47	2.66	NA
Citibank ($)	3.721	3.830	3.814	5.000	6.500
% Increase		3	(.4)	31	30
% of AT	.69	.77	.76	.6	NA
Manufacturers Hanover ($)	2.234	2.566	3.375	2.850	NA
% Increase		15	31	(16)	
% of AT	1.01	1.5	1.47	1	NA
Morgan ($)	2.934	3.159	3.677	4.050	NA
% Increase		8	16	10	
% of AT	1.01	.86	.94	.96	

EXHIBIT 4

CHEMICAL BANK

PROPOSED CONTRIBUTIONS CUTS

	Original 1984 Budget	With Proposed Cuts
Corporate Social Policy/Public Policy Committee	$2,742,450	$2,444,500
Officer-Directors	590,500	490,500
Urban Services	460,000	460,000
Matching Gifts	850,000	850,000
Subtotal	4,642,950	4,245,000
Metropolitan	200,000	200,000
Domestic	100,000	100,000
Overseas	50,000	50,000
Subtotal	350,000	350,000
Total	$4,992,950	$4,595,000

2

THE EMPLOYEE AND THE FIRM

INTRODUCTION

In going to work for a firm, employees assume a number of obligations that accrue to a particular role. Foremost among the role obligations of employees is *loyalty* to the company. The ethical (and legal) basis of this obligation of loyalty lies in the employee's status as an *agent*, which is a person who agrees to act in the interests of another, in this case the employer. The employer, in turn, is a *principal*, who directs the activities of an agent. Specifically, a loyal agent-employee has an obligation to work as directed and to preserve confidentiality. These obligations arise, in part, from necessity: Business activity would not be possible if employees could not be trusted to take direction and to safeguard sensitive information.

Employee loyalty has its limits, most notably in cases of whistle-blowing where an employee becomes aware of unethical and possibly illegal conduct in the organization, especially when it is likely to cause harm to others. In situations of this kind, the obligation of loyalty comes into conflict with an obligation to prevent serious injury or loss. Deciding whether to blow the whistle thus requires employees to thread their way between conflicting moral demands. Managers, too, face challenges in dealing with whistle-blowing subordinates, both before and after the whistle is blown.

"The Case of the Willful Whistle-Blower" is a case study that looks at whistle-blowing from a manager's point of view when a conscientious employee accidentally uncovers a long-buried report with explosive contents. Did the manager, in this case, fail to meet the employee's legitimate concerns, thereby leaving him little choice but to "go public" with the damaging information? And, afterwards, how should the manager deal with disruptive consequences of the employee's act of conscience? This case study shows that whistle-blowing poses difficult choices, not only for whistle-blowers themselves but also for others in the organization.

Company codes of ethics invariably forbid employees to have substantial investments in customers or suppliers or in competing firms. The reason is that an outside financial holding can interfere with the ability of an employee to do his or her job properly. More precisely, an employee has an obligation to act in the interests of the employer, and owning stock in another company, for example, could lead an employee to put this personal interest ahead of the employer's. Such a situation is called a *conflict of interest*. Actual biased judgment or the potential for biased judgment is the most common form of conflict of interest, but also competing against an employer, misappropriating information, and abusing a position, all for personal gain, are also instances of conflict of interest. Some codes prohibit all sources of conflict of interest, but more often they require only that an employee reveal investments or other interests that could create a conflict of interest so the employer can monitor the conflict and protect the interests of the company.

The case of R. Foster Winans illustrates several of the different kinds of conflict of interest. As the writer of the popular *Wall Street Journal* column "Heard on the Street," Winans knew the contents of the column in advance. By trading in the stocks of companies mentioned in the column, Winans and two stockbrokers at Kidder, Peabody & Co. were able to reap a profit of $690,000. All three conspirators were charged with insider trading by the Securities and Exchange Commission (SEC), and Winans was fired by the *Journal* for violating the newspaper's policy on conflict of interest.

Newspapers usually prohibit reporters from writing about companies in which they own stock so as to avoid the possibility of bias. There is no suggestion that Winans slanted his columns to further his insider-trading scheme, but he was in violation of two further provisions of the code of ethics at the *Journal*, which prohibit misuse of position and misappropriation of confidential information. Insider trading by an employee is thus a conflict of interest for several reasons, but whether these are or ought to be the basis for the SEC rule forbidding insider trading is another matter. The SEC position is that insider trading involves a misappropriation of information acquired during the course of employment and hence is a violation of the duty of an employee to use that information solely in the employer's interests. This so-called misappropriation theory is controversial, however. The Winans case was expected to be a legal test of this theory of insider trading, but the question was not settled by the U.S. Supreme Court's decision in the matter.

The case of Steve Charles provides an opportunity to explore the enforcement of a code of ethics when an employee apparently has done nothing wrong except for a failure to report an outside financial interest. Is the mere potential for a conflict or the appearance of one grounds for terminating a valued employee? Codes of ethics can prohibit conflict of interest, but the task of enforcing them fairly still falls to practicing managers.

An obligation to protect confidential information and trade secrets of a company extends beyond its own employees to those of customers and competitors, especially when there is an agreement of confidentiality. Not all information can be rightly protected, however, and employees and other companies have a right to use some sensitive information that a company would prefer not to share. Thus, the knowledge that an engineer acquires during the course of employment constitutes part of his or her marketable skills, and so the freedom of employees to go to another employer or to go into business for themselves would be hampered by stringent protection of confidential information and trade secrets.

A further example is software piracy, which is a breach of confidentiality when the software is obtained with an agreement of confidentiality. It is also a theft of a kind of property, called *intellectual property*, which is commonly protected by patents and copyrights. Thus, the ethics of the unauthorized use of computer software is seldom in question. Are there circumstances, however, in which a company might be justified in making a copy of a critical software program? The case study titled "Agrico, Inc.—A Software Dilemma" probes this question by describing a situation in which loss of access to the original program as written by a supplier's programmers would place the company at great risk. And difficult relations with the supplier increase the possibility of just such a loss. It is instructive to consider in this case the source of the problem—how it arose—and whether copying the program is really a solution to the company's problem.

Information is also central to issues involving employee privacy, although the information in question is usually personal information *about* employees. Privacy, according to one definition, is "the condition of not having undocumented personal knowledge about one possessed by others."[1] Employers are justified in gathering some information of this type so as to make sound hiring decisions and, once employees are hired, to administer health benefit plans and to monitor employee health and safety, for example. The main questions confronting employers are what information will be collected, how it will be used, and who will have access to it. Once a decision is made to collect information, further questions arise, such as: What means will be used to gain the information? What steps will be taken to ensure the accuracy and completeness of the information? And will employees have access to information about themselves?

All of these questions must be answered in developing a justified drug-testing program. The right—indeed, the responsibility—of employers to protect themselves and other employees against the problems of drug abuse in the workplace is beyond dispute. But is a drug-testing program the best way to achieve these ends? A decision must be made, first, about whether the information gained will be used for the benefit of employees and the company alike by opportunities for treatment and rehabilitation, or whether it will be used merely for the purpose of dismissing employees found to be using drugs. Any justified program must also protect the right of employee privacy as well as the right of due process. Taking steps to ensure the accuracy and completeness of information and allowing employees access to information about themselves will help to prevent false accusations of drug use and the resulting unfair treatment.

In the case study titled "Testing Employees for Substance Abuse," the CEO of the fictional United Companies solicits advice on implementing a drug-testing program and receives conflicting opinions, including some from managers who work closely with organized labor at the company's plants. All of the relevant considerations are carefully laid out in this case, but they do not make the CEO's decision any easier.

NOTE

1. W.A. Parent, "Privacy, Morality, and the Law," *Philosophy and Public Affairs*, 12 (1983), 269.

WHISTLE-BLOWING

THE CASE OF THE WILLFUL WHISTLE-BLOWER

Sally Seymour

When Ken Deaver, CEO of Fairway Electric, promoted me to vice president of the nuclear division, I was on top of the world. Now, just a month later, it feels like the world's on top of me. I'm used to having a team to share the problems, but now I'm on my own. At least Ken's door has always been open to me. He's been my mentor since I began at Fairway eight years ago, and he's really responsible for my success here. I owe him a lot. But when I think back over the last few weeks, I have to wonder whether I should have listened to him on this one.

It started the morning I walked into my office to find Jim Bower, one of my old teammates, waiting for me. He apologized for taking my time but said it was really important. I had worked with Jim for more than four years. If he says it's important, it's important.

Reprinted by permission of *Harvard Business Review*. "The Case of the Willful Whistle-Blower," by Sally Seymour, January-February 1988. Copyright © 1987 by the President and Fellows of Harvard College; all rights reserved.

"What's up?" I asked.

"Bob," he said, "I've run up against something I can't handle alone. I hate to dump this on you when you're just starting your new job, but it's the sort of thing I should take to my boss, and that's you now."

"Sure, Jim. Whatever it is, you've got my help."

He took a couple of deep breaths before he continued. "You know how we're cramped for space downstairs. Well, yesterday I asked my secretary to clear out any files over five years old. Before she left for the day, she stacked the old files on my desk so I could glance through them. And I couldn't believe what I found."

Jim pulled a red notebook from his briefcase.

"I found this report written 15 years ago by two engineers in the nuclear division. It's about a flaw in our design of the Radon II nuclear reactor. Apparently there was a structural problem in the containment unit that would show up as the power plant was being built. It wasn't a safety hazard, but it would hold up construction and cost a lot to fix. The report says that Fairway was going to rework the design. But listen to this memo from the head of the nuclear division." Jim opened the notebook and read from a sheet stapled to the inside cover.

"'The potential problems in the design of the Radon II are disturbing. They do not, however, present a safety hazard. It therefore would be counterproductive to discontinue sales of the design. If there are problems with fittings, they will show up as the plant is built, at which point the necessary corrections can be made. The need for retrofitting is not uncommon. Our experience has been that customers rarely complain about such extra costs.'"

Jim closed the notebook and looked up.

"This memo makes me sick, Bob. I can't believe Fairway would risk its reputation by selling plans they knew were flawed. Those customers bought the designs thinking they were the best on the market. But the Radon II took longer to build and cost a bunch more money than what Fairway told customers. That's misrepresentation. Maybe the reason the utilities never complained is because they could pass the cost on to the rate payers. But that's a real rip-off, and the top guys at Fairway knew about it."

Jim threw the notebook on my desk and looked at me, his face flushed.

"Don't you think engineering ought to know about this?" he said.

I'd never seen Jim so steamed up. Of course, I was pretty upset myself. That report was new to me too. But I had a lot of faith in Fairway, so I wasn't going to leap to conclusions. I told Jim I'd ask some questions and get back to him by the end of the day.

I headed straight for Ken's office, recalling along the way everything I could about the Radon II reactor. I knew that we'd had problems with it, but it never occurred to me that our original designs were flawed. Jim was right that no one ever complained about the delays and costs of refitting. But I remembered one instance where a utility converted a Radon II to a coal-fired plant because of the cost overruns. In that case, the utility paid for the conversion and it didn't go into the rate base.

When I showed the report to Ken, he recognized it right away.

"How did Jim get ahold of this?" he asked.

"He discovered it by accident—cleaning out old files," I said. "He's pretty disturbed about it, and I can't say I blame him." Ken's office was suddenly very still.

"I thought this report was dead and buried," he said. "Have you read it?"

"Enough to get the drift," I said. "Apparently we sold a power plant design when we knew there were flaws in it."

"Yes, but you've got to understand the context. Back then we were in the middle of an energy crisis. Everyone was rushing to build nuclear power plants. We were under tremendous pressure to come up with a winning design, and Radon II was what we decided on. After a few plants went under construction, some problems surfaced, so we put a couple of engineers on it. But by the time they wrote this report, it was too late for us to go back to the drawing board. We wouldn't have had any customers left. We figured we'd solve the problem as soon as we could, but we'd sell the original design in the meantime. It was basically a very good one. And it was safe."

"I can't believe we would risk our reputation like that."

"I know it's not the way we usually operate, but that shows you the pressure we were under," Ken said. "The whole division would have gone down. There was no other way."

I was uncomfortable putting Ken on the defensive. I'd always trusted his judgment. Who was I to grill him about something that happened 15 years ago when I wasn't even around? Still, I needed to press the point.

"So what do I tell Jim?" I asked.

"Nothing. It's ancient history. The engineers who wrote that report are long gone. Look at it this way, the fact that we ordered a study of the problem shows that we care about quality. We eventually got the bugs out. Besides, it was never a question of safety. It was merely a matter of some extra work during construction."

"But what about all the cost overruns? If Fairway didn't swallow them, someone else must have—like the utilities or their customers."

"Look, Bob, what's past is past. What would we gain by bringing this into the open today? But I guarantee we've got a hell of a lot to lose. The regulators and some shareholders would love to blame us for all the exorbitant cost overruns. And the antinuclear groups would have a field day. We've got enough problems getting licenses as it is.

"We'd lose a lot of business, you know. I'm talking about hundreds of jobs here, and the very survival of this company. Maybe we're not perfect, but we're the most conscientious, quality-conscious corporation I know of."

"And what do I do with this report?" I asked.

"Deep-six it. As we should have done long ago. Tell Jim Bower what I told you, and explain why there's no reason to make an issue of it at this late date."

I nodded in agreement and headed back to my office. I found Jim waiting.

He scowled when I reported Ken's reaction.

"So you're telling me to forget I ever saw the report? And I suppose that means you're going to forget I showed it to you."

"Look, Ken's got some good reasons for not wanting to make an issue of it. I may or may not agree with him, but he's running the show."

"Damn it, Bob!" Jim shouted. "If we go along with this, we're just as guilty as the people who sold those bad designs 15 years ago."

"Cool down, cool down. I know what you're saying, but Ken is just being realistic. After all, no one got hurt, the cost was spread over a lot of people, and the problem's been corrected. If this gets exposed, it could really hurt us."

"No, I won't cool down. Maybe it seems like ancient history to Ken, but unless we make a clean slate now, it could happen again. One of the reasons I took this job is because Fairway is a company I can respect. What am I supposed to think now?"

"I see your point," I replied, "but I also see Ken's. And he's the boss. Maybe you should talk to him."

"If I can't get through to you I don't see how I'll get through to him. So I guess that's it."

As it turned out, that wasn't it. When Jim left my office, he didn't go straight back to work. First he went to the newspaper, and the story appeared two days later.

FAIRWAY SOLD DEFECTIVE REACTORS
—REPORT WARNED OF HAZARD

Naturally, the reporter got it all wrong and blew the problem out of proportion. He didn't even have a copy of the report. I suppose we hadn't helped matters though. When the reporter called for a comment, Ken asked him to call back in a couple of hours. Then Ken and I met with our public relations officer, Amy Thone, to discuss how to handle the situation. Amy thought we should come clean—admit we made a mistake and stress the fact that our record for the past five years had been excellent. But Ken felt that the less we said, the sooner it would blow over. I went along with him. When the reporter called back, Ken's response was "no comment."

The article did say that the anonymous source still thought Fairway was a reliable builder of nuclear plants and that it was a good company with many skilled and highly principled employees. The source had gone to the newspaper because he felt it was his ethical duty to the consumers who had been forced to pay for Fairway's mistakes. But that part of the story was buried in the next-to-last paragraph.

Needless to say, the public outcry was intense. Antinuke activists went berserk, and politicians made holier-than-thou speeches. After a couple of days hearing phones ring off the hook, we realized that stonewalling was compounding our problems. So we made a clean breast of it. We drafted a statement to the press saying that Fairway engineers had in fact discovered design flaws in 1973 but that the company had corrected the problem within 14 months. Ken made himself available to answer questions, and he and Amy arranged to meet with community leaders. They even invited experts from the university to answer the technical questions. The thrust of these efforts was to assure the public that no flaws had been discovered since 1973 and that all Fairway's designs were safe.

Thanks to Amy and Ken, the controversy finally died down. I was proud of the way they handled things. I was also glad that Ken didn't fire Jim. At the height of the crisis, someone at headquarters had suggested that he "get rid of the troublemaker," but Ken thought that would only make matters worse. I didn't want to fire Jim either. I felt he was still a valuable employee. I knew he was committed to Fairway, and we sure needed his skills.

We weathered those difficult weeks with only a few outstanding lawsuits, but an ugly incident like that never has a simple ending. It keeps unraveling. Now we have another problem. Word got out that Jim was the whistle-blower, and now his life here is miserable. The feeling is that Jim can't be trusted. Last week, Lorraine Wellman, another former teammate, came to talk to me about the problem.

"You know, it's not that anyone hates Jim for what he did," she said. "It's just that no one can understand why he did it. They could understand it if someone had been hurt or killed because of a bad design, but that wasn't the case. In their minds, he risked their jobs for something that happened ages ago.

"Morale is pretty low in the trenches," she added. "One guy told me he used to be proud of where he worked. Now his neighbors razz him about 'Radongate' and 'Three-Mile Radon.' No one wants to work with Jim, and it's affecting our output."

I felt terrible for Jim. Unlike the others, I understood why he did what he did, and I respected his integrity. On the other hand, I wasn't surprised that his coworkers resented him. I just wished everyone would forget the whole thing and get on with their work. But the situation seemed to be getting worse instead of better.

Yesterday Ken came to see me about the mounting problems in Jim's department. He suggested that Jim might want to resign and that we could give him a very generous package if he did. I knew what Ken was driving at. He didn't want to stir up trouble by firing a whistle-blower, but he thought we could get around it by pressuring Jim to leave on his own. That would solve all our problems. Of course Ken just wanted what was best for Fairway, but I resisted the idea. I asserted that the problems were temporary, and threw in a few remarks about Jim's outstanding performance. I figured I should defend him. After all, Jim had done the noble thing, and it didn't seem right that he should get the shaft. But Ken persisted. He was worried about meeting targets and didn't think one person should be allowed to make everyone else look bad. He asked me to talk to Jim.

Jim had been avoiding me since he showed me the report, and maybe I was avoiding him too. The worst thing about this whole situation is that it ruined our friendship. Still, he agreed to see me in my office. I tried to break the ice by extending my hand and saying that I missed seeing him. But he ignored the gesture and mumbled something about being busy. So I decided to jump right in.

"I've heard about the problems you've been having with the team. This thing is taking its toll—on Fairway, your department, and you."

"I can handle it. Or maybe that's not your point. Are you saying that the company doesn't want me around anymore?"

"Look Jim," I said, "I'm real sorry this happened. I hate to see you and your family suffering like this. Maybe a transfer to another office would be the best thing. There are other divisions that could use your talents."

"You just don't get it, do you, Bob? I haven't done anything wrong, and I'm the one who's suffering. People are blaming me for a report I didn't write and bad designs I didn't push on customers. And now I'm the one you want out. I figured the idea of firing me might occur to someone, but I can't believe you agreed to it. That's one I hadn't expected."

"No one has mentioned firing," I said. "I'm talking about a transfer. I see why you're angry about your teammates giving you a hard time, but why come down on me? I'm one of the few who understand your position, and I've tried to support you."

"You've tried to *support* me? Give me a break! I didn't want to get into this, but now that you've brought it up, I'm going to spell it out for you.

"I didn't ask to see that report. It fell into my hands. But once it did, I couldn't just pretend it wasn't there. What the company did was wrong— you know that and I know that. If someone didn't say something, Fairway could get away with it again.

"But I surely didn't figure you'd make me go this alone. I didn't expect you to run to the newspapers, but I did expect you to make a strong case to Ken for the company coming clean on this. And failing that, I expected you—as my supervisor—to take this off my shoulders by assuming the responsibility yourself.

"You've got more power than I have, and you certainly have more influence with Ken. But you acted like this whole thing had nothing to do with you—like you were just a messenger. You dumped Ken's answer in my lap and washed your hands of the whole affair.

"I never thought I'd say this, but it's beginning to look like you care way too much for your fancy new title and your tight relationship with Ken. Well, I won't quit and I won't transfer!"

Before I could respond, Jim was out the door. I don't know how long I sat at my desk in a daze. After a while I tried to get back to work, but I couldn't concentrate. The whole morning I kept going over what Jim had said. How could I defend Jim and the company at the same time? Was Ken wrong? Had Jim really done the noble thing after all?

Conflict of Interest

Steve Charles: Implementing Conflict of Interest Policy

Philip R. Inman

It was Monday, January 7, 1991, when Steve Charles walked into my office. "Alan, I think I'm being fired. As you are aware, it has been discovered that I have had an ownership in a company that has done business with Ridgeway, and I am now being investigated for a conflict of interest. Alan, I promise you I have never acted in anything less than the best interest of Ridgeway, and have never personally profited from directing Ridgeway business toward this company." With that, he walked out the door.

CAREER HISTORY

Steve Charles and I first became friends by working side-by-side as field engineers out of Ridgeway's Houston, Texas, office in 1983. We both had about five years' experience with Ridgeway Energy, a large-sized international oil and gas independent, and we found ourselves as the only two production engineers for the company's Gulf Coast operations. Steve's primary assignment was in the Offshore Division, where he quickly estab-

This case was prepared by Philip R. Inman under the direction of Professor Jeffrey A. Barach as a basis for class discussion rather than to illustrate either effective or ineffective handling of an administrative situation. Copyright © 1991 by Jeffrey A. Barach, A.B. Freeman School of Business, Tulane University, New Orleans, LA 70118.

lished himself as a dedicated, bright, hard-working young engineer who practiced an extremely strong work ethic. This was reinforced when, two years later, he transferred overseas for an international assignment. Family in tow, he moved to a mostly underdeveloped country that was in close proximity to his area of responsibility, but still required extensive travel and lengthy field assignments. In his two years there, he never uttered a complaining word, but continued to gain experience and expertise in oil and gas operations and to perform at a high level for the company.

Steve and I lost touch with each other when he went overseas, and I subsequently transferred to California to supervise Ridgeway's West Coast engineering department. Shortly thereafter, in 1987, Steve returned from overseas to Houston. In his assignment there, he continued to work in an operations engineering assignment, doing major project engineering and construction assignments. His reputation for handling a great amount of work in detail, the ability to achieve results, and his coordination of multiple groups and people in major projects only solidified his strong performance perception in the eyes of those with whom he associated. However, he had worked the same areas before, worked with the same cast of people, and had exhausted most of the opportunities in the area, so his desire for new challenges and assignments began to strengthen. It was not surprising that when a Facility Engineering assignment opened in California in late 1989, I put in a call to Steve.

CALIFORNIA ENGINEERING

Steve arrived January 2, 1990, full of energy and acting like he had stepped into a brand new career. I recruited him to lead perhaps the largest facilities project the California area had seen in many years. His assignment consisted of directing the design, specification, bidding, fabrication, contractor selection, installation, and start-up of a new $2 million production system. To perform this job, Steve was assigned a senior engineer, junior engineer, field construction supervisor, and draftsman on a full-time basis.

This project entailed almost the entire 1990 calendar year. The results that Steve and his project team achieved were absolutely phenomenal. The entire project, which grew in scope during the year to almost $3 million, was performed under budget and on schedule. However, what set his efforts apart was his handling of adversity through almost all phases of the project. Delays, problems, and unpredictable setbacks were a frequent occurrence. Steve handled each and every one, most of them personally, with the utmost precision. It is easy to understand why this effort, and most importantly the results, earned Steve an "Exceptional" rating on his 1990 annual review, and this set the stage for a very high merit raise and possible promotion later in the year.

CONFLICT

The phone rang that morning of January 8 around 11:30. The manager of Ridgeway's Internal Security department was calling to gather some information and requested that I come to his office upstairs. When I entered the room, I also found the manager of Ridgeway's Audit Department there. They wished to discuss Steve Charles.

What followed in the next 45 minutes comes close to being the low point of my career. I was made aware of a situation whereby several years ago Steve had gone into business with another Ridgeway employee (at the time) in the investment of some oil- and gas-producing properties, operating under the name Diversified Energy Management Consultants (DEMC). It was unclear whether these properties were in competition with any of Ridgeway's properties, but what was clear was that Steve had violated Ridgeway's Conflict of Interest Policy by failing to disclose this investment, which may conflict with an employee's ability to perform in the company's best interest. This partnership continued for several years until 1989, when it apparently ceased business owing to bankruptcy.

Unfortunately, it got worse. Internal Security had become aware of Steve's ownership of an oilfield service company named Offshore Instrumentation Specialists of Texas (OIST). The company was owned and operated by Alex Elon, a young, industrious entrepreneur who had known Steve and maintained a friendship for several years. This investment was fine until August 1989, when on an unsolicited basis, OIST worked for Ridgeway on at least two jobs. It was unclear whether OIST did any more work for Ridgeway, but what was clear was that Steve, once again, never disclosed an ownership under the company's Conflict of Interest policy.

Furthermore, Internal Security discovered the presence of a second, independent company owned and operated by Alex Elon named "DEMC." This company provided consulting services to the oil business through the use of contract engineers, inspectors, and other technical personnel. There was no evidence that Steve owned a portion of this company, but the Internal Security people were highly suspicious since both OIST and DEMC were owned and operated by Alex Elon, they operated out of the same address, evidence did exist that Steve Charles owned part of OIST, and Steve had owned a company named DEMC in Texas several years earlier. They were under the belief that it was more than coincidental that a company named DEMC was so close to Steve Charles. But perhaps the biggest concern was that the senior engineer, field construction supervisor, and draftsman were all DEMC employees, contracted out to Ridgeway and working under Steve Charles's direction and in my department.

QUESTIONING ME

Because I was Steve's immediate supervisor, and they were aware that I had known Steve for many years, the Internal Security people were interested in what knowledge I had of all this. I never felt so helpless as I sat there for a considerable amount of time explaining to my interrogators that I knew nothing of any of this. I was shocked and upset that Steve Charles, whom I had entrusted with almost free reign for a full year on a project of such tremendous magnitude, would get himself into a situation such as this. I could not, regardless of the evidence, bring myself to believe that he was guilty of a conflict of interest. And if he was, would I be implicated as well for possible involvement, or at the least, allowing this conflict to exist within my organization? I ended up offering to the Internal Security people a strong character profile of Steve's professional integrity on the job, his outstanding achievement, his reputation, value to the company, and, above all, my personal belief that he was not caught in a conflict of interest between the company and his personal investments.

QUESTIONING STEVE

I was asked to arrange for a direct questioning of Steve by the Internal Security people. I obliged, and early that same afternoon, Steve met for over two hours with them answering questions and providing information as to his ownership and financial benefits. Steve explained that he had indeed owned a company named DEMC several years ago, but those producing properties were nowhere near any properties Ridgeway had and, in his opinion, it was nothing more than an investment and had no bearing with the performance of his job. He admitted to buying a 20 percent ownership in OIST in July 1987, but said he played absolutely no role in its operation, and of special importance, in their business with Ridgeway (it was confirmed that Ridgeway had solicited OIST to perform the work). He stated that no other work had been done by OIST for Ridgeway since then. In addition, Steve claimed he had never played a role in trying to get Ridgeway to even consider OIST for business. He produced evidence showing that he sold his OIST ownership in August 1990 owing to a disagreement with a third minority owner.

As to DEMC, Steve strongly asserted he never had any ownership in the firm. He admitted to a friendship with Alex Elon, and stated that when Alex formed the company, Steve had suggested the name DEMC and Alex ended up using it. But it was strictly circumstantial that his association with DEMC today, as a user of its personnel on a contract basis, was with a company whose name was the same as a former company of his own.

MY MEETING WITH STEVE CHARLES

Steve entered my office late that afternoon in an understandably emotional state. He replayed the events of the previous two hours with Internal Security and repeatedly stated that he had never acted in anything less than the best interest of Ridgeway. I asked him if he received financial benefits from any of these companies at the expense of Ridgeway. He stated an emphatic no. Steve followed with an explanation that the only charge of which he was guilty was the failure to disclose the investments under the Conflict of Interest policy. He then asked me if I wanted him to resign. I said no, and shortly thereafter instructed him to go home. We would talk more in the morning.

MY ETHICAL DILEMMA

I left that night having real doubts about what all was going on. I had known and trusted Steve for so long, and had absolutely no reason to doubt that he was telling me anything but the truth. He readily admitted to never having filed a Conflict of Interest statement, because he knew, in his own mind, that he did not have a conflict of interest. But is it that simple? Steve had to have known that if he was clean, then disclosure would have led to that very conclusion and the company would have granted him permission to have the investment. Why didn't he just file? The more I thought, the more questions I had.

I discovered very early the next morning that the results of the previous day's investigation had been passed to my area manager, the human relations and business managers, as well as the vice-president. These individuals were all two levels above me (minimum) and I knew that my immediate supervisor was unaware of the situation. I was also certain that none of the managers had personally discussed this situation with Steve and heard his side of the story.

A meeting was scheduled for 9:00 A.M. to hear the final report of the Internal Security people and to decide whether punishment was appropriate. The Conflict of Interest policy clearly states that failure to disclose could result in punishment up to, and including, termination. But was the issue the conflict of interest, or was it failure to disclose the investments? And was Steve's failure to disclose grounds for punishment, including termination? If I was to act, it had to be now.

R. FOSTER WINANS

Curtis W. Tarr

Deceptive are the visions the underworld sends to the world above.

—Virgil, *Aeneid*

On the morning of March 29, 1984, *The Wall Street Journal* announced to its readers, in a long and prominently featured article, that one of its columnists, R. Foster Winans, was reported to have told the Securities and Exchange Commission (SEC) that he had provided privileged information on companies to a few investors prior to publication of the data. This was the first public notice of what the press later would term the worst scandal in the history of *The Wall Street Journal*. It also foretold larger dishonorable activities on the stock market that would focus the interest of the American people on white-collar crime.

WINANS'S BACKGROUND

R. Foster Winans, at that time 35, had been a reporter ever since he quit college. After his apprenticeship, covering accidents, courthouses, school boards, fires, and city councils for small-town newspapers, he yearned to live in New York City and to work in business journalism, which he considered a growth field. Life had become too routine at the *Trentonian* in Trenton, N.J., with only an occasional chance to serve as a stringer for *The New York Times* to spice the drudgery of familiar tasks. The opportunity for a new adventure appeared when Dow Jones, publisher of *The Wall Street Journal*, offered Winans a starting position in 1981.

At that time Dow Jones provided each new employee with its policy on ethical conduct, but when Winans joined the staff, the personnel office had run out of the pamphlets detailing the policy. Only after he had begun to talk to the SEC in 1984 did Winans learn about the specifics of the policy. Specifically it stated: "[e]ach employee is expected to bend over backwards to avoid any action, no matter how well intentioned, that could provide grounds even for suspicion that an employee made financial gains by acting on the basis of inside information [including] our plans for running stories." Where other employees hired later had to read the policy and confirm

This case was prepared by Curtis W. Tarr, Dean-Emeritus, Johnson Graduate School of Management, Cornell University. Copyright © 1988 by Curtis W. Tarr.

in writing that they understood its contents, Winans only learned about it after he had committed the most grievous error of his life. He testified later that he knew other employees who were equally unaware of the policy.

Winans quickly impressed his superiors at the *Journal*, even though he started with little knowledge of the business world. In a few months he was given the chance to write about volatile stocks, interviewing analysts and others to determine why prices on these issues were rising or falling. Winans later reported, "[a]lthough I hadn't covered business and had no experience with investing, I found Wall Street as intoxicating as a carnival midway. I seemed to have a Velcro mind for detail and proved to be a quick study of the logic of stocks and the stock market."

In his new assignment, Winans progressed rapidly, pleasing his superiors with his investigative and writing skills. Soon he began to generate his own stories with only modest editorial oversight by others. Within a year and a half, the top people at the *Journal* began to notice his work with pleasure and expectation of what eventually he could accomplish. Winans still lacked the familiarity with the stock market that he needed, but he had the sense to recognize a good story, and he developed a reliable network of sources with whom he worked with skill.

At this juncture, the editors of the *Journal* offered Winans the best assignment of his young life, to be the co-writer of "Heard on the Street," the world's most widely read column on the stock market. Winans had begun his employment with the Dow Jones News Service at a salary of $379 a week. He had been given one merit review with a raise and several contract raises so that when he started with the *Journal* he was making $480 a week. He was told that he could hope for an added $50 a week but that would be the maximum he could expect from his employment there. Only later did Winans learn that the person he replaced on the column earned $8,000 a year more than he did, and that his co-writer earned about $20,000 more. But at this point he did not complain; he relished the increased responsibility and a salary that exceeded greatly what he had earned elsewhere. Although the *Journal* had the same conflict of interest policy as other units of Dow Jones, Winans did not see the statement when he came to his new position. Quite obviously he was coming into a visible and sensitive position of great responsibility, a time when some instruction on ethical conduct might have been most helpful.

Auspiciously, Winans began his new assignment at the start of a prolonged bull market. Price levels for stocks advanced beyond the expectations of all but a few. Many investors gathered fortunes quickly. Winans, close to so much activity and aware of money being made, wondered how he might enhance his modest income. In his investigation, he came upon a health-care company whose stock sold for $4 a share. Winans thought this might be a reasonable risk so he bought a few hundred shares, wrote about the company in his column, saw the price rise briefly and then return to the

$4 level, languish for a while, and finally begin a slow rise. When the price reached $12, Winans sold, but it continued to climb to $20. The young writer then began to consider himself as a stock-picker before the issue took a fall to about 38 cents and eventually investors no longer bid for it.

Some colleagues had told Winans that they did not believe he should invest in a stock while writing about the company. He could see that it was unethical to buy stocks and then write about them in a way that might influence the price. But Winans rationalized his action by reasoning that he had reported truthfully. Emboldened by this logic he took part of his $2,500 profit to invest in another company, about which he also wrote. On this transaction he earned $750.

ENTER PETER BRANT

Besides Winans, the other principal partner in the scandal was Peter Brant, a middle-class native of Buffalo, N.Y., who had gone to Babson College in Massachusetts and then entered the training program at Kidder, Peabody. Brant, a man of abundant confidence to match his fair intelligence, was remembered by friends as having good looks, being a smart dresser, and possessed by entrenched gambling instincts. As a 13-year-old, he had gone often to the racetrack (instead of to the beach as he had told his mother) where he had to convince adults to place bets for him.

Beginning at Kidder, Peabody as a telephone salesman, Brant dreamed of money as he phoned prospects and tried to sell them stocks or bonds. He wanted a life-style rivalling those with inherited wealth, including a country estate, antiques, paintings, horses, memberships in the right clubs. His dreams stimulated his aggressive selling. Within five years he had attained earnings of $600,000 annually, enough to permit him to buy a home on the North Shore of Long Island. It was rumored that he had been blackballed from membership in the exclusive Piping Rock Club, near his home, because he had changed his name.

But Brant did win a friendship among the membership, a New York lawyer named David W.C. Clark, whom he met at a nearby polo club. Clark, three years Brant's senior and a graduate of Deerfield Academy and Columbia University, had a net worth of several million dollars as well as many wealthy clients. The two gained confidence in each other, and Clark entrusted some of his funds to Brant for investment. He also found other clients for their investing schemes. Not content entirely with the glamour of the market, they invested in horses and yachts. But their market activities generated handsome commissions both for Brant and for Kidder, Peabody. By 1983 Clark's account alone produced gross commission revenue of about $100,000 a month, about 30 percent of Brant's total, and of this Brant collected about 50 percent. Those who supervised Brant also got a part of the remaining commission, so that whatever Brant did to enhance his own fortune benefited his superiors in a substantial way. Some of these superiors also received year-end bonuses based upon a profit performance that Brant did much to improve.

By June 1983 Brant had become the number-one broker at Kidder by a wide margin. He owned shares in the firm, and he had aspirations of controlling it. He enjoyed a chauffeured limousine, a corner office with a large lobby, two secretaries, and a generous decorating budget for the furnishings. No one at Kidder, Peabody crossed him; doing so might threaten the goose laying golden eggs for so many; anyone with Brant's contacts could easily switch to another firm if he became unhappy at Kidder.

It was at this pinnacle of Brant's success that Winans met Brant. Winans knew that Brant might be the biggest retail producer in New York, and he wanted to interview him. The two met several times at exclusive clubs where Brant had membership, but Brant curiously sought to avoid the publicity that a published interview would bring. Instead, he developed into a contact for Winans, who admitted later to having been awed by Brant's charisma. After all, here was a man younger than Winans who came to work most days by helicopter from his Long Island home, one who already had won fabulous success.

BRANT'S ECLIPSE

Sadly for Brant, a turn in the fickle stock market during the summer of 1983 ate omnivorously at the broker's fortune. So confident had Brant become in his ability to predict success that he had invested most of his money and that of his clients in Digital Switch. In 18 months, that stock had gone from $7 a share to about $50, and Brant had ridden it all the way. The rising stock generated huge paper profits, and Brant had used these to borrow for greater investments, both for himself and those who trusted him. Thus as the paper profits rose, so did the margin debt. When the price began to fall, Brant and David Clark had no cash to cover their debts, and when they sold the stock, they further depressed the price. By October, both men had lost millions of dollars of paper profits as the market continued to pound Digital Switch.

Brant's stubbornness, perhaps, had prevented him from acting prudently and selling early enough to prevent disaster. Instead he sank into a depression and sought other ways of making up the loss. At this point he called Winans, inviting him to have drinks at his club. Winans, at that time, had no awareness of the disorder that fate had brought to the broker's financial affairs. In the conversation that followed, Brant made a cunning proposal that changed forever the life of a successful but naive business reporter.

As Winans recalled, Brant simply suggested: "You let me know what's going into the paper. . . and I can either go long or go short, depending on whether the story is positive or negative, and we can make some money." Winans understood that the deal was for a split between them of the profits made.

Winans was so flattered that a millionaire broker would want to engage in an arrangement with him that he forgot to ask himself why someone so successful would want to stoop to that means of making money. Also, temptation came at an awkward moment for Winans, who found himself broke despite his $28,000 annual income. He was trying to support a lover and roommate, David Carpenter (formerly a news clerk at the *Journal*), in a small but unprofitable publishing venture, and he was failing to meet his modest commitments. Besides, Winans had observed many deals on the Street that involved questionable ethics, and he had become somewhat hardened. Furthermore, Winans wondered how long his job might last. His superior seldom praised him and often threatened to fire him for minor acts. Apparently bad chemistry plagued their relationship.

But as he considered the offer, Winans found another reason to accept it: He could see no one victimized by what he intended doing. He insisted that he must continue to report as accurately and fairly as he could about stocks that he, not Brant, would choose. Although the SEC lawyers later said that Brant had influenced the content of two columns (one about Digital Switch), Brant generally did not attempt to interfere in Winans's work. Thus the stage was set for Winans's downfall.

THE TRADING SCHEME BEGINS

Although Peter Brant lost on his first venture, he quickly made up for that as he used the information from Winans for his investments. He advanced Winans $15,000 against profits from the scheme, and the reporter quickly paid off his obligations so that he was relieved from financial pressure. Three more payments, totaling about the same amount, were made to David Carpenter, Winans's roommate, in trust for Winans, and $10,000 of this amount was used by the pair for a down payment on a $71,000 home in eastern Pennsylvania, which profits from the manipulations were to pay for in full. Winans apparently did not know what information Brant used or how much he made on the tips; otherwise he would have understood the degree to which Brant took advantage of him. For the time being, Winans felt better about his life.

The scheme worked bountifully. When Winans inserted favorable information in the *Journal* column about a firm, the price, on average, increased about 6 1/2 percent the first day; bearish information depressed a price about 5 1/2 percent. Thus, Brant bought stocks in advance of good news; on bearish tips, however, he worked with "put" options, or short sales. In some cases, the tip from Winans involved material that Winans's co-author had written, but of course the tip worked equally well. Although

Brant and Clark used the tips to greatest advantage, David Carpenter (as agent for Winans) engaged in speculation with smaller amounts at risk, an indication of the resources with which he worked. Brant added another dimension to the developing conspiracy by inviting his college friend and colleague at Kidder, Ken Felis, to join in trading the same stocks for his own account.

As the SEC demonstrated later with evidence at the trial, the plan created some of the greatest profits when the *Journal* column published adverse news about a firm. As an example, on October 26, 1993, Winans reported to Brant that an adverse article on Commodore International Ltd. would soon appear. Acting on that information Felis bought 300 put options on the Philadelphia Stock Exchange for $75,300, and Clark sold short 30,000 shares of Commodore on the New York Stock Exchange. Clark received $1,053,720.10 for his short sale (a short sale is made when an investor sells borrowed shares with an agreement to buy them back later). On October 28, the article appeared. Commodore opened at $30.25 a share, down $1.25 from the previous close. Felis sold his puts for $162,819.55 for a profit of $87,519.55, while Clark bought shares to cover his short position for $919,048.31, resulting in a profit of $134,671.79.

After Brant cautioned Winans not to use his office telephone to send tips, the reporter began to call from a pay telephone near his building; he also initiated fictitious names to allay suspicion.

SUSPICION AND INVESTIGATION

What neither Winans nor Brant knew was that the American Stock Exchange monitors trading activity using a software program that can detect unusual patterns. Within two weeks, the program detected heavy trading by David Clark in stocks mentioned in "Heard on the Street." That information triggered the start of a quiet investigation that eventually produced evidence that the exchange turned over to the Securities and Exchange Commission.

Brant's trading activity also attracted attention at Kidder, Peabody. Because of his success, Brant had a following. His office manager, Evan Collins, had made a habit of studying the transactions of the broker. Relations between the two had not been smooth owing to the way Brant disdainfully treated Collins. Brant once confessed to Felis, "You have to beat a dog [Collins] every so often so it knows it belongs to you." As he filtered through the evidence, Collins noticed the correlation between Brant's recent activities and the information published in the *Journal* column. He shared this with his superiors.

Learning of this, Brant's superiors faced a dilemma that tests the strength of managers. If it were possible that Brant or someone known by him had gained information from someone at the *Journal*, then they faced a scandal of gargantuan size. On the one hand it might invite an SEC investigation (obviously they did not know that an investigation already had begun). On the other hand, if they became too curious they might cause the temperamental Brant to quit the firm and go elsewhere, losing by far their most important source of income.

But something had to be done. Thus, the sales manager of the New York region for Kidder, Peabody asked Brant where David Clark was getting his information for trades. Brant answered that he must be hearing it from someone on the Street. Still troubled, the sales manager elected to turn the Clark case over to the firm's counsel for review. Brant warned that Clark might decide to take his business elsewhere.

Robert Krantz, general counsel for Kidder, Peabody & Co., and a senior partner with 20 years' experience with the firm, mulled over the Clark case and then asked outside counsel, Sullivan and Cromwell, to prepare a paper indicating the legal implications if, in fact, David Clark had gained his information from someone at the *Journal*. Meanwhile, Krantz met with Clark, who stated that he acted on the basis of advice from many friends. Clark also threatened to take his account elsewhere, a possibility that must have made Krantz uneasy. Krantz said that he had no intention of asking Clark to close his account; he merely wondered what a judge would think if he viewed the evidence of numerous trades made just before publication of information in *The Wall Street Journal*.

Krantz told Brant about his conversation with David Clark. Brant asked whether he and Clark had done anything wrong. Krantz admitted that he did not think so, but that the correlation looked bad and he wanted it stopped. Brant wondered aloud if they could continue trading but not every day. Krantz replied that he never again wanted to see evidence of trading before publication in the *Journal* column.

Brant and Ken Felis congratulated themselves on Krantz's admonition because they reasoned that they were not doing anything illegal and that they would not be caught if they traded less frequently. Of course they had not told Krantz how they had received the information, but they rationalized not doing so by convincing themselves that anything that brought in profits was sound business.

A few days later, Evan Collins jolted Felis's complacency when he told him that some of Felis's and Brant's trades had not been made for Clark, an indication that the pair might be involved in the scheme.

As the pressure increased, Clark moved some of his trading to another firm, Bear Stearns & Co. Brant and Felis in turn created the Western Hemisphere Trading Corp. in Costa Rica, supplied it with a mailing address in care of the Bank Institute of Zurich, Switzerland, transferred $275,000 from the Felis account at Kidder to the Swiss bank, and then established an account at Kidder for the dummy corporation. Quickly they began to trade for this new account. But soon investigators at Kidder detected this and insisted that Brant and Felis stop the trading. Meanwhile Clark continued his activity at Bear Stearns. The conspirators decided to explain the payments to David Carpenter, Winans's roommate, if necessary, as settlements for decorating work for Brant.

Although Kidder investigators were pacified, those at the SEC continued their work with zeal. They focused their attention on six transactions by Clark that were timed perfectly to take advantage of stock price changes triggered by information about the stocks published in the *Journal*. On March 1, 1984, Winans received a telephone call from the managing editor of the *Journal*, Norman Pearlstine. At first, Winans thought that he might be given a raise, for he had recently received an offer from *The Outlook*, an investment advisory publication of Standard & Poor's. Instead, Pearlstine told Winans of the SEC investigation. Moments later a lawyer from the SEC called Winans. The SEC had increased the scope of its investigation to a dozen columns and then to 21. Meanwhile the *Journal*, after the March 1 conversation, relieved Winans of the "Heard on the Street" assignment, and on March 2 it published a story about insider trading and added that the SEC was "informally investigating allegations that a stock trader had advance knowledge of certain articles that have appeared in *The Wall Street Journal*." Shortly thereafter, the *Journal* terminated Winans's employment.

These actions naturally placed Winans under heavy pressure, and two weeks later he and David Carpenter went to Washington, D.C., to confess the sad tale to the SEC, offering to supply all of their records. Peter Brant held out until April 9 when he resigned his position as vice president of Kidder, Peabody. Ken Felis had resigned his position shortly before.

Brant and David Clark toyed with the idea of fleeing to Brazil, but Clark abandoned that hope to enter a treatment center for alcoholism. Brant, separately, considered living on his yacht. Clark later told the SEC that Brant had showed him stacks of $100 bills that he estimated to be worth about $20,000. Winans had no resources for such dreams, but he had told the truth and he argued that while he had acted immorally he had not broken the law. Thus, when the U.S. Justice Department asked him to plead guilty to three crimes and avoid a trial, he refused.

INDICTMENTS

On May 17, 1984, the SEC charged R. Foster Winans, David J. Carpenter, Peter Brant, Kenneth Felis, and David Clark with "fraud and deceit" before the federal district court in New York City. The SEC, in a 55-page civil complaint, accused the defendants of violating the antifraud provisions of the federal securities law as well as SEC regulations. It alleged that Winans had profited illegally from stock trading based on market-sensitive information that he had leaked to others, and that he had earned $31,000 from this illicit scheme. The others, it complained, had gained about $700,000. Companies on which they traded involved such prominent names as Schlumberger, Merrill Lynch, International Harvester, Todd Shipyards, Toys "R" Us, International Paper, Caterpillar Tractor, Western Union, Getty Oil, Coleco Industries, Petro-Lewis, G.D. Searle, Greyhound, and Beatrice Foods.

Under examination the defendants or attorneys representing them had somewhat different stories. David Clark stoutly argued that he knew nothing of information coming to Peter Brant from Winans and that he should not have been included in the case. Brant and Ken Felis invoked the Fifth Amendment and refused to testify or to produce documents to coop- erate with the SEC. Winans and David Carpenter, through the same attor- ney, confessed that they had acted unethically but not illegally. Winans apologized profusely for bringing shame to his profession.

The suit immediately caused considerable debate among lawyers. Clearly the SEC sought to widen the net of those who could be considered as inside traders, something the courts had resisted. Thus far, the courts had been clear in their rulings that directors, officers, and employees of a company are subject to the law, specifically Section 10(b) of the Securities and Exchange Act of 1934 and Rule 10b-5 promulgated by the SEC. But the SEC wanted to include as "insiders" anyone who used information in secu- rities dealings that was not generally available to the public. The SEC argued that Winans had a fiduciary responsibility to his employer not to use information for personal gain, and it also argued that Winans had a fiduciary duty to his readers to disclose to them any financial interest he might have in companies about which he wrote. This latter position of the commission caused concern among some First Amendment lawyers who thought that a journalist could not be forced to disclose such matters to readers. If the SEC position were upheld in court, some lawyers wondered where the line on disclosure might be drawn.

On August 28, a federal grand jury indicted Winans, Carpenter, and Felis, charging them with criminal conspiracy, securities fraud, and mail and wire fraud. Winans was named in 61 counts, Felis in 47, and Carpenter in 15. The grand jury also named Peter Brant as a co-conspirator, but Brant already had pleaded guilty in July in order to avoid trial, and he agreed to return $454,437.19 in illicit profits. The SEC made it clear that he would not thereby avoid further charges; in particular, it referred to a suit filed by Roger W. Wilson, a 27-year-old actor, against both Brant and David Clark, seeking damages of $12 million. Wilson claimed the pair had used Wilson's inheritance for insider trading, some of it involving tips from "Heard on the Street." Brant and Clark, four months later, agreed to pay Wilson $1.2 mil- lion in partial settlement of that case.

The criminal indictment maintained the previous SEC position that a journalist had a legal duty to disclose his financial interest in a case about which he or she wrote. Naturally, journalists questioned this, maintaining that their First Amendment rights would be restricted if courts affirmed such a position. *The Wall Street Journal* continued its conflict of interest policy forbidding quick trading and requiring that writers not own any stock in an industry they covered, but it decided not to ask its reporters to disclose financial interests. *The New York Times* had a similar policy, but for the first time required its senior business editors to advise the chief financial officer of the company annually about stock holdings and transactions.

In October 1984, the U.S. Justice Department dropped its controversial charge of breach of duty to readers that had been directed at Winans so that it could expedite the criminal charge against him, Carpenter, and Felis.

TRIAL AND CONVICTION

The criminal trial began in late January 1985, and involved 20 days of testimony. Peter Brant served as the government's chief witness. Questioning involved legal matters much more than questions of fact. The case was heard without a jury.

The government offered two reasons for conviction: that defendants had conspired in a way that violated SEC Rule 10b-5; and that fraudulently they had misappropriated "property" from *The Wall Street Journal*, harming the *Journal*, and thus violating the mail- and wire-fraud statutes. Defendants held that, although they had acted unethically, they had not done anything illegal. The newspaper was the only possible victim of fraud, and the paper had no interest in the securities traded. Furthermore, they had not conspired to take either money or property from the *Journal*.

The provision of the Securities Exchange Act of 1934 in question was:

Section 10: It shall be unlawful for any person, directly or indirectly, by the use of any means or instrumentality of interstate commerce, or of the mails, or of any facility of any national securities exchange. . .

(b) To use or employ, in connection with the purchase or sale of any security registered on a national securities exchange or any security not so registered, any manipulative or deceptive device or contrivance in contravention of such rules and regulations as the [Securities and Exchange] Commission may prescribe as necessary or appropriate in the public interest or for the protection of investors. . . .

Thereupon the SEC had written the following regulation:

Rule 10b-5 EMPLOYMENT OF MANIPULATIVE AND DECEPTIVE DEVICES.
It shall be unlawful for any person, directly or indirectly, by the use of any means or instrumentality of interstate commerce, or of the mails, or of any facility of any national securities exchange,

1. to employ any device, scheme, or artifice to defraud,
2. to make any untrue statement of a material fact or to omit to state a materi-

al fact necessary in order to make the statements made, in the light of the circumstances under which they were made, not misleading, or

3. to engage in any act, practice, or course of business which operates or would operate as a fraud or deceit upon any person, in connection with the purchase or sale of any security.

After study, Federal District Judge Charles E. Stewart, Jr., in a 45-page opinion on June 24, 1985, found the defendants guilty of fraud, Winans on 59 counts, Felis on 41, and Carpenter on 12. The law provided a maximum imprisonment of five years for each count of fraud and conspiracy, and $1,000 for each count of mail and wire fraud.

Judge Stewart accepted the SEC allegation that Winans's actions constituted a theft of confidential information and a fraud against *The Wall Street Journal*. "What made the conduct here a fraud was that Winans knew he was not supposed to leak the timing or contents of his articles or trade on that knowledge," Judge Stewart wrote. "The scheme was also a fraud and not a 'mere theft' because the scheme's object was to filch from [the employer] its valuable property by dishonest, devious, reprehensible means. Here the fraudulent taking and misuse of the confidential information stolen from *The Wall Street Journal* placed immediately in jeopardy probably its most valuable asset—its reputation for fairness and integrity."

On August 6, Judge Stewart sentenced Winans to 18 months in prison, a $5,000 fine, five years' probation, and 400 hours of community service during the probationary period. Observers generally conceded that it was an unusual sentence for a journalist. David Carpenter received three years' probation, a fine of $1,000, and 200 hours of community service. The attorney for Winans and Carpenter announced that he would appeal the conviction, but Winans after the sentencing said "[t]he judge's decision was a fair decision." Winans reported to the judge that his legal fees amounted to $200,000 and that he was trying to find a publisher for a book he wanted to write about his experiences. Winans later agreed to forfeit $4,502 that he and Carpenter had made from their illicit trading activities.

The following day, Judge Stewart sentenced Ken Felis to six months in prison, a fine of $25,000, five years' probation, and 500 hours of community service. Two days earlier, Felis had agreed to forfeit about $160,000 that he had made from trading securities illegally on information supplied by Winans.

Finally, the system cast its net around David Clark, who was indicted on January 21, 1986. A year later he pleaded not guilty to the charge that he had embezzled $3.7 million from his clients to finance his participation in the Winans insider-trading scandal, along with some of his other expensive tastes.

THE APPEAL

On May 27, 1986, the U.S. Court of Appeals in Manhattan upheld 2 to 1 the securities fraud conviction of Winans, Carpenter, and Felis. The majority opinion, written by Judge Lawrence Pierce and joined by Judge Walter Mansfield, held that a person cannot gain a competitive advantage "by conduct constituting secreting, stealing, purloining or otherwise misappropriating material nonpublic information in breach of an employer-imposed fiduciary duty of confidentiality. Such conduct constitutes chicanery, not competition; foul play, not fair play." In his dissent, Judge Roger Miner wrote: "[t]o say that the 'publication schedule' of *The Wall Street Journal* was the nonpublic, confidential information stolen by the defendants is to extend the sweep of [securities laws] beyond all reasonable bounds," adding that securities laws and provisions never were "intended to protect the reputation or enforce the ethical standards of a financial newspaper."

The U.S. Supreme Court agreed on December 15, 1986, to hear an appeal from Winans, Carpenter, and Felis. On November 16, 1987, the Court affirmed the judgment of the Court of Appeals. Justice Byron R. White delivered the opinion of the Supreme Court.

By a vote of 8 to 0, the Court agreed that the defendants had violated the mail- and wire-fraud statutes. Unanimously the justices concurred that the defendants fraudulently took valuable property from the *Journal*, its confidential business information that it should be able to use in any way it sees fit. Property need not be tangible; "[c]onfidential information acquired or compiled by a corporation in the course and conduct of its business is a species of property to which the corporation has the exclusive right and benefit, and which a court of equity will protect through the injunctive process or other appropriate remedy."

By a vote of 4 to 4, the Supreme Court sustained the judgment of the Appeals Court that defendants had violated the securities laws. But a tie vote did not advance an understanding of what constitutes "insider trading" and thus it failed to strengthen the hand of the SEC as SEC lawyers had hoped. Thus, many lawyers and legislators began immediately to ask the Congress to pass new legislation defining more carefully an "insider."

In 1909 the Supreme Court had established a rule that a director of a company either must reveal to the public inside information or not trade in the stock. In 1934 Congress passed the Securities Exchange Act noted above. In 1968, the United States Court of Appeals for the Second Circuit in New York ruled that anyone having inside information of consequence must either disclose that information to the public or refrain from dealing in the stock. In 1980 the U.S. Supreme Court reversed the conviction of Vincent Chiarella, a printer who had assembled information from confidential documents and used it to trade stocks; the Supreme Court, in a decision written by Associate Justice Lewis F. Powell, held that there must be a confidential relationship or fiduciary duty between the defendant and someone else in order to violate securities laws. In 1983 the Supreme Court, again in a decision written by Justice Powell, ruled that a financial analyst, Raymond Dirks, did not violate the law when he urged his clients to sell the stock of a company in which he had uncovered a huge fraud. Thus the definition of an "insider" had not been made clear, and the SEC sought to use the *Winans* case as a means to make it so. Many argued that if Justice Powell had still been sitting on the Supreme Court the split decision sustaining the Appeals Court in the *Winans* case would have been a majority against the government.

Winans believed that the Supreme Court would uphold his claim, and the result disillusioned him as he prepared to enter federal prison. David Carpenter had, by that time, moved to the Midwest in an effort to find anonymity. Ken Felis had returned to Connecticut to take over a family business, serving his prison term on weekends.

For his trial, David Clark engaged F. Lee Bailey, the prominent criminal defense lawyer; the government prosecutor relied heavily upon the testimony of Peter Brant to prove its case. Charged with embezzling $3.7 million from law clients, Clark was free on bail. Personally, Clark's life had taken some unfortunate turns. He had to sell his Long Island home after spending thousands renovating it. His divorce became final on January 12, 1988. He no longer was welcome at some of the private clubs he had frequented so often in better days. Clark had gained so much weight that he no longer could play polo, previously a weekly diversion in his life. Behind him were the days when he could bet $10,000 on a backgammon game. Then, on January 16, 1988, David Clark was stricken beside the pool at his mother's home in Fort Lauderdale, Florida, and he died shortly thereafter of acute hemorrhagic pancreatitis, the consequence of his alcoholism. A friend from his days as a New York socialite concluded that Clark "lost sight of himself and his family and the things he loved; he wanted it all too soon, too fast. It wasn't alcohol that killed David Clark. It was money."

Peter Brant, on February 26, 1988, faced Judge Stewart, who considered Brant "at least as guilty as Mr. Winans, and perhaps more so." But the judge tempered his sentence so that Brant would serve an eight-month prison term over 120 weekends, permitting him to continue his work at a telecommunications firm in West Palm Beach, Florida. Brant was also fined $10,000, given five years' probation, and ordered to volunteer 750 hours to community service. In a separate settlement made earlier with the Securities and Exchange Commission, Brant agreed to give the SEC $454,000, pay the government over $1 million in tax obligations, and be barred from the securities industry for life.

Thus did justice run its course.

TRADE SECRETS

AGRICO, INC.—A SOFTWARE DILEMMA

H. Jeff Smith

George P. Burdelle, vice president of information systems at Agrico, Inc., walked into the computer room with his systems and programming manager, Louise Alvaredo, at 6:30 P.M. on Wednesday, May 27, 1987. Alvaredo typed a few keystrokes on a systems computer console and turned to Burdelle. "So, as you can see, Jane Seymour [the software engineer for Agrico's new AMR system] left the source code on our computer when she left for dinner." She paused, and then asked, "Should I copy it to tape and ship it to our off-site storage facility?"

Agrico's $500 million portfolio of farm-management properties was set for conversion to the new computer system over the upcoming weekend. AMR, a vendor of farm-management software, had been selected to provide the software for the new system. The previous summer AMR had agreed to supply the object code for the system but had been quite reluctant to release the source code to Agrico.[1] The software purchase agreement between Agrico and AMR provided that the source code be placed in escrow to provide protection in case of a natural disaster or in the event of AMR's bankruptcy or inability to provide adequate support for the software. But, despite repeated attempts, Burdelle had been unable to reach an acceptable arrangement with the software company regarding the escrow of the source code.

Burdelle and Alvaredo knew that Agrico would have certain access to the most recent version of the source code should they choose to copy it now and secure it. Given his experience with AMR over the past year, Burdelle was not confident that AMR's proposed arrangements to escrow the source code were adequate. And if Agrico's $500 million portfolio were converted to the new computer system and something happened to the existing object code, the possibility existed that the object code could not be reproduced.

Furthermore, Burdelle had an operational concern. He wanted to be sure that any future modifications to the software were made using the most recent version of the source code, which included all previous modifications. Otherwise, there was a risk that the portfolio data could be altered—or, corrupted—without anyone's knowledge.

Copyright © 1988 by the President and Fellows of Harvard College. Harvard Business School case 189-085. This case was prepared by H. Jeff Smith under the direction of Professor F. Warren McFarlan as the basis for class discussion rather than to illustrate either effective or ineffective handling of an administrative situation. All identities have been disguised.

He recalled the words of Agrico's attorney from a discussion held earlier that week:

> What if you *could* get a copy of their source code through some means? The contract states we cannot have a copy of the software without AMR's written permission. On the other hand, the agreement clearly calls for an escrow agreement that is acceptable both to AMR and to Agrico. If it ever got to court that we took their source code, the judge or jury could well side with us, especially when we explained the trouble we have had with AMR and their unsatisfactory response to our concerns. Still, a lawsuit would be bad publicity and would consume a lot of everyone's time, even if we won. If we lost, it is not clear what the impact might be.

Now, because of an AMR employee's oversight, Burdelle had access to the source code.

"When do you need a decision?" Burdelle asked his systems manager. "Jane said she'd be back from dinner by eight o'clock," Alvaredo replied, "so I need to know in an hour or so."

"I'll give you an answer at 7:30," responded Burdelle, as he walked to his office.

AGRICO—COMPANY BACKGROUND

Agrico, Inc., started by two farmers in Des Moines, Iowa, in 1949, provided farm and ranch management services for 691,000 acres of land in several midwestern states. With market value of its portfolio at $500 million by 1987, Agrico ranked as one of the nation's larger agricultural management firms. Maintaining four regional offices housing an average of five farm managers each, Agrico was able to provide cost-effective management services for more than 350 farms and ranches. The company, acting as an agent, bought equity interests in farms and ranches for their clients (usually pension funds) and managed them to provide operating cash flow and capital appreciation.

Agrico had three different arrangements for the properties. Under crop-share lease arrangements, which represented 47% of their portfolio, tenant farmers would agree to farm land managed by Agrico in return for a portion of each year's crops, which Agrico would ultimately sell in commodity markets. Under cash-rent leases (51% of the portfolio), farmers made cash payments for use of the land. Agrico also directly managed a few properties (about 2% of its total). (See Exhibit 1 for selected data on Agrico and Exhibit 2 for an organizational chart of the company.)

AGRICO'S NEW COMPUTER SYSTEM

During their 1985 business planning process, Agrico's executives decided that their existing arrangement for computer services—an agreement with a nearby commercial real estate concern that provided all services for a yearly fee—was not adequate for their present or future needs.[2] The same year they also identified a need for office automation to improve productivity. Their local contract for computer services expired on September 30, 1987, and as summers were traditionally slow (buying, selling, and leasing of farms took place in the winter and spring and supervising of crop harvests in the fall), June 1, 1987 was set as the target conversion date.

Since Agrico had no internal computer systems staff, they contracted with a large computer consulting firm for recommendations on their computing needs and responsibility for them. The consulting firm assigned several of its employees to the project, including a project manager—George P. Burdelle, a mid-1970s graduate of Georgia Tech who had received his MBA from the Harvard Business School shortly thereafter. The results of the systems planning project indicated that Agrico should do in-house data processing. But as they had little expertise, and to minimize cost and installation lead time, it was recommended that they use a software package rather than attempt to develop a custom-coded system. Thus, a software selection and systems design project was begun in March 1986.

Functional requirements for the system were very complex, since it was expected that a single software package would be used for all three property arrangements under Agrico management. The cash-rent leases offered few problems—that accounting was fairly straightforward. The directly managed properties, though few in number, required a different focus—"all the logistics of running a farm or ranch," according to Burdelle. As for the crop-share leases, since Agrico not only shared all expenses and revenues from these farms, but also often received part of the crops for payment, it was heavily involved in farm commodity markets. So, in addition to the program requirements needed to manage the receiving, selling, and delivering of its portion of the crops, the software had to accommodate the commodity market information.

Agrico insisted that these software requirements be met by a single vendor offering an integrated package. From an initial list of more than 40 potential vendors, only two were identified; each was asked to submit a bid in a "request for proposal" (RFP) process. Agrico selected AMR for their software. As Burdelle later explained:

> When you came down to it, it was a relatively straightforward decision for Agrico. AMR had 12 clients up and running, and they had excellent references. We visited two clients and saw demonstrations of features we knew we needed. The software ran on a minicomputer that also provided excellent office automation capabilities. The only major risk we saw was the fact that AMR was a small company.
>
> Our second choice vendor—a mid-sized software house with about 120 employees—sold software that met most of our functional requirements, but they had only sold three copies, none of which were in production yet. Their software ran on a mainframe, with heavy systems support and operations expertise requirements. In addition, the mainframe had very limited ability to support office automation.

A number of modification and enhancement requirements were identified for the AMR software during the selection process, and the cost and completion schedule were included in the RFP response from the vendor. Work on the system installation project began in July 1986.

Throughout this period Agrico was impressed with Burdelle's grasp of its complex system needs; they offered him the position of vice president of information systems, and Burdelle accepted on July 11, 1986. He said:

> Agrico had a need for someone to build a systems department, and I enjoyed working with the company personnel. The June 1, 1987, conversion target date allowed us adequate time for the installation, and we had the ability to run parallel with the old system before cutting over.

THE AMR RELATIONSHIP

AMR, a small software outfit headquartered in Omaha, Nebraska, had been founded in 1977 by A.M. Rogers. It sold only one software package—a system for managing farm and ranch portfolios. With 12 clients in nine states, AMR appeared to hold the solution for Agrico. Burdelle described them:

> They were a small company with 10 employees, including Rogers himself. We called every one of their customers and got the same story: positive experiences. Rogers was the core of AMR and had his hand in everything, from marketing to software design and programming. The other employees were systems people, but they were more "carpenters" than "architects."

Also in July, Agrico and AMR signed an agreement stating that AMR would provide software consistent with Agrico's needs; AMR would be required to make modifications to its software package. The total purchase price for the software, including modifications, was approximately $200,000. Agrico would also pay one percent of this amount monthly as a maintenance fee. The modified object code was to be delivered to Agrico no later than October 1, 1986; the agreement stated that Agrico's access to the source code was limited to "viewing listings reasonably necessary to test the system." Only AMR was allowed to make modifications to the code. Commented Burdelle:

> We realized that a good percentage of Rogers's revenue came from modifying the software to meet unique client requirements, so we offered to pay more to buy the source code. We acknowledged that if we modified his source he would not be responsible for retrofitting our changes to his new software releases. However, he apparently was afraid that someone would steal a copy of his software. We offered to sign nondisclosure agreements, whatever, but Rogers was really irrational about keeping the source code.

The software purchase agreement required AMR to maintain the software in escrow with a third party to insure adequate backups. (See Exhibit 4 for excerpts from the agreement, which was prepared primarily by Agrico's attorney.)

THE SOFTWARE EXPERIENCE

AMR delivered the object code, as promised, by October. It was installed on Agrico's new computer, which had been delivered in late September. During this same time, Burdelle completed the hiring of his systems staff, which included a systems and programming manager, two programmers, and two operators.

The software acceptance test followed. Both the new Agrico staff and the consultants were involved in the testing. Burdelle related the experience:

> We quickly discovered that all was not right. There was no standard software, as AMR had installed 12 versions—one for each of its clients—around the country. No two were the same—the AMR programmers added or deleted code based upon the needs of each client. We wanted to use practically all of their options, and apparently none of their clients had used them all together. While the individual options worked, they did not always work correctly when combined. We also found out that a number of functions had never been thoroughly tested anywhere.
>
> As it turned out, AMR usually installed and converted the software and then fixed bugs when they were discovered by the client. We were not willing to live with that approach.
>
> Given this situation, we rearranged our schedule to provide more time for software acceptance testing. Our purchase contract required us to pay 20% of the software price upon contract signing, 60% of it 30 days after completion of software acceptance testing, and the remaining balance 90 days after system conversion. We had AMR's attention, because they did not get most of their money until the software passed our acceptance test. I was not going to jeopardize our clients' assets with bug-filled software. Furthermore, I began to see that the escrow of our software was very important, since a standard version literally did not exist.

From October through January, the Agrico team worked at the AMR offices in Omaha. Significant flaws were identified in the software, but AMR had successfully corrected them by March, and Jane Seymour from AMR had begun working on Agrico's computer in Des Moines. But this testing and repair process had exacted its toll on the relationship between Rogers and Burdelle. A contentious tone had crept into their correspondence, which was frequent. On one occasion Rogers complained about the Agrico project team's "tiger testing" of the software, and Burdelle noted, "I instructed the team to be ruthless in identifying bugs. I refused to sign off on the acceptance test until the software was perfect. It was not a pleasant experience."

OFF-SITE ESCROW

During this same period, Burdelle began lengthy discussions with Rogers to define the specific arrangements for the escrow of the object and source code. Burdelle explained:

> When we realized that every one of AMR's installations was unique, we understood just how important it was to have copies of the unique source code for our system stored for backup purposes. Without source code, there was potential for our being forever locked into the existing system with no chance for enhancements or modifications. It was possible we would have to go through the detailed software acceptance testing process again if any changes were made. Given our experience with AMR to date, I was not willing to take it on faith that our source code was adequately protected.
>
> Rogers claimed that we should be satisfied with his backup plan, in which he occasionally took tapes to his bank's vault in Omaha. However, we had no independent way to verify that the source code AMR stated as our escrow copy was in fact the source code that generated our object code. There are companies that store computer tapes in special facilities, like the one we employed in Des Moines for our data tapes, and we wanted that kind of security. Plus, we wanted an independent third party to insure that the latest version was available. The easiest way: escrow the source in the off-site facility we already used.
>
> But Rogers was afraid that we'd modify or sell his source code if it was in the same off-site facility we use, and he was paranoid about keeping control. We talked and talked with him, but our discussions came up empty. He said he thought our concerns about backup procedures were overblown.

Concerned that the June 1 conversion date was fast approaching with backup procedures for code storage still unclear, Burdelle discussed the situation with Agrico's attorney on Tuesday, May 26:

> The attorney said that we had a classic problem of ambiguity. The contract did require AMR to provide us with access to the source code so that we could understand it, but only AMR had the right to copy and store it. Yet, AMR was supposed to store it in a "satisfactory" manner; apparently, we each defined "satisfactory" differently. The attorney felt that if we could get access to the source code we might have a good court argument for storing it ourselves. But technically getting and storing the code did violate the contract.

Burdelle had also considered other solutions, such as discontinuing the relationship with AMR and looking for other vendors. He said:

> Many times along the way, I thought about telling AMR "thanks but no thanks." I realized that the expenses we had incurred were really sunk costs: things like our consultants' bills for debugging the software, which by then had accumulated to $75,000. The biggest problem was that there were few other options: we already knew there was only one other vendor that had even a remotely similar software package, and it used different hardware.
>
> Time was of the essence; any delays in converting to the new system

would cost Agrico dearly. We did not want to start over and develop a custom system; that would have been a monumental project. I was confident that the software now worked as it should, but I was concerned about future modifications.

We had also created much ill will with Rogers, and he was becoming even more irrational as the days went by.

In contrast to the deteriorating relationship with Rogers, Agrico had developed great rapport with Jane Seymour. On Wednesday, May 27, Alvaredo said, in fact, that she believed Seymour may have "looked the other way" in leaving the source code on the computer when she went to dinner. "I think Jane knows the bind we are in with Rogers," she told Burdelle.

BURDELLE'S DECISION

Burdelle, alone in his office, pulled the AMR contract from his file cabinet and read again the words concerning access to source code. He thought once more about the attorney's advice, and he quickly reviewed the ramifications of the potential need for modifications to the software. "While we've had more than our share of disagreements, I have always been honest with Rogers, and I've tried to prove that he had no reason to distrust us," Burdelle mused. "I want to abide by the terms of the contract, but I don't want to jeopardize Agrico's clients' assets."

At 7:30 P.M., Burdelle walked to the computer room to give Alvaredo his decision.

NOTES

1. *Source code* contained a computer program's statements written by programmers in high-level programming languages like BASIC, COBOL, FORTRAN, PL/I, C, etc. It could be printed out on paper or shown on a display terminal and read much like text. A compiler (a special computer program) translated the source code into *object code*, which was in a binary format executed by the computer. Usually, object code could not be read by programmers or easily modified. To make changes to an existing program, programmers usually changed the source code and then recompiled the program, thus creating a new version of the object code. (Most computer software packages purchased by consumers, e.g., LOTUS 1-2-3, contained only the object code. The source code was seldom distributed in such packages.)
2. See Exhibit 3 for a summary of Agrico's experience with its new computer system.

EXHIBIT 1

AGRICO, INC.—A SOFTWARE DILEMMA

SELECTED COMPANY DATA (FOR 1987 UNLESS OTHERWISE NOTED)

Acres under management	691,000	
Market value of properties	$500	million (approx.)
Number of farms	250	
Number of ranches	130	
Number of employees	83	
Number of clients	170	
Tenants:		
Crop-share lease	175	
Cash-rent lease	197	
TOTAL TENANT LEASES	372	

Other data:	1986	1985
Revenues	$5,272,000	$5,157,000
Net income	487,000	436,000
Total assets	3,027,000	2,691,000

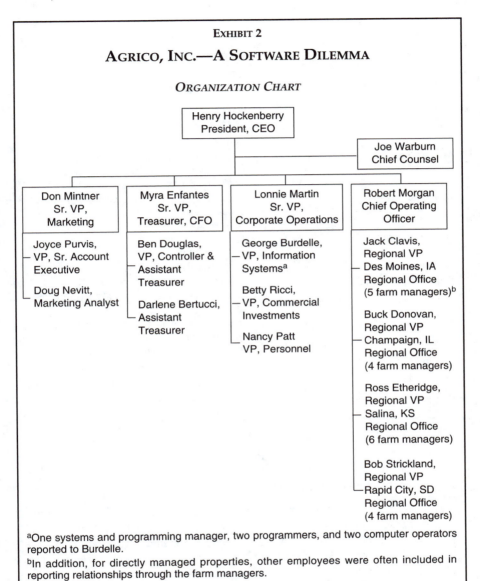

EXHIBIT 2

AGRICO, INC.—A SOFTWARE DILEMMA

ORGANIZATION CHART

Henry Hockenberry
President, CEO

Joe Warburn
Chief Counsel

Don Mintner
Sr. VP,
Marketing

- Joyce Purvis,
VP, Sr. Account
Executive
- Doug Nevitt,
Marketing Analyst

Myra Enfantes
Sr. VP,
Treasurer, CFO

- Ben Douglas,
VP, Controller &
Assistant
Treasurer
- Darlene Bertucci,
Assistant
Treasurer

Lonnie Martin
Sr. VP,
Corporate Operations

- George Burdelle,
VP, Information
Systemsa
- Betty Ricci,
VP, Commercial
Investments
- Nancy Patt
VP, Personnel

Robert Morgan
Chief Operating
Officer

- Jack Clavis,
Regional VP
Des Moines, IA
Regional Office
(5 farm managers)b

- Buck Donovan,
Regional VP
Champaign, IL
Regional Office
(4 farm managers)

- Ross Etheridge,
Regional VP
Salina, KS
Regional Office
(6 farm managers)

- Bob Strickland,
Regional VP
Rapid City, SD
Regional Office
(4 farm managers)

aOne systems and programming manager, two programmers, and two computer operators reported to Burdelle.
bIn addition, for directly managed properties, other employees were often included in reporting relationships through the farm managers.

EXHIBIT 3

AGRICO, INC.—A SOFTWARE DILEMMA

EXPERIENCE WITH NEW COMPUTER SYSTEM—MAJOR EVENTS

Date	Event
1985—Business Planning Process	Executives set June 1, 1987, as target-conversion date.
March 1986	Software selection and systems design project started; consulting team in place (including Burdelle).
July 1986	Work on system installation project begun. Burdelle accepts job at Agrico; resigns from consulting firm. AMR agreement signed.
September 1986	New computer hardware delivered; systems staff on board.
October 1986	AMR delivers object code.
October 1986–January 1987	Software acceptance testing; Agrico team (staff and consultants) work at AMR's Omaha offices.
March 1987	Significant software flaws corrected. Jane Seymour (AMR's software engineer) begins work on Agrico's computer in Des Moines.
May 26, 1987	Burdelle speaks with Agrico attorney.
May 27, 1987	Seymour leaves source code on computer.

EXHIBIT 4

AGRICO, INC.—A SOFTWARE DILEMMA

EXCERPTS FROM AMR AGREEMENT

Agreement made and entered into this 10th day of July 1986, between AMR Software Company, Inc. ("AMR"), a Nebraska corporation with its principal place of business in Omaha, Nebraska, and Agrico, Inc. ("Agrico"), an Iowa corporation with its principal place of business in Des Moines, Iowa.

[Specifics of the sales agreement followed in items 1–14. Included was an agreement that Agrico could examine the source code listings "reasonably necessary to test the system." Item 15 described the monthly maintenance fee—one percent of the purchase price—and defined the support services to be provided.]

16. AMR PROPRIETARY MATERIAL:
   a) The software may not be copied or reprinted in whole or in part without the prior written permission of AMR.

b) Agrico shall not allow anyone other than Agrico or AMR personnel to copy any code or documentation manuals. Agrico shall not give, sell, or allow access to any person not employed by Agrico or to any other company a copy or listing of any of the programs contained in the software, except to *bona fide* consultants of Agrico who, prior to such access, execute with AMR a nondisclosure agreement.

c) The software, including the programs therein and the documentation manuals, is proprietary information of AMR and Agrico shall not disclose any of this proprietary information to any other parties except as otherwise provided in 16.b above.

d) The source code listings shall not be copied or duplicated.

e) Agrico or Agrico's consultants shall not disclose the fact that AMR has provided the source code listings to Agrico hereunder.

f) The source code listings shall not be removed from Agrico's premises.

[Items 17–22 referred to responsibilities of the parties.]

23. ESCROW OF SOURCE CODE: AMR shall place a copy of the source code for programs comprising the software in the custody of a third party (in escrow) that is satisfactory to both Agrico and AMR. AMR warrants and represents that it will update the source code in the possession of the custodian on an annual basis at no cost to Agrico. AMR shall charge Agrico for the cost of escrowing the source code.

AMR warrants that in the event AMR commences a voluntary case or other proceeding seeking liquidation, reorganization or other relief with respect to itself or its debts under any bankruptcy, insolvency, or other similar law now or hereafter in effect or seeks the appointment of a trustee, receiver, liquidator, custodian or other similar official for AMR or a substantial part of AMR's property; or an involuntary case or other proceeding shall be commenced against AMR seeking liquidation, reorganization or other relief with respect to AMR or its debts under any bankruptcy, insolvency, or other similar law now or hereafter in effect or seeking the appointment of a trustee, receiver, liquidator, custodian or other similar official for AMR or any substantial part of its property, and such involuntary case or other proceeding shall remain undismissed and unstayed for a period of 60 days; or an order for relief shall be entered against AMR under the federal bankruptcy laws as now or hereafter in effect; or AMR discontinues marketing or support of the software, and upon Agrico's reasonable belief that AMR is no longer able to provide maintenance of the software, after demand has been sent to AMR at their current address by registered mail, the custodian shall deliver to Agrico the source code and all technical documentation.

Agrico reserves the right to test the escrow disk pack at AMR's office to insure the software is an exact duplicate of the current version of the Agrico software.

24. WARRANTY: AMR hereby represents and warrants to Agrico, such representation and warranty to be in effect as of the date hereof and for so long thereafter as Agrico pays the monthly fee described in item 15 hereof, that the software delivered hereunder is free from defects in manufacture or materials and will continue to meet the specifications and requirements as described in the proposal, the RFP and this agreement after installation, and AMR will, without charge to Agrico, correct any such defects and make such additions, modifications, and adjustments to the software as

may be necessary to keep the system in good operating order and performing in accordance with the foregoing representations and warranties. In addition, AMR warrants that all modifications made to the software meet the business objective of the modification, will be fully unit tested, system tested, documented, and will not adversely affect the system.

[Item 25 detailed several general clauses regarding payment agreements and official addresses.]

IN WITNESS WHEREOF, the parties hereto have executed this agreement under seal in duplicate originals as of the date first written above.

[Signatures followed.]

PRIVACY

TESTING EMPLOYEES FOR SUBSTANCE ABUSE

Alan F. Westin and John D. Aram

United Companies is a conglomerate with two major divisions: (a) a group of oil refinery companies located in four states and employing 7,000 persons, and (b) a multistate financial services division employing 4,500 persons in banking and brokerage operations. United thus has a diverse work force of executives, middle and line management, professionals, salespersons, white-collar clerical and customer service workers, and blue-collar production workers.

Like many firms, United has had incidents of alcohol abuse among its managerial and employee work forces. In 1984 a ring selling cocaine in the printing department of a branch bank was detected by local police and drew national publicity. In the refinery in Baton Rouge, Louisiana, the security department has reported several dozen accidents that security investigators believe to be drug related. And in one of United's banks the controller who embezzled $2 million was found to have been a heavy drug user who said he stole to keep up his habit.

Two years ago, United instituted a "Fitness for Duty" policy, dealing with the detection of alcohol- or drug-impaired behavior on the job. Now United's CEO, Charles Marston, is concerned that this policy may not be sufficient. He has called on various staff groups to reexamine the magni-

Selection from *Managerial Dilemmas* by Alan F. Westin and John D. Aram. Copyright © 1988 by Ballinger Publishing Company. Reprinted by permission of HarperCollins Publishers Inc.

tude of the substance abuse problem and to advise him about possible changes in the company's policy.

You are Charles Marston. After writing a memo on January 4, you have received the replies presented here. What action do you now decide to take?

KEY PERSONS INVOLVED

Charles Marston, Chief Executive Officer
Howard R. Porter, Senior Vice President, Administration
Paula F. Astor, Head of Employment and Labor Relations Group, Law Department
Kevin Holloran, Vice President for Employee Relations

MEMORANDUM

Date: January 4
To: All Department Heads
From: Charles Marston, Chief Executive Officer
Re: Employee Screening for Substance Abuse

I have just returned from last week's National CEO's Association meeting in Denver. One of the more interesting reports presented there concerned the problem of substance abuse in the workplace, which is evidently on the rise almost everywhere and starting to worry a great many executives. Some of the figures cited in the report were truly disturbing. Last year, drug and alcohol abuse resulted in productivity losses estimated at close to $40 billion. When the additional costs of increased medical claims, higher insurance premiums, absenteeism, theft, and accidents associated with substance abuse are figured in, the total drain on American business may have exceeded $100 billion. An equally alarming statistic is that by some estimates, nearly one worker in five uses controlled substances. But the problem isn't limited to these substances—abuse of over-the-counter drugs, prescription drugs, and alcohol is even more common than the use of illegal drugs. (I am enclosing two recent newspaper and magazine articles detailing the scope and magnitude of the situation.)

As you know, we haven't completely escaped these problems ourselves. You will recall that two years ago, a number of workers at our Texas refinery were found to have fairly severe substance-abuse problems—an incident that unfortunately was reported in the local press. It was this episode, coupled with our awareness of earlier problems and incidents, that led us to formulate and issue our Fitness for Duty policy. Despite some initial difficulty with the union, the policy has generally been well received by our employees. (In fact, it has become a model that several other companies have copied.) As you know, this policy provides for breathalyzer or drug testing only when there is some reason to believe that an employee is impaired by alcohol or drugs while on duty. Our strong emphasis—both in our handling of the Texas episode and in the Fitness for Duty policy—is on offering help to our personnel under the Employee Assistance Program; this, rather than more punitive approaches, has certainly been a factor in the acceptance of our policies up to this point.

The question now arises, however, whether these policies are still adequate, and whether they will prove sufficient for dealing with a problem that seems likely to become increasingly severe in the years ahead. At Denver, the focus of the discussions was almost entirely on the issue of drug testing for employees. Estimates of the number of Fortune 500 companies that are now screening applicants or employees for substance abuse, or are seriously studying the implementation of screening programs, range from 30 to 50 percent, depending on whose figures you accept. Many medium-sized companies are following suit. It is widely felt that this approach is the wave of the future. Thus, we at United Companies had best confront the issue head-on:

- Do we need to institute a random screening program for our blue-collar and white-collar work force?
- If so, should we also test management personnel?

I would like your advice on these questions. Please send me your views within the next two weeks, as I intend to make a recommendation to the Management Committee on this subject at its meeting of February 5.

ATTACHMENT

UNITED COMPANIES FITNESS FOR DUTY POLICY

ADOPTED JULY 1, 1986

The unauthorized possession, distribution, sale, knowing transportation, or use of drugs or controlled substances, where admitted or verified, is prohibited. The unauthorized possession or use of alcohol or being under the influence of alcohol on Company property is also prohibited. These provisions apply to all Company employees, and to all persons entering Company premises or facilities. Employees required to meet federal safety qualifications and regulations may be subject to additional restrictions concerning the use of drugs—including over-the-counter and prescription drugs—and alcohol during nonworking hours.

United Companies reserves the right to require an employee to submit to a drug test or breathalyzer test whenever the employee's observed behavior or other convincing evidence provides reason to believe that the employee's use of drugs or alcohol is likely to impair job performance or in any way jeopardize the safety of persons or property. If a drug screen indicates drugs in an employee's system or if a breathalizer test indicates that the employee is under the influence of alcohol, the employee will be terminated. (First offenders will have the option of seeking treatment and/or counseling and/or other rehabilitation services under the provisions of the Employee Assistance Program—see Publication 2-303E.)

ATTACHMENT

Drug, Alcohol Abuse Costs Firms $100 Billion a Year, Report Says

WASHINGTON (UPI)—Drug and alcohol abuse on the job is costing businesses an estimated $100 billion a year, but increased efforts to combat abuse are sometimes hindered by poor information and uncertainties, a business reporting firm said.

In a recent report, the Bureau of National Affairs Inc. said drug and alcohol abuse on the job is receiving "unprecedented attention from employers, unions and public policy leaders, but solutions to the multibillion-dollar problem are proving to be elusive and loaded with controversy."

"Financial costs range from medical bills and insurance premiums to productivity losses and business failures," the report said. "The bottom line losses, according to some estimates, may exceed $100 billion a year."

Lost productivity due to alcohol and drug abuse costs the U.S. $39.1 billion a year, the report said, adding that of the amount, $30.8 billion is attributed to alcohol-related productivity losses and $8.3 billion to drug-related losses.

U.S. industry lost $81 billion in 1984 due to accidents "and people using drugs and alcohol on the job have three to four times the number of accidents as those who don't," the report said.

As a result, the report said testing for drugs and alcohol has increased.

"Surveys cited by the National Institute on Drug Abuse show that the percentage of Fortune 500 companies screening employees or job applicants for drug use rose from 3% to almost 30% between 1982 and 1985," the report said.

However, drug and alcohol screening has its problems.

According to the survey, critics say drug tests produce erroneous results, create employee and union relations difficulties, invade employee privacy and fail to indicate whether an employee is actually impaired by a drug.

Attention has focused on illegal drugs in recent years, but the report finds that legal drugs—alcohol, prescribed medicines and over-the-counter drugs—pose problems for far more employees than do illegal drugs.

"The National Institute for Drug Abuse has estimated that abuse of prescription drugs causes 60% of hospital emergency room admissions for drug overdose and 70% of all drug-related deaths," the report said.

In addition, the report notes that a 1981 study of drug testing labs conducted by the U.S. Centers for Disease Control—the latest such survey conducted—found error rates as high as 100% at some testing labs.

The study warns that employers "should be careful to examine the fairness of drug screens and searches. Innocent victims of errors may challenge managerial intransigence in court. There are clearly grounds for litigation seeking substantial damages in the doctrines of invasion of privacy and defamation."

Other findings in the report:

- Absenteeism among alcoholics or problem drinkers is 3.8 to 8.3 times greater than normal.
- Alcoholics have a two to three times greater risk of being involved in an industrial accident.
- Up to 40% of industrial fatalities and 47% of industrial injuries can be linked to alcohol abuse and alcoholism.
- Grievance procedures by workers appealing drug or alcohol-related firings cost employers an average of $1,050 each.
- Non-alcoholic members of alcoholics' families used 10 times as much sick leave as normal, according to one study.
- Average monthly health care costs in families with an alcoholic member were $207 per person, compared with $107 per person for families with no known alcoholic members.
- Alcoholics' average health care costs increased from $150 a month two years before treatment to $450 during each of the six months prior to treatment, and to $1,370 in the final pre-treatment month.

The Bureau of National Affairs is a Washington-based private company that has 60 publications covering business and economics, law, taxation, labor relations and environmental protection and other topics.

Source: Used with permission of *Investor's Daily*, April 3, 1986.

ATTACHMENT

USING DRUGS? YOU MAY NOT GET HIRED

BY TED GEST

Scores of applicants today are facing more than job-competency exams. They need to pass urine tests as well.

The problem is illicit drugs. Companies are cracking down to prevent accidents, absenteeism and low productivity that they blame on wide use of marijuana, cocaine and other substances ranging from illegal "angel dust" to prescription medications.

A new survey shows that 1 in 5 of the nation's biggest companies now give tests, and an additional 19 percent may join the trend within two years. Employers are beginning to test workers already on the payroll, and a few school systems may test both teachers and students.

The practice is spreading rapidly even though critics say tests are often inaccurate and that the drugs they do detect may have no effect on job performance.

GI Tradition. Testing got its foothold in the armed services, which long have insisted on strict prohibition against drug use by their personnel. In recent years, business owners and government officials have turned up more and more cases of civilian mishaps linked to drugs. Although no one has compiled a national toll of drug-caused accidents, several cases have been documented in the transportation and utility industries.

Drugs were a factor in a Burlington Northern rail crash in Wyoming last year [1984] in which two crewmen were killed. The railroad dismissed an engineer who had been smoking marijuana. Tests of crewmen on a train parked nearby turned up several more drug users, who also were fired.

The crash of a small plane last year in northern New Jersey that killed the pilot and three passengers also was the result of drug use, reports the National Transportation Safety Board. The board suspects that drug use was involved in train collisions in Arkansas, Atlanta and Miami. The Federal Aviation Administration fired three Miami air-traffic controllers found with marijuana and cocaine at work.

To weed out drug abusers, many firms require job applicants to submit urine for analysis that can detect a half-dozen or more drugs. The exam can find cocaine traces for two days after use and marijuana for several weeks.

Critics complain that the test often is inaccurate. Some samples are handled improperly, causing "false positives"—persons tagged as drug users when they are not. A study of 13 laboratories by the federal Centers for Disease Control showed an error rate of up to 66 percent. "Some testing is done by untrained people," notes Richard Hawks of the National Institute on Drug Abuse.

Others say initial indications of drug use should be rechecked on more sophisticated equipment. When that is done, "results are almost 100 percent accurate," contends Claude Buller of North Carolina-based CompuChem Laboratories. Preliminary tests cost only a few dollars, but many firms don't pursue follow-up tests that often cost $50 or more.

When companies use the tests as a screening device, there is little that applicants can do to protest. As long as exams are required of everyone, discrimination claims are likely to fall flat. It may be a different story for tests of those already on the job, and some of these employees are charging that their privacy is being violated.

What may be the first drug-testing dispute to enter the courts erupted last summer in San Francisco at Southern Pacific Transportation Company, which forced nearly 500 workers without warning to submit urine samples. Computer programmer Barbara Luck was dismissed after she refused to participate on privacy grounds. Luck has a lawsuit pending against the company, as does an office manager whose test showed that he had used cocaine—a charge he denies. The man says he was sent to rehabilitation classes even though a follow-up test showed no evidence of drug abuse.

After reports of such cases, San Francisco last month became the first major U.S. city to bar employers from ordering tests unless there is clear evidence that a worker's drug use endangers others. The measure permits tests only for police, firefighters and rescue units.

Even so, more public and private employers whose work involves public safety are likely to continue drug checks. Burlington Northern intensified testing after last year's crash. Unions unsuccessfully challenged a plan by the Federal Railroad Administration to require all railroad job seekers to submit to tests.

Urinalysis may spread in sports. Big-league baseball was embarrassed last summer when the Pittsburgh trial of a drug dealer included extensive testimony on cocaine use by major-league players. Commissioner Peter Ueberroth has asked all 650 players to take tests. But the players' union has balked, arguing that all players shouldn't be made to comply if only a few have a drug problem.

School Barriers. Moves to test teachers and students have run into roadblocks. A New York judge barred urinalysis for teachers on Long Island, and a New Jersey judge ruled December 10 against a plan to test high-school students. The courts said the procedure violated constitutional protections against unreasonable searches.

No court has stopped testing in a private firm, although the question of whether privacy rights are violated by such procedures may eventually end up in the Supreme Court.

In the meantime, the question facing businesses is whether testing is worth the costs. Some companies insist that it is. After Pacific Gas & Electric Company began to screen applicants, injuries among newly hired construction workers fell 40 percent. But North Carolina toxicologist Arthur McBay says he has seen no scientific evidence that the "millions of dollars being spent on handy-dandy screening programs" have reduced drug problems on the job.

> Still, growing public pressure to do something about substance abuse will make screening routine in many employment offices.
>
> *Source: U.S. News & World Report*, December 23, 1985.
> Copyright, December 2, 1985, *U.S. News & World Report.*

MEMORANDUM
Date: January 12
To: Charles Marston, Chief Executive Officer
From: Howard R. Porter, Senior Vice President, Administration
Re: Mandatory Employee Drug Screening

In response to your memo of January 4, I would like to say that I enthusiastically endorse your resolve to face the issue of substance abuse head-on, while it is still a manageable problem rather than a crisis. So far we seem to have escaped the worst, and it is my hope that decisive and farsighted action now will minimize our difficulties in the future.

It is hard to say just how severe the overall problem is at United Companies, but here is what we know about the situation at our various facilities.

1. *Refinery Division.* Our four oil refinery companies in Maine, Texas, Louisiana, and North Carolina currently employ some 7,000 people. About 60 percent of these employees are blue-collar workers, represented by the Petroleum Workers Union (PWU). Our Security Department reports that last year there were ten terminations of employees who were found to be under the influence of alcohol or drugs while on the job. Most of these employees were refinery workers at the Texas and Louisiana facilities, but a computer programmer and an office worker were also fired. In addition, 37 employees who admitted to substance-abuse problems were placed in counseling or treatment programs, at company expense, under the provisions of the Employee Assistance Program.

These figures do not necessarily define the full extent of substance abuse in our refinery operations, however. While no one so far has been caught selling drugs, there were rumors of drugs being readily available for a time at the Texas refinery. (This situation seems to have cleared up with the discharge of several workers there and the rehabilitation of a number of others, as mentioned above.) Moreover—and in some ways more alarmingly—there were a number of highly suspicious accidents at the North Carolina facility, one of which actually endangered the lives of several workers, as well as equipment worth millions of dollars. We have not been able to pinpoint the cause of these incidents, but most of the obvious possible factors, such as inadequacies in training, have been ruled out. Our Security people, though they have no hard evidence, think it quite possible that substance abuse may have been to blame.

2. *Financial Services Division.* Our bank in California and our brokerage firm in New York City together employ nearly 4,500 people, none of them unionized at present. Last year, six employees were terminated for drug use or intoxication at work. The most serious incident involved a small drug-selling ring that was uncovered in the printing office of the New Caledonia State Bank. Three employees were fired, and two of them were subsequently indicted; the cases have not yet come to trial. (In this instance, as in the Texas case of some years ago that you mentioned in your memo, the story made the papers and we received some rather unfavorable publicity.) Here again, we cannot be sure that we know the full extent of the problem; the six cases that resulted in termination may represent just the tip of the iceberg. Twenty-three employees also sought help for substance-abuse or related problems and were referred for treatment under the Employee Assistance Program. The controller at our San Antonio midtown branch bank, as you will recall, said that continuing his drug supply was what led him to embezzle $2 million from the vault reserves.

I think it is important for us to recognize the full extent of the safety and security problems that substance abuse can entail. While some aspects of this are obvious, others tend to be overlooked. Of course, an intoxicated refinery worker could cause an accident that destroys expensive equipment, injures or kills plant personnel, and even endangers people in the surrounding community. (We all remember what happened in the Bhopal disaster.) But this is not just a blue-collar problem. What about the clerical worker who steals company property—or worse, sells confidential information—to support a drug habit? What about the computer operator who embezzles millions of dollars for the same reason, or, while stoned, accidently misdirects huge sums? Such things have happened elsewhere, and they could happen here. We are vulnerable to many sorts of harm that might result from the actions of our workers, and could be held legally accountable for the harm their actions might inflict on others.

It is for these reasons that I feel strongly about the following recommendations:

1. We should immediately begin routine screening of all job applicants. Many companies now do this, and to my knowledge there are no legal impediments. Clearly it is better to head off potential problems than to worry about how to deal with them when they have become deeply rooted. I look upon this approach as "an ounce of prevention."

2. We should institute a program of periodic screening for all Financial Services Division employees, perhaps with special emphasis on the testing of personnel who are likely to be in the possession of sensitive financial information, or who handle large sums of money, or who are involved in electronic fund transfers, and so forth. Such a program could help us eliminate unreliable people whose actions might someday prove

very costly to us. In the absence of union representation, and given the publicity that substance abuse has received recently, I do not anticipate that our employees could successfully resist the implementation of a screening program, or would even attempt to do so. I see no need to extend such testing to management personnel at the present time. Apart from the one case of drug-related embezzlement by a high executive in San Antonio, we have no evidence of management involvement in any of the substance-abuse incidents that have come to our attention. Moreover, many managers would probably regard testing as indicative of a lack of trust. At best, this might lower morale; at worst, it could touch off a serious revolt among the very people whose enthusiastic leadership we most rely on.

3. The situation in our Refinery Division is somewhat different, in that the union strongly opposes random screening. I am enclosing a recent article from *Lifelines*, the health and safety newsletter of the Oil, Chemical, and Atomic Workers [OCAW] Union. This is the "sister union" of our PWU, and the two usually have similar attitudes. The article spells out the union's position on this issue. Briefly, unions feel that any screening program should be an issue for collective bargaining—that is, we cannot implement such a program without their approval. They contend that random screening programs are inherently an invasion of privacy, in that tests can detect evidence of activities that the union feels are not a valid concern of the company (for example, the use of drugs off company property). So long as such activities do not affect an employee's job performance, the unions maintain that they are none of the employer's business. Thus, their position is that any screening should be only for "probable cause"—that is, on the basis of some objective evidence of impaired performance—and that employees found to have a substance-abuse problem should be given an opportunity to obtain treatment under an employee assistance program. (I should point out that what the union endorses is essentially our present policy.) In addition, the union has raised concerns about the accuracy of current testing procedures and the confidentiality of test results.

In view of this opposition, I think we should, as a first step, attempt to negotiate a drug-screening policy that will meet our needs while still being acceptable to the union. The union has expressed a great deal of concern over job-security issues lately. Perhaps we can arrange a trade-off during this summer's collective bargaining: some concessions on our part regarding job security if they will soften their stand against random screening. It may turn out, however, that the PWU feels that it cannot live with *any* program that involves random testing. If this proves to be the case, I think we should still go ahead and institute such a program. Our position should be that it is simply a management prerogative. It is our right to hire and retain the people we think can do the best job for us, and we do *not* feel that the people we want are those who use drugs—legal or illegal, on the job or at home. We must, of course, be prepared for the filing of grievances over the issue, and perhaps even a lawsuit. Nevertheless, other managements have stuck to their guns in the face of similar opposition, and we should do the same. The issue is too important to back away from; it is a test of our resolve.

4. There remains the issue of the test to be used. I am not prepared to make a recommendation on this issue just now: I propose that it be turned over to a committee for study, perhaps under the chairmanship of our Chief Medical Officer, Dr. Thomas Crippen. It should be noted, however, in view of the questions that have been raised about accuracy and confidentiality, that the test selected and the precise testing procedures adopted may be critical to the effectiveness and acceptance of the entire program. The tests currently available vary widely in their reliability, cost, and sensitivity, and in the nature of the substances they can detect. All of these factors should be taken into account before we commit ourselves to a particular procedure.

ATTACHMENT

DRUG TESTING PROGRAMS

RANDOM SCREENING IS NOT THE ANSWER
BY SYLVIA KREKEL, OCCUPATIONAL HEALTH SPECIALIST, OCAW

On April 9, the Conoco Refinery in Denver was invaded by "rent-a-cops." Both Conoco and contractor employees were herded into lunchrooms and trailers for several hours while the hired private security police, assisted by drug-sniffing dogs, searched lockers and cars for drugs, paraphernalia, and firearms. Employees weren't even allowed to go the bathroom.

This is just another example of employers overreacting to perceived drug problems in the workplace.

Why are employers rushing to impose drug screening programs and what is OCAW's response?

WHY THE RAPID GROWTH

Substance abuse, including alcohol, is undoubtedly a problem in some workplaces. It is also probably true that many employers are blaming substance abuse for conditions that arise out of the nature of the workplace itself. A major reason drug testing has become so popular today is that an entire new industry has grown up in the last 4 or 5 years marketing detection kits for drugs in the urine. These drug kits can cost as little as $10 or less per sample, and can be very unreliable.

Another reason for the rapid growth of drug testing is the wide publicity that has been given the issue of testing and its use in professional athletics. Any issue given a lot of publicity will have a bandwagon effect.

Finally a big impetus to drug testing was given by President Reagan's Commission on Organized Crime. The Commission recommended in March, 1986, that all federal agencies immediately implement drug testing programs, and that both the public and private sector make it clear that any and all use of drugs is unacceptable.

OCAW POLICY

More than a dozen OCAW-represented employers, many with multiple locations, have imposed drug screening programs, most in the past few months.

First, we should make it clear that OCAW does not condone the abuse of drugs and alcohol, and are just as concerned as the employer about employees using drugs or alcohol on the job or reporting to work under the influence. However, we also believe that what a member does on his or her own time, away from the job, is none of the company's business, as long as it does not affect the employee's job performance.

OCAW considers any drug screening program to be an issue for collective bargaining under the National Labor Relations Act (NLRA).

As a mandatory issue for bargaining, the company must engage in meaningful, good-faith negotiations with the Union regarding their proposed policy and its implementation prior to putting it in place. Merely advising the Union of the policy does not constitute bargaining and this should be made clear to the company, through NLRA charges if necessary.

OCAW Vice-President Robert Wages and the Health and Safety Dept. have developed a letter that should be presented to the company asking for further information on various aspects of the drug screening program. The letter that should be presented to the company asking for further information on various aspects of the drug screening program. The letter is specifically designed to provide information on the "reasonableness" of the policy. Some of the areas of drug screening programs about which OCAW is concerned are:

- *Random screening.* As far as OCAW is concerned, random screening of employees makes any proposed drug screening program unreasonable and objectionable. Our position is that screening should always be for "probable cause" such as deteriorating job performance, excessive absenteeism, impairment on the job or other objective considerations. Employees found to be "positive" by a valid confirmed drug test should be given the opportunity to go into treatment through an Employee Assistance Program (EAP), without any discipline for a first offense. OCAW is fully supportive of EAPs.

Union intervention accomplished the revision of the drug testing programs of two major oil companies; their programs were changed to exclude random testing in favor of "probable cause" testing. One was a result of a pending court order, the other the result of a stipulation at an arbitration hearing.

- *Reliability.* Many of the new laboratories that offer drug testing are a cause of concern because there are currently no licensing or certification requirements by the government. In some studies, test results from some of these labs have 100% error rates.

OCAW is also concerned about the "chain of custody" of samples and the confidentiality of testing and reporting results.

Any OCAW group that is faced with a drug testing program should immediately contact their assigned representative and Dan Edwards, Health and Safety Director.

Source: OCAW Reporter, May-June, 1986.

MEMORANDUM
Date: January 16
To: Charles Marston, Chief Executive Officer
From: Paula F. Astor, Head of Employment and Labor Relations Group,
             Law Department
Re: Employee Drug-Testing Programs

I hope you will forgive me if I respond to your memo of January 4 at some length. Many people do not realize how complex the whole issue of drug testing really is. While screening for substance abuse has obvious attractions, it also has many legal ramifications that the Management Committee and CEO must take into account before making a decision.

First of all, it should be obvious that substance abuse is a problem of our society as a whole. United Companies did not create this problem, nor can we eliminate it single-handed. Nevertheless, we must make an effort to do our part in controlling it. This is a matter not just of corporate responsibility, but of corporate self-preservation. Our potential legal exposures, should we fail to do everything in our power to curb drug abuse by our employees, are enormous and extremely serious. Consider, by way of illustration, the following hypothetical scenarios:

- A refinery employee, under the influence of drugs or alcohol, ignites a fire that causes the explosion of a petroleum storage tank. A fellow worker is killed; in addition, several nearby houses are destroyed and their occupants injured. The injured parties, as well as the family of the deceased worker, sue United Companies.
- A computer programmer who has an expensive cocaine habit and is employed by our brokerage house diverts a million dollars in client funds to his personal account and disappears, surfacing a month later in a country

with which the United States has no extradition treaty. The defrauded customer sues United Companies for losses incurred.

In our defense, we deny responsibility by demonstrating that in both cases all equipment was properly maintained, employees were well trained, adequate safety and security regulations had been formulated and were in force, sound management procedures had been followed, and so on. We contend that what occurred resulted from the actions of individual employees over which United had no control.

In vain! Under the doctrines of negligent hiring or negligent administration, we could still be found liable if the actions of the employees were the result of their drug use, and United, knowing the potential dangers that an impaired employee might present, had not done everything in its power to detect drug-abusing employees and exclude them from its work force. Thus, we have a substantial responsibility for the actions of our employees, and it is up to us to make sure we do not hire or retain people who might do serious harm to others.

How can we exclude such people from our work force? Some employers, faced with the threat of lawsuits and other challenges to drug testing from unions or employees, have seen the situation as essentially "damned if you do, damned if you don't." The situation, however, is not that bleak. The law is fairly clear: As a private corporation, we are bound only by our collective-bargaining agreements, statutes, and the common law as it pertains to employer–employee relations. We are not bound by the constitutional guarantees of the Fourth, Fifth, and Fourteenth Amendments relating to due process, searches and seizures, and privacy, as a governmental agency would be. Thus, our management can legally screen employees for substance abuse, even in a random-testing program, in order to ensure a safer workplace and limit our legal exposure.

Prudence dictates, however, that in setting up a random-screening program we attempt to follow certain guidelines and satisfy certain criteria that are not currently mandated by law. There are three good reasons for this:

1. By doing more to ensure proper procedures and safeguards than the law actually requires of us, we provide ourselves with an extra margin of protection against potential lawsuits. Litigation is so expensive and inconvenient that it is better to err on the side of safety, and thereby discourage any temptation on the part of employees or unions to sue, than to rely on prevailing in court.

2. It seems likely that in the coming years, many states will pass laws regulating programs such as we plan to establish and setting stringent standards for the protection of employee rights in matters such as privacy and due process. We would do well to anticipate such statutory changes now. That way, we can avoid the unpleasant experience of waking up one day to

find that parts of our program are being successfully challenged in the courts of this or that state.

3. By making sure that our program is as fair as possible, we can blunt potential opposition and minimize the resentment that such programs often arouse. Good employee relations are a valuable asset for any company, and it is important that we do whatever we can to retain the trust and goodwill of our employees, as well as of the general public.

I feel that a successful drug-screening program should have the following characteristics:

- There should be a clearly defined need for such testing. This means that testing should be confined to employees whose activities could pose a danger to the health, safety, or security of their fellow workers, the public, or the company. Thus, many of our refinery workers might legitimately be tested, because if one of them makes a mistake while impaired by drugs or alcohol, the consequences could be disastrous. Similarly, we could justify testing bank tellers and other employees who handle large sums of money. But we would not need to test our sales personnel or clerical workers. The risks posed by substance abuse on the part of a few such workers are not great enough to justify the invasion of individual privacy and abuse to dignity involved in wholesale testing. Although the constitutional protection of the right to privacy is narrow and does not apply to private corporations, such protection could easily be extended to private sector workers by state laws.

  Note that it is not considered discriminatory to screen only certain workers or classes of workers, if the decision is clearly based on the nature of the hazards associated with their work. A decision to screen all blue-collar workers but not white-collar workers, by contrast, or to screen only black workers, might be held to be discriminatory.

- The test used and the associated procedures must meet high scientific standards of accuracy and reliability. (We would probably use urinalysis.) This is necessary to forestall challenges based on the allegation that the tests violate requirements for due process. (Here again, the constitutional guarantee of due process is legally inapplicable to us, but could in the future be granted to workers by state statutes.) For the same reason, positive test results should be double-checked and confirmed by a second test before action is taken against an employee, and employees should be given an opportunity to contest positive results. (It is my understanding that Kevin Holloran intends to address some of the problems associated with tests and testing procedures in detail in a separate memo.)

- The company's policies with respect to drug use and its drug-testing program should be clearly explained in advance to all employees and prospective employees. Ideally, the drug-screening program should be set up with the cooperation of the union at unionized facilities. The drug policies of the company should be included in all employment contracts, and consent to testing should be specified as a condition of employment or continuation of employment once hired.

- The test should be administered with maximum regard for employee privacy, and the results should remain confidential. Test results should not be released to *anyone* outside the company, and should be available to management only on a need-to-know basis. Positive test results should not be shown to anyone until they are confirmed by a second test.

- Employees shown by a *confirmed* test to have a substance-abuse problem should be offered the opportunity to get help through our Employee Assistance Program rather than be discharged. If the employee refuses to use the program, or does not pass it, or is later detected to be using drugs again, we would have no alternative but to discharge him or her.

It should not be too difficult to devise a drug-screening program that satisfies all of these criteria. I have no qualms about recommending the establishment of such a program if the precautions outlined above are taken.

MEMORANDUM
Date: January 17
To: Charles Marston, Chief Executive Officer
From: Kevin Holloran, Vice President for Employee Relations
Re: Drug Testing of Employees

I have seen Paula Astor's memo on the legal aspects of employee drug screening. She has certainly done an excellent job of clarifying some very complex issues. Nevertheless, I feel that before we can be in a position to embark confidently on a course of action, a number of difficult problems need to be considered. These problems involve not only the law but also employee relations, public relations, and our relationship with the union.

One particularly thorny problem is the question of whether to test management personnel. On the one hand, if we do test management personnel, we run the risk of alienating a great many of our executives, who would regard their inclusion in the program as a sign that they are not trusted. We certainly need to attract the best possible people to the executive ranks, and we cannot expect to get or keep such people if we impugn their integrity, even if only by implication. There would also be no easy way to draw lines between different levels of management—we would have to include everyone, from the Chairman of the Board on down. Such a program would be sure to generate a lot of resentment, along with passive if not overt resistance, which could not fail to undermine its acceptance among the rest of the work force. I foresee a great deal of pressure being exerted to exempt management from any screening.

On the other hand, the difficulties created by excluding management could be even worse. At present, the courts have held that there is no legal requirement that a screening program must include the entire work force of a company. This could conceivably change in the future, however, either by the passage of new statutes or simply by a change in interpretation. The courts might well rule that requiring only certain categories of employees to submit to drug testing violates the requirements for equal protection. And even today, some courts have upheld the position that a testing program cannot be limited to certain parts of the work force unless the employer can demonstrate a reason for such selectivity. Given the enormous publicity about cocaine use among professionals and executives, and the potential harm that an addicted executive could do to the company (for example, by embezzlement or by misuse of privileged information), excluding professionals and executives might be very hard to do.

Quite aside from the strictly legal questions, there are psychological and public relations considerations involved in this decision. Many people might consider that testing workers but not managers is unfair, un-American, and so forth. Issues of class and even of race could easily arise; our managers are middle-class and predominantly white, while much of our work force, especially in our refinery operations, is blue-collar and includes a large minority contingent. I would not be surprised to hear claims that a testing program that has a disproportionate effect on minorities represents a violation of EEO requirements.

Another problem is the effect that a drug-screening program might have on our relationship with the union. Our past conflicts with the PWU have largely given way to cooperation in the past year or two, in part owing to the success of our Quality Team Program. It would certainly not be in our interest to jeopardize this greatly improved climate, which has made it possible to resolve many issues (such as those involving quality control, work rules, and the like) that previously gave us a lot of trouble. The union tends to see drug screening as a pivotal issue for this decade, and is likely to dig in its heels.

It should also be noted that our choice of testing methodology could have crucial implications for both the legal standing of the program and our employee relations. At present, the most widely used screening tests require the collection of urine specimens for analysis—a procedure that, since it must be done under observation to prevent fraud, many employees look upon as an embarrassing invasion of their privacy. The use of such specimens means that stringent precautions must be taken at all points in the testing process to prevent mislabeling, contamination, or tampering, as well as misreporting of results. Moreover, the specimens probably need to be saved, at least for a time, in case subsequent tests are required.

There are several different urine screening tests currently available. The most widely used is EMIT, an enzyme immunoassay that can be performed either in a lab or in the workplace. Such tests have the advantage of being quite inexpensive (about $15 per person); however, they are not always very accurate, even when done by a commercial laboratory (as quite a few reported incidents have documented). False negatives—which means that the test fails to detect a drug that is in fact present—are quite common. More seriously, false positives are also common. This means that the test erroneously indicates the presence of a drug that is not present, or confuses a legal substance (such as an over-the-counter cold or cough medication) with a restricted one (such as an amphetamine). I emphasize the danger of false positives because they can cause an employee to be unjustly accused of substance abuse, stigmatized, terminated, and the like. If the test results are contested and then shown to be incorrect, the company must then contend with a very unhappy employee who might well file a grievance or even a lawsuit for libel or slander. The courts have held that if a company acts recklessly or maliciously in disseminating incorrect information about an employee's drug tests, it can be held liable for damages. (In fact, revealing any information about an employee's test results is probably an illegal invasion of privacy, as the confidentiality of medical records is protected under the law.)

The inaccuracy of screening tests means that a positive test should always be confirmed by a more sophisticated (and expensive) test before the employee is confronted with the results or management is informed. Reliable confirmation can be obtained by means of gas chromatography and/or mass spectrometry, which are much more sensitive and accurate and can identify the unique chemical "fingerprints" of hundreds of different substances. Unfortunately, these techniques can be used only by trained laboratory personnel working with complex equipment, and so may cost ten times as much as the screening assays. For this reason, some companies and laboratories deal with the problem of confirmation by simply repeating the original screening test, or performing another screening test of a slightly different type. This approach is dangerous and should be avoided.

There is another problem associated with urine testing, however. Traces of many drugs remain in the body for long periods of time—hours, days, or in some cases even weeks. The length of time that a substance remains detectable in the urine varies with the nature of the drug, and to some extent with the individual involved—his or her weight, diet, body chemistry, and so forth. Thus, when a urine screening test gives a positive result, it tells us only that the individual has used a particular drug at some time in the recent past. It does not tell us that the drug was taken on the job, nor does it tell us whether the user is presently impaired by this substance. The fact that these tests do not measure impairment is a serious drawback, since the main purpose of such screening is to eliminate workers whose job performance is compromised in some way by substance abuse. Workers may contend that it is not the business of United Companies whether they smoked marijuana on Saturday night, so long as they come to work on Monday morning ready and able to do their job. Our only responsibility, they might say, is to ensure that United gets a day's work for a day's pay—not to monitor our employee's life-styles, impose our moral values, or even enforce the drug laws. The fact that our screening tests can detect lingering traces of restricted substances that may have been used off company property, on the employee's own time, puts us in the position of intruding into the private lives of our employees. Although this may not now be illegal for private employers to do, it would appear to be a violation of our own Employee Privacy Policy, instituted in 1981. Let me quote a few of the relevant passages:

- "United Companies will collect only such information about employees as is necessary and useful for hiring and personnel purposes. All such information will be treated as confidential, and will not be released to outsiders unless there is a legal requirement to do so (as in the case of IRS or Social Security records) or such release is consented to by employees (as in the case of information needed to obtain mortgages, etc.)."
- "Only management personnel with a demonstrable need to know can inspect an employee's personnel files."
- "The off-the-job activities of our employees—including, but not limited to, family, community, religious, civic, and social activities—are not legitimate concerns of United Companies, and United Companies will not collect information about such activities."

Fortunately, there is a possible solution to most of the technical problems I have discussed. Screening devices that measure brain electrical activity, rather than the presence of chemicals in urine or other body fluids, will be available shortly. Such noninvasive devices (the first of which, called the MONITOR 1000 system, will be on the market later this year) avoid the embarrassment associated with having to provide urine specimens, as well as the need for concern over the labeling and custody of the specimens. They are fast, cheap, and easy to use, requiring no laboratory work, and they can accurately detect and distinguish among the number of different substances, including alcohol. Most important, they *measure the extent to which the employee is actually impaired at the time of testing*—which is what the company needs to know, and (in the view of some people) all the company needs to know. Thus, the invasion of the employee's privacy is minimized.

It is difficult to weigh so many complex factors and decide on a clear course of action. Nevertheless, since you have requested a recommendation, here is what I suggest:

- I believe that we should institute a screening program for new applicants. Once hired, however, employees should be subject to drug testing only for "probable cause." This is our present policy, and it has worked well; I think the harm involved in expanding the scope of our drug testing would outweigh any potential benefits at this time. This is also what almost all state and federal court rulings in 1986–87 required *public* employers to have as their basis for testing, even when narcotics detectives, prison guards, and U.S. Customs Officers were involved.
- If we do decide to adopt a policy of random or periodic screening for our work force, we should definitely include management personnel in the program.
- Any screening program that we adopt should be based on the MONITOR or similar noninvasive brain-wave test. All positive tests should then be confirmed with a gas chromatography/mass spectrometry urine test.

3

ETHICAL ISSUES
IN EMPLOYEE RELATIONS

INTRODUCTION

The cases in this section all concern discrimination or employee health and safety. These are not the only matters that bear on the ethical treatment of employees. Other ethical issues include fair compensation, job security, notification of layoffs, the process for termination, family leave policies, the restructuring of work, and the quality of work life. However, discrimination and worker health and safety remain among the most serious problems in the American workplace despite decades of legislation and government regulation. A 1993 survey found that more than 20 percent of minority workers believe that they have been discriminated against by their own employer, and only 60 percent of female managers considered their advancement prospects to be "good" or "excellent," compared with a figure of 84 percent reported by males.[1] Findings like these indicate a serious problem, not only in the injustice done to workers but also for the impact on business. The same study revealed that perceptions of mistreatment reduce the loyalty of employees to the company and their willingness to do a good job. Thus, discrimination harms everyone.

It is easy to agree that discrimination is wrong. The main controversies concern what constitutes discrimination and, if it has occurred, what ought to be done to correct it. Many of the cases in the section explore the boundaries of discrimination in its many different forms. Is the mere statistical underrepresentation of racial minorities and women in certain jobs evidence of discrimination? Are employment practices discriminatory when the qualifications used cannot be shown to be reasonably job-related? Or when evaluation procedures cannot be shown to test for those qualifications? Is it discriminatory to exclude women from certain jobs for seemingly legitimate business reasons?

"The Jones Boycott" introduces much of the legal framework developed in Title VII of the 1964 Civil Rights Act. Distinctions between different kinds of discrimination and possible employer defenses are explained in the context of a challenge to the statistical underrepresentation of racial minorities in the work force of a grocery store. Are the managers of this store guilty of nothing more than a failure to scrutinize their hiring practices more closely? Of particular concern in this case is whether hiring and promotion ought to be done "by the numbers" with a view to a certain statistical distribution across all job categories. The Compu-Tech case focuses attention on another aspect of discrimination when female employees are taken off a job because of the reluctance of a prospective foreign client to deal with women. Are the women victims of discrimination if their overall career prospects are not harmed, and if they benefit from the success of the company in gaining the prospect as a client?

Sexual harassment is a serious problem in the workplace, which has been declared by the courts to be a form of discrimination. Unlike other forms, however, sexual harassment involves primarily the behavior of one employee toward another and not, at least directly, the practices or policies of the employer. Still, the organization may have a responsibility to prevent harassment—by developing a strong policy, for example, and communicating it effectively to employees—and also a responsibility to respond appropriately to reported incidents. In the case titled "Propmore Corporation," a male manager is caught between a valued female employee who believes that she has been harassed and others who urge him to treat it as an unfortunate misunderstanding. Complicating the manager's decision are the facts that the alleged harasser works for another company and that the incident occurred outside the workplace.

Discrimination also occurs in women's earnings. Although the Equal Pay Act of 1963 prohibits different wages for men and women who perform essentially the same work, disparities still exist when women's total income is compared to men's. In 1991 (the latest year for which data are available) women earned only 70 cents for every dollar earned by men. Some of this difference is due to education, work experience, and other market factors, but a certain amount can be attributed to discrimination. One strategy for reducing the earnings gap between men and women is "comparable worth," which is a procedure for setting wages according to the features of a job that deserve compensation. Thus, the pay of secretaries and truck drivers would be set, not by market forces—the supply and demand for these services in a free market—but by comparing them with respect to such features as the amount of knowledge, responsibility, and problem-solving ability required to perform the jobs.

The arguments for and against comparable worth address such issues as the extent to which wage differences are caused by discrimination, the possibility of making meaningful comparisons, the effect of comparable worth on the efficiency of labor markets, and the difficulties of implementation. These and other considerations are presented in two opposing memorandums at The Kidd Company (a fictitious name). One is written by a female executive assistant in the Human Resources Department, who is in favor of comparable worth, and the other, a critical assessment, is written by her boss, the manager of the department. After reviewing the arguments contained in these memorandums, the president of The Kidd Company must decide whether to pursue the matter further with the executive committee.

A common but controversial remedy for discrimination is affirmative action, in which companies adopt goals for more equitable distribution of jobs among racial minorities and women and give some preference to these groups in hiring and promotion. Affirmative action may be the only practical means for correcting wrongs committed against some employees, but other employees, usually white males, complain that they are victims of discrimination in reverse. One such person was Daniel A. McAleer, who was passed over for promotion at AT&T so that the company could satisfy a court-ordered affirmative action plan. Without the plan, women and racial minorities could not be compensated for the discrimination that had been committed by AT&T, and yet Mr. McAleer was also forced to pay a price. The U.S. Supreme Court has ruled in several subsequent cases—most notably in *United Steelworkers and Kaiser Aluminum v. Weber* and *Johnson v. Transportation Agency, Santa Clara County*—that properly designed affirmative action plans are permissible under Title VII of the 1964 Civil Rights Act. The AT&T case raises the same question: May employers legally adopt reasonable plans to correct for past discrimination? But because this case was settled out of court, it provides no answer to another question, namely whether an employer might still owe some compensation to employees who are denied advancement because of the company's need to adopt remedial measures.

Occupational health and safety raises at least three distinct issues. One is the extent to which employees have a right to be protected against workplace hazards. In setting permissible exposure limits for cancer-causing agents, for example, the Occupational Safety and Health Administration (OSHA) must decide on the level of acceptable risk when risk cannot be eliminated entirely. Should the level be the lowest that is technologically feasible, or should the benefits be commensurate with the costs? A second issue is the right of employees to refuse hazardous work and the conditions under which such a right can be exercised.

The third issue is perhaps the most controversial: the right of employ-ees and others to know about hazards in the workplace. OSHA requires that all chemicals be labeled with some information, but Congress and many state and local governments have attempted (largely without success) to require companies to reveal more. A pending state law is the subject of the case "Responding to a Sweeping 'Right-to-Know' Proposal," in which a large manufacturing company must decide on an appropriate lobbying strategy. In addition to the merits of the law itself, the case explores some of the problems of choosing a strategy in lobbying a state legislature.

The final case in this section combines issues related to occupational health and safety with those related to discrimination. Here, Johnson Controls, a Milwaukee-based battery manufacturer, struggles with the prob-lem of protecting fertile women from exposure to lead, a substance that is known to adversely affect a developing fetus. The solution adopted by many American companies—to exclude fertile women from jobs that involve lead exposure—invites charges of discrimination, and such so-called fetal protec-tion policies also have some women undergoing surgical sterilization in order to keep their jobs. The main legal issue is whether the policy at Johnson Controls is a violation of Title VII, but among the ethical questions are these: Who is responsible for protecting a developing fetus? The mother or the employer? And do companies have a right to protect themselves against possibly ruinous liability suits for failure to provide protection?

NOTES

1. Sue Shellenbarger, "Work-Force Study Finds Loyalty Is Weak, Divisions of Race and Gender Are Deep," *The Wall Street Journal*, September 3, 1993, pp. B1, B2.

DISCRIMINATION

THE JONES BOYCOTT: A COMMUNITY COMPLAINS ABOUT PERSONNEL POLICIES

Gary B. Frank and Avis L. Johnson

Larry Mason turned to George Paul and said, "This is getting serious, George!"

George Paul, owner of the West Side Market, nodded decisively. "Yes, I think it's time for us to call in the lawyers on this, Larry. I don't know if

This case was prepared by Gary B. Frank and Avis L. Johnson at the University of Akron. Reprinted by permission of the authors.

we are right or wrong; I'm not even sure if it matters. In my mind, there are at least two issues we must consider: legal and ethical. In any case, you will have to continue to manage the West Side store somehow, even if Reverend Jones makes good on his threat of a boycott. I'm sorry, Larry, that we didn't take this matter seriously enough two months ago when this whole mess got started."

BACKGROUND OF THE PROBLEM

The *mess* that George Paul was bemoaning began as a complaint by the Rev. Thaddeus S. Jones to Larry Mason, manager of the West Side Market. Specifically, the Rev. Jones had first called on Larry Mason after one of the minister's parishioners, Aaron Washington, had talked to Rev. Jones about his failure at getting a job at the store. At the time Mr. Washington had applied, he had been told by one of the assistant managers not to bother filling out an application. The assistant manager had responded as he did because the store had just filled the last of its vacant positions; but the assistant manager's choice of words was unfortunate. Mr. Washington took the statement to mean that he was not welcome to apply since he was black.

It was the assistant manager's day off when Rev. Jones arrived at the store, and Larry Mason had no idea what had happened. After listening to the complaint, Larry replied, "I'm sure there was some mistake by Mr. Washington. We're an equal opportunity employer, we have many black employees, and we've never discouraged blacks from applying at any of our stores."

Rev. Jones had looked around and then said, "Yes. Well, I see that a couple of your baggers are black, but that's all I see. Mr. Washington is a qualified butcher, a man with a family to support, and I guess you thought he was probably too old to bag groceries for you."

This confrontation might have been resolved at that point, but Rev. Jones's sarcasm had not been lost on Larry, and he had had a bad day already. He concluded the conversation by saying, "Reverend Jones, we're a good employer. We stand by our record. And I'm sorry if that doesn't suit you."

The next Sunday the minister talked at length from his pulpit about the need of his congregation to support employers who provide meaningful and dignified jobs to the members of the community—and to walk an extra block to shop at stores where the owners weren't just "trying to make a dollar off our people."

That statement may have been unfair as applied to West Side Market, but it did echo the concerns of many of the congregation. The West Side was the older section of town that had been largely abandoned by whites as they moved to the suburbs. For thirty years, the West Side had been predominantly black; however, the tone of the community had started to change in the last six to eight years.

Gentrification had hit the West Side as young, urban professionals rediscovered the magnificent older homes of the district and the convenience of the sector's proximity to both the central business district and the riverside bars and clubs. These yuppies had an impact on the business mix of the area as quiche bars and health clubs started to displace older businesses. For many of the black businessmen on the verge of retirement, the ability to sell at the highest prices in memory was viewed as a godsend; but for others in the community, fear of losing employment made these changes unwelcome.

In this climate, the West Side Market became the unwitting center of community tension. The West Side Market had taken over and remodeled a market that had been vacant for four years. The new store did not displace anyone, and the competition that it provided the single existing food market had resulted in lower food prices in the neighborhood. But in the heat of the current social controversy, the beneficial impact of the West Side Market was largely ignored. The situation escalated as community rallies were held by Rev. Jones. The news media covered these events, and in the course of two months, the West Side Market's hiring practices became an open topic of community discussion.

So, as George Paul discussed these events with Larry Mason, he had good cause for concern. Opening the new store had extended George financially, but his initial projections had been that the store would achieve break-even within a few years. However, an organized boycott, even for several weeks, would force George to close the store with ruinous losses.

INVESTIGATING THE LEGAL ISSUE

It was a very disturbed George Paul who met with his lawyer, Justin Stanhope. After hearing the facts, Justin responded, "George, you're my friend and I hate to see you in a bind, but I have to warn you that your problem may be more than community relations. I'm somewhat surprised that you haven't already had a call from the Equal Employment Opportunity Commission. But I've dealt with the Reverend Jones before and I know that he has strong feelings about community self-help. So, maybe the Reverend Jones has done you a favor that neither you nor he recognizes yet. Reverend Jones pulls a lot of weight in that community and you made a mistake in not meeting with him before this got so far out of hand. At the same time, I think that he can be a reasonable man. He's intelligent and he truly cares for his community. If you can get him cooled off, you might be able to discuss this whole affair more rationally. As to whether you do have a legal problem, I can't answer you yet. We need more facts to go on."

At this point, George Paul jumped back into the conversation. "Justin, you know that I'm always willing to call in the legal eagles when I'm in over my head. At the same time, I know from past experience what you folks charge. What with opening the new store, I am in a real cash bind. Is there anything I can do to help put together these facts?"

"Well, George, I did give a speech a while back to the Small Business Association that covered some of the problems in equal employment opportunity law. If you like, I'll have my secretary run off a copy for you. After you have gone through it, give me a call. I should caution you, though, that the speech was very general and the law in this area changes rapidly."

George took the speech home that night and settled down in his den to read it carefully. The text of this speech is shown in Exhibit 1.

EXHIBIT 1

EQUAL EMPLOYMENT AND THE LAW

PRESENTED TO THE SMALL BUSINESS ASSOCIATION
BY JUSTIN STANHOPE

I'm pleased to be here this afternoon, and I believe the subject you have asked me to cover is a timely one. At one time, only major corporations seemed to have to worry about equal opportunity employment, but this is no longer the case. The impact of the law is being felt by increasing numbers of small firms. In fact, as amended in 1972, Title VII of the Civil Rights Act applies to private employers like yourselves that have as few as fifteen employees on each working day during twenty or more calendar weeks in the current or preceding year. Both the public and employees are far more knowledgeable about their rights, and fewer employees feel disloyal if they pursue those rights.

Most of you try to be fair in all aspects of your employment practices. As business people, you know that "fairness" is just good business practice. You recognize that if you limit employment to one class of people, you miss out on good potential employees. And you recognize that the morale of your current employees will be adversely affected if you act in a capricious, arbitrary, or discriminatory fashion. So I know that all of you try to follow a "Golden Rule" policy in the way you treat employees and applicants. However, despite your best intentions, you can inadvertently violate the law if you don't understand it. This is especially the case in the area of equal employment opportunity law.

So, today I'm going to give you a brief overview of the law and the associated administrative process. Although you should be aware that there are numerous other pieces of antidiscrimination law, which I'll briefly mention later, since our time is limited I will focus first and primarily on Title VII of the Civil Rights Act of 1964, amended by the Equal

Employment Opportunity Act of 1972, the Pregnancy Discrimination Act of 1978, and the Civil Rights Act of 1991.

The thrust of Title VII of the Civil Rights Act of 1964 is put forth in Section 703, where it states that it shall be unlawful for an employer "to limit, segregate, or classify his employees in any way which would deprive or tend to deprive any individual of employment opportunities or otherwise adversely affect his status as an employee because of such individual's race, color, religion, sex, or national origin." As I mentioned, the 1972 amendment extended application to private employers. Since that time the Pregnancy Discrimination Act of 1978 amended Title VII to provide employment discrimination protection to pregnant women through benefits such as health insurance, sick leave, pensions, and vacation time. Two major court cases provided rulings that clarified the meaning of sex discrimination. *Barnes v. Costle* (1977) recognized sexual harassment as a form of sexual discrimination, and in *United Auto Workers v. Johnson Controls* (1991) a company's fetal protection policy, that had been applied to all women of childbearing age, was ruled to be unlawful sex discrimination.

More recently, the Civil Rights Act of 1991 amended Section 703 to make it less difficult for employees to prove they had been discriminated against on the basis of disparate impact, thus overturning *Wards Cove Packing Co. v. Antonio* (1989) and reinforcing the *Griggs v. Duke Power Company* (1971) decision. The burden of proof rests on the employer. For instance, if an applicant can demonstrate that a company's selection practice has caused disparate impact on the basis of race, color, religion, sex, or national origin, then the employer must demonstrate that the practice is job related for the position in question and consistent with business necessity. The applicant then has the opportunity to rebut an employer's defense by demonstrating that an alternative selection practice is available that will reduce disparate impact. If the employer refuses to adopt such a comparable alternative, disparate impact is established.

The 1991 amendment entered into other areas as well. For instance, it held that decisions motivated by race, color, religion, sex, or national origin can establish a practice to be unlawful even when other legitimate concerns also played a part. It broadened the scope of Title VII and the Americans with Disabilities Act of 1990 to cover U.S. citizens employed in foreign countries by American-owned or American-controlled employers, broadened damage awards, and explicitly prohibited discriminatory use of test scores, or "norming" by adjusting scores, using different cutoff scores, or altering the results of employment-related tests on the basis of race, color, religion, sex, or national origin.

Just from this brief description of Title VII and its amendments, you can see that it is far-reaching in terms of your employment practices. It affects recruiting, hiring, performance appraisal, compensation, training, promotions, job transfers, and, indeed, all of your human resource policies and actions. *Connecticut v. Teal* (1982) made it clear that discrimination must not be found in any of these employment areas, judged separately. In other words, if disparate impact is found in any stage of the employment process, that stage must be shown to be job-related, in spite of the fact that the final outcome of the entire process may be equal for a protected class. The Civil Rights Act of 1991 added a dimension to this when it stated that "the decision making process may be analyzed as one employment practice" when the elements of the process can't be separated for analysis, thus allowing an employee to address the entire process when demonstrating that a particular employment practice causes a disparate impact.

As business people, you wish to comply with the law. In the early days after enactment, what constituted discrimination was often unclear. Employers often wondered what their defense would be if faced by a discrimination charge. Today, even though we still see a continuing case-by-case development and interpretation of the law, business does have some general guides to follow. In 1978, the major federal equal employment opportunity enforcement agencies jointly issued the federal *Uniform Guidelines on Employee Selection Processes* (known as *Uniform Guidelines*). These guidelines are significant to you for three reasons:

1. They apply across most of the federal statutes and executive orders which may affect you.
2. They give an operational definition of employment discrimination so you can monitor whether you are likely to have broken the law.
3. They lay out the defenses you have if you are the target of an EEO action.

We will talk about the latter two points at some length; but, first, you must recognize that the law has never said that you must hire or retain unqualified employees. What Title VII does say is that you can't make your human resource decisions based upon race, color, sex, religion, or national origin.

Now, with regard to an operational or working definition of discrimination, the 1978 *Uniform Guidelines* established what is known as the four-fifths or 80 percent rule. Previous case law had developed the concept of disparate or adverse impact to define discrimination. Under the concept of disparate impact, if the effect of your employment practices led to disproportionate selection of a group, you had discriminated. But the employer did not know how equally balanced his or her labor force had to be for protection from a discrimination charge. Now, under the four-fifths rule, the employer has an advance guide to what constitutes disparate impact, and therefore this allows the employer to self-monitor his or her actions.

You should know, too, that the EEOC uses the four-fifths rule as a guide to determine which charges should be pursued and that it has been used in court cases for determining disparate or adverse impact. *Watson v. Fort Worth Bank & Trust* (1988) extended the use of this rule in cases involving subjective employment practices such as interviews, performance appraisals, and job recommendations. Slide one will show you how this works. Thus, this company's selection procedure appears to have adverse impact against blacks, because the selection rate for blacks is less than 80 percent of the rate for whites.

SLIDE 1			
	Applied	Hired	Percent Selected
Blacks	42	4	9.5%
Whites	215	35	16.3%

$$\frac{0.095 \text{ Selection rate for blacks}}{0.163 \text{ Selection rate for whites}} = 58\%$$

To use the four-fifths rule in disparate impact analysis, we need to identify applicant groups and have historic information on numbers applying and selected. The burden of proof to justify the actions falls on the employer. Thus, you should note two facts:

1. The illustration we used was simplified. You would have a more complex analysis by the time you had included whites, blacks, American Indians, Asians, Hispanics, cross-categorized by male and female. Moreover, almost any identifiable group might claim protected status.
2. You are under a strong record-keeping requirement. The legitimacy of your selection procedure will depend on the outcome of the disparate impact analysis. If you don't have records, there is a strong presumption of disparate impact.

At this point, assuming you have done disparate impact analysis and have found that you have violated the four-fifths rule, you may choose to change your selection policies, or you may be ordered to change them. However, if you feel your selection methods are justified, the *Uniform Guidelines* tell you how to defend what you have done. The guides discuss multiple validation methods, but the process essentially amounts to a demonstration that the standards you have used are job-related and are justified for business necessity.

Remember, the law does not require you to hire or maintain unqualified people. The law does require that an employer has the burden of proof to show that these qualifications are necessary for the job if they result in disparate impact.

The actual validation methodologies are quite complex and are beyond the limits of our time today. I do caution you, though, that it is very difficult to validate procedures after you are the target of an EEO suit. In that case, your only hope is if you had previously conducted a full job analysis which identified the knowledge, abilities, skills, and other characteristics (KASOs) that each job required, and your selection procedures were based on these critical work behaviors.

If you are unable to justify your practices, you may be forced to modify your policies. You also may be liable for hefty back pay settlements. The good news is that most cases are settled out of court through compromise. Due to limited resources, the EEOC has been forced to rely on voluntary compliance and negotiated settlements. If a charge is brought to the EEOC, they will make at least two attempts to get a voluntary settlement between you and the parties who have brought the charge. You can help your own case by obtaining a copy of the charge that was filed, respond accurately in writing and, if discrimination occurred, try to reach an equitable settlement out of court. Cooperate with the EEOC, but provide only relevant requested information rather than unrestricted access to your files. If efforts to reach a voluntary settlement fail, it is still unlikely the EEOC will carry the suit against you unless your case is very blatant, involves large numbers, or covers new legal ground—they don't have enough employees to press every case. Moreover, the affected employees or applicants are not likely to sue by themselves unless they can get backing from some outside group, such as the American Civil Liberties Union.

Even though this is the case, it is not something you want to risk because you can't tell in advance which cases the EEOC will press all the way to court. Consequently, your best course of action is to mount a preemptive defense in depth. By this I mean that you should build into your human resource policies protective measures, such as:

1. First, conduct job analyses of your positions.
2. Second, from the job analyses, construct selection procedures that are based on critical job behaviors.
3. Third, monitor the outcome and, if you find that you are getting close to the four-fifths limit, change your policies.
4. And, fourth, the federal enforcement agencies are increasingly taking a "holistic" approach, in that they watch for good faith efforts on behalf of the employer. So you should try to communicate in every way possible to your employees and job applicants that you are an equal opportunity employer, and follow through with actions that back your words. What you do is remembered longer than what you say.

Before closing, I promised that I would mention some of the other pieces of antidiscrimination law. One that applies to those of you who employ twenty or more people each working day during twenty or more calendar weeks in the current or preceding year is the Age Discrimination in Employment Act (ADEA) of 1967, amended in 1986, protecting job applicants and employees of age 40 or over. This virtually removed any mandatory retirement age, and will have growing impact as the labor force ages. More recently, the Older Workers Protection Act of 1990 specified unlawful age-based distinctions in benefits plans. For employers with federal contracts of $2,500 or more, the Vocational Rehabilitation Act of 1973 covers affirmative action toward qualified handicapped people. However, the more recent Americans with Disabilities Act (ADA) of 1990, effective on July 26, 1992, affects all employees with more than twenty-five employees, which will be reduced to fifteen in 1994. The ADA does not require affirmative action but it broadly defines physical and mental impairments that "substantially limit" major life activities, including persons with acquired immune deficiency syndrome (AIDS) and who are HIV (human immunodeficiency virus) positive. Finally, the Immigration Reform and Control Act (IRCA) of 1986 forbids companies with three or more employees to knowingly hire illegal aliens and specifies the consequences for those that do.

If you do all this, it still won't totally protect you from individual charges of discrimination, but it will go a long way in preventing a class action suit, and this is a significant accomplishment.

After reading the speech, George Paul called the manager of the West Side store. "Larry, we need to get together tomorrow morning. Meet me at nine in my office. I've got some material that I want you to read—and it's going to mean that you will have to do a bunch of digging through your employee files."

The next morning, while Larry was in George's office, George Paul called Justin Stanhope. "Justin, I read your speech. I'm going to have my West Side manager pull together the figures for disparate impact analysis. But we're at somewhat of a loss. We could analyze things six ways to Sunday, and we need some direction."

"Well, George, you're right. If you do get hit with an EEOC charge, they will probably go on a fishing expedition that covers all of your human resource policies. If that does happen, we will need to present your best case—and that may mean breaking the data down by store, or trying to lump all the stores together if that gives us better bottom-line figures. But don't get carried away, yet. For now, you aren't facing a charge, and what you want to do is placate Reverend Jones. After we have gone through our own analysis of your employee records, it may be helpful to lay the facts before Reverend Jones. For the analysis, I suggest you focus on the West Side Market's hiring data and break it down by supervisory/nonsupervisory categories, by male/female, and by race. Also, don't accuse me of trying to drum up business, but we might want to set up a review of all of your human resource policies just in case your problem worsens."

"Justin, I think you're right. I had no idea this EEO stuff was so far-reaching. It is time to take a close look at our human resource policies. But one question, how can we validate these policies?"

"George, you're jumping the gun. Don't worry about that yet. Let's see what develops. And get me that data as soon as you can."

Within several days, Larry collected the hiring data on the store's first four months of operation, organized it into the suggested categories, and sent the result to Justin Stanhope's office. These data are shown as Exhibit 2.

Exhibit 2
West Side Market Hiring Data

	Current Employees				Applicants			
	Black		White		Black		White	
	M	F	M	F	M	F	M	F
Supervisory:								
Store manager			1		2		7	2
Assistant manager (produce manager)			1		1		5	
Assistant manager (stockman)			1		2		6	
Butcher			1		3		5	
Deli and bakery		1					4	3
Nonsupervisory:								
Meat cutters	2		3		6		12	2
Stockers	1		3		12	4	25	4
Produce	1		2		5	1	12	
Deli and bakery		3		2	3	12	1	8
Checkers		3		4		17		14
Baggers	4	1	2		24	8	20	5

COMPU-TECH

Idalene F. Kesner

Karen Lowe sat at her desk, angry, upset, and outraged. She had just gotten off the phone with one of her employees, Lynn Brown, who had been told by Roger Reed, senior product manager, that she would not be part of the presentation Lynn's company was making this weekend to the Japanese ambassador. In Roger's words, "The Japanese do not respect women and, therefore, the ambassador may take offense at having to consider a business proposal presented by a woman." According to Roger, the planned joint venture might be in jeopardy if Lynn were included in the presentation. Listening to Lynn on the telephone, Karen realized why she, too, had been pulled from her normal role as presenter. Now she had two dilemmas. At a personal level Karen was angry and upset. She had been pulled from a project presentation not because she was unqualified but because she was female. Moreover, Karen now had an employee of hers in the same boat. Lynn's telephone call was an appeal to her boss to do something about the discrimination she had just encountered.

As Karen hung up the phone, she started considering her options. Clearly, how she handled this situation was important. First, she wanted to send the right signal personally. She had worked long and hard to achieve her current position. She wasn't interested in ruining years of effort by making a political blunder. On the other hand, this most recent incident was certain to send a signal to others in the company. Other women and minority employees were certain to be watching Karen's lead. Moreover, Karen knew that as Lynn's boss she had to deal with Lynn's complaint. As she sat at her desk, she knew she would have to decide to whom she would talk, when, and how.

THE COMPANY

Compu-Tech, a multibillion dollar International Fortune 200 computer corporation, manufactures and sells computers, operating systems, and applications software, as well as chips and microprocessors.

The company is organized in a hybrid type of structure. The first level

This case is based on actual events, but the names of individuals and the company have been disguised. The case was prepared by "Karen Lowe" (name disguised) and Idalene F. Kesner, Kenan-Flagler School of Business, University of North Carolina. Copyright © 1992 by Idalene F. Kesner. Reprinted by permission.

is divided along product and functional lines. There are three major product divisions: (1) mainframe computers, (2) personal computers, and (3) chips and microprocessors. Each division is responsible for developing, manufacturing, and providing product support for that product line.

Each product division has global responsibility for its products, and each carries product verification responsibility. As part of this responsibility, the various divisions have developed demonstration centers. These centers serve three main functions. First, they represent a beta test site. In other words, they are the first "real world" use of the newly tested product in a fully configured system. Thus, beta sites represent live, working demonstrations. In addition to this function, they are also responsible for developing software and user applications. A third function is to provide an environment in which potential customers can see the equipment in operation. Sales and marketing personnel frequently bring major customers to these centers for product presentations. In this way clients can see firsthand demonstrations of the hardware and software they are considering purchasing. This last function is important given that customer purchases can reach upwards of $1 million. For most clients, this investment can represent a significant proportion of their company's income.

Compu-Tech has six demonstration centers worldwide. These centers typically report to a customer service or product support organization, and they have three to fifteen employees supporting each operation. The managers are usually senior-level managers who report to a director.

At the same level as the three main product divisions, Compu-Tech has functional divisions. One of these divisions is marketing and sales. This area is organized by regions, and each segment sells all products within its region. Although the marketing and sales division has no direct control over the product demonstration centers, it is one of the prime users of the facility. As noted earlier, sales personnel consider these centers an important part of their presentation to potential customers.

TECHNICAL INFORMATION CENTER

In the demonstration center where Karen Lowe acts as senior manager, there are fifteen employees. In addition to Karen, there is a Manager of Strategic Support, a Manager of Customer Programs, a Visit Logistics Coordinator, and a departmental secretary, who all report directly to Karen.

Karen's center is considered the premier demonstration center in the company. It was the first one built, and since that time all others have been patterned after it. Moreover, the others are smaller and handle mostly local business. In contrast, Karen's center was the one to which major national and international accounts were brought. During 1990 over 4,500 customers visited the Technical Information Center.

The center had a large lobby, two spacious conference rooms, a customer lounge, a large demonstration area, a full kitchen, and a well-equipped auditorium. On one side of the lobby was a 35-inch television monitor. This screen was used to display animated computer shows with specialized greetings for individual customers. For international visitors, special shows were done using the flag of their country, and messages were written in their own language. Name tags were made using this same program.

When appropriate, the customer lounge was often used to serve hors d'oeuvres to guests. Special care was taken to accommodate the clients' tastes. Chinese guests, for example, preferred soft drinks to be at room temperature, and for snacks they preferred fresh fruits to cheese and crackers. Karen's staff was quite adept at making these subtle adaptations, which signaled that every customer was treated as an individual and that every customer was important. For more formal meals, full service could be provided from the center's kitchen, which was fully equipped with elegant china and glassware. A full-time caterer was employed along with support staff to ensure excellent presentation and service.

Formal product presentations were handled in the auditorium. Here, the equipment was the most up-to-date and included six slide projectors, two overhead video presentation units, a computer used to perform animated presentations, and two overhead projectors. The auditorium was set up like a modern theater with elevated seating. All seats faced a center stage, and at the back of the stage was a large screen used for displaying video presentations. Hidden behind the screen were panels of glass doors. These doors provided access to the test facility. At an appropriate time during the presentation, the screen could be lifted electronically from a remote location. This revealed a complete test site, which customers could tour.

Like everything else at the center, tours were geared toward the needs and desires of customers. For customers with an extensive technical background, presenters would cover the material in as much technical depth as the customer desired. In contrast, for customers interested only in the end result of a new system, the technical aspects were kept to an absolute minimum. Attention was focused instead on user applications and potential uses of the product in the customer's environment. Great care was taken to learn the backgrounds and needs of each visitor, and then presentations were structured accordingly.

According to Karen Lowe, "The strategy for the area was to be 'high-tech/high-touch.'" The product displayed and demonstrated was definitely high-tech and on the leading edge. In fact, if it wasn't presented properly, it could overwhelm people. Thus Karen and her staff went to great lengths to show the "high-touch" side of the strategy. As each customer group arrived, they were greeted in the lobby and escorted to a conference room. Here, they could partake of refreshments, have a product presentation, conduct a meeting, or just relax for a few minutes. From the conference room, the guests were escorted into the auditorium where the appropriate-level presentation or product verification was done, followed by a tour of the test facility. From here the guests were usually escorted into the demonstration area, where, once again, demonstrations were customized for each group.

In addition to the personal service provided by the staff, the high-touch concept was also incorporated into the surroundings. Furnishings were simple but elegant, lighting was soft and variable, and luxurious carpeting extended throughout the facility. Art work included original watercolors of people using the products that Compu-Tech manufactured and sold. Several other artworks were commissioned for the facility.

Karen and her staff worked hard to create an atmosphere where customers felt at home. As Karen noted to her staff many times, "Our chief responsibility is the establishment of an interface so comfortable and transparent that business communications could and would take center stage during the visit." This view was echoed by everyone in the facility. According to one staff member:

> Our number one objective at this center is to provide an inviting atmosphere where potential clients can view Compu-Tech's products and observe first-hand their quality. But, we are also here to give prospective clients a chance to view our service dimension.

According to Karen, her demonstration center was regarded by others in the company as one of Compu-Tech's chief means for showing customers, "We are with you all the way." Through the center, Compu-Tech was able to demonstrate not only that the company was responsible for installing equipment but that it would also help with training. Furthermore, during the demonstration, Compu-Tech could convey to the customer that if any problems developed or if modifications were necessary (e.g., owing to rapid growth of a customer's business), the company would be there to help.

It was clear that, overall, Compu-Tech viewed itself as a high-quality, high-service provider. As such, the demonstration centers were the firm's most important contact point in which to prove the efficacy of this strategy. As Karen Lowe said to her employees many times:

> There are many quality computer companies out there our customers can choose from. What gets them to sign on the dotted line with us is our people and the services we provide after the purchase. We stick with them. They spend a lot of money on our equipment, and so it's our job to help them realize the most out of their investment. If it weren't for our people, we'd be just another computer company. We wouldn't be among the select group of top performers in the industry.

At the close of each visit, the salesperson who brought the group to the center was asked to complete an evaluation form and return it. Composite scores on these evaluations ranged from 4.4 to 4.9 on a 5-point scale, with 5 being excellent. This strong feedback indicated to Karen and her staff that they were indeed meeting their customers' expectations. Elaborating further on this point, Karen noted that:

> Accommodating the customer is our most important means for achieving the corporation's overall goal of quality and service. Tell us what it takes to serve you best and we'll be there. Why do you think we do the things we do here at the demo center? Why host receptions? Why do we go through elaborate presentations and demonstrations? Why have others evaluate our performance? The answer goes beyond wanting you to spend millions of dollars buying our system. The answer to these questions is that we want to prove that we understand your computer needs, and we will do everything in our power to serve those needs. We want to prove to you that when it comes to your computer needs, we can and will go the extra mile.

Karen's boss, Greg Stone, agreed. According to Stone:

> We are prepared to accommodate the customer's every need when it comes to computers, operating systems, and software applications. We know that none of our competitors have better-quality products. We don't want to be—or rather, we won't be—"out-serviced" on the service end.

THE PEOPLE

As senior manager at the center, Karen Lowe was in charge of all aspects of visits to the Technical Information Center, defining and coordinating appropriate marketing messages, developing and delivering presentations, and setting the future strategic direction for the center.

Karen had been with Compu-Tech over seven years; during this time she had been in manufacturing, materials, customer service, and human resources. She had a Ph.D. in Human Resource Development and was considered a "high-potential" employee.

Karen categorized her responsibilities into three main areas. First, she had responsibility for the fifteen employees in the center. She had been in her current position for two years, and during her tenure had led the staff to major innovative improvements in an already well-functioning, well-respected area. Among the many innovations made were local area network (LAN) bridging demonstrations, networking applications, and vertical marketing applications.

Partly as a result of Karen's efforts, the Technical Information Center was recognized as "the place" to take customers in order to showcase Compu-Tech's product lines. Indeed, sales personnel consistently reported closure rates of 90 percent and higher following visits to the center. Thus, it was clear that the center was responsible, in part, for many millions of dollars in revenues annually.

Karen typically handled many of the customer presentations and tours. This was especially true for high-level visitors and for dignitaries from other countries. She had presented to executives and dignitaries from eighteen different nations over the past year, and had a folder with over fifty letters of appreciation from sales personnel and customers hosted at the center. Included was a letter from the CEO of Compu-Tech himself. This was in response to a presentation hosted by the CEO for a group of retired company officers. In his letter of thanks to Karen's vice president, the CEO stated, "The time spent at the Center was well enjoyed by our honored guests. . . . The contribution and support by your staff throughout the planning and execution stage was exceptional and very professional. This event is just another example of teamwork, striving for excellence, and commitment that was demonstrated continuously by your staff."

In addition to Karen, there were quite a few other important people at the center. Lynn Brown, an application engineer, was one of Karen's staff members. She had been with Compu-Tech for about eight years and with the Technical Information Center about one year. Her background was in marketing, and she had handled demonstrations and trade shows for several years. Lynn also had experience in product verification at Compu-Tech before coming to Karen's organization. The product that Lynn specialized in was used to network several mainframe computers. In her presentations she demonstrated surveillance and maintenance functions for the network from a single location. Although this product was only about two months old, Lynn had already done over ten demonstrations for customer groups. Several of these "demos" were presented to very high-level visitors, and four were for visitors from foreign countries.

Roger Reed was the manager for the product Lynn demonstrated. Roger had been one of the developers of the product and had personally trained Lynn, seen her demonstrations, and certified her as competent in this area. Currently in his job as product-line manager, Roger gave product presentations to customer groups, served as a liaison to regional sales personnel, and carried overall responsibility for the continuing development and evolution of the network surveillance product. Roger, an engineer, had been with Compu-Tech for twelve years in a variety of technical functions.

Karen's immediate supervisor was Greg Stone. Greg was the Director of Software Verification. Greg had been with Compu-Tech for seventeen years; much of that time was in the area of mainframe systems installation, but the past five had been in software verification. Greg's facility, known as a FAST office (i.e., First Application System Test), was responsible for verifying the quality of the software prior to its being available for customer purchase.

Greg reported to Dan Parks, Assistant Vice President for Product Verification. Dan had product verification responsibilities for his product line across all marketplaces and coordinated the activities of FAST-type offices in three countries. Dan had been with Compu-Tech for a dozen years. Seven of them were spent in systems installation, and the last five were in software verification.

Dan reported to Tom Clark, who was the Vice President of Product Support. Tom's organization included several areas in addition to product verification: Software Management, Product Integration, and Process Support. In addition to these areas, a finance person and a human resources person also reported to Tom. Tom, in turn, reported to the division president, who reported directly to the CEO of Compu-Tech.

THE INCIDENT

In mid-March, Karen received a call from the coordinator for international visits requesting an unusual Saturday visit by a Japanese ambassador. Karen saw no problem with this request; she agreed to the date, and she began making the appropriate arrangements. She would personally handle the presentation and tour and would have Lynn Brown available to handle the product demonstration. Information was forwarded to the appropriate individuals, citing Karen's name as the prime presenter.

Over the next couple of weeks, Karen learned that the ambassador was a diplomatic agent who was vested with full powers to conduct business on behalf of his government. Part of the discussion with the ambassador was a potential joint-venture agreement that would ultimately transfer certain manufacturing capabilities from the United States to Japan. It would be worth literally millions of dollars to both parties, and completion of this agreement would have a significant impact on the future of the computer business both in Japan and America.

A common practice for visits at this level was for a higher ranking Compu-Tech person to accompany the guest. Because Greg Stone and Dan Parks were going to be out of town, Tom Clark was given the responsibility of accompanying the delegation to the Technical Information Center. From this point, Karen planned to handle the presentation and tour. Lynn's "demo" would be part of the tour.

Ten days before the visit, Karen was approached by Greg who stated that he and Dan Parks had been discussing the need for Doug Paynter (a peer manager of Karen's) to broaden his horizons. They viewed the visit by the Japanese ambassador as an excellent opportunity for Doug, who worked in the highly technical side of the business, to learn more about the customer base. Greg asked Karen if she would be willing to work with Doug to prepare him for the event so that he could make the final presentation. Karen was a little puzzled by this request but agreed that it would indeed be an excellent learning experience for Doug.

Eight days before the visit, Tom Clark notified Karen that he would not be available for the visit; the visit was on a Saturday morning, and Tom would not be back from his European trip to a customer site until that afternoon. Instead, the Senior Vice President of Manufacturing, Pete Westlake, would accompany the guest to the Customer Center.

Three days before the event, Karen received a call from a very upset Lynn Brown, who said she had just been informed by Roger Reed that she could not present because the visitor was "old guard Japanese" who did not respect women. In fact, no women would be present during the presentation. According to Reed, at "Compu-Tech the customer comes first. Compu-Tech's policy had always been to bend over backwards for its customers." Apparently, this was just one more step in setting the right tone for these critical negotiations. At that moment Karen realized the real reason why Doug Paynter was taking over her job of presenter.

Karen hung up the phone and sat stunned. The pieces were falling into place, and she wasn't quite sure what to do from here. Lynn Brown was waiting for an answer. Should Lynn come in on Saturday or not? Would she take part in the presentation? And, most importantly, what was Karen going to do about this outright case of discrimination against a subordinate? Karen herself wondered what she should do. As Lynn's boss, she would have to respond to her employee, but she also felt cheated on a personal level. Moreover, wouldn't others be looking to see how Karen handled the matter? Just how far would Compu-Tech go to "accommodate the customer"?

SEXUAL HARASSMENT

PROPMORE CORPORATION

Peter Madsen and John Fleming

OVERVIEW

Don Bradford was on the fast track at the Propmore Corporation. But he wished he could slow things down a bit, given several hard choices he had to make.

Propmore Corporation was a good place to work. It had sales of about $500 million per year, a net profit margin of 5 percent, and a return on equity of 15 percent. Propmore made several key components used by the aerospace industry and consumer goods market. It was a leader in its field. The company was organized by product divisions, each reporting to the executive vice-president. Its operations were decentralized, with broad

This case was developed by Peter Madsen and John Fleming for the Arthur Andersen & Co. SC Business Ethics Program. Reprinted by permission of Arthur Andersen & Co. SC.

decision-making capability at the divisional level. However, at the corporate level, functional departments (Purchasing, R&D, Personnel, and Marketing) set company policy and coordinated divisional activities in these areas. Propmore was financially successful, and it treated its people well, as Don Bradford's experience showed.

After earning his M.B.A. four years ago from a respected state university, Don quickly rose through the ranks in Purchasing. At age 31, he holds the prestigious position of manager. Before joining Propmore, Don earned a B.S. in engineering and worked for three years in the aerospace industry as a design engineer. During his first three years at Propmore, Don was a buyer and received "excellent" ratings in all his performance appraisals.

As purchasing manager, Don enjoyed good working relationships with superiors and subordinates. He was accountable directly to the division general manager and, functionally, to the corporate vice-president of procurement, Mr. Stewart. His dealings with these people were always amiable, and he came to count upon them for technical guidance, as he learned the role of divisional purchasing manager. Don had several staff assistants who knew the business of buying and were loyal employees. He had done a good job of handling the resentment of those passed over by his promotion to manager, and he had developed a good deal of trust with the buying staff. At least he thought he had—until Jane Thompson presented him with the first in a series of dilemmas.

Jane Thompson, age 34, had been with Propmore for ten years. She had a B.A. in English literature and two years' experience as a material expediter before coming to Propmore. Initially hired as a purchasing assistant, Jane became a buyer after two years. She enjoyed her job and the people she worked with at Propmore. In four years of working with Don, Jane had come to admire and respect his approach to management. She appreciated his sensitive yet strong leadership and saw him as an honest person who could be trusted to look after the interests of his subordinates.

But the dilemma with which Jane now presented Don made him wonder whether he had the skill to be a manager in a major division.

A LUNCHEON HARASSMENT

After a two-hour purchasing meeting in the morning, Bill Smith, an Airgoods Corporation sales representative, had invited Jane Thompson to lunch. They left at noon. An hour and a half later, Jane stormed into Don Bradford's office, obviously upset. When Don asked what was wrong, Jane told him in very strong terms that Bill Smith had sexually harassed her during and after the luncheon.

According to Jane, Bill made some sexual comments and suggestions toward the end of the meal. She considered this to be offensive and unwelcome. Jane, however, told Bill to take her back to the office. He attempted to make light of the situation and said he was only joking, but on the way back he made some further comments and several casual physical contacts to which she objected. When they arrived at the company, Bill was embarrassed and tried to apologize. But Jane entered the office before he could finish.

Jane demanded that the Airgoods Corporation be taken off the bidder list for the raw material contract and that Airgoods' president be informed of the unseemly and illegal behavior of one of his salesmen. She would also consider taking legal action against Bill Smith through the Equal Employment Opportunity Commission for sexual harassment. Also, Jane stated she would investigate suing the Propmore Corporation for failure to protect her from this form of discrimination while she was performing her duties as an employee of the company. At the end of this outburst, Jane abruptly left Don's office.

Don was significantly troubled. Jane played a critical role in getting bids for the raw material contract. He needed her. Yet he knew that if he kept Airgoods on the bidder list, it might be difficult for her to view this vendor objectively.

Don was somewhat concerned about Jane's threat to sue Propmore but doubted that she had a very good case. Still, such an action would be costly in legal fees, management time, and damage to the company's image.

Don wasn't sure what to do about the bidder list. Airgoods had an excellent record as a reliable vendor for similar contracts. Propmore might be at a disadvantage if Airgoods were to be eliminated. On the other hand, Don firmly believed in standing behind his subordinates.

At this point, he needed more information on what constitutes sexual harassment and what policy guidelines his company had established. He examined two documents: the EEOC Definition of Sexual Harassment (Exhibit 1) and the Propmore Corporation's Policy HR-13, on Sexual Harassment (Exhibit 2).

EXHIBIT 1

EQUAL EMPLOYMENT OPPORTUNITY COMMISSION DEFINITION OF SEXUAL HARASSMENT

Unwelcome sexual advances, requests for sexual favors and other verbal or physical contact of a sexual nature constitute sexual harassment when (1) submission to such conduct is made either explicitly or implicitly a term or condition of an individual's employment, (2) submission to or rejection of such conduct by an individual is used as the basis for employment decisions affecting such individual, or (3) such conduct has the purpose or effect of unreasonably interfering with an individual's work performance or creating an intimidating, hostile or offensive working environment.

Applying general Title VII principles, an employer, employment agency, joint apprenticeship committee or labor organization (here-inafter collectively referred to as "employer") is responsible for its acts and those of its agents and supervisory employees with respect to sexual harassment regardless of whether the employer knew or should have known of their occurrence.

EEOC guideline based on the Civil Rights Act of 1964, Title VII

EXHIBIT 2

THE PROPMORE CORPORATION POLICY HR–13

POLICY AREA: Sexual Harassment

PURPOSE: The purpose of Policy HR-13 is to inform employees of the company that The Propmore Corporation forbids practices of sexual harassment on the job and that disciplinary action may be taken against those who violate this policy.

POLICY STATEMENT: In keeping with its long-standing tradition of abiding by pertinent laws and regulations, The Propmore Corporation forbids practices of sexual harassment on the job which violate Title VII of the Civil Rights Act of 1964. Sexual harassment on the job, regardless of its intent, is against the law. Employees who nevertheless engage in sexual harassment practices face possible disciplinary action, which includes dismissal from the company.

POLICY IMPLEMENTATION: Those who wish to report violations of Policy HR-13 shall file a written grievance with their immediate supervisors within two weeks of the alleged violation. In conjunction with the Legal Department, the supervisor will investigate the alleged violation and issue his or her decision based upon the findings of this investigation within 30 days of receiving the written grievance.

GATHERING MORE INFORMATION

Don Bradford had met Bill Smith, the Airgoods Corporation salesman, on several occasions but did not feel he really knew him. To learn more about Bill, Don talked with his other key buyer, Bob Peters. Bob had dealt with Bill on many contracts in the past. After Don finished recounting the incident concerning Jane, Bob smiled. In his opinion, it was just a "boys will be boys" situation that got blown out of proportion. It may have been more than a joke, but Bob did not think Bill would do something "too far out." He pointed out that Bill had been selling for ten years and knew how to treat a customer.

Don's next step was a visit to the division personnel office. In addition to going through Jane's file, he wanted to discuss the matter with Ann Perkins, the division's human resource manager. Fortunately, Ann was in her office and had time to see him immediately.

Don went over the whole situation with Ann. When he had finished his account, Ann was silent for a minute. Then she pointed out that this was a strange sexual harassment situation: it did not happen at the company, and the alleged harasser was not a member of the Propmore organization. The extent of the company's responsibility was not clear.

She had heard of cases where employees held their companies responsible for protecting them from sexual harassment by employees of other organizations. But the harassment had taken place on company premises, where some degree of direct supervision and protection could have been expected.

Ann filled out a slip authorizing Don to see Jane's personnel file. He took the file to an empty office and went through its contents. There were the expected hiring and annual evaluation forms, which revealed nothing unusual and only confirmed his own high opinion of Jane.

Then Don came to an informal note at the back of the file. It summarized a telephone reference check with the personnel manager of Jane's former employer. The note indicated that Jane had complained of being sexually harassed by her supervisor. The personnel manager had "checked it out" with the supervisor, who claimed "there was nothing to it." The note also indicated that Jane was terminated two months after this incident for "unsatisfactory work."

Don returned to his office and called his functional superior, Mr. Stewart, to inform him of the situation. Mr. Stewart was the corporate vice president of procurement. He had known Bill Smith personally for a number of years. He told Don that Bill's wife had abandoned him and their three children several years ago. Although Bill had a reputation for occasional odd behavior, he was known in the industry as a hard-working salesperson who provided excellent service and follow-through on his accounts.

A TELEPHONE CALL

Don felt he needed even more information to make a thorough investigation. He contemplated calling Bill Smith. In fairness to Bill, he should hear his version of what happened during the luncheon. But he knew he was not responsible for the actions of a nonemployee. Furthermore, he wondered if talking to Bill would upset Jane even more if she found out? And would it be a proper part of an investigation mandated by company policy?

As Don considered his options, the phone rang. It was Bill Smith's boss, Joe Maxwell. He and Bill had talked about the luncheon, he said, and wanted to know if Jane had reported anything.

"Don, I don't know what you know about that meeting," said Joe, "but Bill has told me all the facts, and I thought we could put our heads together and nip this thing in the bud."

Don wasn't sure if this call was going to help or hinder him in his decision making. At first, he felt Joe was trying to unduly influence him. Also, he wasn't sure if the call was a violation of Jane's right to confidentiality. "Joe, I'm not sure we should be discussing this matter at all," said Don. "We might be jumping the gun. And what if Jane—"

"Wait, wait," Joe interrupted. "This thing can be put to rest if you just hear what really happened. We've been a good supplier for some time now. Give us the benefit of the doubt. We can talk 'off the record' if you want. But don't close the door on us."

"Okay," said Don, "let's talk off the record. I'll hear Bill's version, but I won't reach a conclusion over the phone. Our policy requires an investigation, and when that's complete, I'll let you know our position."

"Gee, Don," said Joe, "I don't think you even need an investigation. Bill says the only thing that went on at lunch was some innocent flirtation. Jane was giving him the old 'come on,' you know. She was more than friendly to him, smiling a lot and laughing at his jokes. Bill saw all the signals and just responded like a full-blooded male."

"You mean Jane was the cause of his harassing her?" Don asked.

"No, he didn't harass her," Joe said with urgency in his voice. "He only flirted with her because he thought she was flirting with him. It was all very innocent. These things happen every day. He didn't mean any harm. Just the opposite. He thought there was a chance for a nice relationship. He likes her very much and thought the feeling was mutual. No need to make a federal case out of it. These things happen—that's all. Remember when you asked out one of my saleswomen, Don? She said 'no,' but she didn't suggest sexual harassment. Isn't this the same thing?"

"I don't know. Jane was really upset when she came to me. She didn't see it as just flirting that went on," said Don.

"Come on, Don," insisted Joe. "Give her some time to calm down. You know how women can be sometimes. Maybe she has PMS. Why don't you let things just settle down before you do anything rash and start that unnecessary investigation? I bet in a couple days, you can talk to Jane and convince her it was just a misunderstanding. I'll put someone else on this contract, and we'll forget the whole thing ever happened. We've got to think about business first, right?"

Joe Maxwell's phone call put things in a new light for Don. If it was only innocent flirtation, why should good relations between Propmore and Airgoods be damaged? Yet he knew he had an obligation to Jane. He just wasn't sure how far that obligation went.

COMPARABLE WORTH

THE KIDD COMPANY

Scott H. Partridge

Jennifer Andersen, after her graduation from UCLA, accepted a position as a management trainee with The Kidd Company, a Los Angeles–based firm involved in the design and manufacture of high-tech computer components. Organized in 1972, the company took great pride in its ultramodern manufacturing facilities and in a reputation for enlightened employment and personnel practices. The company operated a single-plant manufacturing facility and had approximately thirteen hundred employees.

Jennifer started out as an executive assistant in the Human Resources Department where she administered the company's affirmative action program. Company policy was that the makeup of the company work force should approximate the ethnic makeup of the community in which the plant was located and should have a proportion of male and female workers comparable to the percentages of both sexes in the general work force. Jennifer took pride in the fact that The Kidd Company was in the process of meeting its affirmative action goals. On the other hand, she was much disturbed over the fact that the enthusiasm that provided for ethnic and gender diversity in the manufacturing, technical, supervisory, and managerial staffs did not, in her opinion, extend to the compensation of individuals in those various groups.

Specifically, she felt that women working in what were traditionally female-dominated jobs within the company, such as secretaries and accounting clerks, were not being compensated fairly when compared with men working in traditionally male-dominated jobs, such as electronic technicians, computer operators, and draftsmen (called "drafters" by Jennifer). After some soul-searching, and a great deal of research, Jennifer concluded that the problem was of such importance that it was her responsibility to take some action to bring it to the attention of top management. Working mostly on her own time, she summarized her arguments for a formal comparable worth program in a memo she presented to her immediate superior, Henry J. Brown, along with a request that the material be forwarded up to the Executive Committee for consideration.

Scott H. Partridge, *Cases in Business & Society* (2nd ed.), pp. 120–126. Copyright © 1989. Reprinted by permission of Prentice Hall, Englewood Cliffs, NJ.

MEMORANDUM
October 5, 1988
TO: Mr. Henry J. Brown
            Manager, Human Resources Department
FROM: Jennifer Andersen
            Executive Assistant
SUBJECT: Comparable Worth

The concept of "comparable worth" is now an important social, legal, and political issue facing many employers. Although the Supreme Court has not, as yet, issued a substantive ruling on the issue, advocates are pressing comparable worth class-action suits all over the country, and forward-thinking employers are developing programs that will solve this last area of blatant discrimination against their women employees.

Already, six states—Washington, Idaho, Minnesota, New Mexico, Iowa, and South Dakota—have adopted comparable worth laws. In addition, it is supported by feminist organizations, by politicians from both political parties, by labor unions attempting to include it in collective-bargaining agreements, and by enlightened businessmen attempting to anticipate future problems with their employees.

SOME DEFINITIONS

"Comparable worth" is a system of resolving the problem of gender-based wage disparities based on the fundamental idea that every job has a determinable worth to the employer that can be measured and given a numerical value. This numerical value is based on things such as job skills required, physical effort needed, responsibility, and working conditions. Once jobs are assigned a numerical value, each job with the same value will receive equal pay—in other words, there will be equal pay for comparable worth.

In deciding what is comparable, other factors, such as market factors, will be deliberately disregarded. Thus, comparable worth is premised on the idea that workers should receive equal pay for *dissimilar jobs* where factors such as skill, effort, responsibility, and so on can be proven to be substantially equal or comparable. Therefore, the basic proposition underlying comparable worth is that it is possible to compare different jobs—even jobs that are totally dissimilar—and establish some kind of correct pay relationship between them. For example, in the suit against the state of Washington, the plaintiffs successfully paired clerk typists (usually women) with warehouse workers (usually men) and demonstrated that the two jobs were of comparable worth even though dissimilar and that there was no rational reason why they should have traditionally received significantly different levels of pay.

"Comparable worth" is not the same as "equal pay for equal work." Under the latter, an employer is required by law to pay equal wages to men and women who do the same or basically equivalent work. Thus, male secretaries should be paid the same as female secretaries, and female truck drivers should be paid the same as male truck drivers. The concept of comparable worth carries the idea of "equal pay for equal work" to its logical extension. It arises from the fact that some jobs are traditionally held by women—such as nurses, secretaries, retail clerks, and bank tellers—while other jobs—such as construction workers, truck drivers, and garbage collectors—are usually held by men. Further, women often receive lower pay in the traditional female jobs even though these jobs often require equal—or even greater—levels of skill, knowledge, responsibility, and so on than traditional men's jobs.

In summary, the comparable worth concept says that jobs which differ in work content may be comparable and should, therefore, be compensated for at the same rate. There should be equal pay for all employees—regardless of their gender—whose work is of equal value to this firm.

ARGUMENTS IN FAVOR

It is a fact of life in the United States that women earn, on the average, less than two-thirds of what men earn. In addition, it is also true that very little progress has been made over the past twenty-five years in eliminating this disparity. Those who advocate comparable worth view it as the most efficient and effective method of dealing with this wage gap.

The first argument supporting comparable worth is the claim that there is a bias in wages and salaries paid to women. Not only do women fill a smaller percentage of managerial and administrative positions compared to men, but there also appears to be a pervasive and systematic undervaluation of work done by women that is not only accepted but really unquestioned. It exists in every industry, every occupation, and every profession—even in those dominated by female employees.

The second argument for comparable worth is that it really is possible to develop and apply methods by which the monetary value of various kinds of work can be measured and compared. In fact, techniques have been designed which allow for us to provide not only objective but dependable comparisons of the necessary requirements for different jobs.

The third argument has to do with the cost of implementation. Some businessmen claim that the cost of eliminating sex-based wage differentials will be prohibitively expensive to implement. These critics forget that only about 30 to 40 percent of the male-female earnings gap is due to discrimination. Nondiscrimination factors, such female preference for part-time work, make up the balance. Also, no one has seriously suggested that we eliminate these pay inequalities overnight. It will undoubtedly be a long and tedious process.

To sum up, I believe that comparable worth is an ideal that we should, as a company, adopt on its merits. It makes not just economic sense, but moral sense for the wages that we pay to be a reflection of the intrinsic value of the jobs performed. It can provide a standard that eliminates sex bias and compares wages on the basis of relevant, compensable factors.

SUGGESTED COMPONENTS OF A SYSTEM

Job Analysis. The fundamental core of any job evaluation system is the development of functional job descriptions. The person who knows most about a particular job is, of course, the person performing that job, so the most accurate job descriptions are obtained by interviewing employees. There are numerous guides for obtaining this kind of information through interviews by asking the following kinds of questions:

1. What do you actually do?
2. What are your most difficult duties?
3. What special skills are necessary?
4. What experience is required?
5. What special independent judgment is required to do your job?
6. What is the consequence if you make an error?
7. With whom do you interact?
8. What particular physical skills or effort is required?
9. What unusual working conditions exist?
10. Do you have supervisory responsibility?

Job Evaluation. Although it is not scientifically exact, job evaluation can be a valid method of establishing the relative value of a wide variety of positions within an organization. For The Kidd Company, I recommend the establishment of a Job Evaluation Committee composed of seven members representing the Production, Engineering, Marketing, Data Processing, Secretarial, Maintenance, and Accounting departments, with a chairperson chosen by the group. The ongoing function of the group will be to develop and maintain a system by which each of the job evaluation elements can be applied to the jobs in our company. For example, Exhibit 1 illustrates how this system could be applied to our own company.

With the job evaluation index in hand, we can then compare the maximum salaries that should be paid to the actual salary schedule currently operative within our company as shown in Exhibit 2.

The third column [in Exhibit 2] lists suggested maximum pay scales for each of the job positions illustrated. It is obvious from the data that female-dominated jobs, such as secretary and accounting clerk, are relatively underpaid and that male-dominated positions, such as computer operator and drafter, are relatively overpaid. Assuming that the company decides to implement comparable worth as an official policy, changes will have to be implemented slowly, since it will obviously be difficult to make radical pay rate changes overnight.

EXHIBIT 1

THE KIDD COMPANY: JOB EVALUATIONS

Job Classifications	Knowledge	Experience	Judgment	Independence	Accountability	Interrelationships	Physical Skills	Environment	Physical Effort	Physical Risks	INDEX
Electronic Technician	30	16	15	12	14	8	6	8	8	6	123
Secretary	30	16	18	14	14	14	6	2	4	2	120
Computer Operator	24	24	15	16	14	12	6	2	4	2	119
Drafter	24	24	15	12	14	8	6	4	6	2	115
Maintenance Worker	18	24	12	8	11	6	6	8	12	8	113
Accounting Clerk	24	24	15	14	14	8	6	2	4	2	113

EXHIBIT 2

THE KIDD COMPANY: COMPARATIVE PAY RATES

	Maximum Pay Rates	Job Evaluation Index	Suggested Revised Rates
Electronic technician	$8.87	123	$8.88*
Secretary	8.34	120	8.66
Computer operator	9.19	119	8.59
Drafter	8.34	115	8.30
Maintenance worker	8.11	113	8.16
Accounting clerk	7.91	113	8.16

$$\text{*} \frac{\text{Sum of pay rates}}{\text{Sum of index nos.}} = \frac{\$50.76}{703} = \$.07219 \times 123 = \$8.88$$

Many critics of comparable worth might suggest that the plan I have developed will have a serious impact on the profitability of our business. What they lose sight of is the fact that for the past half-century, wage and salary programs in companies of all sizes have had the same objectives as those who now propose the ideal of comparable worth. In spite of the prophets of doom, the principle of comparable worth can be absorbed within our current systems with only minor disruptions. I hope that you will take this proposal under serious consideration.

MEMORANDUM
October 15, 1988
TO: Mr. Charles J. Ellerbee
               President
FROM: Henry J. Brown
               Manager, Human Resources Department
SUBJECT: Comparable Worth Proposal

Enclosed you will find a copy of a memorandum recently submitted to me by Jennifer Andersen, an executive assistant/management trainee working in my department. She has asked that her memo be forwarded to you and to the Executive Committee, and I am doing so. Along with Jennifer's paper, I am also enclosing the following comments, which express my own opinion on the value of the comparable worth concept and how it would fit into our company.

The best place to start to examine the comparable worth issue is to consider the reasons for gender-based differences in pay. It is, of course, well accepted that women earn, on the average, about 60 percent as much as men. What should not be forgotten, however, is that there are legitimate reasons why this difference exists. Some of these reasons are:

1. Women make up a larger portion of the part-time work force than do men, and this condition seems to be increasing. Since employers believe that the costs of part-time employment are higher than for full-time employment, and since there is a lower commitment on the part of the part-time employee, they usually have less job security and usually earn less than full-time workers.
2. Women tend to reject higher-paying jobs that have less desirable working conditions. As a group they prefer not to work surrounded by high temperatures, noise, or dirt or to accept positions where job requirements include heavy lifting, rotating shifts, or seven-day operation. For a variety of reasons, women tend to prefer weekday work, fixed shifts, light lifting, and pleasant work surroundings.
3. Women tend to reject some jobs out of hand, based on their perceptions of job requirements, even though there is no real reason why they could not perform well and even though the pay is better than jobs dominated by female workers.
4. Women, in general have different external responsibilities than do men, spending more time with children and on home management, and because of this may be less flexible regarding working hours and other job demands.

5. Men and women often approach employment careers with different motivations. A man with little motivation, minimal attachment to his company, and with little interest in his job, may seek advancement because he needs the money to feed his family. On the other hand, a highly motivated woman with an excellent performance record and high aspirations may not accept a promotion because her husband is being transferred or her young children need her attention.

6. One of the crucial differences between employment patterns of men and women is continuity of employment. It is common for women to enter the work force for a few years and then withdraw for an extended period while their children are in their younger years. When they return to the work force, their real wages at reentry are usually lower than at withdrawal, and the reduction is greater the longer the interruption. The amount of the decline in wages has been calculated at 3.3 to 7.6 percent per year of absence from work.[1]

7. Women may earn less because of the occupations they choose. When they choose traditional "female jobs" such as teaching, nursing, and clerical and service work, they encourage the wage disparity to continue. If more women were to set their sights on higher-paying "nontraditional" jobs and acquire the skills needed to land them, this would help reduce the earnings difference.

8. Women may earn less than men because they have less education than men. Over 22 percent of all male workers have a college degree, as compared to 17.5 percent of all female workers. This will change in the future, because among persons age 18 to 24, a larger proportion of women than men are enrolled in college.[2] For the present, though, the educational differential does remain an important contributing factor.

9. Women earn less than men because they are, on the average, less experienced and therefore less productive.

10. Women earn less than men because of an excess supply of women flooding the job market.

11. Finally, women earn less than men because men tend to belong to stronger and more aggressive labor organizations.

DIFFICULTIES IN IMPLEMENTATION

Those who advocate comparable worth base its implementation on extensive use of job evaluation systems. The goal is to present objective comparisons of the skills, effort, and responsibilities required by vastly different jobs. The problem is that a totally objective plan for comparing and valuing dissimilar jobs—one which lacks bias and can be applied in the real world—just does not exist.

Any evaluation system necessarily involves subjective judgment in both its creation and application. There are no universally accepted standards of measurement, and experts differ among themselves about which factors should be measured and how many points should be assigned to each. This can be illustrated in Exhibit 3, which shows how various job evaluators rated five jobs differently in four different states—Wisconsin, Iowa, Minnesota, and Washington.

EXHIBIT 3

JOB WORTH POINTS AS A PERCENTAGE
OF POINTS ASSIGNED TO ELECTRICIANS

	WI	IA	MN	WA
Electrician	100	100	100	100
Licensed practical nurse (LPN)	150	124	79	108
Dental assistant	108	77	50	73
Telephone operator	91	64	49	60
Data entry operator	55	72	43	63

Source: Association of Washington Business, "Comparable Worth in the Private Sector: A Debate," *Pacific Northwest Executive*, July 1985, p. 22.

The chart shows that Minnesota rated LPNs lower than electricians while the other three states rated them higher—in the case of Wisconsin, considerably higher. Similar significant differences are seen in the case of dental assistants.

This chart points out the main illusion of comparable worth—that the different skills, working conditions, and responsibilities of jobs can be expressed in formulas. They can't. The consequence is that it leads us to ask the wrong questions. The right question is not, Do we pay women's (or men's) jobs enough? But, rather, Do we pay enough for specific jobs to get qualified workers? If not, we need to determine what combination of higher salaries and qualifications is needed.

Comparable worth cannot be implemented fairly in the workplace because it is subjective and vague in concept with few objective guidelines, and because it is highly dependent upon the point of view of the job evaluator in comparing vastly dissimilar jobs.

Those who advocate comparable worth have a fundamental misunderstanding of how the labor markets function. Indexes developed from job evaluation systems do not tell us anything about the labor market, which can be capricious and highly localized. Even if two jobs were judged to be equal, one job might be difficult to fill and the other flooded with applicants. For example, in the Wisconsin state government, a legal secretary is paid $14,800 and a public defender investigator (level 3) $20,600. The experimental job evaluation system, however, rates the jobs as almost equal, even though 92 percent of the investigators are men and 100 percent of the secretaries are women. To eliminate "sex bias," the recommendation is to hike the legal secretaries' salary 33 percent to $19,600.[3]

This sort of approach, which is similar to the one proposed for our company, assumes that it is as easy to hire secretaries as it is law school graduates—which is probably just not true. Again, the right question to ask is: What do we have to pay in order to get the quality of workers we need in each job position?

In conclusion, we would have chaos if comparable worth ever became an official policy of this company. Not only would it increase our labor costs, but both labor and management would be forced to abdicate their functions. Decisions we now make based on productivity, profitability, and the interaction of supply and demand would now be made by bureaucrats operating under an illusion of mathematical precision. Wage inequities between the sexes is not, in the final analysis, a problem that lends itself to solution by decree.

NOTES

1. Jacob Miner and Haim Ofek, "Interrupted Work Careers: Depreciation and Restoration of Human Capital," *Journal of Human Resources*, vol. 17, no. 1 (Winter 1982).
2. Sherri Miller, "The Incomparable Problems of Comparable Worth," *Consumers' Research*, October 1984, and Arthur Padilla, "The Economics and Politics of Comparable Worth," *North Carolina Review of Business and Economics* (Spring 1985), 9.
3. Robert J. Samuelson, "The Myths of Comparable Worth," *Newsweek*, April 22, 1985, p. 57.

AFFIRMATIVE ACTION

AFFIRMATIVE ACTION AT AT&T

Earl A. Molander

On December 8, 1975, Daniel A. McAleer, a service representative handling orders for telephone service for American Telephone & Telegraph Company (AT&T) Long Lines out of the Washington, D.C., office, filed a discrimination suit in United States District Court against his employer. In his suit, McAleer alleged he had lost a promotion to staff assistant to a less-qualified female employee because of AT&T's court-ordered affirmative action program. He asked the court for the promotion, back pay, and damages.

After hearing the case and the company's defense that an earlier consent decree obligated it to favor women and minorities over white males, Judge Gerhard Gesell ruled that McAleer was not entitled to the promotion, but was entitled to monetary damages. Judge Gesell noted that McAleer

From Earl A. Molander, *Responsive Capitalism: Case Studies in Corporate Conduct.* Copyright © 1980 by McGraw-Hill. Reprinted with permission of McGraw-Hill.

was "an innocent employee who had earned promotion but was disadvantaged when AT&T rejected his application in order to rectify its past discriminations against women." AT&T immediately petitioned for reconsideration, arguing that it "could not simultaneously be in compliance with, and in violation of, Title VII" of the 1964 Civil Rights Act, and raising additional defenses. In the meantime, the federal district court in Pennsylvania, which had approved the consent decree, reaffirmed the use of overrides such as used in the *McAleer* case. Before Judge Gesell could rule on the motion for reconsideration, AT&T and McAleer settled out of court for a reputed $14,000, including legal fees. Commenting on the monetary settlement, McAleer lamented, "What I wanted was the promotion."[1]

THE CIVIL RIGHTS MOVEMENT IN THE UNITED STATES

The civil rights movement in the United States had its roots in the sit-ins, boycotts, and marches in the American South in the early 1960s. These actions, together with their media coverage, brought to public attention the conditions of black Americans and ultimately led to passage of the Equal Pay Act of 1963 and the Civil Rights Act of 1964, which outlawed discrimination on the basis of race, color, religion, sex, or national origin. In the next decade, other legislation protecting the civil rights of individual Americans followed, including Executive Order 11246, which barred discrimination by federal contractors in employment based on race, color, religion, or national origin, and Executive Order 11375, which barred discrimination by federal contractors in employment based on sex and creation of the Equal Employment Opportunity Commission (EEOC).[2]

The particular interest in discrimination against women followed a growing interest in this area in society and government, catalyzed by the growth of the "women's liberation" movement in early 1970. Of the 16,000 complaints received by the EEOC in the previous fiscal year, 17 percent had involved charges of unfairness to women.[3] By the summer of 1970, a proposed constitutional amendment guaranteeing equal rights for women, later to be known as the Equal Rights Amendment (ERA), was moving rapidly through Congress. In July, the Justice Department filed its first sex discrimination lawsuit against an employer and union.[4]

THE COMPANY

American Telephone & Telegraph Company is the principal producer of telecommunications equipment and service in the United States. It employs close to 1 million people, over half of them women, making it the largest private employer and employer of women in the country. In 1978, assets were $111 billion, sales $41 billion, and profits $5.3 billion. The parent company is organized into geographical companies, such as Mountain Bell and

South Central Bell; a Long Lines Company that handles long distance; Bell Telephone Laboratories, its research arm; and Western Electric, which manufactures telephones and telecommunications equipment.

As the decade of the seventies began, AT&T was beset by a host of problems uncommon in its then 85-year history. Among the more pressing of these problems for the Bell System, as the firm is sometimes known, were a decline in the quality of service in some of its major markets, including New York, Boston, and Washington, D.C.; new competition using technologies pioneered at AT&T's own research and production subsidiaries, Bell Telephone Laboratories and Western Electric; and inexperienced workers with new attitudes toward the repetitive work and indigenous culture in this tradition-bound company. In May 1970, *Fortune* magazine broadcast these problems to the rest of the business world in an article entitled, "The Age of Anxiety at AT&T." According to *Fortune*, nothing was more disturbing to the company than its decline in service:

> "Service comes first," Bell people say again and again, and they honestly believe it. The thought is embedded in their consciousness like a post in concrete, for providing good service is the *sine qua non* of Bell's legitimacy, the company's pledge of performance in return for the privilege of monopoly.[5]

Giving better service and meeting new competition was somewhat hampered by the Bell System's personnel problems. Since the early 1960s, turnover had doubled among operators and quadrupled among switchmen, frame men, and other key artisans, putting additional burdens on supervisory personnel already feeling the pressure of an overall decline in company profits. These supervisory personnel were also irritated with one of the company's most important personnel tools, an extensive system of performance indexes on which salary and promotions were based. Many employees distrusted the indexes and saw them as dehumanizing. In response to this criticism, additional quality measurements, based upon the customer's perception of service, were adopted, and managers began to rely less on the rigorous technical indexes than they had in previous years.[6]

DISCRIMINATION CHARGES AGAINST THE COMPANY

In November 1970, AT&T applied to the Federal Communications Commission (FCC) for a revised tariff schedule to help offset the increased costs in AT&T's long-distance services. In contrast to the electric utilities, AT&T had a history of fighting increased costs with internal efficiencies, rather than running to state and federal regulatory commissions for rate increases. Up to 1968, the company had averaged eleven years between rate increases.[7]

Less than a month later, on December 10, 1970, the Equal Employment Opportunity Commission intervened in the FCC proceedings and asked that the rate increases be denied. The EEOC charged that the rate increases would be "unjust and unreasonable" because the firm had engaged in "pervasive, systemwide, and blatantly unlawful discrimination in employment against women, blacks, Spanish-surnamed Americans, and other minorities."[8] EEOC's decision to use the arena of the FCC to tackle AT&T may have been prompted by the FCC's "get tough" stand on discrimination in broadcasting.[9]

Specifically, EEOC contended that the employment practices by AT&T violated the following:

> Sections 201(b), 202(a), 214, 501 and 502 of the Communications Act of 1934, as amended; Sections 21.307 and 23.49 of the FCC's Rules and Regulations; Sections 703(a) and(d) of Title VII of the Civil Rights Act of 1964; the Civil Rights Act of 1866; the Equal Pay Act of 1963; Executive Order 11246; and the Fair Employment Practices Acts of numerous States and cities.[10]

On January 21, 1971, the FCC denied the EEOC suit any role in the AT&T rate increase decision. In its memorandum opinion, the FCC held "no showing has been made between rate levels and the company's policies and practices in the matter of equal employment opportunity." However, the FCC went on to emphasize that "in divorcing these claims from the subject rate proceeding we are not intimating that they are without merit." The FCC then made provision for a separate hearing to explore the "serious questions . . . of law and fact" raised by the EEOC. These included:

(A) Whether the existing employment practices of AT&T tend to impede equal employment opportunities in AT&T and its operating companies contrary to the purposes and requirements of the Commission's Rules and the Civil Rights Act of 1964;

(B) Whether AT&T has failed to inaugurate and maintain specific programs, pursuant to Commission Rules and Regulations, insuring against discriminatory practices in the recruiting, selection, hiring, placement and promotion of its employees;

(C) Whether AT&T has engaged in pervasive, systemwide discrimination against women, Negroes, Spanish-surnamed Americans, and other minorities in its employment policies;

(D) Whether, and in what manner, any of the employment practices of AT&T, if found to be discriminatory, affect the revenues or expenses of AT&T, or otherwise affect the rates charged by that company for its interstate and foreign communications services, and if so, in what ways is this reflected in the present rate structure;

(E) To determine, in light of the evidence adduced pursuant to the foregoing issues, what order, or requirements, if any, should be adopted by the Commission.[11]

Immediately, the EEOC began to seek allies for its suit against AT&T. Four days after the FCC decision, William H. Brown III, chairman of the EEOC, approached Joseph Beirne, president of the Communication

Workers of America (CWA), which represented the majority of AT&T's hourly employees, and officially invited the union to join EEOC as plaintiff in the case. The CWA respectfully declined. Throughout 1971 (and 1972), the CWA continued to decline EEOC overtures to be joint plaintiff against AT&T or to submit substantive proposals which EEOC could analyze. The CWA did cooperate with the EEOC in collecting some information from union members pertinent to the suit, but otherwise would say only that any proposed changes in personnel procedures would have to be "grieved and arbitrated."[12]

On December 14, 1971, CWA President Beirne wrote a letter to AT&T President Robert D. Lilley noting his concern about sex discrimination by AT&T and suggesting they "begin discussions on this vital matter promptly." AT&T responded affirmatively, and over the next year the company and union met on an informal basis. The union was thus kept abreast of AT&T relations with EEOC by both the company and the federal agency.[13]

Ultimately, the EEOC was able to persuade the International Brotherhood of Electrical Workers (IBEW), which represents a minority of AT&T hourly employees, to petition to intervene as a plaintiff in the case.[14]

FCC HEARINGS ON THE EEOC SUIT

On December 1, 1971, the EEOC followed its charges of a year earlier with 5,000 pages of statistics and testimony supporting its position. Included were charges that AT&T was "the largest oppressor of women workers in the United States" and that for the past thirty years

> Women as a class have been excluded from every job classification except low-paying clerical and telephone-operator jobs. . . .
> The handful of blacks and Spanish-surnamed Americans who were employed held only the most menial and degrading jobs—those of laborer, janitor, and porter.[15]

Eight months later, AT&T responded with an even more voluminous file of statistics and written testimony. Appearing before the FCC, John W. Kingsbury, assistant vice president of AT&T for human-resource development, argued that EEOC had forgotten his firm's principal responsibilities to its communications customers:

> In its zeal in trying this case against the Bell System, the EEOC has failed to recognize that the primary reason the Bell System exists is to provide communications service to the American public, not merely to provide employment to all comers, regardless of ability. . . .
> If the Bell companies were to act upon the EEOC's contention that they should require less skills or abilities of those whom they hire, it would be difficult to provide quality service. . . .

What the EEOC fails to recognize is that if we eliminated all our hiring standards, our training costs would soar astronomically and those costs would necessarily be passed to our customers."[16]

Kingsbury also argued that EEOC was judging past actions by 1971 standards and that the Bell System had adjusted its hiring practices to be more reflective of societal changes. AT&T took particularly strong exception to the EEOC demand that more minority workers be hired and given extra training. The company argued that one-quarter of all newly hired workers over the past three years had been minorities, increasing nonwhite employment by 179 percent. As a result, 10 percent of all Bell employees were black. Nonwhite managers had increased from 947 in 1965 to 5,618 in 1971. Women made up about one-third of all Bell managers, an increase of 43 percent in the previous six years. Finally, AT&T held:

If the Bell companies are to continue to provide good telecommunications service at reasonable rates, they cannot hire without regard to applicant's learning ability or fail to consider service and expense obligations in determining job work rules.
The EEOC's excessive demands for relaxation of standards with respect to selection of employees and working conditions must be rejected as a misguided form of paternalism.[17]

Appearing as an expert witness for AT&T, Dr. Hugh Folk, professor of economics and labor and industrial relations at the University of Illinois, questioned the EEOC's use of statistics as inferential proof of discrimination. He argued that over the decades, many occupations have come to be thought of as "men's jobs" and "women's jobs" and the distribution of sexes along such lines at AT&T had nothing to do with the firm's preferences in hiring. These were the traditional patterns in society. In response to the EEOC demand that AT&T recruit more women for higher-paid, skilled jobs, Folk insisted:

The proportion of women in Bell craft jobs will increase, but it will not approach the proportion of women in the labor force unless and until rather deep-seated attitudes held by women toward clerical work—as being proper for women—and physical and outside work—as being improper for women—are substantially modified over time.[18]

While these hearings were in progress, in spring 1972, AT&T proposed a "Model Affirmative Action Program and Upgrade and Transfer Plan" to the EEOC and other government agencies as settlement in the suit. The EEOC felt the plan was inadequate, but on September 20, 1972, the General Services Administration (GSA), acting as the contract compliance agency *enforcing* Executive Order 11246, approved the plan with some modifications. However, a week later, the Office of Federal Contract Compliance (OFCC), the agency within the Department of Labor (DOL) charged with *administering* Executive Order 11246, notified GSA it was assuming jurisdiction in the AT&T matter. Further, the OFCC asserted that the AT&T plan did not conform to its standards.[19]

Through the month of October, officials of the DOL, OFCC, and EEOC met to discuss the GSA-approved AT&T plan. Meanwhile, negotiations between the EEOC, DOL, and AT&T resumed, and a new agreement was reached on December 28, 1972. On January 18, 1973, the agreement was embodied in a consent decree entered in the United States District Court, Eastern District of Pennsylvania. In the agreement, the company agreed to pay $15 million in back wages to 15,000 women and minority group men against whom it had allegedly discriminated and to give $23 million in raises to 36,000 employees who had moved into higher-paid positions but had not had their rates of pay following promotion figured on the new promotion pay plan. However, as is typical in agreements of this type, there was no admission of wrongdoing by AT&T; the company expressly denied that it had discriminated against these individuals.[20]

Commenting on the significance of the settlement, Randy Speck, chief investigator for EEOC's AT&T task force, explained:

> The most important aspect is that in this case, restitution was given to people who had never complained at all, who were suffering discrimination as a result of company policy which essentially locked them into jobs.
>
> Even though employers may not get any complaints [from employees], they're going to have to evaluate their own company to see if they're susceptible, and make provisions.
>
> The basis for the conclusion that women were excluded from certain job categories [at AT&T] was the statistical disparity. The company was over 50% female and yet there were a large number of jobs held exclusively by men or exclusively by women. In fact, over 90% of the employees in the company were in what might be categorized as sex-segregated jobs.
>
> Such a disparity, we argued, was the result of company policy or practice, which was exhibited in different ways. It may not have been enunciated or codified in a manual, but there were usually different methods of processing male and female applicants who came in the door.[21]

EEOC Chairman William H. Brown observed, "We expect AT&T to have a considerable ripple effect. The EEOC lawsuits are designed to turn the ripples into waves where necessary."[22]

AT&T's immediate explanation for its agreement to an out-of-court settlement when it felt no culpability was captured best by David K. Easlick, an AT&T vice president: "It's just that the rules of the game have been changed."[23]

The company's 1972 annual report, published a month later, noted the settlement of the case, the back wages to be paid, and elaborated:

We view this agreement as a further step in the Bell System's continuing efforts to assure equal opportunity throughout our business and to assure that our practices conform to current legal requirements in this rapidly evolving field. Under its terms, qualifications remain, as they must, the fundamental criterion for advancement in the Bell companies. The further expansion of opportunity now afforded and the incentives it inspires will, we believe, strengthen our business' capability for the long term.

As the press (and our own advertising) has noted, the Bell companies employ a number of male operators and a number of women are employed on outside craft jobs as well. Whether this trend will prove significant, only time and gathering experience will tell. In any case, what should be plain is that we have no male jobs, no female jobs, no black jobs and no white jobs. What counts is the ability to perform the work and a readiness to do one's best.[24]

AFFIRMATIVE ACTION AT AT&T

Following the settlement, AT&T embarked on an extensive recruitment and training campaign to meet its affirmative action obligations. Among the employees selected for companywide programs designed to pinpoint potential managers, one in two was a woman and one in five was a member of a minority group. In establishing affirmative action goals, the consent decree divided employees into ten categories by gender, race, and ethnic group. Goals were then set for each of these groups in fifteen job categories. For example, because the United States labor force contained 38 percent women in 1972, some of the jobs set 38 percent women for a goal. For jobs believed to be less attractive to women, lower goals were chosen. The settlement included the following ultimate goals for women in "craft" jobs: (1) 38 percent of all employees in "inside" positions, and (2) 19 percent of all employees in "outside" positions.

Despite this commitment to equal employment opportunity, the company continued to plead for more realism in enforcement of EEOC objectives. AT&T Assistant Vice President Kingsbury told a Conference Board meeting in June 1973:

> I also feel obligated to stress that equal-opportunity advocates must recognize that there are limits to the burden that the business community can carry, limits in terms of programs that can be effectively implemented in a given period of time, and limits of money that can be allocated.
>
> Initiating programs that are not well conceived and tested and promoting individuals who are not qualified, either by inclination or training, runs the risk of wasting valuable human and financial resources and endangering the entire concept of equal opportunity.
>
> We have attempted, along with hundreds of others, to explain the differences between goals and quotas; and in the end thousands upon thousands of people feel there is but a slight semantic difference, despite our good intention and the intentions of those in government.
>
> While some people will argue that our programs don't go far enough, to

others the law, administrative guidelines, regulations and court decisions seem biased in favor of minority-group members and women.[25]

Initially, AT&T permitted its individual companies to pursue their respective affirmative action goals independently. At the end of the first year, however, a majority of member companies had fallen far short of the consent decree's first-year objectives. For the Bell System as a whole, only 51.1 percent of targets was met. Part of the problem was attributed to confusion as to the intended meaning of the consent decree, e.g., did "job opportunities" include just new hires or also lateral transfers and promotions?

As a result of this failure, AT&T was again forced into court in early 1974 by the Government Coordinating Committee (GCC), which had oversight responsibility for the decree. A second consent decree was then signed in which AT&T agreed to make up in subsequent years the shortfalls of 1973.[26]

At this point it was clear that the consent decree's goals were being viewed as hard quotas by the government. As a consequence, the parent company stepped in and imposed its authority on the personnel decisions of its subsidiaries. The major instrument of this authority was the parent company's own office of equal opportunity and affirmative action—a "mini-EEOC"—with a staff of 750. As a result, in 1974 systemwide performance picked up considerably and the company hit 89.6 percent of targets; in 1975, 97 percent; and in 1976–1978, over 99.3 percent.[27]

"AFFIRMATIVE ACTION OVERRIDE": REVERSE DISCRIMINATION

In the 1973 consent decree, AT&T had agreed to a seniority override, or "affirmative action override." If necessary, to meet affirmative action goals, the company was required to depart from the promotion criteria specified in many of its collective-bargaining agreements with the CWA, IBEW, and independent unions.

One victim of "affirmative action override" was David McAleer, a senior clerk with five years in AT&T Long Lines Company, who applied for a newly created supervisory position in his area. Despite his score of 34 out of 36 on the company's evaluation scale, he lost out in his bid to one Sharon Hulley, who had less seniority and had scored only 30 on her performance rating. On December 8, 1975, McAleer sued for the promotion and damages in excess of $100,000 for lost salary and diminished opportunity. McAleer was joined in the suit by the CWA, which claimed that AT&T "has by this action interfered with the union's ability to represent its members and secure them employment rights under the collective bargaining agreement which AT&T admittedly has disregarded."

On June 9, 1976, United States District Judge Gerhard A. Gesell dismissed the union's case, while ruling that McAleer was entitled to monetary compensation but no promotion. In denying McAleer his promotion Gesell ruled that "such relief might well perpetuate and prolong the effects of the discrimination that the [1973] decree was designed to eliminate."[28] In rejecting AT&T's claim that it was just following the directive of the consent decree, Gesell acknowledged that "ordinarily one who acts pursuant to a judicial order or other lawful process is protected from liability arising from the act." But, he continued, "such protection does not exist where the judicial order was necessitated by the wrongful conduct of the party sought to be held liable." This interpretation represented a further extension of the Supreme Court's ruling in *Franks v. Bowman Transportation Co., Inc.* (1976) that

> an eligible and presently qualified candidate who was a victim of past discrimination could, and indeed generally should, receive a "scarce" benefit given to only a single individual, such as a promotion to a particular position, even at the expense of other, innocent employees.
>
> Judge Gesell, in commenting on the *Franks* decision, noted that: "Apparently common to the various opinions in *Franks* was a recognition of the need to share among the respective parties the burden of eradicating past discrimination and achieving equality of employment opportunities. In particular, it was agreed that courts should attempt to protect innocent employees by placing this burden on the wrongdoing employer whenever possible. . . ." This Court, agreeing with these sentiments, sees no reason why in equitably distributing the burden among the concerned parties the onus should be shifted from the employer responsible for the discrimination to the blameless third-party employee any more than is, as a practical matter, unavoidable.
>
> Accordingly, the Court holds that plaintiff McAleer has a cause of action for monetary damages under Title VII.[29]

In the interim, the federal district court in Pennsylvania, which had approved the consent decree, had reaffirmed the use of an override such as that involved in the *McAleer* case. Shortly after Judge Gesell's decision, AT&T petitioned for reconsideration, charging that the company "could not simultaneously be in compliance with and in violation of Title VII" of the Civil Rights Act of 1964. Before Judge Gesell could rule on the matter, on September 14, 1976, AT&T and McAleer settled out of court, whereupon Judge Gesell withdrew his opinion in *McAleer*, stating "it shall no longer have any force or effect."

Encouraged by the *McAleer* decision, by early 1978 thirteen other AT&T employees who felt themselves to have been victims of reverse discrimination had filed similar suits in federal courts. However, all were eventually either withdrawn or dismissed by the court as having been required by the consent decree, including one case filed in the same court as the *McAleer* case.

Additionally the unions had lost in their challenge to the affirmative action override at the federal district court in Pennsylvania and before the Third Circuit Court of Appeals. They then appealed to the United States Supreme Court, where this appeal was denied.

By 1978, AT&T had made further progress. In the ten-level management pyramid, over a thousand women were in level 3 and above—jobs paying over $30,000—nearly three times the number in 1972, but only four women had reached the sixth level.[30] Minority group managers in level 3 and up had quadrupled since 1972. But ironically, overall minority males had not fared as well as white or minority females, even though they are probably the primary equal opportunity concern of the larger society.[31]

In outside craft areas, women in 1978 held 3.6 percent of the jobs, far less than the 19 percent goal set out in the 1973 consent decree (Exhibit 1). One problem in these positions was the accident rate for women—three times that of their male counterparts. In *semiskilled* inside jobs, the company was having more success. By 1978, 35.5 percent of these jobs were filled by women as compared to a consent decree goal of 38 percent. In meeting consent decree goals, the Bell System's "mini-EEOC" and management had invoked "affirmative action override" more than 36,000 times in the six years of the consent decree in hiring and promoting women, minorities, and white males.[32] This was just 16 percent of the 225,000 women and minorities hired and promoted and slightly more than 6 percent of the 560,000 total job opportunities in the Bell System in the period.

EXHIBIT 1

EMPLOYMENT STATISTICS, END OF YEAR 1972 COMPARED TO END OF YEAR 1977 (CONSENT DECREE SIGNED 13 JANUARY 1973)

	EOY 1972		EOY 1977	
Minorities				
Total:	102,224	13.8%	129,849	16.6%
In mgt.:	8,534	4.6%	18,257	8.7%
Women				
Total craft:	6,417	2.8%	18,110	8%
Outside plant craft:*	244	0.2%	3,624	3.6%
Inside plant craft:*	6,173	6.5%	14,486	15%
In higher mgt.:	34,711	22.5%	48,189	27%
(1st level & above, excluding "administrative")				
Males				
Clerical	8,250	4%	22,686	10.7%
Operators	2,060	1.4%	6.131	6%
Total employment				
Total Bell System:	1,020,000		953,245	
Total excluding WE & BTL:	778,000		767,000	

*Includes skilled and semiskilled positions.
Note: Above figures for minorities, women, and males do not include Western Electric (WE) and Bell Telephone Laboratories (BTL), since they were not a party to the 1973 consent decree.
Source: Peggy Beaumont, American Telephone & Telegraph Company, New York, N.Y., 28 June 1978.

By 1978 American society was on the record as opposing affirmative action, or, more specifically, reverse discrimination. Eight in ten Americans said that ability, as determined by examination, and not preferential treatment to correct past discrimination, should be the main consideration in selecting applicants for jobs (Exhibit 2). Even minorities (55 percent) and women (80 percent) opposed preferential treatment. However, a majority of Americans did not oppose the federal government offering special educational or vocational courses, free of charge, to enable members of minority groups to do better in tests.

EXHIBIT 2

PUBLIC OPINION POLL ON REVERSE DISCRIMINATION

"Some people say that to make up for past discrimination, women and members of minority groups should be given preferential treatment in getting jobs and places in college. Others say that ability, as determined by test scores, should be the main consideration. Which point comes closest to how you feel on this matter?"

	Pref.	Ability	No opinion
Nationwide	11%	81%	8%
Men	10	82	8
Women	12	80	8
Whites	9	84	7
Non-whites	30	55	15
College	15	81	4
High school	9	84	7
Grade school	11	70	19
East	13	77	10
Midwest	8	87	5
South	9	79	12
West	15	82	3
18–29 years	11	81	8
30–49 years	10	84	6
50 years & older	9	81	10

Source: George Gallup, Princeton, N.J., November 1977.

In summer 1978, the United States Supreme Court made its first ruling on reverse discrimination in the *Bakke* case. In compelling the medical school of the University of California-Davis to admit Alan Bakke, the Court ruled that the rigid quota systems, which set aside a specific number of slots for minority applicants, were discriminatory against white applicants. The Court did acknowledge, however, that race could be one of a number of considerations for admission in a school's effort to achieve diversity among its students.[33]

Faced with continuing challenges to its quota procedures, the EEOC in December 1978 adopted guidelines under which employers who adopt AT&T-like affirmative action programs would be protected from reverse discrimination charges.[34] The guidelines took effect January 11, 1979.

On January 18, 1979, the consent decree expired with AT&T having met 99.3 percent of the objectives set six years before. After that date, AT&T was no longer obligated to use "affirmative action override." According to Chairman John deButts, the company would continue to pursue the spirit of affirmative action in its personnel policies, however.[35]

One area where AT&T did expect to ease its affirmative action efforts was in seeking and retaining women for outside craft jobs. It was here the company had fallen the farthest from its goals, partly because of accident rates, partly because, according to John deButts, "There are not many women who want to go down a manhole in New York City."[36]

Although Chairman deButts acknowledged that the need to depart from the "best qualified" criterion had had some impact on efficiency, he felt extensive training programs had made the net effect insignificant.[37] As to the override, Don Liebers, head of the company's equal employment and affirmative action program, concedes he won't miss it: "It was necessary for this period of time. But my personal feeling is that this is not the way promotions should be made—not a way to run a business forever."[38]

In June 1979, the Supreme Court entered a second opinion on affirmative action when it ruled against Brian Weber, a Kaiser Aluminum & Chemical Corporation employee who had filed a discrimination suit against the company. Black employees with less seniority had been admitted to the company's skilled-crafts training program, which had half its slots reserved for blacks, ahead of Weber. The Court ruled that voluntarily giving preference to minorities and women in hiring and promotion in "traditionally segregated job categories" was consistent with the "spirit" of the Civil Rights Act of 1964.[39]

NOTES

1. George C. Lodge, "Equality of *Result*, Not Equality of Opportunity," *Across the Board*, March 1978, p. 59.
2. For a thorough review, see Edwin M. Epstein and David R. Hampton, *Black American and White Business* (Encino, Calif.: Dickenson, 1971).
3. "Equal Rights for Women Workers—A New Push," *U.S. News & World Report*, 3 August 1970, p. 51.
4. Ibid.
5. Allan T. Demaree, "The Age of Anxiety at AT&T," *Fortune*, May 1970, p. 264.
6. Ibid., p. 272.
7. Ibid., p. 264.
8. U.S. Equal Employment Opportunity Commission, "Petition to Intervene," Federal Communications Commission Hearings on AT&T Revised Tariff Schedule, 10 December 1970, p. 1.

9. "FCC Gets Tough on Equal Employment," *Broadcasting,* 9 June 1969, p. 38.

10. See *Equal Employment Opportunity Commission et al., Plaintiffs v. American Telephone and Telegraph Company et al., Defendants,* U.S. District Court, Eastern District of Pennsylvania, No. 73-149, 5 October 1973, in Commerce Clearing House, Inc., *Employment Practices Guide,* ¶19442, p. 5030.

11. Ibid., p. 5031.

12. Ibid.

13. Ibid.

14. Ibid.

15. "Bias Charges in Hiring: AT&T Fights Back," *U.S. News & World Report,* 14 August 1972, p. 67. © U.S. News & World Report, Inc.

16. Ibid., p. 66. © U.S. News & World Report, Inc.

17. Ibid., p. 68. © U.S. News & World Report, Inc.

18. Ibid. © U.S. News & World Report, Inc.

19. *EEOC et al. v. AT&T et al.,* pp. 5032–5033.

20. The provisions of the consent decree are reported in 1 CCH EPG ¶1860 at 1533–3—1533–14 (1973).

21. "More AT&T-Type Settlements May Be Ahead, Says EEOC," *Industry Week,* 29 January 1973, pp. 12–13.

22. M. Barbara Boyle, "Equal Opportunity for Women Is Smart Business," *Harvard Business Review,* 51:86, May-June 1973.

23. "Ma Bell Agrees to Pay Reparations," *Newsweek,* 29 January 1973, pp. 53–54.

24. American Telephone & Telegraph Co., "Annual Report," New York, 1972.

25. "Impact of Spreading Crackdown on Job Bias, *U.S. News & World Report,* 18 June 1973, p. 90. © U.S. News & World Report, Inc.

26. Second consent decree, 1 CCH EPG ¶1860.

27. American Telephone & Telegraph Co., "AT&T Equal Opportunity Brochure," New York, n.d., p. 2. (Mimeographed.)

28. *McAleer v. American Tel. & Tel. Co.,* 416 F. Supp. 435, 1976.

29. Ibid.

30. "Ma Bell's Daughters," *Wall Street Journal,* 28 February 1978, p. 27, col. 1; and Carol J. Loomis, "A.T.&T. in the Throes of 'Equal Employment,'" *Fortune,* 15 January 1979, p. 50.

31. Loomis, "A.T.&T. in the Throes," p. 50.

32. Interview with Dick McKnight, Media Relations, American Telephone & Telegraph Co., New York, 20 December 1978.

33. *Regents of the University of California v. Bakke,* U.S. Individual Slip Opinion No. 76-811, 28 June 1978, 156 pp.

34. "EEOC Adopts Final Guidelines Covering Hiring," *Wall Street Journal,* 12 December 1978, p. 2, col. 2.

35. Loomis, "A.T.&T. in the Throes," p. 57.

36. Ibid., p. 50.

37. Ibid., p. 57.

38. Ibid.

39. "Beyond Bakke: High Court Backs Affirmative Action in Employment," *Wall Street Journal,* 28 June 1979, p. 1, col. 5.

OCCUPATIONAL HEALTH AND SAFETY

RESPONDING TO A SWEEPING "RIGHT-TO-KNOW" PROPOSAL

Alan F. Westin and John D. Aram

International Manufacturing Corporation is a 75-year-old firm that now specializes in producing plastics, mainframe computers, and consumer electronic equipment. It has eight manufacturing plants in the United States and four overseas facilities, in Formosa, Singapore, Hong Kong, and South Korea. Its corporate headquarters are in New Caledonia.

International has regularly been on the *Fortune* list of the ten "most admired" American companies and ranks among the top five "most desirable" firms in surveys of graduating college seniors entering careers in business. In addition to a well-known job-security policy and a "people first" human resources philosophy, the company has been an internationally recognized innovator over the past four decades in developing and implementing advanced manufacturing technologies and computerized information systems.

International also follows a policy of active involvement in industry associations, business educational and research groups, and local community affairs. It has testified often in federal and state legislative hearings on legislation both directly and indirectly affecting business.

You are Roy Lear, president of International, and have called on senior executives to advise you on whether the company should take a public stand on a far-reaching right-to-know bill currently under consideration in the New Caledonia State Legislature.

KEY PERSONS INVOLVED
Roy Lear, President
Phillip LaFolia, Assistant to the President
Fred Regan, Vice President, Labor Relations
Armand Goneril, Vice President, Manufacturing
Louis Cordelia, Vice President, Public Affairs

MEMORANDUM
Date: April 2
To: Fred Regan
           Vice President, Labor Relations
           Louis Cordelia
           Vice President, Public Affairs

Selection from *Managerial Dilemmas* by Alan F. Westin and John D. Aram. Copyright © 1988 by Ballinger Publishing Company. Reprinted by permission of HarperCollins Publishers Inc.

                        Armand Goneril
                        Vice President, Manufacturing
        From: Philip LaFolia
                        Assistant to the President
        Re: Proposed State Right-to-Know Legislation

As you know, President Lear will be attending the New Caledonia Manufacturers Association meeting in two weeks. At that time he would like to be able to set forth International's position on the right-to-know (RTK) bill recently introduced in the New Caledonia State Senate and now being debated in that body. It is therefore essential that we have your views on this matter within a week's time.

In case you have not yet had a chance to study the proposed legislation, let me summarize its key provisions.

- New Caledonia employers who make, store, use, or process "potentially toxic or hazardous substances" must prepare or obtain a separate Material Safety Data Sheet (MSDS) for each such substance. For the purposes of this law, a potentially toxic or hazardous substance is one that appears in the National Institute for Occupational Safety and Health (NIOSH) Registry of Toxic Effects of Chemical Substances—a list that currently comprises some 65,000 chemicals and is continually being expanded. (It should be noted that inclusion on this list does not mean that a substance has actually been found to be dangerous, merely that it has been tested for toxicity. Many of the substances on the list are quite harmless.) The MSDS must include, among other things, the substance's chemical name, common name, and Chemical Abstract Service (CAS) number; the hazards or risks posed by the substance, including acute and chronic health effects and symptoms of overexposure; safety precautions for use of or exposure to the substance; and emergency procedures for spills, fire, disposal, and first aid.
- In addition, labels containing most or all of this information must be placed on containers holding toxic or hazardous substances (as defined above), as well as on storage tanks, mixing vats, reaction vessels, and pipelines or other conduits carrying such substances.
- Employers must keep copies of the MSDSs on file at a central location in the workplace. Any employee who believes that he or she may have been exposed to a toxic substance—or any representative designated by such an employee—can request to see the MSDS for that substance. If the employer does not comply with such a request within 48 hours, the worker(s) has the right to refuse to work with the substance in question. The same is true in the case of unlabeled substances or mixtures of substances.
- In addition to the MSDSs, employers will have to prepare, for use by the state departments of Public Health and Environmental Protection, detailed surveys of the chemicals they have on hand. This information will be made available to emergency response units (for example, local fire departments). It will also be a matter of public record and easily accessible to anyone requesting it.
- Any employer wishing to withhold information from the surveys or the MSDSs in order to protect a trade secret must make formal, written application to the state Department of Public Health. Trade-secret protection will not be granted to any substance known or suspected to be a mutagen, carcinogen, or other health hazard, and can be denied to any other substance at the discretion of the Commissioner of Public Health.

- Employers must implement a comprehensive training program for employees using substances known or suspected of being toxic or hazardous.

You can see from this summary that the bill under consideration is a very sweeping one—perhaps the strongest piece of RTK legislation thus far proposed in any state. However, our legal counsel has pointed out that some portions of this bill, should it be enacted into law, may not survive a challenge in the courts. In the fall of 1985 and the spring of 1986, the long-awaited Hazard Communication Standards of the federal Occupational Safety and Health Administration were phased in. These regulations, in OSHA's words,

> establish uniform requirements for hazard communication in manufacturing. . . . Each employee who is exposed to hazardous chemicals will receive information about them through a comprehensive hazard communication program. . . . All covered employers will be required to provide the information to their employees by means of labels on containers, material safety data sheets, and training.

In a New Jersey case, a federal judge ruled that insofar as the state's RTK statute dealt with hazard disclosure to workers in manufacturing, it was preempted by the OSHA standards and would have to be redrawn to eliminate conflict with federal regulations. A state law mandating *public* access and disclosure, however—a so-called community RTK law—would be valid, since it would cover an area to which the OSHA standards do not apply. Thus, we can expect that the community RTK provisions of the legislation now being debated would most likely survive any legal challenge. The same is true of disclosure provisions relating to workers in jobs other than manufacturing—true, at least, until such time as the OSHA regulations are extended to cover those areas.

Regardless of its legal status, the pending legislation has the enthusiastic backing of a considerable number of unions—including the Chemical and Utility Workers of America (CUWA), which represents the majority of our own work force—and of a broad coalition of consumer, environmental, and other liberal groups such as the Public Interest Protection Alliance and the New Caledonia Coalition of Concerned Citizens. All of these pressure groups are lobbying energetically for the bill and are prepared to press actively to ensure its passage. The New Caledonia Chamber of Commerce and the Allied Industries of New Caledonia (AINC) have already stated their opposition to the bill and are preparing a campaign to defeat it.

It is clear that we cannot support the bill now pending. That being the case, it would appear that we have basically three options:

1. Take a firm stance in opposition to the legislation.
2. Remain silent on the whole issue.
3. Oppose the bill in its present form, but come forward with our own specific proposals for a more moderate and balanced bill.

Clearly each of these positions has its drawbacks. Opposing the bill could make us unpopular with civic groups and the public at large, not to mention unions; supporting an alternative bill, no matter how moderate, would probably alienate us from other firms, many of which are flatly against any such legislation whatsoever. But if we take no position and remain silent, we forfeit the opportunity to exert any influence in behalf of our own interests.

President Lear is eager to receive your input on this difficult question as soon as possible.

MEMORANDUM
Date: April 4
To: Roy Lear
            President
From: Fred Regan
            Vice President, Labor Relations
Re: International Manufacturing's Position on Proposed RTK
            Legislation

In response to Phil's request for an opinion about where we should stand on the pending RTK bill, I have a simple answer: We should take no stand at all. In fact, we should keep as low a profile as possible on the whole matter. I know that International doesn't usually duck tough issues, but there are times when discretion is the better part of valor, and I think this is one of them. If we get involved in this squabble, we have a lot to lose and almost certainly nothing to gain.

First of all, there's the union to consider. As I'm sure you know, our relations with the CUWA have been uneven. Sometimes they've been remarkably amicable, thank heaven. But when they get a bee in their collective bonnet, they can be very tough (remember the confrontation over the mandatory drug-testing issue?). Lately things have been going smoothly. Do we really want to rock the boat by trying to scuttle their pet bill? You may not be aware of this, but Senator Gloucester, who introduced S 3311 (the pending bill), is a big fan of the CUWA, and the feeling is mutual: He is one of the most vociferous union spokesmen in the state legislature, and the unions—the CUWA in particular—back him heavily at election time. The union leadership helped him draft this bill, and has made an all-out commitment to getting it through. RTK is a highly emotional issue with the union membership—and we have a new contract to negotiate this coming November. Why rile them up now?

We should also have some thought for our image with the public at large. We have the reputation of being an enlightened, forward-looking company that takes its social responsibilities seriously. Standing up in opposition to a piece of legislation that many civic groups have endorsed and that large segments of the public see as progressive can only undermine popular trust in International—trust that we have taken a long time to build, and that our advertising people spend millions of dollars each year to reinforce.

Of course, we could try to cozy up to the CUWA and the environmental activists by endorsing RTK in principle and then coming in with an alternative bill (or a lot of amendments to this one) that would be easier for us to live with. But I don't think this strategy would get us anywhere. The unions (and the environmental Nervous Nellies) are very attached to S 3311 in its present form. They see it as pioneering legislation, a model for the rest of the country. They like the idea that it's the toughest bill of its kind ever introduced, and that's the way they want to keep it. If we draft weaker legislation—even if it's better, fairer, more balanced, and so on—the unions and their sympathizers will scream bloody murder about how we've gutted their precious bill, how we're trying to co-opt the movement for worker safety and environmental protection. . . in short, business up to its old tricks.

At the same time, backing *any* other bill would, as Phil suggested, open our right flank to attack from some of the more hard-line business organizations, who will see us as a traitor to the cause. We don't really want to be perceived in the business community as a bunch of sellouts, do we? Remember, some of the firms with whom we do the most business are still in the dark ages as far as environmental and workers' rights issues are concerned. Can't you just see Charley Smythe of Amalgamated getting red in the face when he hears that International is backing an RTK bill? He won't care what's in the bill—just that we even considered supporting it. Smythe hasn't come to terms with workers' compensation or the corporate income tax yet, let alone RTK. But we had nearly $3 million of sales to Amalgamated last year.

I could see risking the wrath of the unions or the business community or even both if we had a fighting chance of accomplishing something worthwhile in terms of the legislation itself, but we don't. As far as our ability to defend our own interests in the state legislature is concerned, this is strictly a no-win situation. It's not likely that we can prevent some sort of RTK bill from being passed; the political momentum is too great. If we dig in our heels for a last-ditch stand against any legislation at all, we'll just get steamrollered. (Look what happened in New Jersey.) But if we bring in a more moderate bill, our position will become ammunition for the enemy. For them, half the battle is to force us to admit that there's a problem in the first place. If we say, "Well, we know there's a problem, and here's the legislation we think is needed to deal with it," they'll be delighted. They'll just reply: "See, even the big corporations admit there's a need for such legislation. They've even drafted a watered-down version of our bill to try to deflect us from our purpose. Very sneaky—but we won't be fooled! This just proves that we really need our original strong bill."

All in all, if we get involved in this we're just going to get our fannies caught in a wringer. And it's not necessary! This isn't our responsibility alone—the bill will affect practically everybody who does business in this state. So why should we stick our necks out for everyone else? Why should we put ourselves in an exposed position and let other people take potshots at us from every direction? Let the Manufacturers Association carry the ball on this issue, or the C of C, or AINC. That's what we pay dues for. It's all very well to be a leader, but let's try to be a leader in popular causes. We're not going to make many friends on this issue, no matter what we do. And since there's no law that says we have to take a position on RTK, let's not. Let's just duck this one publicly. Privately, we can support whatever efforts the Executive Committee of the Manufacturers Association sees fit to make. Their lobbyists should have a good sense of where things stand right now in the legislature and what we might hope to accomplish behind the scenes.

MEMORANDUM
Date: April 7
To: Roy Lear
            President
From: Armand Goneril
            Vice President, Manufacturing
Re: Need to Oppose S 3311

With regard to the RTK bill now pending in the state senate, I don't see how there can be any ambiguity in our position. We've got to oppose it as strenuously as possible—it's poison. I can't think of a worse bill to come along in the past twenty years—not just for us, but for any business trying to get along in New Caledonia. Of course, I am not opposed to the idea that employees should know what harmful substances they're working with and be protected from them; no one at International will quarrel with that. And I believe that members of the public have certain rights to be informed of anything that is truly dangerous to their communities. But this bill typifies the way in which a good idea can be ruined by irresponsible, overzealous proponents who don't take the time to think through the consequences of what they're proposing. (Some of the people behind this measure are probably motivated more by simple hostility to corporations per se than anything else, but let's assume these are in the minority.)

Just listing the flaws in the bill could take all day. Here are a few of the more obvious ones:

- It's completely idiotic to require MSDSs and labeling for every substance in the NIOSH registry. This list contains tens of thousands of chemicals, including things like water, salt, and sugar. Many of them are known to be completely harmless; they're only on the list because they've been tested for toxicity. What is the necessity for labeling harmless substances?
- Most firms (including ours) have, because of federal law, already instituted

safety labeling, hazard communication, and worker training programs. We have spent a great deal of money already in complying with OSHA's Hazard Communication Standards, which covers the "tell the employees" side of RTK. And with threats of lawsuits from persons claiming to have been injured by manufacturer negligence (the "toxic tort" cases) and with insurance costs what they are today, we would be crazy not to have active programs of this kind. Naturally, these programs have been tailored to the needs of individual firms. They therefore vary from company to company, depending on a company's size, the nature of the materials it handles, and so on. The proposed state legislation would only result in duplication of effort, and would shoehorn each company into the same mold, whether appropriate or not. A printer employing five people would have to meet the same requirements as a research and development lab employing five thousand.

- In addition, there are already federal laws and regulations on the books that deal with chemical safety and hazard disclosure: the Federal Hazard Communication Standards of OSHA, the Clean Air Act, the Clean Water Act, the Toxic Substance Control Act—I counted fifteen federal and five state statutes that address various aspects of the "problems" that S 3311 is designed to "solve." What is the point of further and redundant legislation?
- The trade-secret protection provisions of the bill are woefully inadequate. Many substances that manufacturers need to safeguard as proprietary will be unprotectable merely because they are *suspected* of being harmful. And the machinery for obtaining exemption from disclosure, even for harmless substances, is so burdensome to manufacturers as to be almost useless.
- The costs of complying with this law will be crushing to many companies. Can you imagine the amount of paperwork it will entail? That is, assuming that compliance is even possible. Many employers probably won't be able to find out what chemicals are in every product they buy for their own use. How will they label pipelines, which carry different things at different times? The same is true for mixing vats and storage vessels. And what about the cost of enforcement? That, too, is likely to be enormous. Where is New Caledonia going to get the money? From another tax increase? We're trying to attract business to the state, not drive it away! Taxes are already too high—and if the taxes don't drive companies out of the state, the trouble and expense of complying with ill-conceived laws such as this one surely will.
- All of these drawbacks might still be acceptable *if* the law provided any real protection—but I doubt if it will. For one thing, workers don't need to know the chemical name and CAS number of everything they handle. They need to know its common name and, in brief and clear form (preferably by some sort of easily visible color code), what kind of hazard it poses. Labeling *everything*, whether harmful or not, with unpronounceable and incomprehensible chemical names will just confuse people and dilute the warning value of the labels—it will just be ineffective! And for another thing, much of the bill will ultimately be irrelevant anyway. OSHA's Hazard Communication Standards have just been published, and as Phil pointed out in his memo, these preempt many of the labeling and worker protection aspects of S 3311. The company has complied with the OSHA standards. These new provisions in S 3311 will be struck down in court as soon as someone takes the trouble to challenge them, and the only people who will benefit will be a handful of lawyers.
- S 3311 would be a boon, however, for two groups: (a) union organizers and (b) those who wish to harass or discredit businesses. Since virtually anyone would have access to chemical inventory information, could demand on-site

inspections of workplaces, and could act on behalf of workers in demanding to see MSDSs, the door would be open for anyone who wanted to stir up trouble—either with a view to convincing employees that they need union representation (or stronger union representation) to "protect" them from "hazardous" substances, or with a view to convincing the public that communities are in mortal danger from insidious chemical poisons used by irresponsible corporations. It would be child's play to convince residents of any community that they have another Bhopal right in their backyard.

- In fact, however, it is the legislation itself that poses the biggest threat to public safety. Since anyone could use this law to discover the nature, quantity, and precise location of drugs, explosives, or other sensitive materials, it could be exploited by criminals or terrorists. Security for dangerous substances would be almost impossible to achieve. That is why some people are calling this the right-to-steal bill.

- The penalties proposed for violations are unduly harsh, including as they do prison sentences for many infractions. Nor does S 3311 distinguish between deliberate and accidental violations. If this bill were enacted, no sane person would want to be in a position of responsibility in this industry!

- Finally (and I could go on, but I guess that's enough for starters), the law is virtually unenforceable, for reasons that I'm sure must be abundantly clear by now.

RTK is much more than an unwise, costly, and overcomplicated piece of specific legislation. Viewed properly, it is an attempt by U.S. unions to take RTK and parlay it into the kind of radical "union right to information" that European unions have won through even broader "access" legislation and codetermination laws. This is the foot-in-the-door toward the European "democratization"-of-the-workplace ideology, and we should fight it here.

As you can probably see, I think that S 3311 has a few flaws. This legislation is sure to impose unbearable hardships on many businesses. It will make more jobs for bureaucrats in government (and, for that matter, for paper-pushers and record-keepers in our own firms) while costing the jobs of countless workers as some businesses close, others move to less inhospitable states, and still others are forced into layoffs and plant closings. How can we not, then, take a firm stand against such an outrageous piece of legislation? If it passed simply because no one took the responsibility for trying to stop it, we would have only ourselves to blame. But even if the fight proves futile, what will others think of us if we don't at least try to stand up for our own rights?

MEMORANDUM

Date:	April 8
To:	Roy Lear
	President
From:	Louis Cordelia
	Vice President, Public Affairs
Re:	Our Position on State RTK Legislation

For some time I have been keeping abreast of developments in RTK legislation nationwide. Thus, even before your inquiry regarding the bill now pending in the New Caledonia State Senate, I had come to the conclusion that we would sooner or later have to face up to this issue. Having given a good deal of thought to the matter, I feel that it would be a big mistake either to avoid taking a position or to oppose any RTK legislation. Instead, we should carefully consider our own needs as well as those of our work force and the public, and try to present a compromise bill that both we and the RTK proponents can live with.

I realize that this may not be a popular suggestion. Nobody loves a compromise, and in this case we can't even be certain that the compromise bill will pass; we may simply have to absorb a defeat. So many people, I imagine, will say, "Why not at least try for victory?" and opt for an Alamo-style resistance to RTK in any form. Others may say, "If it looks as though we can't win, why not just stay out of the fight?" Both of these positions seem reasonable; however, I don't feel that in the long run they are in our best interests.

First of all, we must consider this problem from a broad perspective. These days, people are nervous about chemicals, and they are nervous about large corporations. When both chemicals and large corporations are involved, they can get downright paranoid. It's no use just saying to them, "Well, don't be nervous—you can trust us." Heaven knows, our PR people spend a good deal of time and money to get that message across to the public, and I don't question the value of their efforts, but there's a limit to how much can be accomplished that way. Everyone has heard about Bhopal; many people remember Love Canal. Just recently New York banned the eating or sale of striped bass because of the presence of PCBs in their tissues. People know how those PCBs got there.

My point is that the public is better informed, more sophisticated, and more anxious than ever before. We must show them that we are making a good-faith effort to address their concerns, or we will just be buried under an avalanche of protective legislation. Much of it will not be at all to our liking—unfair, ill conceived, impractical, ruinously expensive, you name it—but it will be passed. Legislatures ultimately respond to popular pressure. The longer we try to keep the lid on, the more violent will be the explosion, and we will have only ourselves to blame. What we must do instead is to channel these energies (which derive from concerns that are at bottom legitimate, even if somewhat exaggerated) in such a way that our legitimate needs are also addressed.

It is also important that the public not be allowed to view industry (and, of course, International Manufacturing in particular) as an adversary. We are proud of our reputation and have worked hard to gain and hold the public's respect. We have never been concerned with the bottom line to the exclusion of all other concerns. We have always taken seriously our responsibilities to our employees and to the community. If we take a stance against RTK legislation (and no one will care that it was because the bill was a bad one—all they'll remember is that we were against RTK), we will jeopardize a public image that took years to create. All our responsible, voluntary actions—the affirmative action program, the funding of environmental research, our very liberal policies on employee privacy issues, our pioneering of quality circles, and the rest—could be quickly forgotten. These days, one black mark is often enough to brand a company as an enemy of the people.

At the same time, we should understand the intensity of feelings about RTK on the part of the unions. Although we may tend to impute organizational self-interest and liberal-ideological motives to union advocacy, behind these are genuine problems with earlier industry conduct, and we all know that some "outlaw" conduct continues today. I have attached two short articles, one covering the valid emotional concerns that unions express and the other showing the determination that the RTK coalition in nearby Michigan displayed right before they passed their RTK law.

For these reasons, I propose that we develop a bill of our own that attempts to protect our workers, the communities in which we do business, *and* International Manufacturing, and have this new bill introduced by a leading moderate legislator. (Alternatively, we might be able to develop and support amendments to S 3311 that would make it acceptable; that is a determination for our legal staff to make.) I do not believe that these three aims are incompatible, if we are willing to compromise. Nor do I think that the labor and environmental lobbies would be averse to working with us to hammer out such a compromise. After all, they, too, have to worry about ending up with nothing because they asked for too much. They don't want to provoke die-hard opposition, nor do they want to have to contend with legal challenges to an overly ambitious bill that won't stand up in court. They, too, I'm sure, would rather have a law that everyone can live with. In Massachusetts, industry representatives and RTK advocates wound up producing a compromise bill that all sides ultimately supported, even though they were still bitterly apart on matters of principle.

I'm certainly not the person to spell out just what form such a compromise should take or what provisions would make such a bill satisfactory to us. These are matters for our Legal, Health and Safety, Manufacturing, Labor, and Community Relations people to hash out. But I think that even I can see the broad outlines. If S 3311 calls for preparation of MSDSs for 65,000 substances perhaps the list can be limited to a more manageable number—say, only those known to pose serious health or safety hazards. If the paperwork involved in preparing elaborate MSDSs is too burdensome, perhaps some simpler way of providing the same information can be found. If S 3311 calls for labeling all containers that contain *any* measurable amount of a listed substance, perhaps a concentration threshold can be introduced. If S 3311's requirements for labeling and public disclosure would jeopardize trade secrets, perhaps an easier mechanism for claiming an exemption when trade secrets are involved could be built into the law. The provisions for work-site inspections by employees and/or community residents could be modified—for example, by requiring that a petition be filed or a warrant issued before inspection was permitted. Access of community residents to MSDSs could be similarly restricted to prevent frivolous or harassing inquiries. Penalties for unintentional violations of the law could be made less harsh than for willful violations. And so on.

I would like to address briefly two counterarguments to the position outlined above. First, some might object that we should not enter fights unless we are fairly confident of winning them. Since we cannot be sure that a compromise bill will prevail over the original "hard-line" S 3311, why take the risk of entering the fray? My answer is that we have to be concerned with the future as well as the present. State legislatures are extraordinarily volatile; a bill passed today may be heavily amended or even repealed in the next session. It is true that the unsatisfactory S 3311 may win this time around. Nevertheless, it is important that we stake out a position now and that the mass media report our position as part of the debate. Otherwise, the fact that some companies favor a reasonable and practical regulatory system will *not* appear in the mass media, and the public will assume that *all* companies accept the Neanderthal positions that will be offered.

Speaking out will not only help our public image but also give us a great advantage in credibility when the legislature recognizes the shortcomings of its first efforts and tries to formulate a better bill in some later session. At that point we will be in a position to say, "We told you so." I can guarantee that the legislature, anxious to correct its past mistakes, will then treat our serious, well-thought-out proposals with the respect they deserve. In short, we may lose this battle but ultimately win the war.

Second, some might also object that we should not take a position before other businesses in New Caledonia have done so, for fear of damaging our standing with our peers. On this point I feel very strongly. We are leaders and always have been. We don't have to run with the herd or wait for the stragglers. We are proud to be trailblazers—let others follow our example, not vice versa. This is particularly true where issues of social responsibility are concerned. Our record on health, safety, and environmental issues is an enviable one. Just this year, you yourself served on the Conference Board's special panel on the Future of Worker Health in a High-Tech Society. Why should we back down to appease some troglodyte? Let's stay where we belong—in the forefront.

RIGHT TO KNOW

BY MICHAEL KENNY

"What you don't know won't hurt you," the old saying goes.

Baloney.

What you don't know about the substances and the hazards around your workplace can be dangerous. NOT knowing these things can endanger your health—even your life. Remember, you have a right to know.

Toxic effects have been reported for more than 50,000 chemicals that are thought to be in the workplaces of America. New ones are being added all the time. More than 2,000 of these are suspected of causing cancer in humans, based on laboratory animal studies.

There is valid scientific evidence of increased health risks for about 20 hazardous substances. Investigators say future studies may lengthen the list.

Approximately 21 million Americans are exposed to substances regulated by OSHA, the federal Occupational Safety and Health Administration.

The National Institute for Occupational Safety and Health (NIOSH) now includes neurotoxic (nerve poison) disorders as one of the 10 leading work-related diseases and injuries. NIOSH says it added nerve disorders because of their potential severity and because of the large number of workers potentially at risk.

A conservative estimate of the workers exposed full time to one or more neurotoxic agents is 7.7 million, and the number of potentially neurotoxic chemicals found in the workplace exceeds 850, according to the federal agency.

While precise figures are hard to come by, it is roughly estimated that about 100,000 Americans die each year from occupational diseases, and some 400,000 new cases of occupational diseases are recognized annually.

In addition to the toll of illness, employer reports show that about 5,000 workers—nearly 100 a week—die each year in job-related accidents, and 2 million more are disabled.

You have a right to know what causes all this sickness and dying.

No one has the right to expose you to a machine, a chemical, or a work practice on your job that may harm or kill you.

Workers' "right-to-know" is a logical extension of the watershed legislation which created OSHA in 1970—one of the most important gains achieved for all workers under the strong leadership of the trade union movement. That law, among other things, guarantees workers the right to a safe and healthful workplace.

A major victory in the Right-to-Know Campaign was a 1982 ruling by the National Labor Relations Board which gave unions access to lists of chemicals used in the workplace.

OSHA rules provide workers access to a broad range of information, including hazard exposure data and medical records.

Right-to-know laws have been passed in many states and cities. Many union contracts have incorporated right-to-know provisions. Similarly, the right to refuse work under dangerous conditions is recognized in many union contracts.

These are hard-won rights, meant to be understood and used by you or your representative for your protection. But such rights are like muscles—unless you exercise them, they become flabby and useless.

Source: *Utility Workers of America*, LIGHT, October 1986. Used with permission of LIGHT.

ATTACHMENT

RIGHT-TO-KNOW BATTLE CONTINUES: LEGISLATORS ON HOT SEAT

LANSING, MICHIGAN—For the past two years, a coalition of labor, environmental, and community organizations has been battling to enact a state law that would give Michigan workers, emergency personnel, and community residents access to information on toxic workplace chemicals. The battle will resume this September when the Michigan legislature takes up H.B. 4111, the Right-to-Know bill.

The bill, which was introduced by state representative Juanita Watkins (D-Detroit), is similar to legislation which passed the House but died in the Senate Labor Committee in 1984. Again in 1985, industry lobbyists have mounted a campaign to defeat strong Right-to-Know protections for workers and citizens in Michigan.

Because of wide public support for Right-to-Know legislation and because common sense dictates that workers should know the nature of the hazards they are exposed to, industry lobbyists have been unable to oppose the concept of Right-to-Know. Instead, the State Chamber of Commerce, the Michigan Manufacturers Association, and the Michigan Chemical Council, to name a few, are supporting a substitute bill which would gut the major provisions of H.B. 4111. In this way they can claim to favor Right-to-Know, while they oppose specific provisions which give Right-to-Know some teeth.

In September your state representative and state senator will be deciding the fate of your right to information on chemicals which cause cancer, birth defects, lung disease, and other illnesses. They will have to choose between a strong bill which truly gives people access to information or a watered-down substitute which would severely restrict public and worker access. We think it's time Michigan joined the 23 other states which have already adopted effective Right-to-Know legislation.

In August the Right-to-Know Task Force will be sending a survey to every state representative and senator asking for their position on the crucial provisions of H.B. 4111. We are hoping the survey will inform the legislature on the issue, guide our state and local lobbying efforts, and flush out those legislators who claim to support Right-to-Know, but who have opposed the most important sections of the bill. We will be announcing the results of the survey in September when the legislature convenes. We believe voters have a right-to-know where their legislators stand on this critical public health issue.

Source: Right to Know Task Force Action Sheet, September/October 1985.

REPRODUCTIVE HAZARDS

JOHNSON CONTROLS AND PROTECTIVE EXCLUSION FROM THE WORKPLACE

Anne T. Lawrence

In 1990, Cheryl Cook was employed in a nontraditional job: She ran the ball mill, a two-story-tall machine that made lead oxide at the Johnson Controls automotive battery plant in Bennington, Vermont. To get the job, the 34-year-old mother of two had had to undergo surgical sterilization. Under a "fetal protection" policy, adopted in 1982, Johnson Controls had decided to hire only infertile women for production jobs, because of the possible effects of maternal exposure to lead on unborn children. The United Auto Workers, the union representing most of the company's production workers, believed that the company's policy was illegal. In 1984, the union filed suit on behalf of all adversely affected employees, charging sex discrimination under Title VII of the Civil Rights Act. Like many women who worked for Johnson Controls, Cheryl Cook expressed resentment at the company's assumption that she was unable to make responsible reproductive decisions on her own. "[Y]ou should choose for yourself," she told a reporter.

By Anne T. Lawrence, San Jose State University. Originally presented at a meeting of the North American Case Research Association, November 1991. Research was supported in part by the San Jose State University College of Business. This case was written from public sources, without the cooperation of management, solely for the purpose of stimulating student discussion. All events and individuals are real. Copyright © 1993 by the *Case Research Journal* and Anne T. Lawrence.

"Myself, I wouldn't go in there if I could get pregnant. But they [company managers] don't trust you."[1]

Johnson Controls, for its part, vigorously defended its policy of protective exclusion, despite the apparently discriminatory impact of the policy and the tough decisions it forced many female job applicants and employees to make. Medical evidence clearly showed, the company believed, that maternal exposure to lead could interfere with fetal development, causing neurological damage and other birth defects. "To knowingly poison unborn children," the company reasoned, was "morally reprehensible."

Moreover, the company argued that it had a legitimate right to protect itself from the expensive liability lawsuits that could result if a child were born with impairments traceable to its mother's occupational exposure. The company, which was in compliance with Occupational Safety and Health Administration (OSHA) lead standards for adult exposure, maintained that there was no technologically or economically feasible way to reduce lead levels in the battery-making process sufficiently to eliminate risk to the fetus.

After a long journey through the judicial system, the dispute between Johnson Controls and employees who believed themselves victimized by its policy came before the U.S. Supreme Court. In March 1991, after a series of contradictory decisions by lower courts, the high court would decide the legality of the Johnson Controls policy of protective exclusion in a landmark case that appeals court Judge Frank Easterbrook called "likely the most important sex discrimination case in any court since 1964, when Congress enacted Title VII [of the Civil Rights Act]." In the balance hung not only the fate of female employees and job applicants at Johnson Controls, but also that of perhaps as many as 20 million other women whose jobs exposed them to substances potentially hazardous to the fetus.

JOHNSON CONTROLS, INC.

At the time of the Supreme Court decision, Johnson Controls, Inc., was one of the nation's leading manufacturers of automotive lead batteries, particularly for the replacement parts market. Between its founding at the turn of the century and the late 1970s, Johnson Controls was engaged chiefly in the production of environmental controls, automotive seating, and miscellaneous plastic products. In 1978, the company purchased Globe Union, Inc., an independent battery manufacturer that had been in business for over 50 years. In 1990, the Globe Battery Division of Johnson Controls operated fourteen plants, extending from Bennington, Vermont, to Fullerton, California, and accounted for 16 percent of Johnson's sales and 20 percent of its income. That year, the company as a whole posted sales of $4.5 billion and employed 43,500 workers—approximately 5400 of them in the battery division.

Prior to the 1960s, few if any women worked in production jobs at Globe Union, reflecting long-standing historical patterns of gender segregation in which men worked in production jobs and women in office and support roles. In the 1970s, at Globe Union—as in many other businesses in those years—women began moving in increasing numbers into traditionally male occupations. Even by the mid-1980s, however, only a small percentage of women had production jobs. In the Bennington, Vermont, plant, for example, only 5 percent of the production work force was female. Women never penetrated the top echelons of the company: In 1990, the company's fifteen top executives and twelve directors were all men.

The production process used in Johnson's Globe Battery Division plants necessarily entailed exposure to lead, which is the element that enables an automotive battery to store and deliver electricity. As Denise Zutz, director of corporate communications at Johnson, bluntly put it, "[Without lead] no one would be driving a car."[2] To make a battery, Johnson Controls workers mixed lead oxide to form a paste, which was then compressed to form lead plates in the core of the battery. Lead dust and vapors were produced at multiple points in the production process. Johnson Controls, like other battery manufacturers, had made numerous efforts to develop a nonlead-based battery. Although several alternatives were currently in the experimental stage—including a zinc-bromide battery that Johnson had been researching for several years—none had yet been successfully developed for commercial use.

LEAD TOXICITY

Lead, a heavy metal, is one of the oldest known toxins. When lead particles are inhaled or ingested, they damage the central nervous, immune, reproductive, cardiovascular, and excretory systems of the body. At low levels, lead causes fatigue and irritability; at high levels, loss of consciousness, seizures, and eventually death. Lead-exposed individuals run a heightened risk of heart attack and stroke. According to the Centers for Disease Control (CDC), lead becomes dangerous to adults at blood levels of 50 micrograms per deciliter ($\mu g/dl$). Children suffer toxic effects from lead at even lower levels. Lead poisoning in children is caused mainly by inhaling leaded gasoline fumes and by swallowing peeling, leaded paint in older, poorly maintained buildings. At blood levels of around 25 $\mu g/dl$, children begin to show characteristic signs of lead poisoning: irritability, hyperactivity, lowered attention span, and learning difficulties. Higher doses, as in adults, can have even more serious consequences.

Lead also adversely affects the unborn. Lead in a pregnant woman's bloodstream crosses the placenta and enters the fetus's blood, at concentration levels similar to the mother's. Because its central nervous system develops rapidly, the fetus is particularly sensitive to lead. Exposure in the womb may lead to irreversible brain damage, resulting in intellectual and motor retardation, behavioral abnormalities, and learning deficiencies. It can also cause spontaneous abortion, low birth weight, premature delivery, and stillbirth. Adverse effects to the fetus have been detected at blood levels as low as 10 µg/dl, well below the CDC standard for adults.

One of the special difficulties with protecting the fetus is that lead is an accumulative toxicant, building up over time in the blood, soft tissues, and bones. Lead's half-life in the body is 5 to 7 years, and it often remains long after an individual has been removed from a high-lead environment. By a cruel twist of medical fate, pregnancy may actually increase levels of lead in the blood, since bones often decalcify during pregnancy to provide calcium to the developing fetus, mobilizing lead stored in the bones. Studies have shown that maternal lead blood levels may as much as double during pregnancy, even without additional exposure. Thus removing a woman from a high-lead workplace when a pregnancy is discovered—or even when one is planned—does not eliminate the risk of lead-caused damage to the fetus.

The effects of lead on male reproductive health are less well understood and more controversial. Lead affects male reproductive capacity: Lead-exposed men may experience reduced sexual drive and, at high levels, impotence. Lead may also cause genetic damage to sperm, leading to birth defects. Most of the evidence for male-mediated effects comes from animal studies. A 1990 University of Maryland study, for example, found that lead-exposed male rats mated with unexposed females produced offspring whose brains developed abnormally. The researchers were unable to explain the biological mechanisms by which such male-mediated effects occurred, however, and the results of this study were not confirmed for humans.

GOVERNMENT REGULATION OF LEAD EXPOSURE

In view of the medical evidence on the hazards of lead, the Occupational Safety and Health Administration (OSHA) in 1978 adopted a standard requiring that employees be removed from worksites when their blood levels reached 50 µg/dl, based on an average of three consecutive blood tests. These employees were permitted to return when their blood levels fell to 40 µg/dl or below.

In setting its lead standard, OSHA also considered the impact of lead exposure on the fetus and the possible need to exclude pregnant or fertile women from high-lead workplaces. The agency concluded:

> [T]here is no basis whatsoever for the claim that women of child-bearing age should be excluded from the workplace in order to protect the fetus or the course of pregnancy.[3]

OSHA did not set a separate standard for fetal exposure. However, the agency did recommend that individuals of both sexes who planned to conceive a child maintain blood levels below 30 µg/dl "because of the demonstrated adverse effects of lead on reproductive function in both males and females as well as the risk of genetic damage of lead on both the ovum and sperm."[4]

THE JOHNSON CONTROLS LEAD HYGIENE PROGRAM

Well before the OSHA lead standard was established, Globe Union and its successor, Johnson Controls, moved to protect their employees from the adverse effects of lead. In 1969 Dr. Charles Fishburn, then working for Globe Union and later the chief architect of Johnson's fetal protection policy, introduced a comprehensive lead hygiene program at the company. Globe (and later Johnson) instituted "housekeeping" measures and engineering controls to reduce lead dust and vapors in the air. For example, the company installed pumps to supply clean air to workstations and central vacuum systems and powered floor scrubbers and sweepers to keep its plants as free as possible of lead dust.

To prevent workers from carrying home lead particles, work clothing and footwear were provided by the company, and employees were given paid time at the day's end to shower and change into their personal attire. The company provided respirators and taught employees how to use them. Johnson maintained an active program of blood testing, and employees with blood levels above 50 µg/dl were transferred without loss of pay or benefits to jobs where the average level of workers was below 30. After purchasing Globe in 1978, Johnson invested $15 million in additional environmental engineering controls at its battery division plants.

Many observers, including those from the union, agreed that Globe Union, and later Johnson Controls, made significant progress in their industrial hygiene programs during the 1970s and 1980s. During this period, the company remained in substantial compliance with OSHA lead standards.[5]

INSTITUTING A VOLUNTARY POLICY

In 1977, partly in response to the growing number of women in production jobs in its plants, Globe Union established its first policy on women in lead-exposed jobs. In promulgating this policy, the company noted:

> [Protection] of the unborn child is the immediate and direct responsibility of the parents. While the medical profession and the company can support them in the exercise of this responsibility, it cannot assume it for them without simultaneously infringing their rights as persons. . . .
> Since not all women who can become pregnant wish to become mothers, . . . it would appear to be illegal discrimination to treat all who are capable of pregnancy as though they will become pregnant.[6]

Observing that scientific evidence at that time had not conclusively established the risk of lead exposure to the fetus, the company did not officially exclude women capable of bearing children from jobs that exposed them to lead. However, the company issued the following warning:

> [We] do feel strongly that those women who are working in lead exposure. . . and those women who wish to be considered for employment be advised that there is risk, [and]. . . we recommend not working in lead if they are considering a family.[7]

The company also required each woman to sign a statement saying that she understood the company's recommendation.

Globe Union did not guarantee transfers for women requesting removal from high-lead-exposure jobs, nor did it guarantee equal wage rates for those who did transfer.

THE 1982 FETAL PROTECTION POLICY

In 1982, the company—now under the management of Johnson Controls—instituted a new "fetal protection" program in all its battery plants. Citing its ethical obligation not to engage in any activity threatening the well-being of any person, Johnson reversed its voluntary policy and announced its intention to exclude all fertile women from high-lead-exposure jobs in its battery manufacturing plants. It stated its policy as follows:

> [I]t is the [Globe Battery] Division's policy that women who are pregnant or who are capable of bearing children will not be placed into jobs involving lead exposure or which could expose them to lead through the exercise of job bidding, bumping, transfer or promotion rights. This policy is intended to reduce or eliminate the possible unhealthy effects of lead on the unborn children of pregnant employees or applicants.[8]

Johnson defined as "capable of bearing children" any woman under the age of 70 who could not provide medical documentation of sterility, regardless of her age, marital status, sexual orientation, fertility of her partner, use of contraception, or intention to bear children. The company explicitly stated that it was not its intention to encourage surgical sterilization:

> [The policy] is in no way intended to support or encourage women of childbearing capability to seek to change this status. Employees are strongly advised against such action.[9]

For women already employed in lead-exposed positions, Johnson Controls applied a "grandfather" clause: They could continue to work at their present positions as long as they were able to maintain blood levels below 30 µg/dl in regular tests. If blood levels rose, they were permitted to transfer to other jobs without loss of pay, seniority, or benefits.

The fetal protection policy applied to all jobs in which any employee had recorded a blood level over 30 µg/dl, or where any air sample had exceeded 30 µg per cubic meter, during the previous year. Such high-lead-exposure jobs typically made up less than half of all production jobs. In practice, however, Johnson Control's new policy excluded fertile women from virtually all production jobs, since most positions—even if not lead-exposed—were connected by chains of job bidding, transfer, or promotion to jobs that were exposed.

JUSTIFYING THE NEW POLICY

In justifying its move from a voluntary policy to one of protective exclusion, the main argument of Johnson Controls was that the old policy had not worked. Between 1977 and 1982, at least six women in high-lead positions had become pregnant while maintaining blood levels above 30 µg/dl. One of the children born to these mothers, according to the company's occupational physician, showed some signs of hyperactivity, although this condition was never definitively traced to the mother's occupational exposure to lead. In addition, the company claimed that increased scientific understanding of the risk of lead exposure to the fetus since 1977 had heightened its concern for fetal health.

The company informed its employees that it had considered and rejected several less discriminatory policies, including voluntary exclusion, limiting exclusion to women actually pregnant or planning to become so, and transferring women whose blood lead levels rose above certain levels. Many pregnancies are unplanned, the company argued. Moreover, women often are unaware of pregnancy during the initial weeks, and—in any case—removal from the job after pregnancy has begun may be insufficient to eliminate fetal risk. To protect the unborn, therefore, Johnson officials argued they had no choice but to bar fertile women from high-lead jobs altogether.

Although the main stated reason of Johnson Controls for adopting an exclusionary policy was its concern for the unborn, the company was also influenced by fears of liability lawsuits from children adversely affected by their mother's occupational exposure to lead. The company believed it had a legal obligation to avoid injuries to "third parties," such as fetuses, resulting from the hazards of its manufacturing operations. In a brief filed later before the Supreme Court, the company's attorneys maintained:

> In this day and age, it cannot seriously be disputed that a company's desire to avoid direct harm to its employees and their families, its customers, and its neighbors from its own toxic hazards goes to the heart of its "normal operation."

The brief went on to quote with approval an opinion in an earlier court decision:

> [The] normal operation of a business encompasses ethical, legal and business concerns about the effect of an employer's activities on third parties. An employer might be validly concerned on a variety of grounds both practical and ethical with the hazards of his workplace on the children of his employees.[10]

Although it delicately avoided addressing the issue directly, the company's point was clear: It was concerned about potential liability risk.

In assessing the extent of the company's exposure to possible liability lawsuits, Johnson Controls managers faced considerable uncertainty. Although employee suits against employers for injury at work are preempted by workers' compensation laws, most states permit the live-born child of an employee to sue its mother's employer for injuries caused in utero by the employer's negligence. Such suits, however, have historically been difficult to win. The causes of most birth defects are elusive. Moreover, in a situation in which an employer had followed all OSHA regulations and warned the mother of known hazards, a child would be hard-pressed to prove employer negligence. Prior to the time the Supreme Court considered the Johnson Controls case, in only one instance had a child sued an employer for its mother's occupational exposure to lead; this case had resulted in a jury verdict in favor of the employer, even though the employer had violated OSHA's maximum exposure rules.[11]

WOMEN'S WORKPLACE RIGHTS

Johnson Controls' new policy of protective exclusion—at the time probably the most comprehensive of any in place in U.S. industry—represented a bold challenge to the Civil Rights Act of 1964 and its subsequent amendments. The company's position raised serious questions about the nature of women's rights in the workplace, and how these were to be balanced against possible rights of the fetus and the employer.

Title VII of the Civil Rights Act of 1964 prohibits discrimination in employment on the basis of sex, as well as on the basis of race, color, religion, and national origin. In 1978, Congress passed the Pregnancy Discrimination Act (PDA), which amended Title VII by providing that the term "on the basis of sex" include "because of or on the basis of pregnancy, childbirth, or related medical conditions." That is, pregnant workers (and others distinguished by "related" conditions, such as potential for pregnancy) must, for all employment purposes, be afforded the same treatment as other workers with similar abilities.

In interpreting Title VII, as amended, the courts subsequently developed two frameworks for analyzing discrimination claims. If an employment policy is discriminatory on its face—for example, if it overtly excludes women from a particular job—it is permitted only if the employer can demonstrate that gender is a bona fide occupational qualification (BFOQ).

In practice, the courts have interpreted BFOQs narrowly. For example, a department store may legitimately hire only men to model male fashions, but a fire department may not hire only men as fire fighters simply because the position is physically demanding.

On the other hand, if an employment policy is neutral on its face but in fact has an adverse impact on members of a protected class, the courts apply a weaker standard. In such so-called "disparate impact" cases, the employer need only demonstrate that its policy is dictated by a "business necessity." According to the United States Court of Appeals for the Fourth Circuit, "[The] test is whether there exists an overriding legitimate business purpose such that the practice is necessary to the safe and efficient operation of the business."[12]

In practice, the courts have held that employment practices that have a disparate impact are defensible only if they are clearly job-related. For example, a police department may be permitted to use written employment tests, even if minorities perform less well on them than do whites, if it can demonstrate that the tests accurately predict successful job performance.

The entry of increasing numbers of women into hazardous jobs in the 1970s and 1980s—and the subsequent efforts of employers to exclude them in the name of fetal protection—called the legal question: Were gender-based policies of exclusion to protect the unborn legal or illegal? And should specific policies be judged under the more restrictive BFOQ or the less restrictive "business necessity" standard? In 1982, when Johnson Controls managers adopted their fetal protection policy, these difficult matters of law remained unresolved.

THE UNITED AUTO WORKERS LAWSUIT

The union representing Johnson Controls employees, the United Auto Workers (UAW), believed that protective exclusion was unfair—and illegal. In 1984 the union filed suit, charging that Johnson's fetal protection policy constituted illegal sex discrimination under Title VII and the Pregnancy Discrimination Act. Individual plaintiffs in the case included Mary Craig, a young woman who underwent sterilization in 1983 to keep her job; Elsie Nason, a 50-year-old divorcee whose pay was cut when she was forced to transfer out of a high-lead-exposure job; and Donald Penney, who was denied a transfer out of a high-lead area that he requested because he intended to start a family.

The union's key argument was that the policy of Johnson Controls violated Title VII of the Civil Rights Act because sterility was not a bona fide occupational qualification. The UAW brief argued that the company's policy was discriminatory on its face:

Because Johnson Controls policy excludes women—and only women—from certain jobs precisely because of their capacity to bear children—that policy is facially discriminatory under the statute [Title VII] as amended by the PDA [the Pregnancy Discrimination Act].[13]

Therefore, Johnson Controls would have to demonstrate a BFOQ. But sterility, the union insisted, had nothing to do with battery-making: "Fertile women. . . produce batteries as efficiently and proficiently as anyone else."[14]

Since fertile women were just as capable of effectively performing the work as were men and infertile women, the employer had not demonstrated a BFOQ. In response to the contention of Johnson Controls that reproductive risks were mediated exclusively through the mother, the union presented medical evidence showing that lead posed a reproductive hazard for men as well as for women. Thus, the appropriate response was not to exclude women, but to reduce workplace exposures to lead for all workers, male and female. The union did not dismiss the employer's concern for fetal health as trivial or insincere. Indeed, the UAW acknowledged in its brief that "certain ethical and moral goals, including promoting child and fetal health, are widely accepted in this society."[15] However, it maintained that the determinants of fetal health were complex and influenced by many factors in addition to workplace hazards. In fact, the union argued, exclusionary policies themselves may be hazardous to fetal health, by pushing women out of jobs with good pay and medical benefits:

> [T]he relationship between fetal health and female employment is a complex one. There are. . . fetal risks both in the processes and materials used in many workplace situations and in depriving fertile and pregnant women of income through denial of employment opportunities.[16]

The plaintiffs also attacked the policy for assuming that women were unable to make independent, intelligent decisions about the conditions under which to bear children. The plaintiffs' attorney, Marsha Berzon, stated in her oral argument before the Supreme Court:

> The policy. . . is based on a negative behavioral stereotype about how women who are faced with possible fetal harm will behave. . . . In today's day and age, women in general can control whether or not they are going to have children.[17]

The mother, not the employer, she maintained, was best situated to assess possible risks and what was best for the child.

The union also argued that the fetal protection policy violated women's privacy. The UAW brief stated:

> Requiring proof of sterility as a precondition to obtaining or retaining a job is, in itself, a serious intrusion into very sensitive matters, even for those whose personal reproductive situation conforms to the employer's requirement.

The policy had the effect, furthermore, of pressuring some women to undergo sterilization, although the company explicitly denied that this was their intent.

Some women workers, the union noted, "are as a practical matter forced to choose between their job opportunities and their childbearing capacity. Since many women are economically dependent on their jobs, putting women to that choice conditions employment for women, but not for men, upon the ability to exercise 'the right to have offspring. . . one of the basic civil rights of man.'"[18]

Finally, the union argued that the policy of Johnson Controls, if upheld, would open the door to the exclusion of women from a very wide range of jobs entailing possible hazards to the fetus, thus effectively resegregating the work force. According to studies by the Bureau of National Affairs cited by the union, as many as 20 million jobs held by women involved exposure to possible fetotoxins; many millions more involved exposure to other risks, such as infectious agents, stress, noise, radiation, or even ordinary physical accidents such as falls or automobile accidents.

The union also noted that in practice fetal protection policies had generally been limited to male-dominated occupations. For example, policies like Johnson's were most common in production facilities in the chemical, automotive, and paint industries—all areas in which women constituted a minority. By contrast, women had rarely, if ever, been excluded on the basis of fetal protection from surgical nursing, childcare, or secretarial jobs, where they dominate the work force—even though anesthetic gases, rubella viruses, and radiation emitted by video display terminals were all documented fetal hazards. The union maintained that employers had not excluded women from these work settings, despite the possibility of fetal risk, for the simple reason that women were indispensable.[19]

If upheld by the courts, the union argued, fetal protection policies would therefore have the practical effect of reversing many of the gains women had made in the 1970s and 1980s in moving into formerly male-dominated occupations and industries. Union attorney Berzon told the court:

> The net effect of upholding a policy of this type. . . would be the resegregation of the work force, particularly because the economics of the situation are that employers are going to install fetal protection policies in instances in which they are not dependent on women workers for the work force and not instigate them where they are highly dependent on women workers, because they would have nobody to do the job.[20]

By upholding the position of Johnson Controls, the union concluded, the court would "cut the heart out of Title VII and out of the Pregnancy Discrimination Act."

NOTES

1. Peter T. Kilborn. "Who Decides Who Works at Jobs Imperiling Fetuses." *The New York Times*, 2 September 1990: Al, A12.
2. Cathy Trost. "Business and Women Anxiously Watch Suit on 'Fetal Protection.'" *The Wall Street Journal*, 8 October 1990: A3.
3. Brief for the Petitioners at 2–3. International Union, United Automobile, Aerospace, and Agricultural Implements Workers of America. *UAW v. Johnson Controls, Inc.*, 111 S. Ct. 1196 (1991) (No. 89-1215).
4. *International Union UAW v. Johnson Controls*, 886 F. 2d 871, 918 (7th Cir. 1989), rev'd., 111 S. Ct. 1196 (1991).
5. Kilborn, A1.
6. Brief for the Petitioners, at 2.
7. *International Union UAW v. Johnson Controls*, 886 F. 2d, at 876.
8. *International Union UAW v. Johnson Controls*, 886 F. 2d, at 877
9. *International Union UAW v. Johnson Controls*, 886 F. 2d, at 878.
10. Brief for the Petitioners, at 18–19.
11. The case was *Security National Bank v. Chloride, Inc.*, 1985; it is discussed in the circuit court opinion in *International Union UAW v. Johnson Controls*, 886 F. 2d, at 886.
12. Margaret Post Duncan. "Fetal Protection Policies: Furthering Sex Discrimination in the Marketplace." *Journal of Family Law*, 28 (1989–1990): 733.
13. Brief for the Petitioners, at 20.
14. Brief for the Petitioners, at 31.
15. Brief for the Petitioners, at 37.
16. Brief for the Petitioners, at 39.
17. Official Transcript of Proceedings before the U.S. Supreme Court, at 8. *International Union UAW v. Johnson Controls*, No. 89-1215, October 10, 1990.
18. Brief for the Petitioners, at 16.
19. For further discussion of this point, see Mary E. Becker, "From *Muller v. Oregon* to Fetal Vulnerability Policies," *University of Chicago Law Review*, 53 (1986); M. Paul, C. Daniels, and R. Rosofsky, "Corporate Responses to Reproductive Hazards in the Workplace: Results of the Family, Work, and Health Survey," *American Journal of Industrial Medicine*, 16 (1989); and Deborah A. Stone, "Fetal Risks, Women's Rights: Showdown at Johnson Controls," *American Prospect*, Fall 1990.
20. Official Transcript of Proceedings before the U.S. Supreme Court, at 11–12. *International Union UAW v. Johnson Controls*, No. 89-1215, October 10, 1990.

4

ETHICS IN MARKETING AND PRODUCT SAFETY

INTRODUCTION

Marketing involves a wide range of decisions, from what products will be produced to how they will be packaged, priced, and sold to the public. The main concern, in all these decisions, is that customers are treated fairly, which is to say, that companies not deceive or manipulate consumers and that they provide adequate information so that consumers can make informed choices. In addition, manufacturers are responsible for the impact of their activities on consumers and the public at large and, in particular, for product safety. Some products cannot be made completely safe, but they should at least be free from any defect that could cause serious injury or death when the product is used properly.

The opening case in this section raises questions about the responsibility of marketers for the social impact of advertising and, especially, the images that advertising can create or perpetuate. The idea of a toy enemy soldier who is all the more dangerous for being a paranoid schizophrenic might seem humorous to children and their parents, but not to the people who suffer from this mental disorder and their families. With countless units of the product on retailers' shelves, what steps should the manufacturer take to meet the angry response of mental health groups? Beyond this case lie questions about the responsibility of advertisers for harmful stereotypes of racial groups or images of beauty or success that have destructive consequences.

160

The Federal Trade Commission (FTC) is charged with the task of protecting consumers against deceptive advertising. Whether an ad is deceptive depends on more than the truth of the claims that are made, since consumers can also be deceived by claims that are implied but not stated or by partial claims that omit certain crucial information. Advertising claims that are supported by statistical evidence are especially problematic, because of questions about the reliability of polls and other data-gathering techniques. In the case "Litton Industries, Inc.," an official of the FTC is called upon to evaluate the research design of a study conducted to compare makes of microwave ovens, which Litton subsequently used in advertising for their own brand. The company believes that the claims are true and supported by the evidence, but should the FTC insist on a higher standard of proof?

Health claims for foods are of great concern to both the FTC and the Food and Drug Administration (FDA), which regulates the labeling on packaged foods and the information provided for over-the-counter and prescription medications. The claim that a cereal can help prevent cancer, for example, requires a higher level of support and a more careful statement of the facts in order to avoid misrepresentation. The "Natural Cereals" case provides an opportunity to evaluate a number of different marketing strategies in which the need to mount an effective advertising campaign must be balanced against legal considerations and considerations of being a responsible marketer.

Marketing sells products, in part, by a shrewd understanding of consumer psychology. Ads and other sales practices play on our hopes and fears, our deepest needs and most ephemeral whims, and also on ordinary human weaknesses. This persuasive function of marketing is not inherently objectionable, but there is a line beyond which certain kinds of advertising and sales practices become manipulative and coercive. A skilled salesperson may have the ability to sell a product to some consumers in a way that deprives them of a truly free choice. Determining the line between acceptable and unacceptable persuasion is difficult and requires a close consideration of specific cases. The interview with David Namer, a self-professed expert salesman, provides a revealing look at a number of sales practices along with Mr. Namer's own evaluation of the ethics involved.

Pharmaceutical firms and manufacturers of medical devices are frequently criticized for their marketing practices. Two of the most publicized cases in recent years involve Burroughs Wellcome and its pricing of AZT, the most effective drug on the market for the treatment of AIDS, and Dow Corning for its response to safety concerns about silicone breast implants. Another controversy on the horizon is the potential marketing in the United States of a drug, already available in some countries of Europe, that can be used to terminate pregnancy. The drug, RU 486, dubbed "the morning-after pill," is avidly sought by women's rights groups as a safe and economical alternative to surgical abortion. It is opposed, for the same reason, by antiabortion groups, which fear an increase in the number of abortions if they can be performed quickly and privately in a doctor's office.

Although the companies in question are in the same industry, the issues in each case are different. For Hoechst-Roussel, the French manufacturer of RU 486, a crucial question is the extent to which public opinion and the possibility of adverse public reaction should influence a decision on whether to market the drug in the United States. The enormous medical benefits of RU 486 have to be balanced against potential liability costs, the costs of gaining FDA approval in a difficult political environment, and also the costs of possible boycotts and other forms of protest. Where do the interests of shareholders lie in this matter? And, finally, should the debate over the ethics of abortion enter into the marketing decision?

The pricing of products is determined largely by market forces, and whatever price a product can command in a free market is generally considered to be fair. Can the price of a drug be set by market forces alone, however, when it is the only treatment for a dreaded, fatal disease? The manufacturer should be allowed a reasonable return on research and development (R & D) costs, but a price beyond a certain level is sure to bring charges of profiteering. But how much is too much? What considerations should the company use to determine a fair price? And how should the company defend its pricing decision in the face of critics who can, perhaps, never be satisfied? The case of "Burroughs Wellcome and the Pricing of AZT" leads onto questions about pricing in a complex regulatory environment where government, private insurers, and other interests play a large role.

The discovery of a dangerous defect in a widely used product poses a critical test for any company. Under the close scrutiny of the media, government, and worried consumers, company executives must evaluate their past actions in bringing the product to market and formulate a plan to resolve the complex set of problems that they now face. Mistakes of the past cannot be corrected, but should a company admit to them and attempt to compensate the victims? The company may disagree with its critics about the extent of the hazard or the best course of action, and yet it must devise a realistic strategy that meets the legal challenges, satisfies government regulators, and preserves the company's reputation, which depends on a respect for the highest ethical standards. At Dow Corning, Keith R. McKennon was brought in as chairman and CEO to make the most difficult decision of his career, a decision on which the survival of the company depended. From the multitude of facts presented in the case, the reader is invited to formulate a course of action that best meets all of the conflicting demands on the company.

ADVERTISING

ZARTAN THE ENEMY
HASBRO BRADLEY, INC.:
ETHICAL RESPONSIBILITY
FOR PRODUCT MARKETING

Denise Y. Etheridge

On Tuesday, December 18, 1984, Stephen D. Hassenfeld, 42, chairman of the board of Hasbro Bradley, Inc., sat and looked out the window of his Pawtucket, Rhode Island, office. In his hand he held a newspaper article headlined GROUP WILL BUY OFFENSIVE DOLLS. The article began:

> Officials of a psychiatric rehabilitation facility said Monday they will begin purchasing dolls labeled as "paranoid schizophrenic" by their manufacturer because the label is offensive and should not be on the market.

"Zartan the Enemy," manufactured by Hasbro, Inc., is sold in a box that describes the doll as "an extreme paranoid schizophrenic. Zartan grows into various multiple personalities to such an extent that the original personality becomes buried and forgotten," the label says.

Jerry Dincin, executive director of Thresholds, which deals largely in the treatment of schizophrenics, says the doll is "incredibly insulting to all mentally ill people and their families."[1]

As he looked out the window, Hassenfeld reflected on the events of the past month. Hasbro initially had become aware of complaints of the "paranoid schizophrenic" label after receiving a letter from the national Mental Health Association in Washington.[2] Several other mental health associations had subsequently complained about the references to the mentally ill contained in the "psychological profile" of the Zartan the Enemy doll.[3]

Donald M. Robbins, vice president of and general counsel to Hasbro, had quickly responded with a public apology, a promise to delete the offensive wording from the description of the toy, and a pledge to donate money to mental illness research.[4] Robbins, however, had stated that it would be too difficult to recall those packages containing the reference to the mentally ill because almost a million dolls had already been distributed nationwide.[5] Reaction to Hasbro's response had generally been favorable, and

This case was prepared by Denise Y. Etheridge, under the supervision of Professor Alexander B. Horniman. Copyright © 1986 by the University of Virginia, Darden Graduate Business School Foundation, Charlottesville, VA. All rights reserved.

Hassenfeld had felt that Hasbro had successfully defused a potentially damaging controversy.

Hassenfeld's feelings of success had been short-lived, however. Jerry Dincin, executive director of Thresholds, a schizophrenic treatment facility, had become outraged that a commercial toy company had manufactured a doll that, in his opinion, would further society's negative perception of the mentally ill. Dincin and other members of the board of Thresholds, after reading of Hasbro's apology and promises, had written to Hasbro demanding that the company recall the doll from the store shelves. A representative of Hasbro had responded by letter, reiterating its apology and affirming its promise to delete all references to mental illness from the package.

Hassenfeld looked down and read the article again. Dincin and the other Threshold board members had evidently not been placated. Hassenfeld wondered to what extent Hasbro had fulfilled its social and ethical responsibility to society. More specifically, Hassenfeld wondered whether the company should recall the doll.

COMPANY BACKGROUND

Hasbro Bradley, Inc., was founded in 1923 by Stephen Hassenfeld's grandfather and great-uncle.[6] The company, initially called Hassenfeld Brothers Company, was founded as a textile-remnant company. During World War II, under the direction of Stephen Hassenfeld's father, Hasbro entered the toy business by selling junior air-raid-warden kits. Since then, Hasbro had become a major manufacturer of a variety of toy products for children of different age groups.

The path to becoming a major U.S. toy company had not been smooth. Until the mid-1970s, despite being profitable, Hasbro was often plagued by cash shortages because of overstocked inventory, overdue receivables, and heavy advertising for products that did not sell.[7] Also, in 1970, Hasbro tried to diversify into day-care centers, but the diversification was a failure. "We'd get phone calls saying, 'We can't find one of the kids,'" said Hasbro management. "The whole company would stop." Another attempt at diversification was equally doomed; Hasbro admitted failure at selling Galloping Gourmet cookware when termites ate the wooden salad bowls stored in the warehouse. "I knew we had trouble when I saw the sawdust," commented a Hasbro officer.

In an effort to get Hasbro back on track, Stephen Hassenfeld, who had joined Hasbro in 1964 and become president in 1974, hired a financial team to review proposed ideas for the company. The team was a failure. For example, because the team rejected numerous ideas for toys in 1977, Hasbro suffered a severe product shortage in 1978, contributing to a $2.5 million loss and heavy debt. Strapped financially, and with no electronics expertise, Hasbro was unable to compete with its then-rival, Milton Bradley Company, when the latter introduced an early version of an electronic toy in 1978. At the 1979 Toy Fair, Hasbro was still not offering a single electronic toy, despite the fact that electronic games had become a booming business.[8]

In 1980 Stephen Hassenfeld, whose goal was to make Hasbro the top U.S. toy company, became chief executive officer. Although the company was now earning more than $100 million in revenues, however, its troubles were still not over. By 1980 Hassenfeld's uncle had become disenchanted with the management of Hasbro, and Hassenfeld settled the family spat by splitting off a pencil business to the disenchanted uncle. Then in 1982 Hasbro turned down the opportunity to manufacture and market the Cabbage Patch Kids; the company felt that children would reject the dolls because they were too ugly.[9] The Cabbage Patch Kids became the rage, earning the manufacturer, Coleco Industries, Inc., millions in revenues.

In an effort to achieve his goal, Hassenfeld concentrated his efforts on weeding out losing products and ventures and pursuing an aggressive acquisition program and an innovative product-development program. As early as 1983, Hassenfeld's efforts began to bear fruit. That year Hasbro's revenues of $225.4 million ranked it sixth in sales among U.S. toy companies. Profits zoomed 117 percent from $7.0 million in 1982 to $15.2 million in 1983.[10]

The increase in sales in 1983 (from $137.7 million in 1982) was caused by several factors. First, Hasbro had been highly successful in introducing new or modified products. New products such as My Little Pony, colorful plastic or stuffed miniature ponies, and Charmkins, miniature, scented jewelry characters, were high-revenue earners in 1983.[11] Additionally, sales from G.I. Joe, which had been reintroduced in 1982 in a modified version, earned Hasbro $80 million in 1983.

A second factor contributing to the increase in sales in 1983 was the acquisition by Hasbro of several product-related companies. By the end of 1983, Hasbro had acquired Knickerbocker Toy Company from Warner Communications, Inc., which added Raggedy Ann, Raggedy Andy, Miss Piggy, and other Sesame Street and Disney characters to Hasbro's product line and resulted in $24 million in sales in 1983.[12] Hasbro had also acquired Glenco Infants Items, Inc., one of the world's largest manufacturers of baby bibs, which also manufactured infant clothing, small toys, and feeding items. Hasbro planned to update and expand Glenco's product line and market the products under the Hasbro Baby logo starting in 1985.[13]

A third factor leading to increased sales in 1983 was Hasbro's insulation from the collapse of the electronic-game market in the early 1980s. While industry experts had criticized Hasbro in 1979 and 1980 for failing to partake in this boom, Hasbro's decision to remain with its conventional toys now seemed wise. Other toy companies were suffering large losses because of the electronic-game bust.

The year 1984 saw a continuation of Hassenfeld's efforts to become No. 1. Pursuing his acquisition strategy, he made a winning bid of $360 million for Milton Bradley, whose stock had been depressed by the collapse of the video-game market.[14] This acquisition was desirable for several reasons. First, by adding Milton Bradley's Playskool product line, Hasbro would be second only to Fisher-Price in preschool toys. Also, Milton Bradley was the industry's largest game-maker; the addition of games to Hasbro's product lines would allow Hasbro to enter an area of business that was less susceptible to fads than were toys.

In addition, Milton Bradley had strong foreign operations; overseas sales, while contributing only 37 percent to Milton Bradley's $337 million of revenues, accounted for 70 percent of the company's 1983 profits. Hasbro, with little overseas sales or operations, intended to capitalize on Milton Bradley's strength in foreign markets.

Finally, the acquisition of Milton Bradley nearly doubled Hasbro's size. The combined projected sales of Hasbro and Milton Bradley, at $350 million and $400 million, respectively, could allow Hasbro to replace Mattel, Inc., as the second largest U.S. toy company and possibly tie General Mills as the top U.S. toy manufacturer.

Although Hassenfeld was committed to his goal of making Hasbro the leader in the industry, he was also committed to identifying and serving "the needs of children in the community."[15] Hasbro participated in, if not initiated, many programs that helped disadvantaged children. For example, Hasbro funded several projects aimed at helping children either overcome or understand disabilities. One such project was the "Reading Is Fundamental Program"; funds from the program were used to purchase reading books to distribute to children with poor reading skills or reading disabilities. Hasbro also provided funding for "My Way, Your Way," an exhibit at the Children's Museum of Rhode Island designed to give visitors the opportunity to learn about and understand various disabilities. In addition, Hasbro provided financial support for the National Captioning Institute, which offered closed-captioned television to hearing-impaired children.

Hasbro had also initiated several programs designed to aid needy children. Through Hasbro's Happy Holidays Program, thousands of children received toys at Christmas time via selected charitable organizations. Hasbro sponsored another program at Christmas time, the Children's Giving Tree, in which the toy company pledged one of its toys to a Rhode Island foster child for every handmade ornament hung on the tree. In 1983 Hasbro organized Operation Toylift, an airlift of toys to be given to each of the 3,600 children of Grenada.

PRODUCT DEVELOPMENT

Each Hasbro toy was the result of a rigorous product-development program. The idea for the product was first conceived either by members of the Research and Development staff or by outside inventors or designers who submitted their ideas to the company. After the concept crystallized, the product idea was submitted to Marketing, Research and Development, and Sales personnel for review. A design team was then responsible for determining what "play characteristics" would appeal most to children. Studies were also conducted to determine what market opportunities existed for the toy.

Early in the product-development stage, the toy was tested by children and parents for "play characteristics" and safety. In addition, the toy was taken home by Hasbro employees so that their families could evaluate the product for aspects such as clarity of instructions and ease of assembly. Focus groups were held nationwide for the generation of ideas to improve the product.

The final product was tested "to determine if the toy [was] fun, aesthetically appealing, manufacturable, cost-effective, and above all, safe." Product Development then worked in conjunction with Engineering and Quality Assurance to ensure that quality was an integral part of the final product. Finally, the product was released for manufacturing.

G.I. JOE AND ZARTAN THE ENEMY

Hasbro's G.I. Joe doll, an 11½" plastic soldier figure, had enjoyed immense popularity among children when first introduced. High plastic prices and strong competition from similar figures (such as the Six Million Dollar Man), however, had prompted Hasbro to discontinue the production of the doll in 1977.[16]

In the early 1980s, Hasbro management, despite Hassenfeld's strong urging not to do so, decided to reintroduce the G.I. Joe doll. The company then hired the Marvel Comics Division of Cadence Industries Corporation to create a cast of "good guys" and "bad guys" to accompany G.I. Joe. Consequently, in 1982 Hasbro introduced a smaller version of the former G.I. Joe doll, now 4" tall, a Mobile Strike Force, composed of "good guys" who were to help G.I. Joe maintain peace and order, and a COBRA army of evil and violent adversaries intent on destroying the "G.I. Joe team." Each member of the Mobile Strike Force and COBRA army had its own distinct personality, which was vividly described on the back of the box in which the toy was packaged.[17]

Zartan the Enemy, a member of the COBRA army, was described as a "master of disguise. . . out to spy on G.I. Joe."[18] The literature printed on the back of the box (as shown in Exhibit 1) further revealed that Zartan could change colors to blend in with his environment and was "a master of make-up and disguise, a ventriloquist, a linguist (over 20 languages and dialects), an acrobatic-contortionist and a practitioner of several mystic martial arts." Included in the description of Zartan's personality was the following psychological profile: "Extreme paranoid schizophrenic. Grows

EXHIBIT 1

MASTER OF DISGUISE

```
Code Name: ZARTAN
File Name: Unknown
Aliases: Too numerous to list
Birthplace: Unknown
```

```
Zartan can alter his skin color at will to blend in with his
environment. He is also a master of make-up and disguise, a
ventriloquist, a linguist (over 20 languages and dialects), an
acrobatic-contortionist and a practitioner of several mystic
martial arts. Very little is known of his background and origins,
but most security agencies agree that he must have had European
military academy training (probably St. Cyr).
```

```
Psychological Profile: Extreme paranoid schizophrenic. Grows
into various multiple personalities to such an extent that
the original personality becomes buried and forgotten.
```

into various multiple personalities to such an extent that the original personality becomes buried and forgotten."

The description and psychological profile, along with Zartan's code name, aliases, and birthplace, were printed on the back of the package in such a manner that the child could cut out the information to make a "file card." The instructions urged the child to save the file card for his "G.I. Joe Command Files," ostensibly so that any Mobile Strike Force member could have the information readily accessible in case of an encounter with the COBRA adversary.

Hasbro recommended the doll for children five years of age and older. By December 1984 between 900,000 and 1,000,000 Zartan dolls, which retailed for $8.99, had been distributed to retail stores.

THE CONTROVERSY

Hasbro first became aware of the controversy surrounding Zartan's characterization as a "paranoid schizophrenic" when it received a complaint from the national Mental Health Association for insensitivity. Hasbro immediately halted production of the doll so as to delete the controversial wording from the description of the toy.

Meanwhile, Hasbro received other complaints from several state mental health organizations and approximately one hundred consumers.[19] The complaint registered by Paul C. Messplay, executive director of the Mental Health Association of Indiana, was typical. Messplay objected to the description of the evil Zartan as a "paranoid schizo-phrenic" because it reinforced "the public misconception about the mentally ill" and depicted "the toy as a person who [was] violent in nature." Messplay explained, "Only a small percentage [of the mentally ill] ever cause any harm or destruction. Most of them are passive. Part of their illness is this passiveness."[20] Messplay then requested that Hasbro recall the dolls from retail stores.

Hasbro responded to the complaints with a public apology, which was first carried on the news wires on December 4, 1984. Donald Robbins, in expressing "the company's deep regret over the incident," explained that "the card slipped through company proofreaders and that the error should never have occurred."[21] Robbins refused to recall the dolls already containing the controversial wording, however, claiming that most of the 900,000 to 1,000,000 Zartan dolls distributed had been sold.[22]

Hasbro went one step further and pledged to donate an undetermined amount of money to mental illness research:

> "This is just to show we're concerned about mental illness and we certainly did not mean any harm," [Robbins] stated. "It [calling the doll schizophrenic] was just an error that was made—a poor judgment—and we're embarrassed by it. We hope to make amends to the mentally ill by donating money to help alleviate the illness."[23]

In an early December 1984 Associated Press article, Messplay, of the Mental Health Association of Indiana, commended Hasbro for its action, which he termed a "very positive reaction." Messplay, evidently satisfied with Hasbro's response despite Robbins's refusal to recall the dolls, stated:

> I think that this [donating money to mental illness research] is a most tangible method of apologizing for an irresponsible act. I must say, I'm encouraged by their responsiveness to this issue and I trust this will give a message to other manufacturers. Perhaps we won't see something like this happening in the future.

Dincin of Thresholds, a nonprofit psychosocial rehabilitation facility, first read the aforementioned article with mild interest and "amusement." After he had "slept on it," however, he "woke up furious" that Hasbro would market a toy that, in his opinion, perpetuated negative images of the mentally ill. On reaching his office on December 6, Dincin fired off a scathing letter to Hassenfeld, the text of which is presented in Exhibit 2. In his letter, Dincin accused Hasbro of gross insensitivity and seeking profit to the detriment of the mentally ill.

Dincin then consulted other members of the board of directors of Thresholds concerning the incident. An informal letter campaign ensued, in which numerous members of Thresholds' board wrote to Hasbro demand-

EXHIBIT 2

Mr. Stephen E. Hassenfeld
Chairman of the Board
Hasbro Bradley, Inc.
1027 Newport Avenue
Pawtucket, Rhode Island 02862

Dear Mr. Hassenfeld:

To put it quite simply, I am disgusted, horrified, aghast, and over-whelmingly outraged that you would produce a TOY for *children* that depicts the horror of mental illness called paranoid schizophrenic. How grossly insensitive. There are several million people who SUFFER with their illness and desperately struggle to overcome their handicapping condition. I know, because Thresholds has served them for 25 years. I can attest to the courage of this struggle.

One difficult obstacle we must continually overcome are stereo-types about what mental illness is and isn't. The stigma is expressed by employers' reluctance to hiring the mentally ill, and by neighborhood outrage when the mentally ill move in. How difficult it is to overcome these hurdles without a schizophrenic doll with multiple personalities.

Your toy is the epitome of avarice, seeking to make a profit by making fun of "crazy" people. How could you ever come to the decision to make the toy in the first place? That is what boggles my mind. Did your toy inventors sit around a table and say, "How about this idea for the Christmas Spirit?—A toy that demeans and humiliates several mil-lion people in the United States that sounds like something that Hasbro should do."

I wonder, did you eliminate your "Hemophiliac Special" which oozes blood until it dies (batteries optional, of course). Too bad. There must be a market for it. Or how about a "Cancer Cutie" that will depict a debilitating patient writhing in pain. Hey, that's a beauty. Do you have a special macabre toy inventor on your payroll? Where is your sensibility; your humanness?

Stephen, it is time for you to apologize, recall this stupid product from the shelves, eat the loss, and make your profits from GI Joe.

Yours in Toy Inventiveness,

Jerry Dincin, Ph.D.
Executive Director

ing that the dolls be recalled. The following letter, received by Thresholds board member Sylvia Atros, was representative of the replies that Thresholds members received from a Hasbro representative:

> Thank you for taking the time to write us about your concerns with our Zartan Package. We are truly upset that we offended you and others. When the matter was first brought to our attention sometime ago, we immediately deleted all references to mental illness from the package. At that same time we made a public apology and announced that the company would make a donation to the research of mental illness. Please accept our sincere apologies for our insensitivity.[24]

NOTES

1. United Press International story, December 17, 1984.
2. "Hasbro Apologizes for 'Schizo' Doll," *The Daily Progress*, December 9, 1984, p. D9.
3. "Toy Maker to Remove 'Schizophrenic' Label," *The New York Times*, December 6, 1984, p. C9.
4. Ibid., p. C9.
5. "'Schizophrenic' Doll Has Mental Health Officials Concerned," Associated Press story, December 4, 1984.
6. "Hasbro: Merging with Milton Bradley to Get Nearer the No. 1 Spot," *Business Week*, May 21, 1984, p. 90.
7. Information on this period of Hasbro's history and the quotations come from "Tough Game: New 'Terror' Toys, License Pacts Help Hasbro Bradley," *The Wall Street Journal*, December 13, 1984, p. 23.
8. "Hasbro: Merging with Milton Bradley," p. 90.
9. "Tough Game," p. 23.
10. "Hasbro: Merging with Milton Bradley," p. 93.
11. Company *Annual Report*, 1983, p. 4.
12. "Hasbro: Merging with Milton Bradley," p. 93.
13. Company *Annual Report*, 1983, p. 6.
14. Information in the following paragraphs comes from "Hasbro: Merging with Milton Bradley" or "Tough Game."
15. Information on Hasbro programs and product development comes from the company annual reports of 1982 and 1983.
16. "Hasbro: Merging with Milton Bradley," p. 93.
17. "Tough Game," p. 1.
18. Information on G.I. Joes comes from "'Schizophrenic' Doll."
19. "Company Apologizes for 'Schizophrenic' Toy," United Press International story, December 5, 1984.
20. "'Schizophrenic' Doll."
21. "Company Apologizes for 'Schizophrenic' Toy."
22. "'Schizophrenic' Doll."
23. This and the following quote are from "Toy Maker to Remove 'Schizophrenic' Label," p. C9.
24. *Thresholds Newsletter*, Spring 1985, p. 2.

LITTON INDUSTRIES, INC.

Kenneth L. Bernhardt
and Larry M. Robinson

INTRODUCTION

Fridays were always the worst day of the week for Marc Stillwell. As an Administrative Law Judge for the Federal Trade Commission (FTC), he frequently considered his workload burdensome, but Fridays always seemed the worst. While many civil servants spent the afternoon clearing off their desks preparing to start off fresh the following Monday, Stillwell was cramming his briefcase with case files and court briefs that would require his attention over the weekend. He felt he would be lucky if he could spare the time to watch a little football on Sunday, judging by the bulge in his briefcase.

The Litton Industries case decision had to be made soon, and as the presiding administrative law judge he would have to prepare a detailed decision, including his reasoning for the conclusions reached. The FTC staff attorneys and the Litton attorneys had both filed their final statements containing their arguments and findings of fact, and he would have to sort out from these conflicting documents what was actually correct.

Although it was not surrounded by the heavy publicity that characterized some of the more dramatic cases on which he had worked in the past, the Litton case was important because it contained some important issues concerning the use of surveys in advertising, and the increasing use of comparisons between competitors in advertising with actual names of competitors being used. He knew it was FTC policy to encourage advertising that uses factual data, such as that obtained from surveys, and that the agency also wanted to encourage comparative advertising. At the same time, he had to decide, in this case, if these goals conflicted with another FTC policy—that no advertising should be unfair or deceptive.

In addition to deciding if Litton had engaged in unfair or deceptive advertising and if they had adequate substantiation for the claims made, he also had to determine an appropriate remedy if the company was found guilty. A proposed order had been recommended by the FTC staff attorneys, and he would have to decide if that was reasonable or whether some other order would be better.

Copyright © 1981 by Kenneth L. Bernhardt, Georgia State University, and Larry M. Robinson, Nationwide Insurance Company. Reprinted by permission.

THE COMPANY

Litton Industries, Inc., was founded in November 1953 as a small electronics firm in San Carlos, California. Revenues that year were less than $3 million. By the end of fiscal 1978, Litton was the ninety-ninth largest U.S. corporation, with revenues exceeding $3.65 billion.[1] But Litton's management still held to a strategy laid out in the company's first annual report:

> The company's management [has] planned to first establish a base of profitable operations in advanced electronic development and manufacturing. Utilizing this base, the plan contemplates building a major electronics company by developing new and advanced products and programs and by acquiring others having potential in complementing fields. . . . This plan is designed to establish strong proprietary product values and a "broad base" on which to grow—a profitable balance between commercial and military customers and an integrated but diversified line of electronic products.[2]

By 1980, Litton had grown to become a widely diversified, international industrial conglomerate with 175 manufacturing and research facilities in the United States and around the world, employing over 90,400 people. The corporation produced such products as business computer systems, business furniture, calculators, copiers, Royal typewriters, Sweda cash registers and POS/retail information systems, machine and hand tools, material-handling systems, specialty metal products, electronic components, biomedical equipment, paper and printed products, medical professional publications (including the *Physicians Desk Reference)*, textbook publications, airborne navigation systems, electronic signal surveillance equipment, and so on. Litton's Ingalls Shipbuilding subsidiary built U.S. Navy destroyers and nuclear submarines.

Litton Industries produced primarily commercial, industrial, and defense-related products. However, the company's Electronic and Electrical Products division successfully produced and marketed at least one major consumer good—microwave ovens.

Litton's history in electronic technology allowed the company to be one of the first manufacturers of consumer model microwave ovens. By 1979, the company was the largest manufacturer with a 25 percent market share. Amana, a division of the Raytheon Corp., and another early pioneer in the microwave cooking field, was the second largest producer with 20 percent of the market, followed by Sharp, General Electric, and Tappan with 15, 10, and 10 percent shares, respectively. Litton's microwave sales contributed almost $180 million in revenues to the company in 1978.

PRIMARY DEMAND

Until 1978, microwave oven sales for the industry had been increasing at an annual rate exceeding 45 percent, and it was estimated that by 1985 almost 50 percent of American households would be using the product.

Microwave ovens were capable of handling over 80 percent of a household's normal cooking.

Demand for microwaves began to fall off sharply in mid-1978, surprising analysts who expected sales to begin to decline only after market penetration of America's 80 million households exceeded the 20 percent level. In the first six months of 1978, unit sales were only 14 percent ahead of the same period in the previous year. Comparatively, the growth rate for the first six months of 1977 was 43 percent. This represented a shakeout period in the industry, with two manufacturers, Farberware and Admiral, dropping out of the American microwave market.

Industry experts generally concurred on several reasons for the unexpected slump. By 1978 there were 35 different manufacturers with microwave models on the U.S. market. The proliferation of brands, each with its own array of special features, was believed to have injected a great deal of confusion into consumer purchasing decisions. The complicated controls on many of the models also were believed to have scared off potential buyers.

Because it was a new and fairly expensive product, the proper marketing strategy called for knowledgeable salespeople to explain and demonstrate the microwave oven's many uses. Industry analysts pointed out that by 1978 most dealers were not putting enough effort into actual cooking demonstrations and other "push-type" marketing strategies. This became especially true as mass merchandise retail chains began selling the product. Such stores had neither the time nor the trained salespeople to devote to the kind of personal selling required for such a product.

Although it remained slightly ahead of the industry, with a 20 percent growth rate in 1978, Litton felt the effects of the general sales slump. The company reacted aggressively. The 1978 advertising budget already had been increased by 13.5 percent to over $21.5 million. To counter declining demand, the 1979 ad budget was increased to about $50 million. The company decided to stress product education as the key to market growth, and a large portion of the budget was earmarked for sales training, dealer promotions, and in-store demonstrations. Over 2,000 home economists were hired across the country to demonstrate the product in appliance and department stores, shopping malls and grocery chains.

THE FEDERAL TRADE COMMISSION COMPLAINT

On January 31, 1979, the Federal Trade Commission formally issued a complaint against Litton, stating that some of their earlier advertisements constituted "unfair and deceptive acts or practices in or affecting commerce and unfair methods of competition in or affecting commerce in violations of Section 5 of the Federal Trade Commission Act."[3] The complaint concerned a series of 1976 and 1977 ads in such publications as *Newsweek* and *The Wall*

Street Journal that featured the results of an "independent" survey. The FTC charged that the ads claimed that:

1. The majority of independent microwave oven service technicians would recommend Litton to their customers.
2. The majority of independent microwave oven service technicians are of the opinion that Litton microwave ovens are superior in quality to all other brands.
3. The majority of independent microwave oven service technicians are of the opinion that Litton microwave ovens require the fewest repairs of all microwave brands.
4. The majority of independent microwave oven service technicians have Litton microwave ovens in their home.[4]

The FTC stated that such claims were deceptive and unfair and that there was "no reasonable basis of support for the representations in those advertisements, at the time those representations were made."[5]

The FTC formally alleged that the survey in no way could be described as "independent." They claimed that Litton hired Custom Research, Inc., to conduct the survey but that Litton designed the survey instrument and analyzed the results themselves and that Custom Research had only engaged in telephoning the respondents, who were selected from a list of names supplied by Litton.

The FTC also claimed that the list of respondents was drawn exclusively from a list of Litton-authorized microwave service agencies. The surveys also failed to show that the respondents knew enough about competing brands of microwave ovens to make a comparison to Litton's ovens. The commission also stated that the base number of respondents was too small to have any statistical significance.

In summary, "the sample surveyed was not representative of the population of independent microwave oven service technicians and the survey was biased . . . ."[6]

The filing of the FTC complaint was accompanied with the usual notice stating the time and place of an administrative hearing at which Litton would have to show cause why it should not be subject to a cease-and-desist order. Litton did not choose to enter into a consent agreement, whereby the company would not have admitted any of the charges and would have negotiated an order outlining an agreed upon remedy.

At the time the complaint was originally issued, a Litton spokesperson made the following public response to the charges:

> We employed an independent research firm to survey our authorized independent microwave service agencies numbering over 500 throughout the U.S. Litton surveyed only those servicemen who repaired at least two brands of ovens, and tabulated their response only as to the brands they serviced. Litton feels the claims made in the ads, that up to 80 percent of the servicemen would recommend purchase of Litton microwave ovens, were accurately represented, and that the FTC's concerns are unfounded.[7]

Exhibit 1

Quality is No. 1 at Litton!

76% of the independent microwave oven service technicians surveyed recommend Litton.

Litton Model 419
microwave oven.

Litton leads all brands.

PREFERENCE FOR SPECIFIC BRANDS AMONG TECHNICIANS SERVICING THOSE BRANDS				AVERAGE PREFERENCE FOR LITTON VS. ALL COMPETITION – (weighted average)
Brand To Brand	Litton vs. G.E.	Litton vs. Amana	Litton vs. Magic Chef	
Which Microwave Oven Brand would you recommend to a friend?	59% vs. 23%	66% vs. 18%	81% vs. 1%	76% vs. 8%
Which Microwave Oven Brand is easiest to repair?	68% vs. 5%	65% vs. 8%	71% vs. 0%	72% vs. 4%
Which Microwave Oven Brand is the best quality?	48% vs. 16%	50% vs. 26%	69% vs. 1%	63% vs. 9%
Which Microwave Oven Brand requires fewest repairs?	38% vs. 22%	42% vs. 24%	59% vs. 3%	53% vs. 12%
Which Microwave Oven Brand do you have in your home?	48% vs. 19%	59% vs. 18%	70% vs. 5%	67% vs. 10%

Among independent technicians servicing Litton and competitive microwave ovens, an average of 76% of those surveyed said they would recommend Litton to a friend. And an average of 63% identified Litton brand ovens as having the best quality.

You'll find it in our full line of advanced countertop microwave ovens, double-oven and combination microwave ranges.

Respondents represent independent microwave oven service agencies, who service at least two brands of microwave ovens, (one of them Litton) and do not represent a factory owned service agency. Percentages add to less than 100% due to other responses (other brands and no preference).

© 1976 Litton Systems, Inc.

*Survey conducted by Custom Research, Inc. Complete survey results available on request.

And in such Litton features as Vari-Cook® oven control, Vari-Temp® automatic temperature control and new Memorymatic™ microwave program cooking. Innovative ways to microwave more foods better.

Need any more reasons to buy Litton? Ask your Litton dealer for a microwave cooking demonstration. For his name and number, call us right now, toll free 800-328-7777.

⊞ LITTON
Microwave Cooking

Litton... changing the way America Cooks.

THE FEDERAL TRADE COMMISSION

The Federal Trade Commission is an independent law-enforcement agency charged by the Congress with protecting the public—consumers and businesspeople alike—against anticompetitive behavior and unfair and deceptive business practices.

The commission has authority to stop business practices that restrict competition or that deceive or otherwise injure consumers, as long as these practices fall within the legal scope of the commission's statutes, affect interstate commerce and involve a significant public interest. Such practices may be terminated by cease-and-desist orders issued after an administrative hearing, or by injunctions issued by the federal courts upon application by the commission.

In addition, the FTC defines practices that violate the law so that businesspeople may know their legal obligations and consumers may recognize those business practices against which legal recourse is available. The commission does this through the *Trade Regulation Rules and Industry Guide* issued periodically as "do's and don'ts" to business and industry, and through business advice—called Advisory Opinions—given to individuals and corporations requesting it.

When law violations are isolated rather than industrywide, the FTC exercises its corrective responsibility also by issuing complaints and entering orders to halt false advertising or fraudulent selling or to prevent a businessperson or corporation from using unfair tactics against competition. The commission itself has no authority to imprison or fine. However, if one of its final cease-and-desist orders or Trade Regulation Rules is violated, it can seek civil penalties in federal court of up to $10,000 a day for each violation. It can also seek redress for those who have been harmed by unfair or deceptive acts or practices. Redress may include cancellation or re-formation of contracts, refunds of money, return of property, and payment of damage.

The commission defines its role, in its literature, as:

> . . . protecting the free enterprise system from being stifled or fettered by monopoly or anti-competitive practices and protecting consumers from unfair or deceptive practices.[8]

DECEPTIVE PRACTICES

Deceptive or fraudulent trade practices affecting consumers have centered around the misuse of advertising. The trend in the agency has been to identify and counter the more subtle forms of false advertising. Businesses, in arguing against the FTC's jurisdiction, have relied heavily on the First Amendment's protection, specifically freedom of speech. In 1976, the U.S.

Supreme Court held in *Virginia State Board v. Virginia Citizens Consumer Council* that:

> Although an advertiser's interest is purely economic, that hardly disqualifies him from protection under the First Amendment. . . . It is a matter of public interest that [private economic] decisions, in the aggregate, be intelligent and well informed. To this end, the free flow of commercial information is indispensable.[9]

The Court was reaffirming the First Amendment rights of business enterprises through the right of the public to know facts relevant to decision making in the marketplace.

The Supreme Court, however, held in *Bates v. State of Arizona* in 1977 that this First Amendment protection of advertising was entirely dependent upon its truthfulness. "The public and private benefits from commercial speech derive from confidence in its accuracy and reliability."[10] In other cases, the courts have gone on to say that truthfulness in advertising includes completeness of information, as well as the absence of misleading or incorrect information.

The key legal requirement of advertising is that the advertiser have a "reasonable basis" to substantiate the claims made before an ad has been run. Not having a reasonable basis beforehand has been found by the courts to be a violation of Section 5 of the FTC Act as an unfair marketing practice, even if the ad is not deceptive.

It has long been argued that the FTC's simple enforcement power to issue cease-and-desist orders in regard to false advertising was largely ineffectual, since it occurred after the fact and offered no remedial sanctions. Unscrupulous advertisers could get by with a simple admonition to "go and sin no more." Recently, however, the FTC has been increasing the use of such remedial actions as corrective advertising, the most severe of possible penalties facing legitimate marketers.

In 1975, for example, the FTC ordered the Warner-Lambert Co. to include a corrective message in their next $10 million of advertising. The message would have to say that Listerine was not effective against colds and sore throats, a statement which contradicted the company's earlier advertising. The commission argued that if, under Section 5(b) of the FTC Act, it had:

> . . . the authority to impose the severe and drastic remedy of divestiture in antitrust cases in order to restore competition to a market, surely it had the authority to order corrective advertising to restore truth to the marketplace.[11]

On April 3, 1978, the Supreme Court upheld the FTC order by denying a request to review a lower court's decision.

The FTC, as a rule, has required corrective advertising only when it found that such ads are necessary to present to the public "the honest and complete information" about an advertised product to dispel "the lingering effects of years of false advertising."[12] Without such measures, advertisers would:

> . . . remain free to misrepresent their products to the public, knowing full well that even if the FTC chooses to prosecute, they will be required only to cease an advertising campaign, which by that point will, in all likelihood, have served its purpose.[13]

SUMMARY OF THE FTC'S ARGUMENTS AGAINST LITTON

In a national advertising campaign that stretched over a year and a half in at least 26 states, Litton Microwave Cooking Products promoted the results of a survey of microwave oven service technicians (see Exhibit 1). The advertisements represented the majority of service technicians as recommending Litton microwave ovens on the basis of quality, fewest repairs, and ease of repairs. These advertisements are held by the Federal Trade Commission to be unfair and deceptive in that the survey as conducted does not substantiate the advertisements' claims.

The survey is represented as an independent survey conducted by Custom Research, Inc. In fact, Litton designed the survey, developed the questionnaire, provided the sampling frame, and analyzed the results. Custom Research personnel made the actual phone interviews.

Errors existed in the survey design, which biased the results of the study, thus precluding the results being projected to the population of service technicians as represented in the ads. Litton was aware of these biases prior to the implementation of the ad campaign, but ran the advertisements anyway. A memorandum, sent to executives by Litton's manager of marketing analysis, noted that the surveys were likely to be biased and recommended that the source of the sample be kept confidential. The sample used for the survey was limited to those service technicians on a list of 500 Litton-authorized service agencies. No attempt was made to draw a sample from technicians authorized to service other brands of microwave ovens.

Only one technician from each agency, who was the technician selected by the person answering the phone, was interviewed. Even with this limited, easily accessible sample, response rates were between 42 and 47 percent. Little was done to improve the response rate, and what was done is uncertain since no written instructions were provided for interviewers.

With the majority of respondents authorized only by Litton, their familiarity with Litton products would tend to bias their responses. In addition, no screening was conducted to determine whether the respondent had recently or ever serviced Litton or the brand compared, thereby failing to establish a level of expertise necessary for answering the questionnaire.

With the survey biased to the point that it could not be held to substantiate the advertisements' claims, the FTC proposed an order for Litton

Industries, the parent corporation, and all divisions, to cease and desist ads and representations based on faulty survey techniques or testing. This "strong order," which referred to all of Litton's consumer products and representations, was necessary to "protect the public interest and to deter respondents from future unfair and deceptive acts."

SUMMARY OF LITTON'S DEFENSE

The original complaint in this action challenged certain advertisements run by Litton Industries as being in violation of Section 5 of the Federal Trade Commission Act. The complaint was preceded by a two-year investigation of a limited number of magazine and newspaper ads run October through December of 1976 and August and September of 1977.

Complaint counsel has not met the burden of proving that the advertisements were "deceptive" within the meaning of Section 5. Complaint counsel and their witnesses did nothing more than identify "potential" deviations from *ideal* survey procedures that "might" have influenced the survey results. The procedures used were perfectly reasonable, were in accord with generally accepted survey practice, and yielded reliable results.

Even if one were to assume that a technical violation of Section 5 has occurred, the unintentional, minor nature of any such violation, and the public policy implications of the proposed order, dictate that no order should be issued. The proposed order, covers all products of Litton Industries. As such, it is punitive in nature, sweeping far beyond the violations, if any, that occurred.

In essence, the complaint charges that the ads contained three categories of representations: (1) alleged representations concerning the actual superiority of Litton microwave ovens over competitor brands, (2) alleged representations concerning the opinions of the "majority" of independent microwave oven service technicians relative to the superiority of Litton microwave ovens over competitive brands, and (3) alleged representations that the Litton surveys "proved" the first two representations. Only the third category is alleged to be false and misleading. Complaint counsel did not seek to prove that Litton was *not* superior to competitive brands on the attributes listed or even that independent service technicians were *not* of that opinion. The main issue was not the specific allegations in the ads but, rather, the sufficiency of the surveys upon which the ads were based.

The key issues, then, are (1) whether the ads were interpreted by the readers of those ads in the manner alleged in the complaint, and if so, (2) if the survey provided a "reasonable basis" for any representations that were made. On both issues, complaint counsel bears the burden of proof. A careful examination of the record reveals that complaint counsel misconceived the nature of their burden of proof and fell far short of meeting it. What the record does reveal is that Litton Industries attempted in good faith to conduct reliable surveys aimed at guiding its future marketing and engineering decisions. The surveys were designed and conducted in a manner that would lead to results upon which a "reasonably prudent businessman" could rely.

The surveys were designed and conducted as part of the business planning function at Litton. Specifically, the surveys were in response to advertising and point-of-sale literature by Amana, which directly and implicitly raised questions concerning the quality of Litton microwave ovens. These Amana ads emphasized the fact that Amana had received an exemption from a warning label requirement and caused certain Litton dealers to question the quality of Litton microwave ovens. As a result of the Amana ads, Litton dealers began encountering problems on the sales floors. Their concerns were communicated to Litton management.

The problems caused by Amana's attacks on the quality of Litton microwave ovens persisted. As a result, product quality became a frequent subject of discussion. The Litton Marketing Division President and Litton Microwave Consumer Products President became very concerned that perhaps the quality of Litton microwave ovens was in fact deteriorating and that they were not being adequately informed. Thus, in the early spring of 1976, Litton decided to investigate the quality of Litton microwave ovens through market research studies.

It was only after Litton conducted its studies for internal management purposes and analyzed the results that the idea of incorporating the results into advertising germinated. That possibility was not even seriously considered until September 1976. In fact, the ads were not included in the advertising budget for 1976–1977. As a result, special approval had to be obtained from the President of Litton Microwave Consumer Products in order to prepare the ads.

The advertising copy that ultimately emerged from the surveys presented the results fairly, at a level of detail so complete that it threatened their effectiveness as an advertising tool. The decision to present the data fully was made so that the ads would withstand any subsequent scrutiny.

This case was chosen by Federal Trade Commission staff as a "test" case for establishing industrywide standards for the advertising of survey results and for the procedures which must be followed in such surveys. Indeed, the Commission press release announcing the issuance of the complaint identified it as a test case that would set standards for advertising surveys and tests. Thus, the key issue is whether Litton had a "reasonable basis" upon which to make the claims included in the ads.

NOTES

1. "The Forbes 500s," Forbes (May 14, 1979), p. 234.
2. Litton Industries, Inc., Annual Report, Fiscal 1978, p. 4.

3. Federal Trade Commission Complaint, Docket No. 9123 (January 31, 1979), p. 5.
4. Ibid., p. 2.
5. Ibid., p. 4.
6. Ibid.
7. "Litton Industries, Inc.'s Microwave Oven Ads Deceptive, FTC Says," *Wall Street Journal* (February 2, 1979), p. 4.
8. This section is based on *Your FTC: What It Is and What It Does*, pamphlet published by the Federal Trade Commission, Washington, D.C.
9. William Sklar, "Ads Are Finally Getting Bleeped at the FTC," *Business and Society Review* (September 1978), p. 41.
10. Ibid., p. 42.
11. "Corrective Ad Order Not Anti-Free Speech: FTC," *Advertising Age* (September 13, 1976), p. 2.
12. Ibid.
13. Ibid.

MARKETING STRATEGY

NATURAL CEREALS

Norman E. Bowie and Patrick E. Murphy

Breakfast Foods, Inc. (BFI) is a national manufacturer of food products with three dry cereal divisions—children's, family, and natural. BFI also sells frozen breakfast entrees such as waffles and pancakes.

BFI's marketing department has just hired three assistant branch managers. One of these, Sally Thompson, received her MBA from a major midwestern university. Before joining BFI, Sally spent two years with the marketing group of a large food manufacturer. Although her experience at the former firm was educational, Sally often felt frustrated by the lack of responsibility.

Moving to BFI was good for Sally. BFI is a decentralized, progressive company, and management believes in giving people significant responsibility as soon as possible. Sally learned early that BFI management is quick to reward success but does not tolerate those who do not accept responsibility and its ramifications.

THE ASSIGNMENT

Sally's first major project is to improve market share in the adult cereal market through advertising and labeling strategies. Her charge is to suggest a new or modified marketing campaign for the Natural Cereals

This case was developed by Norman E. Bowie and Patrick E. Murphy for the Arthur Andersen & Co. SC Business Ethics Program. Reprinted by permission of Arthur Andersen & Co. SC.

Division. Natural Cereals' brands are Fiber Rich, Bran Breakfast Flakes, Natural Bran, and Bran Bits. Sally is excited. This project allows her to work with two of the marketing department's best professionals, Tom Miller and Joe Bradley.

Tom Miller, a group product manager for the Natural Cereals Division, is a 20-year veteran of BFI and has greatly influenced company policy. Tom is well-known throughout BFI as a fair, yet demanding, manager with a high degree of integrity. He transferred from the Family Cereals Division five years ago, having made his reputation as the product manager for Winkies, the number-two brand in the company. Since Tom's time is limited, he assigned Joe Bradley to informally supervise Sally on this project.

Joe, recently promoted to product manager, has been with BFI for four and one-half years, most of which were spent in the Family Cereals Division. His best-known campaign was for Sparkles, a children's cereal. Joe joined forces with a well-known toy manufacturer to give away a miniature character toy with each box of Sparkles. The box also contained an order form so parents could purchase the remaining set of characters directly from the manufacturer. This campaign increased market share of Sparkles by 10 percent. Sally knows she can learn a lot from Joe. She also knows he is Tom's friend and protégé. Sally suspects Joe will one day take Tom's position.

Another reason this is the perfect project for Sally is the fact that she is extremely health conscious. She believes too many cereals contain excessive amounts of sugar, which can encourage unhealthy eating habits in children and adults. An avid reader of health food literature, she has seen a number of scientific studies showing a correlation between high fiber and cancer reduction. For example, people who have a diet rich in fiber tend to have a significantly lower incidence of colon cancer.

Sally is well aware of the public's fear of cancer and has faced the trauma of cancer herself. She had a lump removed from a breast only a year ago. Fortunately, it was benign. Her father was not so lucky. Three years ago he succumbed to lung cancer. Sally believes cancer shortens lives and, given the agonizing deaths it causes, leaves severe emotional scars on surviving family members. She has such scars, as well as considerable anxiety about her own fate. She is committed to doing whatever she can in the war against cancer.

COMPETITIVE/MARKET ANALYSIS

After consulting Joe, Sally examines a file of articles compiled by her predecessor about competitors in the cereal industry. The articles point out that intense industry competition is due to strong brands and high levels of advertising. Competitors spend $75,000,000 on advertising, two-thirds of which goes for television commercials. The good news is that adult ready-to-eat bran/fiber cereals grew twice as fast as the market, and sales increased over 20 percent last year.

In 1984, one competitor launched the first health claims advertising campaign for any food product—its high fiber bran cereal. The company included information from the National Cancer Institute (NCI) on its packages and its advertising copy, which it had worked out in advance with NCI. The claims linked a specific product with the prevention of a particular disease—cancer. Although the Food and Drug Administration (FDA), which has jurisdiction over health claims, was not completely happy with this ad campaign, they did not block the ads. The following statement appeared on the back of the company's cereal box:

> The National Cancer Institute believes eating the right foods may reduce your risk of some kinds of cancer. Research evidence indicates high fiber foods are important to good health. High fiber foods, like bran cereal, are considered to be part of a healthy diet. Bran cereals are one of the best sources of fiber.

Also, this competitor's television ads made the following claim:

> Cancer! It doesn't worry me as much since I learned that I can fight back by a healthy diet. The National Cancer Institute believes a high fiber, low-fat diet may reduce your risk of some kinds of cancer. High fiber is important to a healthy diet, just like training is important to an athlete. I run, bike, and swim regularly. But that isn't enough. They say it's a matter of eating right too. My health is really important, so I made some changes, like eating foods high in fiber.

This campaign proved quite effective. Annual sales of the company's cereals grew from $2,100,000 in 1983 to $2,800,000 in 1985. Sally found a study in *Public Health Reports*[1] that examined the effect of this campaign on sales. The article showed that in the 24 weeks following the start of the health claim campaign, there was a sharp increase in sales of this competitor's high fiber cereal. Its share of the total cereal market rose from 0.99 to 1.46 percent, a relative increase of 47 percent.

This competitor followed up its initial campaign with other campaigns that made health claims for its other high fiber cereals. Since 1984, the competitor has increased its advertising by one-third and introduced six new brands aimed at adults. These ads using the cancer preventative message were rather controversial. Certain people objected to the ads because they did not say what kinds of cancer they were referring to and how much of the cereal you had to eat. This statement by Dr. Timothy Johnson (medical director for a major television network) on a "Nightline" program raised several additional questions.

> [W]hen it comes specifically to diet and cancer connection, there is considerable uncertainty. I spent several months this past year looking very carefully

at this hypothesis and talking literally to cancer experts all over the world, and found that opinion was divided and that the studies were inconsistent. Now, the language of the. . . ad is really quite accurate. It says, "Some studies suggest that it may. . . ." Problem is, there are other studies that suggest it may not. And the evidence is there for inconsistency. Now, you might say, so what? It's a diet that won't hurt, it may help, why not hedge our bets? And I really don't have any problem with that approach, but I do have two further concerns. One is that we may squander our scientific credibility in suggesting certainty where it does not exist, and then when we come to the public and really need to talk to them, they may not believe us. And I worry about what may happen on the fringes, not so much with the. . . ad but in health food stores or in other ways in which products and pills and books are promoted as a surefire answer to cancer with a particular diet program.[2]

Another competitor has also jumped on the fiber bandwagon by introducing four new high fiber products. It has promoted its brands with a health claim using a variation of the initial NCI message on the back panel of its bran cereal package. Although this strategy did not increase total sales, the company was able to hold its market share position.

In studying company and trade data, Sally finds that Breakfast Foods, Inc., has lost two percentage points since 1985 and that its overall cereal market share is currently 14 percent. This is far behind the 40 percent share of the market leader and somewhat lower than its main competitor, which holds 20 percent. The data confirm the company has been losing market share to competitors that make a connection between high fiber cereals and a possible reduction in the risk of getting certain kinds of cancer.

Prepared with these facts and figures, Sally schedules a meeting with Joe. She knows the approach she wants to take but decides it would be best to get Joe's advice before developing her preliminary ad campaign.

PRELIMINARY AD CAMPAIGN

As Sally enters Joe's office, he holds up her analysis summary. "Good work, Sally! Your analysis makes the picture clear. We've got to move before our market share drops any lower, and a health-oriented campaign is the way to go." Joe leans back in his chair, clasps his hands behind his head, and motions for Sally to have a seat.

Sally, pleased by Joe's support, replies, "I think the best approach is to follow our competitors' general strategy. People simply don't know enough about their health. Cancer isn't something to take lightly. People need to become more aware of. . . ."

"You're right," Joe interrupts. "A hard-hitting health campaign is what we need. We've probably benefited from the bran-cancer connection indirectly. Making it official with a clear, powerful message should benefit us even more. What we don't want to do, though, is waste our efforts. Tom just sent this memo us." Joe slides an open trade report across his desk.

Sally picks up the report and reads the part circled in red:

> It costs just as much to run a lousy commercial as a good one. More than most products, cereal is "marketing sensitive"; that is, dollars spent on mediocre marketing simply fall into the void, while the same amount spent on a well-aimed pitch can dramatically increase sales.[3]

"This is what it's all about, Sally. We have to come up with a blockbuster campaign for Natural Cereals. Otherwise, we're going to lose our shirts. Let's meet with Tom to get his input. I know he'll support our approach 100 percent."

THE MEETING

Fortunately, Sally and Joe were able to schedule a meeting with Tom for that afternoon. As they walk into Tom's office, Sally feels a little uneasy. She remembers Tom's comments over lunch last week. He had made it very clear he feels marketing and advertising must be truthful as well as persuasive. Sally wonders whether Tom will be concerned by the objections to the competitor's campaign she had read during her analysis.

"Well, this was quick work!" Tom says. "I'm glad to see you've come up with some ideas already. You got my note, I assume. This is going to be one tough campaign—we have to make it count."

"Yeah," says Joe, "Sally has worked around the clock on this. I think you will be pleased with what we've done." Joe smiles and turns to Sally.

Tentatively, Sally begins. "I've read a lot about bran cereals, and it looks like our major competitor has been quite successful. We can build on the health claims they've started. We really wouldn't be providing a new message, but it seems clear health claims will sell."

Tom leans back in his chair, closes his eyes and pauses. After what seems like an eternity to Sally, he says, "I don't know. That's an interesting approach, but it isn't the only one. I'm pretty hesitant about all this new emphasis on health claims. I'm not sure our competitors are presenting the whole picture."

Joe jumps in. "I agree, Tom. I spent a lot of time pondering this issue. But Sally convinced me. I think a carefully developed health campaign is the way to go."

"Well, Sally," says Tom, "I'm not saying no. You've obviously done your homework. But I want to make sure you consider the implications. You know the FDA has been looking into this matter and has issued a directive." Tom rummages through his file drawer, hands Sally a folder, and continues. "Take it and read it. Then come back next Monday with several campaign options. You've put a lot of effort into this so far. Now let's just take some time to consider the alternatives."

CAMPAIGN OPTIONS

Sally goes to work immediately. From the information Tom gave her, she finds that in November 1987 the FDA proposed regulations allowing manufacturers to print messages on food labels about the health benefits of their products. Specifically, the FDA listed four criteria for evaluating health related claims and information on food labeling:

1. Information on the labeling must be truthful and not misleading to the consumer.
2. Information should be based on and be consistent with valid, reliable scientific evidence that is publicly available.
3. Available information regarding the relationship between nutrition and health shows that good nutrition is a function of total diet over time, not of specific foods.
4. The use of health-related information constitutes a nutritional claim that triggers the requirements of FDA's regulations regarding nutrition labeling.

The next morning, Sally makes a copy of the criteria and heads for Joe's office to get his thoughts.

After reading over them, Joe is silent. He shakes his head slightly and says, "I'm not sure these criteria will have any impact on our plans."

"Well," says Sally, "I think we might want to tone down our approach a little, don't you?"

"Not really." Joe smiles. "I did a little research myself last night and I learned the Federal Trade Commission, which regulates advertising, is pretty sympathetic to our competitors' ads. They believe the claim that some people might actually avoid cancer of the colon or rectum by eating their cereals is generally accurate. I think the FTC would allow advertising claims based on this labeling information."

"I don't know how seriously we should take the FDA's position, Joe. But I do know we should stick with the health orientation. Let me think of some specific options and I'll get back to you."

"Okay, it's your show." "But," says Joe, "keep in mind we can't blow this campaign. It's got to have an impact."

Sally feels uneasy as she leaves Joe's office. She knows Joe is right. Her career is at stake. This is a highly visible campaign. Yet, she knows Tom is right too. She starts to think of ideas for her marketing campaign. The FDA proposal would allow her to coordinate packaging and advertising, and that would give consumers a consistent message.

ADVERTISING AND PACKAGING OPTIONS

To determine the best approach, Sally plans to develop several advertising and packaging alternatives for the natural product line. She will take the alternatives to Joe to see what he thinks. She just received from the research department the cereal's side panel containing nutritional and ingredient information (see Exhibit 1). Now she has to work on the marketing options.

Besides the ad linking high fiber cereals with cancer risk reduction she reviewed earlier, she found a recent ad for another product noting it was high in vitamin B and provided an energy boost. As the first option, she thought of a possible hard-hitting strategy using the statement "Vitamin Enriched" on packaging and in advertising.

The report she recently received from BFI's research department indicated that Natural brands contained 13 essential vitamins and minerals. She would feel comfortable putting this on the package and in advertising. In closely investigating the side panel listing nutritional information, she finds that Natural Bran Cereal, by itself, contains no fat. She knows a large part of the market is conscious of the levels of fat in foods. This could be another good claim to make.

But there are problems. Sally knows that the vitamin content is similar in all bran cereals. She also knows from internal company documents that most Americans are not deficient in B vitamins, nor does the amount of B vitamins contained in the cereal give one instant energy.

The second option she thinks of focuses exclusively on the appeal of bran and fiber as possible preventatives to cancer. She learns from company records that the amount of bran in Natural Cereals has increased by 40 percent in the last two years. One label alternative is: "With 40 Percent More Bran." Sally also knows this amount is equal to the most bran in any cereal. Therefore, another label or ad option is: "Containing the Highest Level of Fiber—Help prevent cancer by eating high fiber foods." She could place these statements in large boldface print on the package label and use them in advertising. This would reiterate the competition's strategy of linking cancer reduction with bran.

Another label she considers as part of this second option uses "natural" in the title for Bran Breakfast Flakes or Bran Bits. The slogan "Fiber for Health" is also a possible package label and advertising tag line.

Although these two options would probably be most effective, the FDA criteria keep running through her mind. As a result, she develops a third option downplaying health claims.

Option Three would point out that her product is a high-fiber, low-fat natural food. The label and the ads would feature energetic, healthy young people eating her breakfast cereals before an early morning tennis match. However, other traditional selling devices would be used, and the link to cancer reduction would not appear. From a marketing standpoint, she believes coupons on the back of the package might appeal to a broader market. She could also promote BFI's new "Resealable Pack," which allows the inside bag to be resealed for freshness. Other possibilities include discounts on a T-shirt and a cookbook featuring recipes using Natural's cereals. All of this would add up to a broad-based marketing

EXHIBIT 1

EACH SERVING CONTAINS 10 GRAMS OF DIETARY FIBER.

Nutrition Information Per Serving
Serving Size: 1 oz. (About 2/3 Cup) (28.35 g)
Servings Per Package: 20

	1 oz. (28.15 g) Cereal	With 1/2 Cup (118 ml) Vitamin D Fortified Whole Milk
Calories	90	160*
Protein	3 g	7 g
Carbohydrate	28 g	34 g
Fat	0	4 g
Sodium	230 mg	290 mg

Percentages of U.S. Recommended Daily Allowances (U.S. RDA)

Protein	4%	10%
Vitamin A	25%	30%
Vitamin C	**	**
Thiamine	25%	30%
Riboflavin	25%	35%
Niacin	25%	25%
Calcium	**	15%
Iron	45%	45%
Vitamin D	10%	25%
Vitamin B_6	25%	30%
Folic Acid	25%	25%
Vitamin B_{12}	25%	30%
Phosphorus	15%	25%
Magnesium	15%	20%
Zinc	10%	15%
Copper	10%	10%

** Contains less than 2% of the U.S. RDA of these mutrients

Ingredients: Whole Wheat, Wheat Bran, Sugar, Natural Flavoring, Salt and Corn Syrup.
Vitamins and Minerals: Iron, Vitamin A, Palmitate, Niacinamide, Zinc Oxide (Source of
Zinc), Vitamin B_6, Riboflavin (Vitamin B_2), Thiamine Mononitrate (Vitamin B_1), Vitamin B_{12},
Folic Acid, and Vitamin D.

Carbohydrate Information

	1oz. Cereal	With 1/2 Cup Whole Milk
Starch and Related Carbohydrates	13g	13g
Sucrose and Other Sugars	5g	11g
Dietary Fiber	10g	10g
Total Carbohydrate	28g	34g

appeal without relying totally on fiber and health claims. She thinks Tom might like this approach.

Sally knows these ideas are somewhat sketchy, but she wants Joe's input. She schedules a meeting for the following morning. She grabs a quick sandwich at the cafeteria and goes back to her desk to review her notes and reasoning for the meeting.

EVALUATING THE OPTIONS

Joe listens quietly to Sally's options. As she describes each, he jots down a few notes.

When she finishes, he simply says, "Combine Options One and Two."

"But I'm not sure that's the best way," Sally begins. "They are persuasive, but I think we should consider the implications."

Joe shakes his head. "The implication *is* that you need to increase market share and increase it quickly. Option Three won't do it. Options One and Two will. Everything we put on the package and the ads will be the truth. We could simply say 'Vitamin Enriched and Contains Vitamin B.' We don't need to say anything about vitamin B and an energy boost. Plus, we know the FTC won't object to cancer-reduction claims.

"There is nothing wrong with this approach. Besides, as you said yourself, we're doing people a favor. It isn't our responsibility to make people health experts. That's not our job, but selling cereal is."

Sally frowns. "What do you think Tom will say?"

"Look," Joe responds, "I talked with Tom about this over dinner. He said, basically, what I decide goes. Even if he doesn't agree totally, he won't overrule me. Tom is an excellent manager but doesn't have to concern himself with the details. The bottom line is that if we don't go with a hard-hitting campaign, we're going to lose our shirts. I've made my reputation around here, Sally. Now it's your turn. I want you to develop a full campaign combining Options One and Two."

Sally walks out of Joe's office. The project she wanted so badly isn't turning out the way she expected. She knows that, technically, Joe is supposed to just advise her, but could she realistically ignore his request? Besides, maybe he is right. What he said makes sense. Options One and Two are literally true. And is it her responsibility to make people health experts?

She sits down at her desk and begins to clear her mail. An envelope there from Tom contains a note and list of questions:

SALLY / JOE:

Here are a list of questions I use to evaluate the legal and ethical impact of advertising I have done. Please look them over. We do not want any legal or pressure-group problems!

- Are your claims accurate?
- Do you have competent and reliable evidence to support your claims? It should be evidence that the scientific or medical community is willing to support.
- Have you disclosed important limitations or qualifications to the claims you have made about your product?
- Have you misrepresented or cited out of context the contents of a report or scientific study? Have you suggested there is a consensus of medical opinion on an issue when there is not?
- Have you suggested that a report is government sponsored when it is not?
- Is your advertising inconsistent with information on the label? Has FDA found the food ingredient in your product to be ineffective for your advertising purpose?[4]

Sally quickly scans the list. Exasperated, she phones Joe and blurts out, "Have you read the note from Tom?"

"Yes, Sally, I did," sighs Joe. "I read it this morning, and my position is the same. We can answer yes to each question." Sally slowly replaces the receiver and thinks aloud, "Now what?"

NOTES

1. Alan S. Levy and Raymond C. Stokes, "Effects of Health Promotion Advertising on Sales of Ready-To-Eat Cereals," *Public Health Reports*, July-August 1987, pp. 398-403.
2. Transcript of "Nightline," program 1181. December 2, 1985, ABC News.
3. Quoted in Pamela Sherrid, "Fighting Back at Breakfast," *Forbes*, October 7, 1985, p. 127.
4. Dianne L. Taylor, "Health-Related Food Advertising: 'The Time Is Ripe for Change,'" *Food Engineering*, December 1984, p. 21.

SALES PRACTICES

DAVID NAMER: AN INTERVIEW WITH A PROFESSIONAL SALESMAN

Ladd Cutter and Brad McKean

In February 1975, a professor of business administration and two of his students were researching the ethics of salesmanship. In the course of their research, they met and interviewed David Namer, a professional salesman

This case was prepared by Ladd Cutter and Brad McKean under the direction of Associate Professor Jeffrey A. Barach. The casewriters would like to acknowledge the help and cooperation of David Namer, without whom the case could not have been produced. Copyright © 1975 by the Graduate School of Business Administration, Tulane University.

for 14 years, vice president of a marketing research organization, and author of a manuscript entitled *The People Business*. In his manuscript, which was intended to be a training manual, Mr. Namer was deeply concerned with salesmanship as a profession. He wanted to change the image of the salesman and provide what he felt were the basic tenets of salesmanship.

The following is an edited transcript of the interview, wherein Mr. Namer is asked to answer specific questions about how his manuscript relates to the many "gray areas" encountered in the day-to-day pursuits of the professional salesman. As stated, the interview was edited, and, in several instances, passages from Mr. Namer's manuscript have been included to clarify his responses.

The exhibits include two "hard-sell" pitches provided by Mr. Namer, wherein he illustrates common sales techniques used in door-to-door encyclopedia sales.

Question: Mr. Namer, your book entitled *The People Business* puts the sales profession on a very high plane. It appears that you are saying salesmanship is practiced to some degree by everyone.

Namer: Everyone, all of us, is involved in the people business. But what is the people business? Nothing less than the day-to-day contact and involvement of people, which I call selling. From the first days of Adam and Eve, people have been trying to sell others ideas, beliefs, viewpoints, or services. Eve was the first salesman when she sold Adam on the idea of eating the apple. And what a salesman she was! Here was Adam, all the comforts of paradise and no worries, and yet Eve convinced him that he would have a *"better"* life if he ate the apple.

One would think that man could recognize on his own what is beneficial and what is necessary for his betterment or for his existence, but he really can't.

Man is resistant to change; he will resist change, and will fight change all the way down the line. Man is ignorant of change; he does not recognize the beneficial value of it. He must be sold, sold on an idea, sold on a product, sold on a service. This is why the salesman is so important in society today and has been since the beginning of time. He will probably continue to be no matter how far man progresses.

Question: Do you feel then that, for instance, this is why the artist and the writer, who are both innovators, are attacked by society? Do you mean that the consumer is too dumb to know what is good for him?

Namer: I don't mean that they're dumb in the sense of not being educated or not knowing what's going on around them. What I am saying is that they're ignorant about the *new things* going on around them—about the changes being made.

The fundamental aspects of persuasion are suggestion and logical reasoning—suggestion taking precedence and probably more important than logical reasoning. The human species is not essentially a reasoning creature. In fact, most people scarcely reason at all. All of their actions are usually the result of imitation, habit, or suggestion. Most of their actions, and psychologists will bear this out, are only reactions. The average person accepts as true every idea or conclusion that enters his mind unless a contradictory idea blocks this acceptance. Additionally, the average person will act according to an idea of action which enters his or her mind unless it is blocked by a physical obstacle or a contrary idea. This is the principle upon which the foundation of most of our modern-day advertising is based; the fact that statements which are repeated and not denied will tend to be accepted. The salesman uses those principles during the presentation and close. The salesman will fill out the order, thereby suggesting an act of writing. When he hands the prospect a pen with the suggestion "Please okay this agreement at the X or where indicated," the prospect will generally go along with this idea.

Question: Something disturbs me here, and that is the targeting of your book. A Peace Corps worker in South America trying to teach Indians to drink only water that has been boiled would be less inclined to pick it up than would be a less scrupulous type who wishes to utilize persuasion to sell me something I didn't need.

Namer: I take issue with that. When I sat down to write the book, I reflected on my 13 years in sales; I really like sales. During that time, my mind was constantly thinking of ways to improve the occupation, of upgrading it, of making it more professional. I wanted to bring salesmanship out of the "drummer" image and to spread that professionalism to all salesmen regardless of what they are selling. That is why I named my book *The People Business.* The Peace Corps worker would be just as apt to pick it up as would the vacuum cleaner salesman.

Originally, the book was to be targeted at salesmen; however, as it developed it turned out to be applicable in all phases of life. As I've said before, I feel that I've compiled something that can be used by everyone. My main contention is that everyone is selling in day-to-day interactions with other people. I'm selling my ideas to you and vice versa. Whether or not I get my ideas across to you determines the success of my presentation, whether or not I make the sale.

Question: Many people have the wrong impression of salesmen, through either naiveté or bad experiences, actual or perceived.

Namer: The best example of what you are talking about has occurred in the insurance industry. In the last 15 or so years there was a time when people had a definite image of an insurance salesman. The sloppy, shirt-sleeved person driving through rural sections, banging on doors to get people to buy insurance through high pressure. Threatening people with out-and-out coercion, loss of life, limb and/or property; the last thing people wanted to see was the insurance salesman. The industry spent, therefore, great sums of money promoting the image of the neat, trained professional counselor.

Question: Do you feel that salesmanship is inherent? Are there born salesmen?

Namer: There are no, or at least very few, born salesmen. To be an efficient, successful salesman one must be trained. This training doesn't only consist of attending a seminar and listening to someone who is successful tell of his achievements. Selling is individualistic; when one hears how a salesman makes a sale, that particular strategy may or may not apply to him. What works for you may not work for me. The concepts of selling are universal. Unlike the means, they must be formulated, nurtured, and grasped—then the means will fall into place, just like a puzzle.

Question: What selling experiences have you had?

Namer: I've sold just about everything: encyclopedias, magazines, coffee; recently I've been selling commodities, including flour, rice, wheat, cement, lemon oil, etc., all in bulk lots.

Question: What about product knowledge? I think it would be difficult to sell cement without specific knowledge about its applicability.

Namer: Absolutely, the salesman must have working knowledge of his product; he must have all the answers for anticipated questions. I followed my own advice and researched each item. I don't have an engineering degree in structural concrete, but I know what, where, and how to produce a product to meet desired specifications. I also listen a lot. One must listen to customers and people around him. It's fine to talk, but if you don't get a dialogue going it's almost impossible to get indications of your progress—feedback, as it were.

Question: What about the sales pitch itself? There are some encyclopedia companies that entice a customer by promising a "free" set of encyclopedias as a neighborhood demonstration unit. The only catch to this is that the customer must furnish a letter extolling the virtues of the encyclopedia to the company and must keep the encyclopedia up to date for 10 years with yearbooks, which add up to the full cost of the encyclopedia.

Namer: I can continue that! You know, Mr. Jones, that works out to less than one half the price of a pack of cigarettes a day for a year. Now you know, $70 a year for 10 years, that's kind of ridiculous. Sending a check out every year, that's time-consuming for both of us. Tell you what I'm going to do. If you will agree to pay the $720 or the $20 a month over a period of three years, we will give you, tonight, this beautiful bookcase, unlimited research service on the subjects of your choice, and so on. Isn't that fair?

Question: That's what I had in mind. Is it successful?

Namer: Absolutely. It's a beautiful pitch. By far it and its many variations are highly successful.

Question: In this light, then, are people dumb or ignorant? Why do they fall for it?

Namer: I don't think people are dumb. I don't think they're ignorant either. I think people are unaware. They are ignorant in that they're not exposed to the business atmosphere. They don't know how things are done. In other words, a salesman can enter the home and create the illusion that you're getting something for nothing. There is a little bit of larceny in everyone. Realistically, if people thought they could do something and get away with it, they would do it 99 percent of the time. In fact, even if they had only a fairly good chance of pulling it off they'd try.

Question: Well, do you think that this is fair play? Would you use that pitch?

Namer: No. That is not fair, in the sense that you are taking advantage of people who are unaware or are less aware than you are. You are using your experience and your knowledge.

Question: Could you possibly provide us with an example of what you consider to be an unscrupulous sales pitch? What I'm looking for is an expansion of the pitch that you just gave us.

Namer: Certainly. As a matter of fact, I have an example in my files and will send it to you. [Note: The pitch, as supplied by Mr. Namer, is included in its entirety as Exhibit 1.]

Question: You agree with what you wrote in your book? You stress honesty.

Namer: Yes—honesty and straightforwardness. To be truthful, however, I have used this pitch in my early selling days with both encyclopedias and magazines. I like to consider those early days, tinged with deception and dishonesty, as being my learning period. The latter portion of my career has been dedicated to honesty and legitimacy.

Question: There is no one more vehement about honesty than a reformed thief! Now, can you draw a line as to what is good and evil, black and white, so to say? The pitch that we've been talking about is obviously over the line, but you are not going to go completely the other way—for example, here are the issues, here are the pluses and minuses. That would constitute a judicial approach—your approach would seem to be more advocative.

Namer: I don't think you can draw a line. Each case must be approached individually. It depends on the product you are selling and the needs of the people to whom you are selling. Suppose I was selling quality encyclopedias to a family who could afford it. Assume that their children need and want the set. In this case I would apply pressure to the extent that I wouldn't normally use. I wouldn't take the approach that the children would grow up ignorant, that they will fail in society, that they won't complete high school, or will never get into college, etc. What I would say is that the children would not have the advantages of their peers. In the schools today, given the overcrowded classrooms, teachers do not have time for individual instruction. They tend to give class projects. They say,

"Go home and look this up in your reference set," assuming that all families have reference sets. Now, sure you can look that up in the public library if one is available. But can you see 30 or 40 people descending upon a single reference volume all at once? What usually happens is that after five or six people, someone gets tired of waiting around the library and rips out the page for home study. What does your child do then?

I deliberately referred to *any* reference set as opposed to my own set because I didn't want to imply that without my set the kids will grow up ignorant. It's a case of semantics. You are doing something that you believe is beneficial for that family. You know that sooner or later someone is going to sell them a set of encyclopedias. That salesman could be selling a "flim-flam" product, so I feel that it would be to their advantage to get something of quality, something that the family can make good use of.

Question: OK. We will include what you consider to be an unethical sales pitch in the case, but we don't have any idea of what you consider to be a fair approach. Can you give an example of what you consider to be within the bounds of ethical behavior? What I want is something to demonstrate how you would handle the sale of a set of encyclopedias today; perhaps a hard-sell situation, given the rules of conduct by which you govern yourself.

Namer: That's not difficult. Instead of a canned approach, let me give you a scenario which will demonstrate quite graphically, I hope, the dynamics of the sale, the events leading up to it, how I would handle objections, and several closes which I would use. [Note: The scenario as given by Mr. Namer was quite lengthy and, therefore, is included as Exhibit 2.]

Question: Do you have to have absolute faith in your product before you step in the door? Have you sold items you didn't believe in?

Namer: At one time, when I was a lot younger, I was able to sell something I wholeheartedly didn't believe in, or that I thought was inferior. I think, and my ego confirms this, that I can sell anything to anyone because I'm a very good salesman. But morally, now, I wouldn't sell if I didn't perceive a genuine benefit to the purchaser.

Question: Many products sold door-to-door are first-rate, top of the line, and, therefore, expensive. Why are lower- and middle-class neighborhoods preferred by salesmen? Is it right to sell a quality $10 knife to a housewife in a ghetto?

Namer: Let me tell you something about selling quality products in the ghetto. That woman will purchase a shoddy knife for a dollar. Two weeks later, that knife will break, she'll have to purchase another, and so on. Over a period of time she will have invested more money in knives than the $10 she could have if she had bought quality. This would have benefited her.

Question: In the case of an insurance salesman who convinces someone that he needs a policy and sells a quality product, how does this fit in?

Perhaps after the sale the guy becomes dissatisfied with the premium and gives the salesman a lot of grief. How does the salesman handle this?

Namer: The salesman must consider himself in a positive light. He must believe in the beneficial aspects of his product. Sure, the premiums are a bit of a drag now, but look at the future—the customer will soon have something of value, probably more than he would have had if he had tried saving alone. If you do something deceitful, it is difficult to visualize yourself as beneficial. If you view yourself as beneficial, it is easy to live with criticism.

Question. Periodically, there are times in order to close a deal you must use every. . .

Namer: You have to border on things which might be construed to be devious, sly, or cunning—but I hate to use those words.

Question: Taking another tack, then, nobody has ever spoken to me the way door-to-door salesmen have, except my mother. Why is it when that salesman leaves the door, the sweat is pouring off your forehead?

Namer: I think it is important to delineate between a warm prospect who comes to you with the realization of need for your product and service and a cold one whom you approach and is completely in the dark as to who you are and what you have. The guy who approaches you has a need, a problem, and is seeking help. This is problem solving. The cold prospect doesn't know he has need of your product or service. A mental trauma takes place in the cold prospect; chances are that he went all through his life without knowing or caring that he needed a set of encyclopedias. The moment you hit him, you have thrown cold water on him. The way in which you arouse his awareness has a profound effect upon the outcome of your presentation.

Question: Why then do so many door-to-door salesmen prefer less-affluent neighborhoods? Is it because we can consider those people to be more susceptible to a given pitch?

Namer: You must realize that you're dealing with individuals. You cannot stereotype people. You can't go into a home with the feeling that those people are dumb or less worldly or more susceptible. Look at the Beverly Hillbillies!

Question: On another track, there are times when a salesman has built up the customer to the point of purchase—you say you can sell anything, disregarding ethical practices. At that point, to what extent is the customer begging the salesman to help make the purchase decision? Is the fact that the customer was dumb enough to set himself up reason to rip him off—the way the tennis player who refuses to come to the net asks to be "chopped" at?

Namer: I don't think that people should be taken advantage of, unless they are aware of the rules. Tennis is a win-lose situation; when you enter the court you intend to take advantage of every weakness your opponent possesses, subject to strict and unbending rules.

Question: You have stated in your book that life is a game, that America is competitive, as is selling. How far towards the tennis court do you feel the salesman should go?

Namer: You are right, but the rules and boundaries must be clearly stated to all contestants. You must be sure that all contestants play by the same set of rules. This is one of my major points. It's all right to take advantage—this might be a quirk of my thinking—of someone to whom you have clearly stated the rules. If you use a rule or fine print but you've made him aware that the fine print exists, he has the equal opportunity of using that against you.

Question: Give me an example.

Namer: Take a company purchasing agent and a salesman. When a contract is written it clearly states the rules whereby the product is delivered and under what conditions. Generally there exist penalty clauses. The purchasing agent specifies a delivery date. The seller accepts, knowing that he cannot deliver on time, but he needs that contract. The buyer has covered himself, knowing that the penalty clause will cover his company and ensure speedy delivery. Each has taken advantage of the other.

Question: Who is responsible for the sucker? What about the guy who has got to have something for nothing? Does this give license to the salesman to teach this guy a lesson?

Namer: It is not the duty or place of a salesman to teach the customer a lesson. The sole function of the salesman is to sell his product, period. He may, by his function as product advocate, teach the customer a lesson, but subsequent bad publicity may be detrimental to him and his product. The salesman must pay heed to public relations, despite the fact that he's dealing with a complete idiot. He must maintain a professional approach, similar to that of a physician dealing with a hypochondriac. He will generally give that patient the benefit of the doubt.

Question: What about the obligation of the buyer?

Namer: The buyer has no obligation to the salesman. The obligations of the sale rest solely on the shoulders of the salesman.

Question: What about the buyer who elicits a great deal of time, technical drawings, surveys, etc., from the seller? Don't you think he has created an obligation in his own part? He is stringing him along, in effect stealing the salesman's time, which is incidentally his stock in trade.

Namer: Why is the salesman allowing this to happen?

Question: To make a sale, obviously.

Namer: Precisely. If there was no sale involved, would the salesman allow himself to be taken advantage of? The salesman allows this only because he foresees taking advantage of the buyer when the sale is made.

Question: If you, the salesman, did allow yourself to get strung along too far, you would have overlooked selling's tenet number two—qualify your client. You went too long with a nonproductive client.

This brings me to a very interesting point. When industrial sales are made, big-ticket items are moved. Corporate salesmen do a lot of entertaining, some involving large gifts and the like. Do the ends justify the means using these sales techniques? Do kickbacks fall within the same category?

Namer: I would say that kickbacks do fall within the same category. My contention, as I've stated before, is that the buyer's role is to get what he wants at the lowest possible price. Any means that he has of achieving that is completely justified on the part of the buyer. The salesman is the professional. It is his business to distinguish what constitutes a legitimate buyer from a phoney or unqualified buyer. If he cannot, he doesn't belong in the business.

Question: What if the salesman encounters evidence of collusion or price-fixing? What if, in a client's office, he spots a competing bid on the desk which indicates price collusion?

Namer: That is of no concern to the salesman. That is a top-management affair.

Question: I worked for a used-car dealership and when asked about speedometer settings we were told to respond, "As far as I know, they were not set back." What are your thoughts on this aspect?

Namer: My book covers the fact that the salesman must know his product, and every step in the production of that product.

Question: What about cribbing information on your customers? When I used to sell, I would look across the client's desk and, if I saw competing bids, I would try to read the quotes.

Namer: That's not unethical. You have to know what other people are doing in order to compete. It's a dog-eat-dog world out there; they're doing it to you. You also need to know about your competitors so as to judge your own product.

Question: Many firms consider salesmen to be their intelligence-gathering force. What about the ethics of divulging privileged information?

Namer: It's the duty of the salesman to scout out his competition. If you see something on my desk, it is public because I made no effort to hide it. If you rifle my desk, or if I tell you that something is off the record, it would be unethical of you to divulge it. However, the salesman is almost morally obligated to utilize any information obtained ethically to his benefit. Observance is not dishonest, nor is it unethical.

Question: How about handling receptionists and secretaries? Is it ethical to woo them or to bribe them from time to time with little gifts?

Namer: When you go into a firm, the first person you meet is a secretary or a receptionist. You must woo this girl to get her on your side. She helps you with your sale by making the buyer more accessible. I don't believe that is unethical or immoral. You are selling yourself, and that is a very good quality. I make a strong point in my book on how to handle receptionists and secretaries. That falls neatly into the category of intelligence gathering.

Question: Let's consider retail selling for a moment. When a customer is trying to decide between two items, what is the salesman's role here, and how does he avoid losing the sale because the customer can't make up his mind?

Namer: Three things come into play here. First, the salesman must be an astute listener. He must sense which way the customer is leaning. Second, he must give the customer greater confidence to make up his own mind. And in order to do this, the salesman must be able to adapt to the customer's needs.

Question: Can you expand on the role of adaptability in selling?

Namer: I have found that adaptability is a trait that all salesmen must possess. The salesman must always be ready to confront new selling situations and be able to cope with them. He must realize that he cannot change people, that people change only when they want to, that he must change himself first, and that he must always be positive in his mental outlook.

Question: How does self-confidence fit in?

Namer: As I state in my manual, the basic principle on which the world of selling is founded is confidence or trust. Therefore, it is the salesman's job not only to exude these qualities but also to create a trusting relationship with his customer.

There's another aspect to self-confidence, and that is pride and the desire to feel important. All of us want to be appreciated and to be complimented. Not only must a man feel that he is of some importance, but he craves recognition from his fellows. An appreciation of this very human trait makes it natural for the salesman to use indirect methods in place of the often offensive direct method. It's more tactful to use indirection because this recognizes the right of the other person to feel important. We, therefore, merely suggest instead of dictate. We all resent backseat drivers. The prospect must be made to feel that he did the buying, that he made a wise decision of his own free will.

Question: In other words, you are saying that adapting to the customer's viewpoint is part of the process of building his confidence in his decision. That's an important point. Can you give us an example of how this would work in practice?

Namer: OK. Let's see what happens when Bob Simon walks into Lookwell Clothing Store and is approached by a salesman. Bear in mind that, unless the customer and salesman have met before, there is no association and each appears neutral to the other.

If Salesman Art is inexperienced or untrained, the encounter might go something like this:

Art:	"Good morning, sir; can I help you?"
Mr. Simon:	"Yes. I'm looking for a suit."
Art:	"Right this way, sir; these suits are just the thing for you. I think that they will look very well on you."

At this point, Art has committed himself. Mr. Simon, on the other hand, might find the suits undesirable by virtue of their price or appearance and thus would tend to hold Art in the same undesirable light or lose respect for Art's suggestions.

This would be the end of the sales attempt in the majority of cases, for even if Mr. Simon found a suit that he liked, there would be an inconsistency between his like for the suit and dislike for the salesman.

If, on the other hand, Salesman Art is experienced and more skillful, the encounter would be different.

Art:	"Good morning. My name is Art. Can I help you?"
Mr. Simon:	"Yes. I'm Bob Simon and I'm looking for a suit."
Art:	"Right this way, Mr. Simon. Is there anything in particular that you are looking for and what price range?"

By not at once revealing his own preferences, Art has allowed Mr. Simon to look over the possibilities and express his taste. When Mr. Simon likes something, Art will hasten to agree, thus making Art consistent with Mr. Simon's attitude and way of thinking. When Mr. Simon criticizes, Art will hasten to agree, again making him consistent with his customer. This establishes Art as a man of good taste consonant with Mr. Simon's attitudes.

At this point, Art can use his new position to suggest a suit which might be mildly negative to Mr. Simon, and use this position to change Mr. Simon's mind about it as follows:

Art:	"Mr. Simon, I know that this suit is slightly more than you wanted to pay, but I think that it is just what you are looking for."
Mr. Simon:	"Yes, Art. I think that you're right. I'll take it."

Art has successfully eliminated the inconsistency in Mr. Simon's mind created by the higher cost of the suit and his preference for that suit. This resulted in the sale.

Of course, the salesman's expressions of agreement with a customer's taste, after that taste has already been expressed, are somewhat suspect because of their obvious instrumentality. If the salesman has an alert mind and if the customer's choices follow some pattern, he will be able to anticipate and project ahead to another suit. This will be stronger than after-the-fact association. This consistency principle is the basis of what we, in sales, call the *Depth Theory* of selling.

The principle recognized in depth selling is that often the buyer approaches the salesman with a need or want before it is expressed in terms of a specific product or service. Through conversation the salesman can assist the buyer in exploring and focusing on his need and can also explore his own capacity in terms of goods or services to satisfy this need. This interchange of ideas leads to a clarification of the buyer's problem and also to an understanding of how the salesman can help solve it.

Question: Should a salesman push a sale in light of obvious dysfunction? How hard should a salesman push a higher-ticket item despite the fact that it appears incongruous with the customer's appearance?

Namer: Yes, the sole function of the salesman is to make a sale, within the ethics and morality of sound business practice. Anything he does to make that sale befits his function in life. A customer that comes in and wants to spend his money should be able to, and if the salesman can coax him to spend more than intended, that's fine. This really is a gray area of ethical behavior. Usually, if the salesman can convince the customer to buy, that is sufficient justification [of the idea] that the customer wants the product. It's the customer's, not the salesman's, taste that matters. Sometimes, of course, it is more important in the long run for the salesman to be sure that the customer gets what he really needs. This is particularly true in industrial selling, where the salesman is trying to solve the buyer's problem, and if he doesn't do it, he will lose the business to the salesman who can.

Question: OK. Let's continue that train of thought. I'm concerned with the buyer's right to control his destiny when he walks into a store. Generally, the buyer's aim is to get the best possible deal, regardless. If, for instance, I went to a camera store selling many brands and ask for advice, suppose the salesman recommends a certain brand of camera because he is paid "push money" by the manufacturer. Now, I would have to have a good working knowledge beforehand to know what was the best camera for the money. Is push money ethical? Again we return to the judicial versus the advocacy [by virtue of the push money] approach.

Namer: I would say that this would be an ethical approach to sales, if taken in the light that, even though the store sells many brands, it tends to specialize in one. Furthermore, if a person enters a store, asks for a specific model item, is satisfied with the price as quoted, you, the salesman, are justified in making that sale regardless of the underlying motivations inherent in that sale.

Question: OK. Here is the final question. If, for instance, I am not mentally ready, not all fired up to lead a marketing class case discussion, what is lost? When I do my damnedest to present a case, what is the value-added in the difference between low-pressure, judicial teaching, and high-pressure, advocative teaching—am I really selling?

Namer: Yes, I think you are. You're selling yourself and your ideas. What you're interjecting into the situation is a touch of realism, humanity, and warmth. You're getting away from the mechanistic process where you say this is A, B, C, etc.; choose any one, all, or none. Just because the facts are stated in black and white doesn't mean there isn't a human element in there somewhere. You're placing yourself in the role of human being by expressing this humaneness, this enthusiasm. By doing so, you are conveying your thoughts; you are imputing to your listeners your excitement and enthusiasm; and you are drawing them out of their apathy, their blaséness.

They get excited—maybe not to the point of agreeing with you, but even if you get them to the point that they disagree, you will have brought out their spirit. You have them thinking, you have them using what makes them unique, God's gift—their brains.

EXHIBIT 1

ENCYCLOPEDIA AS ADVERTISING PREMIUM PITCH

AT DOOR

(KNOCK ON DOOR)

Hello! I'm Dave Namer with the Marketing Division of the Intercontinental Encyclopedias, Inc.* What is the family name here? (GET NAME.)

Mr. (or Mrs., depending on who answers the door) _____, I'm not here to sell you anything. In fact, I am part of an advertising and promotional campaign making a survey of your neighborhood's ideas on education. If I may step in, I can better explain to both you and your _____ (wife or husband) what this is all about. (STEP TOWARD THE DOOR. IF ONLY ONE SPOUSE IS PRESENT, RESCHEDULE TO COME BACK WHEN BOTH ARE THERE.)

INSIDE

(POSITION YOURSELF SO YOU ARE SEATED NEXT TO YOUR PROSPECTS; MAKE SURE THAT TV AND STEREO ARE OFF, THEN PROCEED.)

Mr. and Mrs._____, as I previously stated, I am taking a survey of your neighborhood. The purpose of this survey is to select one qualified family to participate in a rather unusual offer.

You see—Intercontinental has just come out with a new edition of its educational library. After many years of planning and over $30 million investment, we are now ready to market and sell our library. In order to make the salesman's job a lot easier, we have decided to place our library in the home of a selected family. This is done at no cost or obligation to the qualified family.

(SHOW A PICTURE OF SET AND EXPLAIN.)

Now, I know what you must be thinking. No one comes into your home and gives away over $500 worth of merchandise for nothing. There has to be a catch, right?

Well, Mr. and Mrs. _____, there is a catch. See, we realize the value of word-of-mouth advertising, especially between friends and neighbors. Therefore, as you use your library, you will be so impressed that you will tell your neighbors and friends about it. This will increase

*Fictional company name.

sales. But—equally important—when our salesmen are out in the field, they can use you as a testimonial for our set.

In order to accomplish this, we will require three things from you:

- First, 60 to 90 days after you have received the library and had a fair chance to look it over, we ask you to write us a letter giving your frank and honest opinion of the library. A letter of testimony, so to speak.
- Second, the company reserves the right to photostat this letter and use it as sales material. You see, they're going to send their regular professional sales staff into your community in three or four months, and experience tells them the first question asked them is who actually owns a library of this type here in town. Now, if they can truthfully tell these people the Browns over here and the Jones over there already own a library of this kind and can show them a letter of recommendation—well, you can get the sales psychology behind this, I am sure.
- Third, that you keep the set up to date with our yearbooks. Remember that your neighbors will be coming to see your set. We want them to see, and for you to have, an updated set. You understand. (EXPLAIN YEARBOOK AND BRING OUT A PICTURE.) After all, if we *gave* you a Cadillac, would it be too much to ask you to buy the gas from our station? (GET A VERBAL "NO" FROM BOTH.)

Exactly the way that we feel about it, too. The yearbooks cost us $50 a year, which is the cost of a daily newspaper, and that is all that we will charge you. All we ask is that you maintain your set current for 10 years. Isn't that fair? (DO NOT WAIT FOR AN ANSWER; CONTINUE. . . .)

Needless to say, to do our work properly, we must make placements intelligently. We must place these libraries with families who have a genuine use and appreciation for material of this type in their home. After all, if we place this library with families who have accepted it only because it was something for nothing, and stored it in the attic or used it as a doorstop, it would defeat the advertising purpose completely.

So, I would have to ask another question: If we could extend to you the invitation, would you and your family appreciate material of this type in your home? In other words—if there was nothing else involved and they would send you a complete 24-volume library and even pay the shipping expenses to get it here, would you be willing to give them the advertising help they ask for by writing a letter of testimony? (GET COMMITMENT FROM BOTH.)

(IF ANSWER IS IN AFFIRMATIVE). . . Well, is this something that you and your family would use and appreciate over the years as well as now if you had it in your home? (GET COMMITMENT FROM BOTH.)

In summary, then, folks, all that we ask in return for this magnificent free library is that you:

1. Send us a testimonial letter.
2. Give us permission to use and reproduce it.

3. Agree to keep your set current for the next 10 years.

In order to help you with the yearbook we will send you an Intercontinental Calendar Bank. (EXPLAIN BANK.) By saving 15 cents a day, the cost of a daily newspaper, you can keep your set up to date.

Quite frankly, though, Mr. and Mrs. _____, the only objection that we've run into is that nobody wants to fool with 15 cents a day for ten years. Not to mention the cost of bookkeeping and accounting that we would incur by this.

Therefore, we have another proposition that will benefit both of us. If instead of taking ten years, you would pay for the yearbooks in three years, you would not have anything to pay for the other seven years. Also, you would save us seven years of bookkeeping costs.

So, if you will do this—prepay the yearbooks in three years—we will pass on our accounting savings to you by way of extra merchandise.

If you agree, we will send to you, at no cost, the following:

1. 15-volume Junior Set (EXPLAIN).
2. 10-year Research Service (EXPLAIN).
3. Bookcase (SHOW PICTURE).

Thus, for your advertising cooperation and your agreement to pay for the yearbooks in three years rather than ten, you will receive:

1. 30-volume Intercontinental Encyclopedia.
2. 15-volume Junior Set.
3. Bookcase.
4. 10-year research service.
5. Yearbooks for 10 years.

Now, if I can get some information from you, I will see if your family qualifies for this program. (FILL OUT AGREEMENT AND CREDIT APPLICATION.)

Well, Mr. and Mrs. _____, from all the preliminary information, your family qualifies. If you will fill out this Registered Owner's Card, then OK the application here (PUT X ON SIGNATURE LINE OF AGREEMENT), I will submit it to the home office for final approval.

Now all I need is ten dollars to cover the shipping charge, and we will process your application.

(PACK UP MATERIALS WHILE THEY WRITE CHECK OUT. AFTER BEING HANDED THE CHECK, STAND UP, . . . WALK TO DOOR. . . AND SAY:)

Congratulations, and welcome to the Intercontinental Family of Library Excellence. (WALK OUT OF DOOR.)

EXHIBIT 2

ENCYCLOPEDIA SALES SCENARIO

Namer: OK. Let me set it up this way. Take the Braswells, Joan and Ted, who live in a lower-middle-class neighborhood, comprising mainly one-story, single dwellings. The homes have wash on the line, automobiles and pickup trucks occupy cluttered carports, and toys and young children fill most front yards. Ted holds a decent job as day-shift foreman at a local manufacturing plant; his salary barely covers month-to-month expenses. Joan helps out with the monthly budget occasionally by taking in wash and working part time for a caterer. They have two children, Anne, 10; and Ted, Jr., 8.

Several weeks earlier Ted noticed an appealing coupon insert in a national magazine, filled it out, and mailed it. The advertisement promised a free booklet entitled "Views of Tomorrow," which offered hitherto unimagined worlds to its recipient in print, in glorious color photographs, and in illustrations.

The postage-free card arrives in the national sales headquarters of Intercontinental Encyclopedias, Inc. (IEI). We'll use a phony company so we don't step on any toes. It is catalogued and then sent to the regional sales director in charge of the territory where the Braswells reside.

Mike McNamara, our fictitious salesman, receives the card as a lead, after paying a modest service charge to the company. Mike is an independent sales agent who contracts with IEI to market their encyclopedias in his territory. Mike telephones the Braswell home to make an appointment.

"Hello, Mrs. Braswell. My name is Mike McNamara. I'm a representative of IEI. We received a request that you made for some information regarding the special offer we have on the Intercontinental Encyclopedia set. I'm calling to find out the best time to get together with you and your husband to show you the details of this special program. I was wondering if perhaps you had time this evening; or possibly Friday or the weekend would be better for you?"

At this point Mrs. Braswell replies that they wouldn't be home that evening.

Mike continues, "I see. Well, how about Saturday—will your husband be home then?"

Joan answers in the affirmative.

"Aha, great; how about if we make it this Saturday at eleven o'clock, or say between eleven and eleven-thirty? Is that OK?"

Joan agrees.

"Great, I'll be looking forward to seeing you then. Thank you."

Mike is punctual. At eleven on Saturday, he parks his car at the curb, walks to the front door, and rings the bell.

Ted Braswell answers the door. Mike takes two steps backward and introduces himself.

"Mr. Braswell? Hi, I'm Mike McNamara from IEI. I have come to deliver the booklet you requested several weeks back depicting the wealth and knowledge and pleasure available to you from Intercontinental."

Ted scowls and says that he didn't expect any salesman, only the booklet.

Mike continues, "Mr. Braswell, Intercontinental is so excited about their new edition that they asked me to bring you free and without obligation their 60-page colorful and informative booklet entitled "Views of Tomorrow," and complete details. . . ."

Ted interrupts, saying that he is not interested.

Undeterred, Mike goes on, ". . . and complete details on how to receive this magnificent set direct from the publisher on the special monthly payment plan."

Ted asks if there is any way that Intercontinental could put the booklet in the mail.

Mike responds, "Yes sir, there is. In fact, we do have a booklet that we can mail out to you. Unfortunately though, there is nothing contained in that book that will probably give you the specific information that you are looking for. In other words, information on the quality of the bindings, the prices, and so on and so forth. This is why the company has requested that I take about fifteen to twenty minutes of your time to give you a review of what we've come out with. I feel that this would be twenty minutes of your time well invested insofar as your future and the future of your family is concerned. Whether you buy the set or not, at least you would have a more enlightened view of the set; and in the future, when you do get ready to buy, you'll be in a better position to make a decision."

Ted indicates that he has no intention of buying a set at this particular time, and apologizes for causing bother and inconvenience to Mike.

"Well, Mr. Braswell, it is my job to show this set on a public relations basis. Whether you buy it or not is up to you; in other words, all I ask is that you look at it. If you like it, you buy it; if not—I thank you for your time.

"I feel that by showing it to you, it will not only give you an awareness of just what Intercontinental is but also will help to dispel a lot of rumors which may or may not crop up about Intercontinental. It will also make you a very good representative of our company. When someone comes to you and starts talking about encyclopedias, you will be able to give them the benefits of your education in that field."

Ted raises no further objections and, still skeptical, grudgingly allows Mike to enter the room. Mike requests that Mrs. Braswell be present for the demonstration. Ted goes toward the rear of the house to summon Joan.

The most outstanding features in the room are an imposing leatherette bar grouping, a new 25-inch color television set, and a huge leatherette lounge chair. The rest of the furniture is old and scratched; both the sofa cover and the curtains are tattered chintz.

Mike hears Ted Braswell's loud voice from the rear of the house, which indicates that he is venting his frustrations on Joan for granting the interview in the first place. Shortly thereafter, the Braswells enter the room.

Mike reintroduces himself to Joan, "Hi, Mrs. Braswell. I'm Mike McNamara. I spoke to you on the phone the other day."

Joan reacts pleasantly, noting that the soothing voice that she recalled from the phone call is attached to a well-dressed, handsome young man.

Ted mumbles that it is about time to get "this thing" over with and sits down in the lounge chair. Joan follows suit on the edge of the sofa. Mike kneels down and delves into his presentation case.

First he brings a sample volume of the encyclopedia out of the presentation case and hands it to Joan Braswell. She accepts the book with the rich, dark brown leather binding and gives it an admiring gaze. She starts thumbing through the volume while paying close attention to Mike.

"Mr. and Mrs. Braswell, as I indicated earlier, the reason I'm here is to demonstrate IEI's new edition, which we feel is a real breakthrough in the field of encyclopedias. We sincerely believe that no other reference set can touch this new edition and Intercontinental is so excited about it that they have decided to introduce the set, complete with convenient credit terms, so that everyone can take advantage of our offer."

Mike proceeds carefully, step by step, in company-approved fashion. His pitch is intentionally slow and deliberate, eliciting favorable responses from Mrs. Braswell at the close of each train of thought. Ted Braswell occasionally nods or grunts, but remains generally silent.

Mike describes the bindings and paper as the finest available. Joan agrees and passes the sample volume to Ted, who glances at it, flips it over twice, and then tosses it on the table. Mike continues unperturbed. He then emphasizes the star-studded panel of contributors, scientists, professors, businessmen, etc., who have lent their expertise to IEI's new edition. It is a lengthy and impressive list. Mike then goes on to describe the attention to detail inherent in the set; the time it took to collect and assemble the data; and the cost to finally produce the new edition. The figure is staggering.

Mike then begins to explain some of the valuable services that IEI provides for owners of reference sets. He decides that he will start to work on Ted Braswell.

"Perhaps some day, Mr. Braswell, you might want to go into business for yourself. The Intercontinental research staff is at your disposal to answer any questions that might come up, be they on engineering, management, merchandising, taxes, accounting, or any other subject. At any rate, any technical question you might have about your present job would gladly be handled by IEI, too. Don't you think this could be very helpful to you?"

Ted replies that it might come in handy sometime. Mike goes on, "Mrs. Braswell, we can help you in the home to save time, steps, and money—three things I'm sure you're very interested in. Also, we'll help you with your outside activities. For example, if you were on the entertainment committee of the PTA, write and tell us how big your group is; what kind of budget it has; what kind of things were done in the past; and we'll supply you with information on what other groups like yours have done in other parts of the country." Joan nods enthusiastically and adds that such a service could be "invaluable" to her. Ted maintains his silence.

Mike keeps the pitch moving. "Incidentally, are your schools crowded in this neighborhood like they are everywhere else?" Joan replies that they "sure are." Mike continues, "Then you know that the brighter child has just as much a problem as the child who gets behind. It seems that our schools are geared only to the average. But, with our service, your children can use this excellent learning tool to pursue their own interests and to help them if they have difficulty with any particular subject. You know, the curiosity of our children is probably our nation's most important asset. If we don't help them to find out how to get the right answers and encourage them to keep their interests in things, how will our country ever get the doctors, scientists, and leaders that we so desperately need?"

Joan Braswell responds immediately, "I want the very best for my children and this encyclopedia set could be the key to their future. If Anne and Ted, Jr., could grow up to be rich and famous, I'd pay almost anything."

At this point, Mike briefly outlines the credit terms which IEI offers. Neither Ted nor Joan objects to the payment plan he presents. Mike now has qualified his clients, created a need for the product, and arranged reasonable financial terms—the three key elements of a successful close. He then makes his first move toward wrapping up the sale. "Let me ask you, can you folks see how our encyclopedia set and services could be a great benefit to the future of your family?"

Ted Braswell replies, after a slight pause, "Well, it looks like a pretty good deal, but I don't think I want to spend the money right now. Why don't you come back in a few months."

Mike begins to push, "Mr. Braswell, let me ask you just three questions before I go. Do you think your family would use and enjoy our encyclopedia set?" Ted nods yes. "Do you feel that IEI's $600 selling price is fair?" "Yes, I guess so," Ted answers. Mike counters, "You guess so, sir. Do you feel we're being excessive with the charges?" "No, not really. It seems to be a fair price," Ted finally replies. Mike then pops the most crucial question, "Can you afford the set?" Ted, a bit indignant answers, "Yeah, we can afford it, but I just don't want to buy it."

Mike then thinks he has them and starts to push harder. "Mr. Braswell, you've just informed me that you feel your family will use and enjoy the set, that the set is worth it to you, and that you can afford it. I really don't think it would be fair of you to deprive your wife and children of this educational opportunity any longer. The price is bound to increase if you delay because of inflation. Besides, we're both here now. You've given me your time; I've given you my time and knowledge." Mike then decides to use what he hopes will be the clincher. "Mr. Braswell, if I could bring into your home a magician who could give you access to 10,000 of the world's greatest minds, who could re-create 10,000 of the world's greatest historic moments—all at your personal request— would you want him?" Ted says, "Sure, why not?" Mike quickly proceeds. "The magician has only one drawback. You must give him a pack of cigarettes once a day. Wouldn't it be worth it to you to be able to have this magician for only one pack of cigarettes?"

"Yeah," Ted answers, "but it's not the same as a bunch of books sitting in a corner."

Joan Braswell suddenly blurts out, "Ted, you're being stubborn. You're hurting the future of this family. If you won't come up with the money for this, I don't know what I'll do!"

Mike glances around the living room, eyeing the new bar set and the big color TV. He is forced to play his ace in the hole. "There are only two basic reasons why a person won't buy this encyclopedia set. One, that person is absolutely destitute, completely broke. And looking around this room, I'd have to say you're living pretty comfortably. I think you'll agree with me there. The second reason is that the person is plain ignorant! But, I don't think you're ignorant either. In fact, I believe you're an intelligent man. I think this encyclopedia is something you want, something your family wants, and particularly something your wife wants. Now, you don't want her to cut you off, do you? You're the one that's got to live with her. . . . I really believe you'd be helping your family by taking this reference set."

"I guess you're right," Ted eventually answers.

Mike brings out his order pad while Joan and Ted whisper to each other. The details of the credit terms are easily worked out within a few minutes. Mike feels that he has performed another mutually profitable transaction. As he gathers up his possessions, Mike thanks the Braswells for their courtesy and adds, "Thank you for the order. I'll be on my way to get things moving on it properly. You should have the complete set by dinnertime tonight. Welcome to the IEI family!"

PRODUCT POLICY

HOECHST-ROUSSEL PHARMACEUTICALS, INC.: RU 486

Jan Willem Bol and David W. Rosenthal

INTRODUCTION

In July 1991, the management of Hoechst-Roussel Pharmaceuticals had, as yet, made no public announcement as to their plans for marketing RU 486 in the United States. The product had been available for testing in very limited quantities, but the steps necessary to bring the new drug to market had not yet been taken.

RU 486 was a chemical compound which was commonly referred to as "the morning-after pill" in the press. The compound had the effect of preventing a fertilized egg from attaching to the uterine wall or ensuring that a previously attached egg would detach. The pill had been thoroughly tested in several European countries with significant success.

RU 486 had become the focus for a great amount of publicity, press coverage, and industry speculation. The compound was also the center of a series of United States Senate hearings. Activists, both in support of and in opposition to RU 486, had sought to influence the company's course of action since the product's inception.

Pharmaceutical industry observers suggested that the company was not marketing the product aggressively in order to "maintain a low profile." It was clear that the Hoechst-Roussel management had an ongoing and very complex issue to resolve as to the disposition of RU 486.

THE DRUG INDUSTRY

The drug industry consisted of three primary components: biological products, medicinals and botanicals, and pharmaceutical preparations. Pharmaceuticals were generally classified into one of two broad groups:

- Ethical pharmaceuticals—drugs available only through a physician's prescription
- Over-the-counter (OTC) drugs, both generic and proprietary (drugs sold without prescription)

This case, by Jan Willem Bol and David W. Rosenthal, was originally written by Laura Case, Gail Geisler, Chris Peacock, Sherri Thieman, and Elisabeth Wolf. It was taken from public sources, without the cooperation of management, solely for the purpose of stimulating student discussion. All incidents and individuals are real, although some names have been changed at the request of the individuals. Copyright © 1993 by the *Case Research Journal* and Jan Willem Bol.

The pharmaceutical industry had grown steadily since 1970 as a result of rising health care costs throughout the world and continuing product innovations from manufacturers. From 1970 to 1980 worldwide sales grew at an average of 10 to 12 percent in real dollars. In the 1980s growth was slightly lower, about 7 percent, and real growth rates were expected to decrease slightly during the early 1990s, the projected rate being from 6 to 8 percent. The growth rates varied considerably among countries and product categories. An estimated breakdown of 1987 worldwide sales of ethical pharmaceuticals by country or region, with projected growth rates, is shown in Exhibit 1.

SIZE AND COMPOSITION

In the late 1980s the industry was not particularly concentrated; the top four firms comprised slightly less than 10 percent of the market. Within specific product categories, however, there were much higher concentration levels, the top four competitors often sharing 40 percent to 70 percent of total sales. Exhibit 2 lists 1987 pharmaceutical sales of the leading global pharmaceutical companies.

EXHIBIT 1

LEADING PHARMACEUTICAL MARKETS

Country	1987 Sales U.S. Millions	1990–1995 Growth Potential
United States	23,979	Moderate
Japan	15,690	Moderate
Germany	6,527	Moderate
France	5,992	Moderate
China	4,890	Low
Italy	4,690	High
United Kingdom	3,370	Low
Canada	1,710	Moderate
South Korea	1,500	High
Spain	1,480	Moderate
India	1,400	High
Mexico	1,300	Declining
Brazil	1,180	Declining
Argentina	856	Declining
Australia	685	Moderate
Indonesia	590	Moderate
Others	33,200	High

Source: Thompson from Arthur D. Little Inc.

RESEARCH AND DEVELOPMENT

The overall health of the pharmaceutical industry was measured by the number of products it developed, the value of its exports, and the high level of its profits. These factors were, in turn, directly affected by the amount of dollars spent on research and development (R&D).

The U.S. drug industry spent some $6 billion on R&D in 1988, up from $5.4 billion in 1987 and $4.7 billion in 1986. As a percentage of sales, the drug industry spent more on R&D than any other major industry group. In 1988 research accounted for more than 15 percent of revenues. Exhibit 3 lists research and development expenditures for some of the leading pharmaceutical companies.

THE OUTLOOK IN 1991

There were a number of positive factors affecting the industry at the beginning of the 1990s. The demographic growth trend in the over-65 segment of the population presented both a larger and more demanding market. The nature of the pharmaceutical business tended to make sales and revenues

---

EXHIBIT 2

TWENTY LEADING GLOBAL PHARMACEUTICAL COMPANIES

Company	Country	1987 Sales, $US000
Merck & Co., Inc.	U.S.	$5,060,000
American Home Products Corp.	U.S.	5,020,000
Pfizer Inc.	U.S.	4,910,000
Hoechst Corp.	Germany	4,610,000
Abbott Laboratories	U.S.	4,380,000
Smithkline Beckman Corp.	U.S.	4,320,000
American Cyanamid Co.	U.S.	4,160,000
Eli Lilly & Co.	U.S.	3,640,000
Warner-Lambert Co.	U.S.	3,480,000
Schering Plough Co.	U.S.	2,690,000
Upjohn Co.	U.S.	2,520,000
Sterling Drug Inc.	U.S.	2,300,000
Squibb Corp.	U.S.	2,150,000
Schering Corp.	U.S.	1,900,000
E.R. Squibb & Sons Inc.	U.S.	1,800,000
Hoffman-LaRoche Inc.	Switzerland	1,500,000
Miles Inc.	U.S.	1,450,000
Glaxo Inc.	U.S.	937,000
Rorer Group Inc.	U.S.	928,000
A.H. Robins	U.S.	855,000

Source: Estimates based on various industry sources. The figures should be regarded as approximations due to differences in fiscal years of companies, and variations in data due to different definitions of pharmaceutical sales.

EXHIBIT 3

RESEARCH AND DEVELOPMENT EXPENDITURES
(SALES IN MILLIONS OF DOLLARS)

Company	1986		1987		1988	
	Sales	%	Sales	%	Sales	%
Abbot	$259	8	$361	8	$455	8
Bristol-Myers	311	8	342	8	394	7
Johnson & Johnson	521	7	617	8	674	7
Hoechst Group	395	10	540	10	608	10
Eli Lilly	420	13	466	13	541	13
Merck	480	12	566	11	669	11
Pfizer	336	7	401	8	473	9
Rorer Group	70	8	82	9	103	10
Schering-Plough	212	9	251	9	298	11
SmithKline	377	10	424	10	495	10
Squibb	163	9	221	10	294	11
Syntex	143	15	175	16	218	17
Upjohn	314	14	356	14	380	14
Werner-Lambert	202	7	232	7	259	7

Source: Annual Reports.

recession-resistant. High and increasing profit margins tended to attract capital in order to support ambitious R&D needs of the industry.

Not all conditions were positive. Pharmaceutical firms had been increasingly criticized for their drug-pricing policies. Critics argued that relatively low manufacturing costs should be reflected in the pricing of drugs, and that high profit levels proved their point. Generic (unbranded) drugs continued their trend of high growth, supplanting the higher-profit, proprietary segment of the market. Liability costs and the costs associated with compliance with increasingly complex and restrictive regulation continued to soar.

Drug companies in the United States were essentially free to price their products as they wished. This was contrary to the policies in many countries outside the United States, where pharmaceutical prices were strictly regulated by governmental agencies. However, as a result of the rapid increase of health care costs during the 1970s and 1980s, there was a movement toward a more restrictive pricing environment both at the state and federal level. In order to make their operations more efficient and acquire economies of scale, many companies had chosen to form alliances with other firms. A trend toward consolidation through merger and acquisition resulted.

The growth of the generic drug segment posed a significant problem to the industry because generic products were priced much lower than proprietary products. The price of a generic drug was often as much as 50 percent lower than the price of the corresponding proprietary drug. All 50 states had laws that permitted substitution of generic drugs for proprietary drugs. As a result, the generic drug market doubled in sales from 1983 to 1987.

Pharmaceutical companies faced extensive product liability risks associated with their products. This was especially true for "high risk" products such as vaccines and contraceptives. The cost of liability insurance to cover these adverse effects had forced many companies to coinsure or curtail their research efforts in these areas. In 1991 liability insurance coverage for the manufacture and sale of contraceptives was in most cases impossible to obtain. As a result of this "insurance crunch," the industry had become polarized. Only small companies with few assets and large corporations with the ability to self-insure tended to market contraceptives.

The pharmaceutical industry's high profit levels and "heavy" expenditure on marketing made it a frequent target for attack by political figures and consumer advocates. Critics suggested that the pharmaceutical companies priced drugs so high that only wealthy patients could afford treatment. Marketing expenditures were blamed for "overprescribing," or the tendency for physicians to rely too heavily on drugs for treatment. Marketing was also blamed for hiding from physicians information regarding side effects and contraindications in order to boost sales.

OUTPATIENT DRUG COVERAGE

Regulation of health care played an important role in the pharmaceutical industry. Increasingly complex regulations both at the state and federal level resulted in corresponding increases in costs of compliance. Further, the political nature of the regulatory system often resulted in uncertainty for the industry. For example, the outpatient drug coverage provision of the Medicare catastrophic health insurance bill was expected to have both a positive and negative impact on the U.S. market, with the overall impact uncertain. Scheduled to begin a three-year phase-in period in 1991, the plan was to cover 50 percent of Medicare beneficiaries' approved drug expenditures, after an annual deductible of $600 was met. Although the new coverage was expected to expand the overall market, it also made the industry more dependent on the federal government, whose reimbursements were increasingly affected by cost constraints. Further, policies regarding other social issues, such as race or sex discrimination, abortion, and even environmental protection came into play for those health care facilities which dealt with Medicare recipients. The documentation necessary to show compliance with the relevant regulation was sure to result in increased costs for facilities. Pharmaceutical company managers were uncertain what effect such regulation would have on specific products.

HOECHST CELANESE

Hoechst Celanese was a wholly owned subsidiary of Hoechst AG of Frankfurt, Germany. Hoechst AG and its affiliates constituted the Hoechst Group, one of the world's largest multinational corporations, encompassing 250 companies in 120 nations. The Hoechst companies manufactured and conducted research on chemicals, fibers, plastics, dyes, pigments, and pharmaceuticals. The United States was the largest and fastest-growing segment for the Hoechst product lines and was often the key to establishing worldwide marketing capability.

Within its Life Sciences Group, Hoechst Celanese, in affiliation with Roussel-Uclaf (a French pharmaceutical company), provided leading products to the prescription-drug markets in the United States. The division was referred to as Hoechst-Roussel Pharmaceuticals Incorporated (HRPI). Exhibit 4 lists the primary prescription drugs provided by HRPI to the United States health care market.

The company also marketed stool softeners and laxatives, including Doxidan and Surfak, directly to consumers, and was developing potential drugs for many conditions, including Alzheimer's disease, cardiovascular disease, some kinds of tumors, and diabetes. HRPI had not previously invested in research into contraceptives or abortion drugs.

EXHIBIT 4

HOECHST-ROUSSEL'S PRESCRIPTION DRUGS

Drug Name	Description
Lasix (furosemide)	A widely prescribed diuretic.
Clarofan (cefotaxime)	One of the largest selling third-generation cephalosporin antibiotics used to treat infections.
Topicort (desoximetasone)	A steroid applied to the skin.
Streptasea (streptokinase)	A product used to dissolve clots in blood vessels, e.g., in the treatment of heart attack.
Trental (pentoxifylline)	Improves arterial blood flow, and is used to treat intermittent claudication (leg pain associated with arteriosclerosis).
Diabeta (glyburide)	An oral antidiabetic agent used in the treatment of non-insulin-dependent diabetes.

Source: Hoechst AG 1988 Annual Report.

ROUSSEL-UCLAF

Roussel-Uclaf, founded in Paris, France, was engaged in the manufacturing and marketing of chemical products for therapeutic and industrial use; perfumes; eyeglasses; and nutritional products. In addition, Roussel was one of the world's leading diversified pharmaceutical groups. Within its pharmaceutical group, Roussel poured its research dollars into a wide range of product categories, including antibiotics, diuretics, steroids, and laxatives.

Roussel employed 14,759 people, and its 72 subsidiaries yielded a total net income of over $84 million in 1988. Ownership was held by two groups: the German company Hoechst AG, with 54.5 percent of common stock, and the French government, with 36 percent.

In 1979, George Teutsch and Alain Belanger, chemists at Roussel-Uclaf, synthesized chemical variations on the basic steroid molecule. Some of the new chemicals blocked receptors for steroids, causing inhibition of the effects of the steroids, including the hormones involved in sexual reproduction. Because of the controversy surrounding birth control, Roussel had maintained a company policy not to develop drugs for the purpose of contraception or abortion and did not want to pursue research into the type of compounds that had been synthesized by Teutsch and Belanger. However, Dr. Etienne-Emile Baulieu, one of Roussel's research consultants, argued persuasively that such compounds represented a revolutionary breakthrough and might have many important uses other than those involved with reproduction, and Roussel continued its research. The research led directly to the discovery, by Dr. Baulieu, of RU 486, and Roussel began manufacturing the drug in the early 1980s.

HISTORY

The trade name for RU 486, a synthesized steroid compound, was Mifepristone. The company referred to the product as a "contragestive," something between a contraceptive and an abortifacient, and marketed it as an alternative to surgical abortion. Like birth control, it could prevent a fertilized egg from implanting on the uterine wall and developing. It could also ensure that an implanted egg "sloughed off" or detached, making the product more like a chemical abortion. Its use was primarily intended for first trimester pregnancies, because if taken up to 49 days after conception, it was 95 percent successful. In the office of the doctor or woman's health center a woman would take a 600-milligram dose of RU 486. She would return 2 days later for a prostaglandin injection or pill, which would result in a vaginal blood flow 2 to 5 days later which was comparable to that of a menstrual period and which lasted approximately 1 week. A follow-up visit to her doctor would then determine whether the abortion was complete and make sure the bleeding had been controlled. If the fertilized egg was not completely expelled, a surgical abortion could then be performed. Researchers believed that the success rate would approach 100 percent when dosage levels were more defined. A few patients did feel slight nausea and cramps. Complications were rare, but it was recommended that the drug be taken under a physician's care because of the potential for heavy bleeding or the failure to abort.

The drug was first offered to the French market in September of 1988. During the time it was on the market, 4,000 women used the drug, reporting a 95.5 percent success rate. However, during this period strong protests and proposed worldwide boycotts of Hoechst products (Roussel's German parent company), brought about the removal of RU 486 from the market and all distribution channels. Dr. Baulieu said the company's decision was "morally scandalous." At this point the French government, which owned 36 percent of Roussel-Uclaf, intervened. Two days after the pill's removal, Health Minister Claude Evin ordered RU 486 back into production and distribution in France, saying, "The drug is not just the property of Roussel-Uclaf, but of all women. I could not permit the abortion debate to deprive women of a product that represents medical progress." Since then, the product had been sold only to authorized clinics. Over 100 French women took the drug each day. Thus, approximately 15 percent of all French abortions were conducted through the use of RU 486.

Because RU 486 triggered such strong emotion for and against its use, Roussel management was hesitant to make it available to the world. A Roussel researcher, Dr. Eduoard Sakiz, commented: "We just developed a compound, that's all, nothing else. To help the woman. . . . We are not in the middle of the abortion debate." Roussel held the patent to the compound, but willingly supplied it for investigations around the world.

The only U.S. research on RU 486 was a joint effort of the Population Council, a nonprofit research organization in New York City, and the University of Southern California. Early results showed a 73 percent efficacy rate. Shortly after the drug became legal in France, China was able to officially license the use of the drug and by 1991 was close to manufacturing the drug itself. In 1990, Roussel management decided to market RU 486 to Great Britain, Sweden, and Holland as well.

It was generally believed that groups opposed to abortion under any circumstances had been largely responsible for keeping the drug out of the United States. Similarly, interest in research on the drug in the United States had apparently been curtailed by the intimidating tactics of the antiabortion groups. No U.S. drug maker had sought a license from Roussel. However, other compounds, similar to RU 486, were in the process of development by pharmaceutical companies both in the United States and worldwide.

No long-term risks or effects had been found to result from continuous use of the drug, nor were any problems expected from its occasional use. There was no information about how the drug might affect a fetus if the woman decided to continue her pregnancy after RU 486 failed, because the limited number of reported failures had all been followed by surgical abortions. Some studies reported that the drug seemed to suppress ovulation for 3 to 7 months after use. One medical journal did report that use of the drug created birth defects in rabbits, but the results could not be duplicated in rats or monkeys.

RU 486's primary function was obviously that of an abortifacient. It was thought that the drug was particularly beneficial for three segments of the population. First, it would be important in the developing nations, where many women lacked access to medical facilities and the anesthetics needed for surgical abortion. Second, it would be useful among teenagers, whose use of contraceptives was erratic at best. Third, it would be useful for women who for various reasons were unable to use other methods successfully.

Secondary markets were potentially available as well because RU 486 functioned by inhibiting progesterone. The drug could, therefore, be beneficial in the treatment of Cushing's disease, in which an overactive adrenal gland releases too much of a steroid similar to progesterone. The drug could also be used to treat types of cancer that depend on progesterone for growth, such as tumors of the breast and other cancers of the reproductive system and endometriosis (abnormal growth of uterine lining). In addition, RU 486 had potential for treatment of the nearly 80,000 women yearly who have ectopic pregnancies, a dangerous condition in which the egg develops outside the uterus.

In France, the availability of RU 486 was limited, and the product was used only under medical supervision. Because of these conditions the price was high, about $80 (U.S. dollars). Industry analysts believed that with larger markets and an increased production scale, the cost of the drug could be reduced in the United States. U.S. industry consultants believed that when drug companies identified the large profit potential associated with RU 486, U.S. interest in the drug would grow.

POLITICAL AND LEGAL ENVIRONMENT

The management of Hoechst-Roussel faced considerable problems with the introduction of RU 486 into the United States. The process of obtaining FDA approval was not likely to begin without the vocal support of American women who saw the drug as an important means to achieve more personal and political control over their fertility. The process of satisfying FDA requirements was likely to require considerable time and expense. Despite criticisms, the FDA had shown little inclination to reduce the time required for licensing new drugs, and the politically sensitive aspects of RU 486 were unlikely to speed the process.

Although the approval process for RU 486 could have in theory been significantly shortened because of the test data already generated by foreign researchers, no American company had yet petitioned the FDA to even begin the process. The standards required before the FDA would approve a new drug were (1) safety for the recommended use and (2) substantial evidence of efficacy. The clinical trials and testing occurred in three phases. Statistically, of 20 drugs which entered clinical testing under the FDA, only 1 would ultimately be approved for the market. It frequently cost a pharmaceutical company up to $125 million and 15 years to move a contraceptive from the lab to approval for the market.

With RU 486, the FDA had apparently resolved to be even more restrictive than normal. Special policies and exceptions to their normal FDA rules had been enacted. Under normal circumstances the FDA allowed patients to ship certain unapproved drugs into the country if the drugs were to be used to treat life-threatening conditions. The agency refused to apply these rules to RU 486. FDA Commissioner Frank Young had written to a Congressional representative that the FDA would not permit RU 486 to be imported into the United States for personal use—for *any* reason.

The FDA did not, however, change an established rule that might permit RU 486 to be imported for the purpose of a "secondary use" such as the treatment of breast cancer. The FDA did not have jurisdiction to regulate the administration of a drug by a physician, so a doctor could theoretically prescribe the RU 486, which had been presumably imported for treatment of breast cancer, for the purpose of inducing abortions. However, the potential liability for a physician who chose to prescribe RU 486 in this manner was probably sufficient to render this possibility remote.

RU 486 was not without its advocates. The National Academy of Sciences recommended that RU 486 be marketed in the United States, but also reported that for that to be possible, the FDA would have to streamline its stringent rules for the approval of new contraceptives. It also recommended that pharmaceutical companies be given federal protection from liability suits so they would be encouraged to reenter the contraceptive business.

If the federal government approved the pill, an individual state could not limit a doctor's decision to prescribe it. The fundamental tenet of the United States Supreme Court decision *Roe v. Wade* was that abortion in the first trimester should remain free from intrusive regulation by the state. Thus *Roe v. Wade* would permit U.S. use of RU 486 as an abortifacient to be administered under close medical supervision. The remote possibility of use of RU 486 as a monthly antifertility drug would also be well within abortion law, and perhaps would allow RU 486 to be treated under law as a contraceptive.

Paradoxically, some observers argued that the United States was most likely to witness the appearance of RU 486 if the *Roe v. Wade* decision were overturned and abortion again became illegal. It was suggested that a black market for the pill would evolve to meet the need for illegal abortions. Dr. Sheldon Siegel of the Rockefeller Foundation stated, "If there is a serious attempt to constrain further progress and further knowledge about RU 486, then it is likely that a black market manufacturer and supply system would develop."[1] The black-market scenario posed very serious health risks for women. Many could suffer side effects, especially in the absence of medical supervision. Still more frightening was the idea that women using the pill illegally would not have access to the backup of safe surgical abortion.

THE CONTRACEPTIVE INDUSTRY

As of 1991 there were nearly 6 million unwanted pregnancies each year in the United States, and as a result, there were 1.5 to 2 million abortions. Yearly, there were 500,000 pregnancy-related deaths, and 200,000 of those were from improperly performed abortions.[2] Up to half of these unwanted pregnancies and deaths could have been prevented if women had more birth control options. In 1991 American contraceptive research had come to a virtual halt, causing the United States to fall far behind other countries in developing new techniques. In the early 1980s, eleven companies in the United States did research in the contraceptive field, but by 1991 only two were engaged in such studies. Political opposition and the possibility of large liability suits appeared to be the most important reasons for the decline in focus on these drugs.

In 1991 several "morning-after" abortifacients had been approved by the FDA for use in the United States. These drugs, based on prostaglandins, which are powerful hormones that can cause serious side effects, were distributed only to hospitals approved by the manufacturer, the Upjohn Company. The drugs were only available by prescription and under the most controlled conditions. The FDA allowed the drugs to be used only for second trimester pregnancies. The drugs were neither advertised to the public nor promoted to physicians by company sales representatives. Likewise, samples of the drugs were not provided to the medical profession. Jessyl Bradford, spokeswoman for Upjohn, stated, "We believe that our commitment to provide a safe and effective alternative to saline and surgical procedures is a responsible one. However, we do not promote abortion. It is an individual decision, made in consultation with a physician. We make no effort to influence such decisions."[3]

The contraceptive market was relatively small, its value being about $1 billion yearly worldwide. Within this market, $700 million was accounted for by the use of oral contraceptives. There were, however, nearly 3 million women in the United States who used nonoral methods.[4] The profit margin on contraceptives was very high. To illustrate, the U.S. government, buying in bulk for shipment overseas, was able to buy a monthly supply of birth control pills for about 18 cents, whereas the average consumer paid about $12 a month. The leader in the contraceptive field was a company named Ortho, which sold contraceptive pills, diaphragms, spermicides, and other products for family planning (e.g., home pregnancy kits). Ortho was continuing to develop improved oral contraceptives that would provide better cycle control and have fewer side effects; however, as mentioned previously, the cost of development of a contraceptive from the laboratory to the market was estimated at $125 million.

Although pro-life forces attributed the decline in contraceptive development in the United States to their efforts, companies and outside experts argued that the reduction was the result of three main factors: high research costs, relatively low potential profit, and the enormous risk that liability suits presented. Robert McDonough, spokesman for Upjohn Company, said, "[Upjohn] terminated its fertility research program in 1985 for two reasons. There was an adverse regulatory climate in the U.S.; it was increasingly difficult to get fertility drugs approved. And there was a litigious climate. . . . Litigation is terribly expensive, even if you win."[5]

In 1988, an $8.75 million judgment was passed against G.D. Searle in favor of a woman injured by the company's Copper-7 intrauterine device. Similarly, Dalkon Shield cases forced the A.H. Robins Company into bankruptcy. In the late 1980s, A.H. Robins was forced to establish a $615 million trust fund to compensate victims of IUD-caused pelvic infections and deaths. Such settlements made liability insurance for contraceptive manufacturers nearly impossible to obtain.

One of the few organizations in the United States that continued research on contraceptives was the Population Council, a nonprofit organization backed by the Rockefeller and Mellon foundations. The Population Council had been conducting U.S. studies of RU 486 on a license from the French developer. Additional support for contraceptive development was evident in proposed [federal] legislation that would provide $10 million for the "development, evaluation, and bringing to the marketplace of new improved contraceptive devices, drugs, and methods." If passed, the legislation would put the federal government into the contraceptive marketing business for the first time.

TECHNICAL ISSUES

RU 486 acts as an antiprogesterone steroid. Progesterone is a hormone which allows a fertilized embryo to be implanted on the inner wall of the uterus. Progesterone also reduces the uterus's responsiveness to certain contractile agents which may aid in the expulsion of the embryo. Additionally, progesterone helps the cervix to become firm and aids in the formation of a mucous plug which maintains the placental contents. All of these steps are necessary for an embryo to properly develop into a fetus. Without progesterone, which initiates the chain of events, an embryo cannot mature.

RU 486 masks the effects of progesterone by binding to the normal receptors of the hormone and prohibiting a proper reaction. The embryo cannot adhere to the uterine lining, so the subsequent changes do not occur and the normal process of menstruation (shedding of the uterine wall) begins.

The Population Council sponsored two studies (1987 and 1988) at the University of Southern California which examined the efficacy of RU 486. The tests were all conducted on women within 49 days of their last menstrual cycle. In the 1987 study 100 milligrams per day for 7 days was 73 percent effective and 50 milligrams per day was 50 percent effective. In the 1988 study one 600-milligram tablet was 90 percent effective.

The studies were conducted without prostaglandin, a compound which dramatically increases the effectiveness of RU 486. With prostaglandin, RU 486 was tested at 95.5 percent efficacy.

The general conclusions drawn from the Population Council research were that RU 486 was more effective at higher doses and that the earlier it was administered in the gestational period, the greater its efficacy.

OPPOSITION AND SUPPORT

The National Right to Life Committee of the United States played an important role in keeping RU 486 from being introduced in the United States. The group referred to RU 486 as the "death pill," claiming that a human life begins at conception and that RU 486 intervenes after conception. A former vice president of Students United for Life said in 1990:

> RU 486 is a poison just like cyanide or other poisons. Poisons are chemicals that kill human beings. . . . RU 486 is such a poison which kills the growing unborn human being.[6]

Antiabortionists also resisted the marketing of RU 486 because in clinical testing, women were required to agree to surgical abortions if the drug was unsuccessful. Pro-lifers also suggested that by simply taking a pill to end a pregnancy, a woman was evading the moral significance of the act. One antiabortion legislator, Republican Congressman from California Robert Dornan, wrote a letter to his colleagues in 1986 to gain support to curtail federal funding for the testing of the pill. He stated his concerns as follows:

> The proponents of abortion want to replace the guilt suffered by women who undergo abortion with the moral uncertainty of self-deception. Imagine with the Death Pill, the taking of a pre-born life will be as easy and as trivial as taking aspirin.

Pro-life groups reacted strongly and even violently to prevent the drug's introduction into the U.S. market. The U.S. Right to Life group began its campaign by pressuring the French company which originated the pill, Roussel-Uclaf. At one point, as a result of the efforts and the influence of this group, which included bomb threats on Roussel executives, the company temporarily discontinued its production of RU 486. Subsequently, the strategy of the group was focused on preventing the drug's introduction in the United States. The transfer of pressure to the U.S. domestic market occurred as a result of RU 486's expansion into the British and Chinese markets and the resultant fear that the United States was the next logical market for introduction.

Pro-life groups continued their letter-writing campaign to Roussel and extended the campaign to Roussel's parent company, Hoechst AG. Further, they threatened to boycott Hoechst's American subsidiary, Hoechst Celanese. The right-to-life campaign succeeded in getting Hoechst to place a "quarantine" on the drug, limiting its distribution to current markets.

Another strategy used by antiabortionists included putting pressure on the U.S. Congress to limit federal funding for research on the drug. Such limitations would strongly impede the Food and Drug Administration approval process. At the same time, pro-life members of Congress continued to lobby for legislation to prohibit further testing. The position of the President, and the increasingly conservative character of the Supreme Court, suggested that the introduction of RU 486 would meet stiff resistance.

In addition to the antiabortion concerns, pro-life groups and some feminist groups were concerned over the short- and long-term physical dangers associated with the use of the drug. Advocates for the pill stressed that a main advantage of the drug was that it was a "safe" method of abortion as compared to the probabilities of injury associated with surgical abortion. The safety claim was largely unsubstantiated, however, due to the lack of available objective test results. According to the *Yale Journal of Law and Feminism*, "The level of ignorance about the long-term effects of RU 486 makes it premature to apply the adjective 'safe.'"[7] Although Dr. Baulieu stated that studies had been performed using rabbits and immature human eggs, no direct objective evidence from these tests had been provided to substantiate his claims of safety.

There were additional concerns that the drug could harm subsequent offspring or cause malformation in unsuccessful abortions. Baulieu admitted that there had been cases where the drug was unsuccessful in causing the abortion and the women had foregone surgical abortion. He indicated that there had been no evidence of maldevelopment. RU 486 was said to be "quickly flushed from a woman's system, making long-term effects less likely." This claim had not yet been proved through empirical evidence.

Although the efficacy of RU 486 was increased significantly when used in conjunction with a prostaglandin, the possibility of incomplete abortion remained. Such a condition was dangerous because of the potential for the tissue remaining in the uterus to cause infection. The threat to the health and life of the woman was, therefore, a reasonable concern.

The final concern that pro-lifers had about the dangers of RU 486 was that it had been proved to be ineffective on ectopic pregnancies, pregnancies which occur in the fallopian tubes or the ovary rather than in the uterus. The concern was that the number of ectopic pregnancies in the United States was on the rise and that women with ectopic pregnancies who used RU 486 and thus believed themselves no longer pregnant were in danger of dying if their fallopian tubes burst.

Gynecologists and obstetricians were mixed in their views toward the introduction of RU 486 into the United States. Pressure from doctors belonging to the World Congress of Obstetrics and Gynecology had forced the French government to require Roussel-Uclaf to resume distribution of the drug after its 1988 withdrawal. However, some doctors considered the product to be unnecessary. One prominent gynecologist and obstetrician believed that there were other chemical alternatives available and stated:

> The drug will be a fiasco for whoever decides to market it due to the stink from Right to Life groups. . . . We already have similar forms of chemical abortifacients that are legal and are used in the U.S. For example, Ovral is used as a "morning-after" pill. In residency. . . when a rape victim came into the emergency room, she was given one dose of Ovral then and another one in the morning. This makes the uterus incapable of conception, which is similar to the effects of RU 486. This method is 95.5 percent effective whereas RU

486 alone [without prostaglandins] is only up to 90 percent effective. Not many people are aware that this goes on so there is not much publicity.[8]

RU 486 was not without supporters. The controversy surrounding the drug elicited the attention of many consumer and political groups. Family planning establishments such as Planned Parenthood Federation of America, World Health Organization, and the Population Council, and feminist groups such as the Committee to Defend Reproductive Rights, Boston Women's Health Book Collective, and the National Women's Health Network, all supported the drug. During the period that Roussel had stopped production and sales of RU 486, the World Congress of Gynecology and Obstetrics had planned to ask physicians to boycott Roussel products if the company did not reverse its decision. Kelli Conlin, president of the National Organization for Women in New York, called for a campaign urging U.S. pharmaceutical companies to test abortion drugs such as RU 486. She said, "Companies cannot let these [anti-abortion] groups push them around. And that group is really a minority."[9]

Right-to-life groups considered RU 486 to be a particular threat because one of their main avenues of action had been picketing abortion clinics and making the process more difficult for those people who chose to terminate their pregnancies. RU 486 could be used in a doctor's office, thus making pickets and public demonstrations less effective. Further, the drug was to be used within the first 7 weeks of pregnancy, and the emotional appeal of showing developed fetuses in danger of abortion would be limited since all that is observed is bleeding similar to menstruation. One fear of pro-life groups was that if RU 486 became common, the very term "abortion" could become obsolete. Dr. Baulieu told the *MacNeil-Lehrer Newshour* in September 1986, that "Abortion, in my opinion, should more or less disappear as a concept, as a fact, as a word in the future."

If RU 486 were authorized for use, it would be possible for a woman to take the pill safely and privately very soon after missing her period without ever knowing whether she was actually pregnant or not. In fact, if used monthly, there was some question whether it should actually be labeled an "abortion drug." Depending on when it was taken, RU 486 worked virtually the same way as the "pill" or an IUD. Normally, the pill prevented pregnancy by suppressing ovulation, but certain forms (containing lower doses of hormones to reduce the side effects) occasionally failed to suppress ovulation and instead prevented the fertilized ovum from implanting in the uterus. The IUD, too, worked by irritating the uterus and preventing implantation. If RU 486 was used within 8 days of fertilization, it brought about the same effect.

One of the reasons given most often in support of RU 486 was safety. The United States had one of the highest percentages of accidental pregnancies in the industrialized world. According to the World Health Organization, "Surgical abortions [in the world] kill 200,000 women each year. Companies are retreating from research in abortion for fear of controversy, special interest pressure, and product liability questions—creating a major health care crisis."[10]

Likewise, there were increased safety problems when the abortion was postponed until later stages of pregnancy. Women facing an unwanted pregnancy often attempted to avoid the physically and emotionally painful abortion decision by ignoring it. If the abortion options were less harsh, it was thought that many women would face up to their situations more immediately and, therefore, more safely. Polls indicated that "Americans tend to oppose early abortions much less fervently and in fewer numbers than late abortions."[11]

Pro-life groups argued that conception is equivalent to fertilization, thus making RU 486 a form of chemical abortion. However, the federal courts and the American College of Obstetrics and Gynecology defined "conception" as implantation. In 1986, a federal appeals court overturned an Illinois law that had used the pro-life definition in its legislation pertaining to abortion. The implantation definition was based on the fact that 40 to 60 percent of all fertilized ova fail to implant. Some pro-choice advocates suggested that if the pro-life argument were carried to its logical (but absurd) conclusion, women should be required to take progesterone to encourage implantation and prevent accidental death of the fertilized ova.

One of the most significant reasons for support for the introduction of RU 486 was the improvement it provided over other abortion options. With RU 486, there would be "no waiting, no walking past picket lines, no feet up in stirrups for surgery." In many cases, abortion clinics would be unnecessary. The clinics, instead, could be replaced by a few 24-hour emergency clinics that could treat any potential complications. It would make the abortion decision much more a personal matter. In some cases it would remove the psychological agony of deciding on an abortion at all. Women who took the pill just a few days after missing their period would never even know if they had been pregnant. Considering the extreme emotional trauma an abortion often caused, this was considered by supporters to be a great benefit. Finally, the cost of RU 486 would make it much more attractive than other methods. According to a *Newsweek* article, "If RU 486 is approved, Planned Parenthood plans to make it available free or 'at cost' at its family planning centers."[12]

A number of industry observers suggested that the availability of RU 486 in the U.S. market was inevitable. They argued that there were enough people who supported RU 486 for a black market to develop. Such a market was even more likely because the drug was already legal and easily available in other countries. Some radical groups even called for their members to support the illegal use of RU 486. Norma Swenson of the Boston Women's Health Book collective argued that RU 486 would save so many women from death by "botched abortions" that it would be worth it for women's groups to encourage its underground use. According to Swenson, "Using RU 486. . . would be a type of civil disobedience."

CONCLUSION

The management of Hoechst-Roussel held the legal and moral responsibility for the decision regarding introduction of RU 486 to the United States. It was clear that, regardless of its direction, the decision would have far-reaching implications for vast numbers of people—not only Hoechst–Roussel's stockholders and customers, but also U.S. society as a whole. It was also evident that the pressures being brought to bear would continue to build.

NOTES

1. *60 Minutes*, April 9, 1989.
2. *Time*, February 26, 1990, p. 44.
3. "Letter to Columbia from Upjohn," 1987.
4. *Business Week*, April 1, 1985, p. 88.
5. "Letter to Columbia from Upjohn," 1987.
6. Personal telephone conversation, April 1990.
7. *Yale Journal of Law and Feminism*, 1(1989), p. 96.
8. Personal telephone conversation, April 1990.
9. *The New York Times*, October 1988, pp. A1, B18.
10. *Business Week*, November 14, 1988.
11. Mishel, D.R., *American Journal of Obstetrics and Gynecology*, June 1988, pp. 1307–1312.
12. *Newsweek*, December 29, 1988, p. 47.

PRICING

BURROUGHS WELLCOME
AND THE PRICING OF AZT (A)

Jeanne M. Liedtka

Early in 1987, the prescription drug azidothymidine (AZT) was cleared for distribution by the governments of England and France. Approval for commercial distribution in the United States was believed to be imminent. Produced under the brand name Retrovir by the Wellcome PLC, a U.K.-based pharmaceutical firm, AZT would be the first drug approved for the treatment of acquired immune deficiency syndrome (AIDS), a fatal disease believed to afflict millions worldwide. In the United States, where pharmaceutical firms enjoyed almost complete freedom in pricing their products, the announcement of the wholesale price of Retrovir by Burroughs Wellcome, the U.S.-based Wellcome subsidiary, was eagerly awaited by investors, insurers, federal health officials, the press, and AIDS activists.

This case was written by Jeanne M. Liedtka, Associate Professor of Business Administration, Darden Graduate School of Business Administration, University of Virginia. Copyright © 1991 by University of Virginia, Darden Graduate Business School Foundation, Charlottesville, VA. All rights reserved.

AIDS

By 1987, AIDS had become a household word in most of the world.[1] The virus that causes AIDS—a retrovirus, HTLV-III/LAV (human T-cell lymphotropic virus type III/lymphadenopathy-associated virus—was isolated by Luc Montagnier at the Pasteur Institute in Paris in May 1983. The virus works by destroying the body's immune systems, making it vulnerable to a host of diseases. The virus incapacitates a special type of white blood cell—a cell that coordinates the activities of other immune cells. Without this "helper" cell, the body cannot respond effectively to many external challenges and is likely to succumb to a variety of opportunistic infections that would pose little threat to healthy immune systems.

After infection with HTLV-III/LAV, the infected person enters one or more of the following medical classifications: antibody positive or seropositive, AIDS-related complex (ARC), and/or AIDS. After infection, most people become seropositive within two to three months. A seropositive individual does not show symptoms of ARC or AIDS but can transmit the virus to other people.

Research in 1986 indicated that HIV-positive patients would eventually develop either ARC or AIDS. The period from initial exposure to the onset of AIDS could range from one to as many as 14 years. The development of ARC did not bring with it the serious opportunistic infections that occurred with AIDS, and ARC by itself was not fatal. AIDS, the most serious condition caused by HIV infection, was the complete collapse of the immune system and, thus, the complete vulnerability of the body to invasion of infectious diseases. In 1986, the average life expectancy, after diagnosis of AIDS, was 12 months.

Between one and two million Americans were estimated to have already been infected with HTLV-III/LAV by 1986. Whether all these people would eventually develop AIDS was not known, but scientists believed that anyone who carried the virus could infect others. By the end of 1985, some 19,000 cases of AIDS had been diagnosed in the United States, and 10,000 of these people had already succumbed to the disease. In 1983, cases were doubling every six months. The most recent doubling had taken 11 months, and the next predicted doubling was in 13 months. Because of the long time between initial infection with the virus and the appearance of AIDS (up to five or more years), predicting the overall impact of the disease on the population was extremely difficult. At year-end 1986, 4 million to 6 million people worldwide were estimated to be infected with the virus.[2] The prediction was that, by 1991, cases of AIDS in the United States alone would be over 270,000.

Some 94 percent of AIDS cases in the United States as of 1986 were in specific target groups: individuals who received blood or blood products before techniques were developed to safeguard the blood supply; homosexual males; and intravenous drug abusers and their sexual partners. Chances of contracting AIDS in the general population stood at one in one million for those not in a risk group. The cities hardest hit were New York, San Francisco, Los Angeles, Miami, Washington, D.C., and Houston. Chances of single men in Manhattan or San Francisco contracting AIDS were 260 to 350 out of 10,000 (roughly the incidence of cancer in the general population).

Transmission was thought to be primarily through sexual contact, as the virus was present in blood, semen, and vaginal secretions, or through the practice of using unsterile needles passed from AIDS victims to others. Most blood transfusions were routinely screened for the AIDS virus by 1986.

THE DEVELOPMENT OF AZT

AZT, an anti-viral agent, while not a cure for AIDS, did appear to prolong life by keeping the virus from reproducing and by postponing the opportunistic infections to which AIDS patients were vulnerable. Researchers expected that AZT might double the life expectancy of an AIDS patient. In the first clinical trials of AZT on humans, conducted during 1985, fifteen of seventeen patients showed improvement within a short time period.

In September 1986, Burroughs Wellcome and the U.S. Food and Drug Administration (FDA) called an early halt to extensive clinical trials of AZT using placebo control groups. "People were dying, and you had clearly statistically significant findings that indicated it would be unethical to continue with the Phase II [placebo-based] trials," an FDA official commented.[3] Whereas 23 percent of the 137 patients on placebos had died, only 6 percent of the 145 AZT patients had died.

The drug did, however, have serious side effects; foremost among them were anemia and other blood ailments. Almost half of the AZT takers in the 24-week Phase II study required a blood transfusion. Concerns also existed that the effectiveness of the drug for a given patient would decrease over time.

The compound AZT was originally synthesized by a researcher at the Michigan Cancer Foundation in 1964. It was abandoned when it failed to work against cancer. In 1984, an organic chemist at Burroughs Wellcome, Janet Rideout, who had been studying AZT's effectiveness against common bacteria, recognized the drug as similar in structure to a chemical that retroviruses needed to reproduce and sent the drug to the National Cancer Institute (NCI) for testing on samples of the AIDS virus. At that point, no pharmaceutical firm had in-house containment facilities to handle the live virus. The cooperation of the federally sponsored NCI was believed to have cut years off AZT's development time. Despite the assistance provided by NCI and the fact that Burroughs Wellcome had not discovered the compound, Burroughs Wellcome management was confident that it would be granted a U.S. patent giving the company exclusive rights to market AZT for AIDS treatment for a period of seventeen years.

THE FDA APPROVAL PROCESS

All new drugs made available for commercial distribution in the United States require the approval of the FDA, which mandates a multiphase process[4] beginning with a request for "Investigational New Drug" (IND) status. In support of this request, which permits the testing of the drug on humans, a firm presents the results of research conducted on animals. The FDA then has 30 days to respond to the request for IND status.

Having received IND status, the three-phase IND testing process can then commence. In Phase I, safety tests are conducted on a small group of people. During Phase II, safety and efficacy tests are conducted on a larger group, and dose levels are set. During Phase III, drug dosages are fine-tuned.

Depending on the success of IND testing, the firm can then request new drug approval (NDA), which permits commercial distribution of the drug and requires, on average, 20 months for NDA approval.[5] AZT earned the quickest FDA approval in history—a five-day review for IND status and four months for NDA status—which was testimony to the urgency of the search, within both the pharmaceutical industry and the federal government, for some kind of weapon with which to combat the AIDS scourge.

THE PHARMACEUTICAL INDUSTRY

Since World War II, the pharmaceutical industry had enjoyed a level of success that few other industries could match. Its research and development facilities had produced a large number of "miracle" drugs that had made pharmaceuticals the most cost-effective means of treatment in health care and had saved countless lives. Pharmaceutical firms were expected to expend in excess of $6 billion on R&D in 1987. The financial performance of the industry was equally impressive. In 1986, the industry earned an average of $0.13 on each dollar of sales—triple the average for manufacturers in general. Similarly, industry return on equity averaged 22.9 percent, compared with 9.6 percent for all manufacturers. The average gross margin for pharmaceuticals was 85 percent.[6]

The industry was not without its critics, however. As early as 1959, the Senate Committee on Antitrust and Monopoly, led by Senator Estes Kefauver, had convened hearings on pharmaceutical-industry practices. In 1968, other hearings were convened, in which the following testimony came from Harvard Professor Seymour Harris:

> Many are concerned that an industry which comes close to being a public utility achieves the highest profits in relation to sales and investment of any industry; is highly concentrated in its control of the market; reveals serious monopolistic trends; increases the cost to consumers by differentiating the product at a dizzy pace, with the differentiated product usually similar to or identical with existing products; and greatly inflates the cost through record expenditures on selling. The competition among companies to overwhelm the

doctors by repetitious and often misleading advertising, and a failure to give as much publicity to the bad side effects as to the immediate beneficial effects, are unfortunate. Thus competition forces even highly moral firms to become less ethical in their behavior. . . . The cost of drugs is too high. I say this, though I am aware that the research contributions of the industry are important and that the lives saved, the suffering averted, and the acceleration of recoveries are worth more than the $4 billion spent on drugs. But the cost could be substantially less.[7]

Drug industry supporters countered that drug treatment, at current prices, was by far the most cost-effective therapy available; and that pricing controls would have the effect of reducing incentives for the development of new drugs, which was not in the public interest.

Between 1981 and 1986, drug prices increased 79 percent in the United States; the overall consumer price index rose 28 percent.

Governmental efforts to curtail rising health care costs had taken different approaches worldwide. (In the U.K., for example, drug pricing was controlled through stringent guidelines set by the National Health Service to prevent "excessive profit margins."[8]) This left open the possibility of significant price differentials across countries for a particular drug. Wellcome's drug Zovirax (for the treatment of herpes), for example, was 70 percent cheaper in the United States than in the United Kingdom; the drug Lanoxin (a digitalis), on the other hand, was 200 percent more expensive.[9] The level of U.S. government interest in AZT pricing was particularly keen, because it was estimated that up to 40 percent of U.S. AIDS patients lacked private insurance.[10]

WELLCOME PLC

Prior to the early 1980s, Wellcome was a little-known drug maker, ranked 24th in prescription-drug sales worldwide in 1985, that concentrated on the marginally profitable search for cures for diseases that afflicted primarily third world countries.[11] Its stock was privately held by Wellcome Trust, a nonprofit foundation that channeled profits into medical research. Prior to the development of AZT, its major products were the antiviral drug Zovirax, approved in 1984 for the treatment of genital herpes, and its over-the-counter cold remedies Sudafed and Actifed.

In February 1985, 25 percent of Wellcome's stock was sold in a public offering. New senior management brought in that year shifted the firm's historical emphasis to more potentially lucrative drug markets, and Wellcome's overall health-care segment earned a 17 percent margin in fiscal (FY) 1986.[12] For the five years prior to the development of AZT, Wellcome was estimated to have spent over $700 million on R&D that produced no big winners.

The U.S. market was a particularly important one for Wellcome. Burroughs Wellcome was expected to account for 40 percent of total firm sales and 50 percent of pre-R&D profits in 1987.[13]

PRICING AZT

Burroughs Wellcome would determine the wholesale price of AZT. The pharmacists who would distribute the drug were expected to take an additional markup, determined at their own discretion, but expected to be approximately 20 percent.

The pricing of AZT was made difficult by uncertainty surrounding the drug's production costs, its ultimate dosage and market size, and the appearance of competing AIDS drugs. As of early 1987, Wellcome was estimated to have spent approximately $80 million on capital improvements and raw materials for AZT-related research.[14] Most costs were incurred after the drug was found to be effective in the test tube at the National Cancer Institute.

The production process for AZT was lengthy and complicated; it took seven months and required 23 separate chemical reactions to produce.[15] The major raw material used in the production, thymidine, was expensive and in short supply.

FDA approval for AZT was expected to permit its use only for those kinds of patients studied in IND trials—those with full-blown diagnoses of AIDS. At present, that category was estimated to include approximately 30,000 patients in the United States.[16] The recommended dosage for these patients was 1000–1200 milligrams per day. Asymptomatic patients, who numbered approximately 100,000 in the United States, would not be approved to use the drug until further research was conducted on AZT's efficacy in ARC patients. Concerns about the drug's long-term toxicity, however, cast doubt on its use over long periods of time.

A number of other drugs were being tested in the fight against AIDS, and the dominance of AZT as the preferred treatment was potentially short-lived. The development of a vaccine was also underway.

Speculation concerning Burroughs Wellcome's decision on the price of AZT drew the attention of the investment analysts who followed the drug industry. E.F. Hutton's Lynne Pauls commented in December 1986:

> At $2.00 per day of therapy, this translates to $20 million–$40 million in sales. At $3.00 per day, $30 million–$60 million is achievable. Sales past this level are linked to several factors, including the outcome of clinical trials on other new drugs in development.[17]

Just one month later, in January 1987, she noted,

> We believe that the company will be able to price AZT at a minimum of $5 per day of therapy per patient [$1,800 per year] without any adverse public reaction. Therefore, we estimate AZT's potential at approximately $140 million on the basis of current statistics on patient numbers—which, as we are all aware, are growing as the AIDS infection spreads.[18]

At the same time, the *New York Times* noted that,

> most Wall Street analysts expect AZT to be priced between $5,000 and $7,000 per patient per year, placing it among the costliest drugs, including Sandimmune, the Sandoz Inc. brand of cyclosporine, for preventing rejection of organ transplants, and Protopin, Genentech Inc.'s synthetic human growth hormone for dwarfism.[19]

Dr. David Barry (Burroughs Wellcome vice president of research) declined to project the price, saying only that, because AZT cost more than $80 million to develop and test, "There's no question it's going to be an expensive drug."[20]

NOTES

1. This section is based primarily on the Institute of Medicine and National Academy of Sciences report *Mobilizing Against AIDS* (Cambridge: Harvard University Press, 1986) and on Pamela Hamilton's "AIDS in the Workplace: Ethical, Economic and Legal Considerations," 1990 Darden Directed Study.
2. Lynne Pauls, "AIDS Drugs in Development: A Follow-up Report," *E.F. Hutton Industry Review*, December 4, 1986.
3. W. Alpert, "Good News, Bad News," *Barrons*, March 9, 1987, p. 42.
4. "Weapons Against a Modern Scourge," *Chemical Week*, May 6, 1987, p. 48.
5. Ibid.
6. A. Pollack, "The Troubling Costs of Drugs That Offer Hope," *New York Times*, February 9, 1988, pp. 1, D23.
7. Cited in Hearings of the U.S. Subcommittee on Monopoly of the Select Committee on Small Business, *Competitive Problems in the Drug Industry* (Washington, D.C.: U.S. Government Printing Office, 1968), p. 1813.
8. J. Walton, S. Adkins, and I. Smith, "Wellcome," *Shearson Lehman Hutton Analyst Report*, July 1987, p. 12.
9. Ibid.
10. J. Davidson, "Medicaid Spending on AIDS to Increase Six Fold by 1992, Health Official Says," *New York Times*, September 10, 1987, p. 4.
11. "A Quiet Drugmaker Takes a Big Swing at AIDS," *Business Week*, September 9, 1987, p. 32.
12. *Barron's*, March 9, 1987, p. 42.
13. Walton, Adkins, and Smith, "Wellcome," p. 8.
14. *Chemical Week*, May 6, 1987, p. 48.
15. Ibid.
16. Alpert, "Good News," p. 42.
17. Pauls, "AIDS Drugs in Development."
18. Lynne Pauls, "Wellcome," *E.F. Hutton Drugs Equity Research*, January 19, 1987, p. 2.
19. M. Chase, "Wellcome Unit's AZT Is Recommended as First Prescription Drug to Treat AIDS," *Wall Street Journal*, January 19, 1987, p. 11.
20. Ibid.

BURROUGHS WELLCOME
AND THE PRICING OF AZT (B)

Jeanne M. Liedtka

On Friday, February 13, 1987, Wellcome PLC of London announced a "provisional" AZT wholesale price of $188 per bottle containing one hundred 100-milligram (mg) capsules. At a dosage level of 200 mg every four hours, this translated into a wholesale price of $8,300 per year, making AZT the most expensive prescription drug known. The anticipated retail cost of the drug was expected to be approximately $10,000 per year.[1]

Investors reacted with enthusiasm to the announcement, sending the price of Wellcome shares up 24 percent on the London exchange by the close of business on Friday. Gross profit margins on the drug at that price were estimated by investment analysts to range between 40 and 80 percent.[2] One New York analyst commented, "We expect Retrovir [AZT] to be . . . the company's largest contributor to revenue and earnings by December and that the profit margin will be about three times the company's 13 percent average."[3]

The reaction of other groups was less positive. The U.S. House Subcommittee on Health and the Environment scheduled hearings in March to discuss the cost of AZT. Questions, as reported by the *Wall Street Journal*, "ranged from sharp to hostile."[4] Representative Ron Wyden queried Wellcome managers, "How did you arrive at a price of $10,000? Why didn't you set it at $100,000?" Representative Henry Waxman, a leader in the fight for emergency funding for patients unable to afford the drug, later commented, "Our system is to award monopolies to innovators; but we cannot allow private enterprise to price sick people out of the market."[5] The New York State Consumer Protection Board began an investigation of "price gouging" on the part of both Burroughs Wellcome and pharmacies.[6]

Physicians were equally concerned. "Only the privileged and rich will be able to handle the cost," Lionel Resnick of the Mount Sinai Medical Center in Miami commented. "It doesn't take much to realize that we have a very big problem." Dr. Jerome Grossman of New England Deaconess Hospital in Boston echoed the concerns: "I think the extraordinarily high price of the drug needs to be justified by the company in very clear terms, because it will clearly limit access to patients who could benefit." Another

This case was written by Jeanne M. Liedtka, Associate Professor of Business Administration, Darden Graduate School of Business Administration, University of Virginia. Copyright © 1991 by the Darden Graduate Business School Foundation, Charlottesville, VA.

physician warned, "Either it'll be on the taxpayer's back or patients will be robbing pharmacies. . . . These are desperate dying patients."[7]

A *New York Times* editorial entitled "Forcing Poverty on AIDS Patients" noted, "The cost is personally devastating to those who must spend down to poverty, but the burden of paying for AZT in the end is borne by everyone through higher taxes and insurance costs."[8]

Some AIDS activists were less philosophical in their response. Nineteen people were arrested in a demonstration at the Burroughs Wellcome distribution center in Burlingame, California, in what was believed to be the first civil disobedience protest against a drug price.[9] Others demonstrated on Wall Street, carrying signs that read "Burroughs Wellcome = Greedy Bastards."[10] "I think it's outrageous, in a life-threatening situation," said Archie Harrison, a 32-year-old AIDS patient. He noted that many seriously ill AIDS patients were living on fixed incomes and would be unable to pay for AZT.[11] Federal health officials were concerned with the effects of the drug price on Medicaid costs, expected to reach $150 million for AZT in the fiscal year beginning in October 1987.[12] Not all AIDS activists supported government regulation of AIDS drug pricing, however. Some maintained that such action would reduce the incentives for drug companies to "step forward to help." In an editorial in the *Wall Street Journal*, a San Francisco AIDS activist argued that "even if the [proposed] amendments have the effect of temporarily lowering some drug prices. . . the chief beneficiaries would not be people with AIDS but rather public and private health insurers."[13]

Throughout the clamor, Wellcome defended its pricing of the drug, arguing:

1. high R&D, production, and material costs required the price;
2. uncertainty over the arrival of newer AIDS drugs necessitated a short-term focus on recouping costs;
3. AZT drug therapy was far less expensive than alternative treatments (namely, hospitalization of acutely ill patients).

"I have no compunction about charging this price," Dr. David Barry, Burroughs Wellcome vice president of research, explained, "No one flinches at hundreds of dollars a day in hospital costs, but everyone expects a drug that prevents hospitalization to be much less."[14]

The *Wall Street Journal* heralded Wellcome in an editorial noting:

Burroughs Wellcome is the only organization that has so far done anything significant to help AIDS victims. . . . [I]ts achievement with AZT was accomplished almost entirely with its own resources—scientific, organizational and financial. . . . Wellcome is learning, though, that one of the risks of doing good is getting criticized. . . . "[15]

Industry analysts defended the AZT pricing decision as consistent with standard industry practice for an important new drug with no available substitutes.

Despite repeated requests from government and activist groups, Burroughs Wellcome refused to release any details or costs or to explain the calculations on which the price was based. "We operate in a free enterprise system," Burroughs Wellcome President Ted Haigler explained. "We're not required to tell all." Commented Wellcome's chairman, Sir Alfred Shepperd, "If we wrapped the drug in £10 note and gave it away, people would say it cost too much."[16]

NOTES

1. M. Chase, "Wellcome PLC Sets Price of AIDS Drug at $8,300 a Year, Higher Than Expected," *Wall Street Journal*, February 17, 1987, p. 7.
2. "Now that AIDS Is Treatable, Who'll Pay the Crushing Cost?," *Business Week*, September 11, 1989, p. 118.
3. B. Feder, "Drug Expected to Spur Growth and Profits of its Maker," *New York Times*, March 21, 1987, p. 32.
4. M. Chase, "AIDS Drug Comes to a Worried Market," *Wall Street Journal*, March 23, 1987, p. 6.
5. H. Schwartz, "Weak Drug Patents Would Inhibit Innovation," *Wall Street Journal*, April 29, 1987, p. 22.
6. T. Morgan, "State Studies Pricing of AIDS Drug," *New York Times*, October 9, 1987, p. B3.
7. Chase, "AIDS Drug Comes to a Worried Market," p. 6.
8. "Forcing Poverty on AIDS Patients," *New York Times*, August 30, 1988, p. A18.
9. "Civil Disobedience Over Price of AIDS Drug," *New York Times*, February 9, 1988, p. D23.
10. Schwartz, "Weak Drug Patents," p. 22.
11. Feder, "Drug Expected to Spur Growth," p. 32.
12. J. Davidson, "Medicaid Spending on AIDS to Increase Six-fold by 1992, Health Official Says," *Wall Street Journal*, September 19, 1987, p. 4.
13. J. Driscoll, "Consumer Protection Could Kill AIDS Patients," *Wall Street Journal*, March 6, 1991, p. A8.
14. Chase, "AIDS Drug Comes to a Worried Market," p. 6.
15. "AIDS Research: Who's in Charge?" *Wall Street Journal*, April 20, 1987, p. 22.
16. B. O'Reilly, "The Inside Story of the AIDS Drug," *Fortune*, November 5, 1990, p. 128.

DOW CORNING AND THE SILICONE BREAST IMPLANT CONTROVERSY

Anne T. Lawrence

The corporate jet lifted off from Washington's National Airport, en route to Dow Corning Corporation's headquarters in Midland, Michigan. February 19, 1992, had been a grueling day for Keith R. McKennon. Named chairman and chief executive officer of Dow Corning less than two weeks earlier, McKennon had just testified before the Food and Drug Administration's Advisory Committee on the safety of the company's silicone gel breast implants. Although not the only maker of mammary prostheses, Dow Corning had invented the devices in the early 1960s and had been responsible for most of their medical testing. Now, the company was faced with the task of defending breast implants against numerous lawsuits and a rising tide of criticism from the FDA, Congress, the media, and many women's advocacy organizations.

The company's potential liability was large: As many as two million American women had received implants over the past three decades, and perhaps 35 percent of these implants had been made by Dow Corning. In December 1991, a San Francisco jury had awarded a woman who claimed injuries from her Dow Corning implants an unprecedented $7.3 million in damages. Although the company believed its $250 million in product liability insurance was adequate to meet any possible claims, some felt that the company's liability exposure could be much, much larger.

The hearings had been contentious. Critics had repeated their allegations, heard often in the press in recent weeks, that the implants could leak silicone into the body, causing pain, scarring and—most seriously—debilitating autoimmune diseases such as rheumatoid arthritis and scleroderma. They also charged that the silicone prostheses could interfere with detection of breast cancer by mammography. In response, McKennon had testified that implants served an important public health need and did not pose an unreasonable risk to users. On the job less than a month, however, McKennon had had little time to sort through the thousands of pages of rel-

By Anne T. Lawrence, San Jose State University. Originally presented at a meeting of the Western Casewriters' Association, March 1993. Research was supported in part by the San Jose State University College of Business. This case was written from public sources, including internal company documents released by Dow Corning Corporation in February 1992, solely for the purpose of stimulating student discussion. All events and individuals are real. Copyright 1993 by the *Case Research Journal* and Anne T. Lawrence.

evant documents or to talk with the many managers who had been involved with the product's development over the past twenty-five years.

The breast implant controversy would surely be a litmus test of McKennon's crisis management skills. Recruited from Dow Chemical Corporation, where he had been executive vice president and head of domestic operations, McKennon came to his new position with a reputation as a "seasoned troubleshooter."[1,2] At Dow Chemical (which owned 50 percent of Dow Corning), McKennon had earlier managed his firm's response to charges that its product Agent Orange, a defoliant widely used during the Vietnam War, had caused lingering health problems for veterans. Later, he had managed Dow Chemical's problems with Bendectin, an antinausea drug alleged to cause birth defects. At the time of his appointment as chairman and CEO, McKennon had served on Dow Corning's Board of Directors for nearly six years.

The unfolding breast implant crisis showed every sign of being just as difficult—and potentially damaging—as any McKennon had confronted in his long career. Would Dow Corning become known as another Johnson & Johnson, renowned for its skillful handling of the Tylenol poisonings in the 1980s? Or would it become another Manville or A.H. Robins, companies that had declared bankruptcy in the wake of major product liability crises? McKennon was well aware that the future of the company, as well as his own reputation, might well hinge on decisions he and his top managers would make within the next weeks and days.

DOW CORNING, INC.

Dow Corning was founded in 1943 as an equal joint venture of Dow Chemical Company and Corning Glass Works (later known simply as Corning, Inc.) to produce silicones for commercial applications. The term *silicone* was coined by British chemist F.S. Kipping to describe synthetic compounds derived from silicon, an abundant element commonly found in quartz and sand. In the 1930s, Corning researchers working on possible applications of silicone in glassmaking developed a number of resins, fluids, and rubbers that could withstand extremes of hot and cold. In 1940, Corning approached Dow Chemical with a proposal for a joint commercial venture, and by 1942 a small plant in Midland, Michigan (Dow's hometown), had begun production. In an important early success, the fledgling venture produced a sealant that prevented the ignition systems of Allied fighter planes from failing at high altitudes. Dow Corning also made products used by the U.S. military in radio and radar systems, aboard Navy ships, and in wartime matériel factories.

At the close of World War II, Dow Corning moved successfully to develop multiple commercial applications for silicone. Within a decade, the company had introduced more than six hundred products and doubled in size three times, making it one of the fastest growing firms in the booming chemical industry. Its varied product line included specialty lubricants, sealants, and resins as well as a variety of consumer items ranging from construction caulk, to adhesive labels, to Silly Putty. When astronaut Edward H. White walked in space in 1965, he was connected to the space capsule by a hose made of Dow Corning Silastic silicone rubber. By 1992, the company was producing nearly five thousand separate products based on silicone.[3-5]

Dow Corning soon developed a reputation as an innovator in organizational design as well as research and development. In 1967, the company reorganized from a conventional divisionalized structure to a global-matrix form of organization, which the company called "multidimensional." At the time pathbreaking, this structure was featured in an article in the *Harvard Business Review* and received considerable attention from management theorists and other practitioners. Under the multidimensional form, the company had ten "profit centers," or basic businesses, each with its own manager and Business Board. Within each profit center, cross-functional product management groups (PMGs) were vested with responsibility for individual product families. Most professionals within this system were in dual authority relationships, reporting both to business group and functional managers. The company was further organized by geographical region, with area managers around the world enjoying significant autonomy. The effect of the company's multidimensional structure was to decentralize authority, push decision making down, and put a premium on cross-functional teamwork and communication. The culture of Dow Corning became known as open, informal, and relaxed.[6]

DEVELOPMENT OF THE FIRST BREAST IMPLANT

Although most uses of silicone were industrial, by the mid-1950s Dow Corning scientists had become interested in possible medical applications and developed several implantable devices, including a heart pacemaker and a hydrocephalic shunt. In the early 1960s, a physician working for the company, Thomas Cronin, became intrigued by the possibility of using silicone to make a breast prosthesis for mastectomy patients. Building off Cronin's preliminary ideas, Dow Corning engineers developed the first prototype of a breast implant by encapsulating a firm-density silicone gel within an elastomer (silicone rubber) bag. First marketed in 1963, this device—known as the Cronin implant—was used initially almost exclusively in reconstructive surgery performed on breast cancer patients following mastectomies.

When Dow Corning first developed and marketed breast implants (as well as its other medical products), the company was operating with virtually no government oversight. Unlike pharmaceutical drugs, regulated since 1906 under the Pure Food and Drug Act and its several amendments, medical devices—even those designed for implantation in the body—were for all practical purposes unregulated. Under the Food, Drug, and Cosmetics Act of 1938, the FDA had the authority to inspect sites where medical devices were made and could seize adulterated or misbranded devices. The agency could not require premarket approval for safety or effectiveness, however, and could remove a product from the market only if it could demonstrate that the manufacturer had broken the law.[7]

Although not required to prove its implants safe by law, Dow Corning—in accord with standard "good manufacturing" practices at the time—attempted to determine the safety of its own medical products before releasing them for sale. In 1964, Dow Corning hired the Food and Drug Research Laboratories, an independent contractor, to undertake several studies of the safety of medical-grade silicones, including those used in breast implants. Several different kinds of silicones were injected or implanted in experimental animals. No evidence was found that the silicones caused cancer, but one study found that silicone fluid injected in dogs created "persistent, chronic inflammation." Company scientists dismissed this finding, concluding that the test animals had experienced a "typical foreign body reaction" that was "not material specific," that is, not specific to silicone.

More troubling were the results of another study conducted by the same lab and reported to the company in 1969. Silicone fluids injected into mice and rats had spread widely, becoming lodged in the lymph nodes, liver, spleen, pancreas, and other organs of the test animals. Again, the company appeared unconcerned, noting that it did not advocate the direct injection of silicone. By the late 1960s, the company had in hand evidence that silicone might cause chronic inflammation and scarring and that, in fluid form, it could migrate widely within the body. The company's responses to the studies, however, suggested that it firmly believed silicones to be biologically inert and safe for internal use.

In the early 1970s, Dow Corning's breast implant business for the first time experienced a serious competitive threat. In 1972, five young men—all scientists or salesmen at Dow Corning—left the company to work for Heyer-Schulte, a small medical devices company in Goleta, California, where they used their experience with silicones to develop a competing breast implant. Two years later, the group—led by Donald K. McGhan—left Heyer-Schulte to form their own company, McGhan Medical Corporation, based in Santa Barbara, California. Their idea was to modify the basic technology developed over the past decade by Dow Corning to make a softer, more responsive implant that more closely resembled the natural breast. In this effort, they relied completely on prior research and development done at Dow Corning;

McGhan's group apparently undertook no independent tests of the safety of silicone materials used in their products. By 1974, both Heyer-Schulte and McGhan Medical had competing products on the market.

The Heyer-Schulte and McGhan implants quickly gained favor with plastic surgeons, and Dow Corning's market share began to erode. By 1975, Dow Corning estimated its market share had declined to around 35 percent, as plastic surgeons switched allegiance to products offered by the small company start-ups. Dow Corning managers became alarmed.

THE MAMMARY TASK FORCE

In January, 1975—responding to the challenge from its California competitors—Dow Corning dedicated a special cross-functional team, known as the mammary task force, to develop, test, and bring to market a new generation of breast implants. The group's main goal was to reformulate the silicone gel to create a softer, more pliable implant competitive with the new products recently marketed by McGhan and Heyer-Schulte. The task force also aimed to develop implants with varying "profiles" and improved sterile packaging. The group of about twenty—all men—hoped to have the new implants ready for shipment by June 1975. The company believed it was justified in bringing the new implant to market quickly, without extensive medical testing, because the new product would be based on materials substantially similar to those used in the older Cronin implants. The safety of the existing line, management maintained, had already been satisfactorily documented on the basis of earlier studies and the history of their use.

One of the questions that quickly arose in the task force's deliberations—as reported in the minutes of its January 21, 1975, meeting—was: "Will the new gel. . . cause a *bleed through* which will make these products unacceptable?" (emphasis in original). Dow Corning scientists clearly recognized that a more watery gel (dubbed "flo-gel")—while softer to the touch—might also be more likely to permeate its elastomer envelope and "bleed" into surrounding tissue. Two product engineers, Thomas D. Talcott and William Larson, were assigned to investigate this issue. A week later, task force leader Arthur Rathjen reminded the group in forceful terms:

> Per the Task Force Time Table, there is only a two week period before the new "flo-gel" is scheduled to be formulated and filling begins. A question not yet answered is whether or not there is excessive bleed of the gel through the envelope. We *must* address ourselves to this question immediately, determine what the facts are, and decide whether the plant is to proceed with the filling of the current inventory [of envelopes]. . . . Question—does the proposed mammary bleed any more than our standard product? If the product does bleed more, is it substantial enough that it will affect the product acceptance? A "go or no go" decision will have to come from the Business Board. The stakes are too high if a wrong decision is made. (January 28, 1975)

On February 4, Talcott and Larson reported that their two and three week experiments "*to date* indicate that the bleed with new gel is no greater than what we measure from old gel controls." They also added, however, that they viewed their early results as inconclusive, and they remained concerned about "a possible bleed situation."

Biomedical tests were contracted out to an independent laboratory, which proceeded with tests in which the new gel was injected into experimental rabbits. Early reports back from the lab on February 26 showed "mild to occasionally moderate acute inflammatory reaction" in the test animals around the injected gel, but the pathologist concluded it was probably due to the trauma of insertion, not the product itself. The task force expressed exasperation at the ambiguity of the lab report:

> G. Robertson wants a clarification on their definition of "mild to occasionally moderate acute inflammatory reaction." Suggested he call Biometrics. (February 26, 1975)

The task force also ordered biomedical testing on migration of gel into the vital organs of monkeys. The laboratory results showed "some migration of the [flo-gel] formulation. . . ." However, the task force agreed that the bleed was still not any more or less than standard gel.

The task force continued to move along at a breakneck pace. On February 20, Rathjen praised the group:

> Mel Nelson and the Business Board members, along with the PMG, were very complimentary of the Task Force/Consultant progress in the mammary program. This has been possible because of your cooperation and open channels of communication. Certainly this last month has demonstrated what can be accomplished when we all pull together. Let's keep it going.

The pace of product development, however, seemed to overwhelm the group's ability to conduct conclusive research on safety, particularly on the issue of whether or not the more liquidlike gel would bleed through the envelope and into body tissues. The March 7 minutes include the following notation:

> T. Talcott still not satisfied [with the elastomer envelope]. A. Rathjen challenged Talcott—if there *is* something TS&D can do to assist in improving envelopes, do it. We are past the point of discussion about getting together to look into it. (emphasis in original)

"THE BEST WE HAVE EVER MADE"

Development proceeded so rapidly that by March 31, ten thousand new flo-gel mammaries were ready for packaging. The task force minutes reported that the products were "beautiful, the best we have ever made." Now six weeks ahead of schedule, the company was able to ship some samples of the new product to the West Coast in time for the California Plastic Surgeons meeting on April 21. However, early demonstrations did not go flawlessly. The task force got back the following report:

> In Vancouver, and elsewhere on the West Coast introduction, it was noted that after the mammaries had been handled for a while, the surface became oily. Also, some were bleeding on the velvet in the showcase. (May 12, 1975)

The task force asked that the high-bleed samples be returned, and Talcott and Larson set about testing them. Tom Salisbury, a marketing representative on the task force, wrote the company's sales force on May 16 to advise them on how to handle "oily" implants:

> It has been observed that the new mammaries with responsive gel have a tendency to appear oily after being manipulated. This could prove to be a problem with your daily detailing activity where mammary manipulation is a must. Keep in mind that this is not a product problem; our technical people assure us that the doctor in the O.R. [operating room] will not see any appreciable oiling on product removed from the package. The oily phenomenon seems to appear the day following manipulation. You should make plans to change demonstration samples often. Also, be sure samples are clean and dry before customer detailing.

The task force ordered samples from the West Coast for examination, but no further discussion of this issue appeared in subsequent minutes.

As the flo-gel implants came on line, the focus of the task force's discussion shifted from production issues to marketing strategy. The task force debated various aggressive marketing approaches, such as rebates, distribution by consignment, price breaks for "big users," and free samples for surgeons known to perform augmentations. Noting that June and July were the "peak months" of the "mammary season," managers called for a big push to grab back some of Dow Corning's eroding market share. Rathjen exhorted his troops:

> With the changes in the plastic surgery business that are happening, RIGHT NOW (McGhan Medical, Heyer-Schulte, etc.) it was felt that aggressive development and marketing activity in the next four months will make a tremendous difference in Dow Corning's position in this market. The time to act is NOW. (May 12, 1975)

The group felt that their market share, which they estimated had eroded to around 35 percent, could be lifted back to the 50 to 60 percent range if they moved aggressively.

By September, Dow Corning was producing 6,000 to 7,000 units per month and aimed to phase out the older Cronin models by early 1976.

However, many bugs in the production process remained to be ironed out. The reject rate at inspection was high—as high as 50 percent on some lots. Among the problems: floating dirt, weak bags, and thin spots in the envelopes. Doctors had returned some unused mammaries, citing breakage and contamination. Overall, however, plastic surgeons liked the product. One task force member later recalled that when plastic surgeons saw and felt the new material, "their eyes got big as saucers."[8] Besides feeling more natural to the touch, the new softer devices were easier to insert and were more suitable for small-incision, low-trauma cosmetic procedures.

In 1976, engineer Thomas D. Talcott, who had been an active member of the mammary task force, quit his 24-year job at Dow Corning in protest, citing the company's decision to market a product of unproven safety. He later said that he felt Dow Corning was conducting "experimental surgery on humans." Talcott later testified as an expert witness for the plaintiff in several trials in which women sued Dow Corning for product liability. The company dismissed his charges, saying that he "left as a disgruntled employee. You've got to question to some degree his motives."[9,10]

A BOOM IN BUSTS

Although breast implants first became available in the 1960s, it was only in the late 1970s and 1980s that the rate of implant surgery took off. The increase was due entirely to a fast rise in the number of so-called "cosmetic" procedures; by 1990, fully 80 percent of all implant surgeries performed in the United States were to increase the size of normal, healthy breasts, rather than for reconstruction following mastectomy.

One cause of the rise in cosmetic augmentations, of course, was the availability of the softer, more pliable implants, which could be inserted through smaller incisions with less trauma to the patient in less expensive, outpatient procedures. In 1990, 82 percent of all breast augmentation procedures were performed on an outpatient basis. Other, broader trends within the medical profession and the wider culture also played important roles, however.

One factor behind the boom in breast augmentation surgery was the growth of the plastic surgery profession. Although procedures to graft tissue from a healthy part of the body to another that had been damaged or mutilated were developed early in the century, plastic surgery as a distinct subdiscipline within surgery did not emerge until the 1940s. During World War II, military surgeons struggling to repair the wounds of injured soldiers returning from the front pioneered many valuable reconstructive techniques. Many of these surgeons reentered civilian life to start plastic surgery programs in their home communities. Within a couple of decades, plastic surgery had become the fastest-growing specialty within American medicine.[11] Between 1960 and 1983, the number of board-certified plastic surgeons quintupled, during a period when most other medical specialties were growing much less quickly (and the U.S. population as a whole grew by just 31 percent). The draw for newly minted M.D.s: regular hours, affluent customers, and high incomes—averaging $180,000 per year after all expenses in 1987.

As their numbers soared, plastic surgeons faced an obvious problem: developing a market for their services. Demand for reconstructive surgery was not fast growing, and cosmetic procedures were often elective and typically not fully covered by medical insurance. In 1983—following approval by the Federal Trade Commission—the American Society for Plastic and Reconstructive Surgery [ASPRS] (a professional association representing 97 percent of all board-certified plastic surgeons) launched a major advertising (or, as the society called it, "practice enhancement") campaign.[12] Other ads were placed by individual surgeons. In one appearing in *Los Angeles* magazine, a seductive, well-endowed model was shown leaning against a sports car. The tag line: "Automobile by Ferrari. Body by [a prominent plastic surgeon]."

Plastic surgeons also campaigned to redefine female flat-chestedness (dubbed "micromastia" by the medical community) as a medical disease requiring treatment. In July, 1982, the ASPRS filed a formal comment with the FDA that argued that:

> There is a substantial and enlarging body of medical opinion to the effect that these deformities [small breasts] are really a disease which in most patients results in feelings of inadequacy, lack of self confidence, distortion of body image and a total lack of well-being due to a lack of self-perceived femininity. The enlargement of the underdeveloped female breast is, therefore, often very necessary to insure an improved quality of life for the patient.[13]

The ASPRS later officially repudiated this view.

By 1990, breast augmentation had become the second most common cosmetic procedure performed by plastic surgeons, exceeded only by liposuction. Since it was a more expensive procedure, however, breast augmentation was the top money maker for plastic surgeons in 1990. That year, ASPRS members collected almost $215 million in fees from women for breast implant surgery (Exhibit 1).

For a variety of reasons, plastic surgery has not been subject to the same degree of oversight as most other medical specialties. Cosmetic procedures are often carried out on an outpatient basis, thus escaping oversight by hospitals. Elective procedures that are not considered medically necessary usually are not reimbursed by insurance, thus avoiding review by another external agency. Although plastic surgery patients typically return to their surgeons for follow-up treatment related to complications of the surgery itself, they rarely return for long-term care. Thus, complications that arise months or years later are more often seen by internists or family physicians, who may be unaware of earlier surgical procedures. Thus, as

EXHIBIT 1

NUMBER AND AVERAGE FEES OF COSMETIC SURGERY PROCEDURES PERFORMED BY ASPRS MEMBERS, 1990*

Procedure	Number	Average Fee	Total Fees (000s)
Liposuction	109,080	$1480	$161,438
Breast augmentation	89,402	2400†	214,565
Collagen injections	80,602	250	20,151
Eyelid surgery	79,110	1360‡	107,590
Nose reshaping	68,320	2590	176,949
Facelift	48,743	3880	189,123
Retin-A	37,338	45	1,680
Tummy tuck	20,213	3430	69,331
Dermabrasion	16,969	1260	21,381
Forehead lift	15,376	1980	30,444

Source: "Estimated Number of Cosmetic Surgery Procedures Performed by ASPRS Members in 1990" and "Treatment Locations and Surgeons' Fees for 1990," fact sheets distributed by the American Society for Plastic and Reconstructive Surgery, 1992.

*Only the ten most common procedures are included. These figures do not include operations by the many physicians who perform plastic surgery procedures without receiving specialized residency training in the field. In most states physicians certified in general surgery may perform cosmetic surgery; in some states, any licensed physician may do so. Thus, this exhibit significantly underestimates the total number of procedures performed and the total fees collected in the U.S. each year.

†Fees for a breast implant operation in 1990 ranged from $1,000-$5,500.

‡Uppers only. Some eyelid surgery involves both lids, which is more expensive.

plastic surgeons moved increasingly into cosmetic procedures, they operated with less institutional oversight than many other specialists.

Another factor contributing to the rise in cosmetic augmentation may have been changing cultural standards of feminine beauty in the 1980s, a decade characterized by social conservatism and, according to some commentators, by a backlash against feminism and female liberation. In the 1970s, women appearing in the glossy pages of fashion magazines were often tall and lanky, with long, straight hair tied at the nape of the neck, menswear "dress-for-success" suits, and distinctly boyish figures. The 1980s ideal woman was very different: The typical fashion model by this time was more likely to sport 1940s retro-look fashions, thick, full curls, sweetheart lips—and lots of bosom. A number of top movie actresses and celebrities—including Mariel Hemingway, Cher, and Jenny Jones—spoke openly of their surgically enhanced breasts. In a special one-hundredth anniversary edition, published in April 1992, *Vogue* magazine summed up current standards of female beauty in this sentence:

And in women's bodies, the fashion now is a combination of hard, muscular stomach and shapely breasts. Increasingly, women are willing to regard their bodies as photographic images, unpublishable until retouched and perfected at the hands of surgeons.[14]

Ironically, the same issue also ran an ad, placed by trial attorneys, in which "silicone breast implant sufferers" were invited to come forward with legal claims.

A STREAM OF SICK AND INJURED

As the rate of implant surgeries rose in the 1980s, so did the number of unfortunate and unintended results. Women who were sick, injured, and in pain from their breast surgery began appearing in the offices of doctors and product liability attorneys. Their stories began to be told—at medical conferences, in legal briefs, and by women's and consumers' advocacy organizations. As they were, Dow Corning and other implant makers were forced to respond to a growing crisis of confidence in their products.

The most common adverse side effect of implant surgery was a phenomenon known as "capsular contracture," a painful hardening of the breast that occurred when the body reacted to the implant by forming a wall of fibrous scar tissue around it. In severe cases, the breast became as hard as a baseball and painful to the touch. The FDA has estimated that severe contracture occurred in about 25 percent of all patients; some hardening may have occurred in up to 70 percent. In fact, capsular contracture was so common that the journal *Plastic and Reconstructive Surgery* advised its physician readers to refer to the phenomenon as an "expected result" or "consequence," rather than a "complication," of implant surgery.

Implants could also rupture, spilling silicone gel into the body and often necessitating repeat surgery to replace the damaged implants. Dow Corning's data, based on voluntary reporting by surgeons, showed a rupture rate of only 1 percent. These figures were challenged by researchers who pointed out that ruptures often are asymptomatic and do not show up on mammograms. Scientists at Washington University in St. Louis and the University of Pittsburgh, for example, estimated rupture rates of 5 to 6 percent; individual doctors reported rates as high as 32 percent, according to evidence presented to an FDA panel.[15] Ironically, rupture was sometimes precipitated by a procedure called "closed capsulotomy," in which physicians attempted to treat capsular contracture by exerting force to the breast, manually tearing the scar tissue capsule. In many cases, the procedure inadvertently broke the implant. Ruptures could also be provoked by programs of strenuous massage recommended by some surgeons to prevent formation of fibrous scar tissue. Once the device had ruptured, silicone could and did travel via the lymphatic system throughout the body, lodging in a woman's spleen, liver, and other internal organs.

Also worrisome was the tendency of silicone implants to obscure cancerous tumors that otherwise would be revealed by mammography. Dr. Melvin Silverstein, a surgical oncologist, conducted studies from 1986 to 1991 showing that mammograms performed on women with implants had a "false negative" rate almost four times as high as those among women without implants; in 39 percent of implant recipients with tumors, the tumor was completely obscured by the implant.[16]

More controversial and less well documented were allegations that silicone implants could lead to so-called autoimmune disorders—diseases in which the body's immune system attacks its own connective tissue. According to the FDA, by 1991 around six hundred cases of autoimmune disorders—such as rheumatoid arthritis, scleroderma, and lupus erythematosus—had been reported in women with implants.[17] Some scientists speculated that some women were, in effect, allergic to silicone, and that their bodies had attacked their own tissues in an attempt to rid itself of the substance. Such reactions were most likely in the presence of ruptures, but even small amounts of gel bleeding through the envelope—or silicone in the envelope itself—could provoke an autoimmune response.

Other physicians believed, however, that the appearance of autoimmune disorders in women with implants was wholly coincidental. In any substantial population—and two million women with implants was clearly substantial—a certain number would develop autoimmune disease purely by chance. Peter McKinney, a plastic surgeon and professor at Northwestern University, articulated this view in an interview in the *Journal of the American Medical Association* in which he called the association between autoimmune disorders and breast implants a "crock of baloney. . . . People get immunological diseases and they just happen to have breast implants."[18]

The question, clearly, was an epidemiological one that could be resolved only with long-term controlled studies of the incidence of autoimmune disorders in populations of women with and without implants. The problem was that absolutely no studies of this type were initiated or even contemplated until 1991. In fact, no comprehensive registries of women with implants existed. Data submitted to the FDA by implant manufacturers in 1991 included no studies that had lasted more than two years, and none that included any questions on autoimmune disease. All relied on the records of plastic surgeons—who were, in any case, unlikely to treat or know about subsequent immune disorders. The question about the relationship between implants and autoimmune disease was, on the basis of existing data, wholly unanswerable. Congressman Ted Weiss (D-New York), who reviewed data submitted to the FDA in 1991, later angrily concluded: "For thirty years, more than one million women have been subjects in a massive, uncontrolled study, without their knowledge or consent."[19]

VICTIMS SEEK REDRESS

Some women who had suffered from breast implants sued. In 1984, Maria Stern of Nevada was awarded $1.5 million by jurors in a San Francisco court, who concluded that Dow Corning had committed fraud in marketing its implant as safe. Stern claimed that her implants had caused joint pain, swollen lymph glands, fatigue, and weight loss. The case was later settled for an undisclosed amount while on appeal, and the court records were sealed. In a posttrial ruling, a federal judge who had reviewed the case records called Dow Corning's actions "highly reprehensible." In the wake of the Stern case, Dow Corning changed its package insert to include a warning that mentioned the possibility of capsular contracture, silicone migration following rupture, and immune system sensitivity.

As other cases slowly made their way through the courts, some victims spoke out publicly. One of the first was Sybil Goldrich, a doctor's wife who had received implants after undergoing a bilateral mastectomy for breast cancer in 1983. In an article published in *Ms.* magazine in 1988, entitled "Restoration Drama," Goldrich told of her experience with silicone implants:

> After two mastectomies, I made every effort to learn about breast reconstruction. . . . Nothing in my research suggested that this "simple" procedure [reconstruction with silicone implants] would turn into five operations, over a period of 10 months, requiring more than 15 hours under anesthesia and countless days of pain and discomfort. The implants hardened, became misshapen, changed position ("migrated" is the word generally used for that) so that they never matched. . . . At one point, the implants nearly passed through the weakened skin, and had to be surgically removed. After this last set of implants failed, I was no closer to restoration than when I started; I simply had several more glaring scars on my disfigured torso.[20]

Goldrich later joined with Kathleen Anneken, a nurse who had experienced a failed augmentation procedure, to found the Command Trust Network, an advocacy organization that became instrumental in providing information, support, and legal and medical referrals to implant victims.

Other women's and public health advocacy groups also played a role in publicizing the risks of breast implants. One of the most active was the Health Research Group (HRG), a Washington-based spin-off of Ralph Nader's Public Citizen. Headed by a consumer activist, Dr. Sidney M. Wolfe, the HRG in 1988 began a systematic effort to pressure the FDA to ban silicone breast implants. The group petitioned the FDA, testified before Congress and other government agencies, issued regular press releases, and distributed information to consumers. The HRG also initiated an information clearinghouse for plaintiffs' attorneys.[21,22] Another active advocacy organization was the National Women's Health Network, a public-interest group that widely distributed information on silicone-related issues.

DEVISING REGULATION FOR DEVICES

The agency in charge of regulating implants—and thus the object of these and other advocacy organizations' pressure—was the U.S. Food and Drug Administration. In 1976—the year after Dow Corning's mammary task force developed its new generation of flo-gel implants—Congress passed the Medical Amendments Act to the Food and Drug Act. Enacted in the wake of the Dalkon Shield controversy—in which thousands of women claimed they had been injured by a poorly designed intrauterine device— the amendments for the first time required that manufacturers of new, implantable medical devices be required to prove their products safe and effective before release to the public. Devices already on the market were ranked by risk, with the riskiest ones—designated "Class III"—required to meet the same standards of safety and effectiveness as new devices.

In 1978, during the initial review of the 1,700 known existing devices, the FDA's General and Plastic Surgery Devices Advisory Panel—which was dominated by plastic surgeons—recommended that breast implants receive the less restrictive Class II designation. The FDA disagreed and, in 1982, proposed a Class III rating. For 6 years, however, the agency failed to take action on its own recommendation. The commissioner later explained that the agency had simply been overwhelmed by the sheer volume of premarket approval applications it had received from manufacturers; he told reporters that reviewing devices in over 130 different categories had been "an enormous undertaking." Finally, in January 1989, the FDA identified silicone implants as Class III devices and gave their manufacturers 30 months—until July 1991—to submit safety and effectiveness data to the agency.

Four breast implant manufacturers submitted premarket approval applications (PMAs) to the Food and Drug Administration in July 1991: Dow Corning, INAMED (formerly McGhan Medical), Mentor (formerly Heyer-Schulte), and Bioplasty. Surgitek, a unit of Bristol-Myers Squibb, withdrew from the implant business, saying it was unable to meet the FDA's deadline. Together, the four PMAs filled 15 large file boxes; Dow Corning's application was by far the most extensive. On August 12, the head of the FDA Breast Prosthesis PMA task force submitted a review of Dow Corning's clinical studies, stating that they were "so weak that they cannot provide a reasonable assurance of the safety and effectiveness of these devices." He noted:

> [The studies] provide no assurance that the full range of complications are included, no dependable measure of the incidence of complications, no reliable measure of the revision rate and no quantitative measure of patient benefit. . . . [Physicians surveyed were instructed] to report only complications associated with the implant. As a result the only complications reported are those at the implant site. This prevents these investigations from detecting

systemic adverse effects. . . . [This] causes an underestimate of both the types and incidence of complications.[23]

Staff reviews of the PMAs submitted by other manufacturers were, if anything, even more scathing. On September 25, the FDA ordered implant makers to give doctors more information about the risk of implants as an interim measure while its PMA reviews continued.

Finally, on November 13, the FDA convened its Advisory Panel to consider the PMAs and to take further testimony. The hearings were highly contentious. The panel heard, once again, arguments concerning the dangers of implants. But the FDA hearings also generated intense support for implants from plastic surgeons, satisfied implant recipients, and breast cancer support and advocacy organizations. Among the most vocal defenders of the implants were women who had experienced successful reconstruction following mastectomies, including representatives of such peer support organizations as Y-Me and My Image After Breast Cancer. Several spoke of the positive psychological benefits of reconstruction, and warned that if the FDA took implants off the market, some women—knowing that reconstructive surgery was unavailable—would delay regular checkups for breast cancer, endangering their lives. Other witnesses argued that women should be free to choose implants, so long as they were fully informed of the benefits and risks of the devices.

The advisory panel debate was, by all accounts, heated. In the final analysis, the panel split hairs: It voted that although breast implants "did not pose a major threat to the health of users," the data submitted by manufacturers was "insufficient to prove safety." However, citing "a public health need," the panel recommended that the devices be left on the market.

The regulatory decision, at this point, passed to the FDA Commissioner, Dr. David A. Kessler. Appointed just a few months earlier, Kessler had brought a new commitment to regulatory activism to an agency marked by what some viewed as a pattern of weak government oversight during the Reagan administration.[24] Now, the fledgling commissioner had two months—until mid-January—to rule on the panel's recommendation on breast implants.

UNAUTHORIZED LEAKS

Unfolding events, however, forced Kessler's hand sooner. In December, a San Francisco jury returned a verdict in *Hopkins v. Dow Corning*, awarding Mariann Hopkins $7.3 million—by far the largest victory ever for a plaintiff in a breast implant suit. Hopkins' attorney claimed that his client's implants (made by Dow Corning in 1976) had ruptured and spilled silicone gel, causing severe joint aches, muscle pain, fatigue, and weight loss. Hopkins had been disabled by a disorder her doctors diagnosed as "mixed connective tissue disease." The woman's attorney told the jury that "this case is about corporate greed and outright fraud." Dow Corning immediately moved to have the legal records in the case—which included hundreds of pages of internal company memos Hopkins' attorney had subpoenaed—sealed.

Somehow, however, the documents from the Hopkins trial ended up in Commissioner Kessler's hands. Their contents evidently alarmed him. On January 6, 1992, Kessler abruptly reversed the FDA's November decision and called for a 45-day moratorium on all sales of silicone gel breast implants pending further study of their safety, and he recalled the advisory panel to consider "new evidence." Both the plastic surgeons and Dow Corning were furious. Dr. Norman Cole, president of the American Society of Plastic and Reconstructive Surgeons, took the unusual step of calling a press conference to brand Kessler's action as "unconscionable—an outrage." Cole said that the sudden moratorium on implant sales had "created hysteria, anxiety, and panic" and called on Kessler to reconstitute the advisory panel, which he called unqualified to judge the safety of the devices. For its part, Dow Corning demanded publicly to know what "new evidence" Kessler had obtained and restated the company's intention to block any release of "nonscientific" internal memoranda. Robert Rylee, chief of Dow Corning's health care business, called a press conference to repeat the company's contention that "the cumulative body of credible scientific evidence shows that the implants are safe and effective."[25,26]

"RANKING RIGHT UP THERE WITH THE PINTO GAS TANK"

Dow Corning's efforts to block release of the Hopkins documents, however, failed. On January 13, *New York Times* reporter Philip J. Hilts—saying only that he had obtained the material from "several sources"—broke the Hopkins case memos in a page one article, under the headline "Maker Is Depicted as Fighting Tests on Implant Safety."[27] In a summary of the contents of several hundred internal company memos, Hilts charged that Dow Corning's safety studies were "inadequate" and that serious questions raised by its own scientific research and by doctors' complaints had not been answered.

More damaging revelations were yet to come. Over the next several weeks, newspaper readers learned of the following incidents, drawn from the company's internal documents:

- In a 1980 memo, Dow Corning salesman Bob Schnabel had reported to his marketing manager that he had received complaints from a California plastic surgeon who was "downright indignant" because the implant envelopes were "greasy" and had experienced "excessive gel bleed." "The thing that is really galling is that I feel like I have been beaten by my own company instead of the competition. To put a questionable lot of mammaries on the market is inexcusable," Schnabel wrote his manager. "It has to rank right up there with the Pinto gas tank."

- In 1985, Bill Boley, a company scientist, had warned that a particular formulation of the gel could cause cancer, and called for further testing. "Without [it]," he argued, ". . . I think we have excessive personal and corporate liability exposure."
- Marketing manager Chuck Leach had reported in a memo that he had told a group of doctors that he had "assured them, with crossed fingers, that Dow Corning had an active study [of safety issues] under way." (Leach later angrily disputed the interpretation given his remarks by the media, saying in a letter to the Associated Press that he had meant the term "crossed fingers" in a "hopeful" rather than a "lying" sense.)
- Dr. Charles Vinnik, a Las Vegas plastic surgeon, had had an extensive correspondence with the company reporting his dissatisfactions with the product. In one letter, he charged that he felt "like a broken record" and told of an incident in which an implant had ruptured and spilled its contents—which he described as having the "consistency of 50 weight motor oil"—onto the operating room floor.

Whether wholly justified or not, the memos created a strong impression that Dow Corning had been aware of safety concerns about its implants for many years and had failed to act on this knowledge. The press moved in aggressively, attacking Dow Corning for its "moral evasions"; a widely reprinted cartoon depicted a Dow Corning executive apparently deflating as silicone gel oozed from his body.

A MODEL ETHICAL CITIZEN

That Dow Corning was being labeled publicly as "a company adrift without a moral compass"—as one *New York Times* columnist put it several days after the internal memos broke in the press[28]—struck many in and around the company as deeply unjust. Ironically, Dow Corning Corporation was widely regarded in the business community as a model for its efforts to institutionalize ethical behavior.

At the center of Dow Corning's efforts was a formal code of conduct and an unusual procedure for monitoring compliance. In 1976—the first full year of sales for its new generation breast implants—the company's board of directors had appointed a three-person Audit and Social Responsibility Committee and charged it with developing a corporate code of ethical conduct. Top managers were motivated, in part, by a breaking scandal at that time in which several large companies had been accused of questionable payments to foreign heads of state to secure contracts. With a substantial portion of its operations overseas, Dow Corning wanted its behavior to be above reproach.

In 1977, the company published its first corporate code of conduct

(Appendix A), laying out a comprehensive statement of ethical standards. In order to ensure compliance, the company initiated a series of annual audits, in which top managers would visit various cities around the globe to evaluate corporate performance against code standards. Audits typically involved five to fifteen people and lasted a full day. Issues covered in the audits were wide-ranging, including, for example, competitor and customer relations, distribution and purchasing practices, employee welfare, and product and environmental stewardship. In addition, the company held training programs on the code, and its semiannual employee opinion survey included a section on business ethics.

Yet, for whatever reason, the company's widely admired procedures had failed to flag the safety of breast implants as an ethical concern. A routine 1990 ethics audit of the Arlington, Tennessee, plant that manufactured silicone implants, for example, did not bring to light any concerns about the product's safety. When later questioned about the apparent failure of the audit procedure, Jere D. Marciniak, chairman of the conduct committee, pointed out that normally product safety issues would come before the relevant business board, not the ethics review. "It wouldn't have been necessary to bring up [the implants' safety] inside a code-of-conduct meeting unless an employee thought the [Medical Device Business Board's] process wasn't working well and wanted to raise the issue," he noted.[29,30]

A "HARDBALL" STRATEGY

As the controversy widened, Dow Corning's response, in the words of one *Wall Street Journal* reporter, was to "play hardball."[31] On January 14—eight days after the FDA had announced its moratorium on implant sales and one day after the first leaked documents appeared in the press—Dow Corning took a $25 million charge against fourth quarter 1991 earnings to cover costs of its legal liability, unused inventory, and efforts to prove implants safe. The company also suspended implant production and placed workers at the company's manufacturing facilities on temporary layoff, with full pay and benefits. Investors, apparently alarmed by this turn of events, knocked down the stock price of both Corning, Inc., and Dow Chemical as they contemplated the parent firms' potential liability.

Implant recipients and trial lawyers were also contemplating the liability question. During the week following the FDA's decision to place a moratorium on implants, one prominent plaintiff's attorney reported he was fielding phone calls from fifty to sixty potential clients a day. By March, as many as 600 lawsuits had been filed against Dow Corning and other breast implant makers, according to Karen Koskoff, co-chair of the breast implant litigation group of the Association of Trial Lawyers of

America. The National Products Liability Database estimated that Dow Corning had been sued at least 54 times in federal court and possibly more than 100 times in state courts. Frank C. Whiteside, Dow Corning's attorney, disputed these figures, saying that there were far fewer than 200 cases pending against his client.[32]

The unauthorized leaks created tremendous pressure on Dow Corning to release its own documents to the public. The FDA publicly called on the company on January 20 to release the material so that women and their doctors could evaluate the new evidence for themselves, rather than simply relying on news reports. (The agency, although in possession of the documents, could not release them because they were still protected under court order.) The company responded two days later by releasing a group of scientific studies—but not the infamous "Pinto" memo and other internal materials that the company dubbed "unscientific."

Suspension of breast implant sales and release of the scientific studies did not slow down the crisis engulfing the company. On January 29, in an apparent acknowledgment of the severity of the situation, the company hired former Attorney General Griffin B. Bell—who had performed a similar role at Exxon Corporation following the Valdez oil spill and at E.F. Hutton following the check-kiting scandal—to investigate its behavior in making implants.

Finally, on February 10—following a top-level intervention by the chairmen of Corning, Inc., and Dow Chemical, both of whom sat on Dow Corning's board—the Board of Directors executed a stunning management shakeup. Dow Corning demoted chief executive Lawrence A. Reed to the position of chief operating officer and forced longtime board chairman John S. Ludington to retire. Keith R. McKennon was named chairman and CEO. Simultaneously, the board announced that it would release to the public fifteen scientific reports and ninety-four nonscientific memos or letters from company files, including the "Pinto" and "crossed fingers" memos, as well as other potentially damaging materials that had not yet been reported by the media.

Several top executives, including Robert Rylee and Robert LeVier, technical director of Dow Corning's Health Care Businesses, met the press the same day to present the company's perspective. Rylee defended the company's decision not to release the documents earlier, saying:

> Our motives are simple. First and foremost, these memos do not answer fundamental questions and concerns that women have about breast implants. And by focusing attention on the memos rather than the science that supports the device, we do nothing but further raise the anxiety level of women and physicians and scientists.

Rylee told the packed press room that "while we are not happy with the memos, we have nothing to hide, and we believe that each memo put in its proper context can be understood and explained." For example, in the case of the infamous "Pinto" memo, Rylee stated:

> The memo was written by a salesman who had an unhappy customer, so obviously he, as a salesman, was unhappy. . . . We believe the doctor was unhappy about the way the implant appeared, rather than the safety or effectiveness of the product. . . .

Rylee categorized many of the memos as "sensational and anecdotal reports, versus true science." Many, he said, were best understood as part of the normal give-and-take that occurs within a technical organization, "one part of a multifaceted dialogue or communication or discussion that goes on," and did not reflect fundamental problems. By pulling various statements out of context, Rylee implied, the press had misrepresented questions scientists might legitimately raise in the course of their inquiry as final conclusions.

He closed the press conference by denying categorically that implants could cause autoimmune disease or cancer.[33]

FACING A CRUCIAL DECISION

On February 20, the day after his testimony before the FDA, McKennon received word from Washington. After three hours of tense debate, the FDA advisory panel had voted just after 5 P.M. to recommend that implants be taken off the market, except for women needing reconstruction following mastectomies or to correct serious deformities. All implant recipients would be required to enroll in clinical studies. Cosmetic augmentations would be strictly limited to those required by the design of the clinical trials. Commissioner Kessler would have 60 days to rule on the panel's recommendation.

McKennon would have to lay a plan of action before his board soon—he certainly could not wait another two months for the FDA's next move. The breast implant business, he had learned, had not made any money for Dow Corning for the past five years. Even in its heyday, it had contributed no more than 1 percent of the company's total revenues. Some of his top executives had urged him just to get out of the implant business altogether and let the attorneys mop up the liability problems. Many in the company felt that the huge settlement in the Hopkins case would be greatly reduced on appeal, and the company's $250 million in insurance would be sufficient to cover their liability. McKennon reflected on these issues as he contemplated his next actions. Certainly, he needed to act decisively to stem Dow Corning's financial losses. But, he pondered, did the company not also have—as he had put it to a reporter a few days earlier—an "overriding responsibility. . . to the women who have our implants"?[34] And what of the company's reputation, so carefully nurtured, for always upholding the highest standards of ethical behavior?

Dow Corning Corporation Corporate Code of Business Conduct, 1977

A MATTER OF INTEGRITY

Dow Corning believes in private enterprise. We will seek to establish an atmosphere of trust and respect between business and members of society, an atmosphere where business and the public understand, accept, and recognize the values and needs of each other.

To establish and promote this atmosphere of mutual trust and respect, Dow Corning accepts as our responsibility a recognition, evaluation and sensitivity to social needs. We will meet this responsibility by utilizing our technological and management skills to develop products and services that will further the development of society.

The watchword of Dow Corning worldwide activities is integrity. We recognize that due to local differences in custom and law, business practice differs throughout the world. We believe that business is best conducted and society best served within each country when business practice is based on the universal principles of honesty and integrity.

We recognize that our social responsibilities must be maintained at the high standards which lead to respect and trust by society. A clear definition of our social responsibilities should be an integral part of our corporate objectives and be clearly communicated to every employee.

STATEMENT OF GENERAL CONDUCT

We shall not tolerate payments in any illegal or questionable form, or non-standard commissions or other compensation, given or received, that may influence business decisions.

We shall not make any political contribution nor participate in partisan political activity as a company, recognizing however the rights of employees to participate in legal political processes as private citizens.

We shall be knowledgeable of local laws and customs and operate within them. On the other hand, when we are not being treated legally or ethically we will pursue whatever legitimate recourses are available to us.

RESPONSIBILITIES TO OUR EMPLOYEES

Relations with employees are based on the understanding that attracting and retaining talented and dedicated employees is vital to the accomplishment of financial and social objectives.

Our responsibilities to our employees are:

To manage our activities in such a way as to provide security and opportunities for our productive employees.

To hire, train, evaluate, and advance on the basis of individual ability, contribution, potential, interest and company needs without distinction as to nationality, sex, age, color or religion.

To compensate in accordance with local, national or industry practice.

To provide a safe and healthy work environment that at least meets the applicable governmental laws and regulations.

To provide a work environment that encourages individual self-fulfillment, open communication and free interchange of information and ideas.

RESPONSIBILITIES TO HOST COUNTRIES IN WHICH WE OPERATE

Activities in host countries are based on the premise that we can and wish to contribute to the economic objectives of the host government while concurrently meeting our corporate objectives.

Our responsibilities to host countries are:

To preserve and, where possible, enhance the environment through elimination or control of pollution.

To conserve natural resources.

To design and modify facilities which meet or exceed current and anticipated environmental and safety laws and regulations.

To hire, train, and qualify host country nationals for positions of responsibility consistent with their demonstrated capabilities.

To pay our required share of taxes and duties but resist inequitable or double taxation between countries.

To resolve any government relations problems or conflicts among overlapping jurisdictions through prompt, direct and open discussions with responsible government officials.

To follow responsible monetary and credit practices and conduct foreign exchange operations not for speculative purposes, but in accordance with normal business requirements and to protect our exposure fluctuations.

To encourage the flow of our technology across borders to the extent needed and appropriate in our local operations and markets, and to receive adequate compensation and protection of this technology.

APPENDIX B:

TIME LINE

1940s: Dow Chemical Corporation and Corning Glass Works form a joint venture to develop and produce military applications for silicone as lubricant, sealant, and coolant.

1950s: Dow Corning develops numerous commercial applications for silicone.

1962: Dow Corning invents the silicone breast implant.

1975: Dow Corning develops and markets new generation of softer, more responsive breast implants.

1976: Congress gives the FDA power to regulate medical devices. However, breast implants are excluded because they are already on the market.

1976: Materials engineer Thomas Talcott quits Dow Corning in protest, citing company inattention to safety concerns with the new implants.

1976: Dow Corning establishes an ethics program, publishes its first Code of Conduct, and initiates annual ethics audits.

1984: Maria Stern successfully sues Dow Corning, claiming foreign body reaction to silicone.

1985: Dow Corning warns doctors and women of possible side effects, including capsular contracture and inflammation.

1989: FDA reclassifies breast implants as Class III devices and order their makers to provide evidence of implants' safety within 30 months.

September, 1991: Surgitek drops out of the breast implant business, saying it can not meet the FDA deadline.

November, 1991: FDA panel finds that safety data submitted by the industry inadequate, but recommends silicone breast implants be left on the market to meet "a public health need."

December, 1991: Mariann Hopkins receives $7.3 million judgment against Dow Corning in San Francisco federal court.

January 6, 1992: FDA calls for a 45-day moratorium on the sale and use of silicone breast implants, citing insufficient evidence of their safety, and asks its advisory panel to examine new evidence.

January 13, 1992: *The New York Times* publishes unauthorized leaks from internal Dow Corning documents.

January 14, 1992: Dow Corning suspends production of breast implants and takes a $25 million charge against fourth quarter, 1991, earnings to cover costs of legal liability, unused inventory, and efforts to prove implants safe. Workers at the company's manufacturing facilities are placed on temporary layoff.

January 20, 1991: The FDA asks Dow Corning to make public documents on implants so that women and their doctors can evaluate evidence for themselves.

January 22, 1992: Dow Corning releases a group of scientific studies to the public.

January 29, 1992: Dow Corning hires former Attorney General Griffin B. Bell to investigate its behavior in making implants.

February 10, 1992: Dow Corning names Keith R. McKennon chairman and chief executive officer, demoting CEO Lawrence A. Reed, who becomes chief operating officer. John S. Ludington, Chairman, retires.

February 10, 1992: Dow Corning releases to the public several hundred additional pages of internal documents, annotated by the firm, including the "Pinto" memo.

February 18, 1992: FDA opens three days of hearings to reconsider whether or not silicone breast implants should remain on the market.

February 20, 1992: FDA panel recommends that silicone breast implants be limited to women who have had mastectomies or who have seriously deformed breasts, and that all implant recipients be required to participate in clinical trials. FDA Commissioner David Kessler has until April 20 to make a final decision on the panel's recommendation.

NOTES

1. Lois Ember, "Silicone Breast Implants: New Dow Corning Chief to Tackle Crisis," *Chemical and Engineering News*, February 17, 1992, pp. 4-5.

2. Larry Reibstein, "Fighting the Implant 'Fire,'" *Newsweek*, February 24, 1992, p. 9.

3. Don Whitehead, *The Dow Story: The History of the Dow Chemical Company* (New York: McGraw Hill, 1968).

4. Eugene G. Rochow, *Silicon and Silicones* (Berlin: Springer-Verlag, 1987).
5. Barnaby J. Feder, "P.R. Mistakes Seen in Breast Implant Case," *New York Times*, January 29, 1992.
6. William C. Coggin, "How the Multidimensional Structure Works at Dow Corning," *Harvard Business Review*, January/February 1974, pp. 54-65.
7. Office of Technology Assessment, *Federal Policies on the Medical Devices Industry* (New York: Pergamon Press, 1984).
8. Philip J. Hilts, "Maker Is Depicted As Fighting Tests on Implant Safety," *New York Times*, January 13, 1992, pp. A1, A12.
9. Tim Smart, "This Man Sounded the Silicone Alarm—in 1976," *Business Week*, January 27, 1992, p. 34.
10. Leslie Berkman, "Implant Whistle Blower Says He Warned Dow," *Los Angeles Times*, February 19, 1992.
11. Bradford Cannon, "The Flowering of Plastic Surgery," *Journal of the American Medical Association*, February 9, 1990, 263(6), pp. 862-864.
12. Susan Faludi, *Backlash: The Undeclared War Against American Women* (New York: Crown, 1991), pp. 217-18.
13. American Society of Plastic and Reconstructive Surgeons, "Comments on the Proposed Classification of Inflatable Breast Prosthesis and Silicone Gel Filled Breast Prosthesis," July 1, 1982, pp. 4-5, reported in Joan E. Rigdon, "Plastic Surgeons Had Warnings on Safety of Silicone Implants," *Wall Street Journal*, March 12, 1992, p. A8.
14. Marsha F. Goldsmith, "Image of Perfection Once the Goal—Now Women Just Seek Damages," *Journal of the American Medical Association*, 267(18), May 13, 1992, p. 2439.
15. Philip J. Hilts, "Studies See Greater Implant Danger," *New York Times*, February 9, 1992.
16. Felicity Barringer, "Many Surgeons Are Reassuring Their Patients on Silicone Implants," *New York Times*, January 29, 1992. 17. Philip J. Hilts, "Panel to Consider What Sort of Rules Should Control Gel Implants," *New York Times*, February 18, 1992, p. A14.
17. Philip J. Hilds, "Panel to Consider What Sort of Rules Should Control Gel Implants," *New York Times*, February 18, 1992, p. A14.
18. Marsha F. Goldsmith, *op. cit.*, p. 2439.
19. Philip J. Hilts, "Panel to Consider What Sort of Rules Should Control Gel Implants," *op. cit.*, p. A14.
20. Sybil Niden Goldrich, "Restoration Drama," *Ms.*, June 1988.
21. Marilyn Chase, "A Consumer Crusader With An M.D. Is A Pain to the Health Industry," *Wall Street Journal*, April 7, 1992, p. A18
22. Public Citizen Health Research Group, *Health Letter*, various issues.
23. Diana Zuckerman, Memo to Congressman Ted Weiss, "PMA Applications for Silicone Breast Implants," September 12, 1991.
24. Christine Gorman, "Special Report: Can Drug Firms Be Trusted?" *Time*, February 10, 1992, pp. 42-46.
25. Philip J. Hilts, "Maker of Silicone Breast Implants Says Data Show Them to Be Safe," *New York Times*, January 14, 1992, pp. A1, A13.
26. Felicity Barringer, "F.D.A. Accused of Creating Panic Over Breast Implants," *New York Times*, January 16, 1992.
27. Philip J. Hilts, "Maker Is Depicted As Fighting Tests on Implant Safety," *op. cit.*, A1, A12.
28. Steven Fink, "Dow Corning's Moral Evasions," *New York Times*, February 16, 1992, p. F13.

29. John A. Byrne, "The Best Laid Ethics Programs...Couldn't Stop a Nightmare at Dow Corning," *Business Week*, March 9, 1992, pp. 67-69.
30. Barnaby J. Feder, "P.R. Mistakes Seen in Breast Implant Case," *The New York Times*, January 29, 1992.
31. Thomas M. Burton and Joan E. Rigdon, "Management Shake-up at Dow Corning Signals a More Conciliatory Attitude," *Wall Street Journal*, February 18, 1992, pp. A3, A10.
32. Don J. DeBenedictis, "FDA Action Spurs Implant Suits," *American Bar Association Journal*, March 1992, p. 20.
33. Federal News Service, "News Conference: Dow Corning Corporation Regarding Breast Implants," February 10, 1992.
34. Thomas M. Burton and Scott McMurray, "Dow Corning Still Keeps Implant Data From Public, Despite Vow of Openness," *Wall Street Journal*, February 18, 1992.

5

THE CORPORATION
AND SOCIETY

INTRODUCTION

The corporation is the dominant form of economic organization in the United States and the rest of the developed world. As a result of their size and reach, corporations have an immense impact on the welfare of countless people, many of whom are far removed from the centers of corporate power. Corporations also exert a strong influence on their own members, which is capable of leading ordinary employees and high level executives to commit unethical and even illegal acts.

The first two cases in this section focus on the factors, both personal and corporate, that contributed to scandals at two of America's best-known corporations. One of these, Beech-Nut Nutrition Corporation, is a household name in the baby food industry, where consumer confidence is a necessity. This did not prevent its two top executives from ignoring evidence that the "apple juice" it was selling for babies contained no apples. The company pleaded guilty to 215 counts of violating federal food and drug laws and agreed to pay a $2 million fine, and the president and vice president were each sentenced to a year in prison and fined $100,000. The second case concerns the brokerage firm E.F. Hutton, which is also a household name, in part because of its advertising slogan "When E.F. Hutton speaks, people listen." This once-proud company pleaded guilty to 2,000 counts of mail fraud and paid a $2 million fine for a complicated system of overdrafts at 400 banks that allowed it to draw interest on more than $1 billion dollars of uncollected or nonexistent funds.

Many corporate crimes result from unbridled greed. The scandals at Beech-Nut and E.F. Hutton, however, involved executives who were, to all outward appearances, deeply loyal to the corporation and concerned only with its success. Saul W. Gellerman has described such employees as basically decent individuals—often proverbial "pillars" of their communities—who are led into a series of damaging mistakes by self-serving rationalizations. In a *Harvard Business Review* article, "Why 'Good' Managers Make Bad Ethical Choices," he cites four causes of this type of misconduct:

- A belief that the activity is within reasonable ethical and legal limits—that is, that it is not "really" illegal or immoral.
- A belief that the activity is in the individual's or the corporation's best interests—that the individual would somehow be expected to undertake the activity.
- A belief that the activity is "safe" because it will never by found out or publicized.
- A belief that because the activity helps the company the company will condone it and even protect the person who engages in it.[1]

These rationalizations are abundantly displayed in the two cases, but a full explanation of the course of events at Beech-Nut and E.F. Hutton also requires us to look beyond the individuals involved to the moral environment of the corporation. Unethical conduct was not explicitly encouraged at these companies, but a climate was inadvertently created that contributed powerfully to the moral blindness that occurred. Lessons can be drawn from these cases about creating and maintaining an ethical corporate environment.

International business involves some especially perplexing ethical dilemmas for corporations, because a company's convictions about acceptable practices have a way of becoming unsettled when business is conducted in other countries with pronounced cultural, social, legal, and economic differences. One common problem arises from the existence of different standards in other parts of the world. When standards conflict, which ones should a corporation follow? —Those of the host country or those observed at home? Or, are there special standards that apply in international business?

Bribery, for example, is an unethical business practice in the United States, and a federal law, the Foreign Corrupt Practices Act, forbids American firms to bribe foreign government officials, even in countries where bribery is legal or, at least, commonly practiced. The wisdom of this piece of legislation has been widely debated, with some arguing that U.S. morality should stop at the water's edge, while others contend that American firms should adhere to the same high standards of morality around the globe. The Foreign Corrupt Practices Act, which was passed in 1977 and amended in 1988, permits some kinds of payments and, more importantly, exonerates companies from responsibility for acts by their agents under certain conditions. In drafting a code of ethics for international business, corporations have a choice, therefore, between minimal legal compliance and stronger policies that go beyond the law.

The case "Wait International and Questionable Payments" describes the choices faced by a fictional company with extensive foreign dealings that is reviewing its code of ethics. The person responsible for recommending any changes is concerned not only that the code give adequate guidance to employees so that they will not inadvertently violate the law but also that the company maintain a high level of integrity in its dealings abroad. This case vividly illustrates the dilemmas posed by different standards in international business as well as the interplay between ethical considerations and the practical demands of business in decision-making situations.

In "H.B. Fuller in Honduras," a foreign subsidiary of a Minnesota-based corporation is called upon to stop the abuse of one of its products by street children in a Central American country. "Glue sniffing" by youngsters in the slums of Honduras and elsewhere is known to cause irreversible brain damage that further exacerbates the social problems of the region. A similar situation was faced by The Gillette Company when news stories revealed that children in the United States were pouring bottles of their popular correction fluid White Out into plastic bags and inhaling the vapors. However, Gillette was able to work with government and nonprofit agencies to develop an effective drug-education strategy. H.B. Fuller, by contrast, had to cope with an uncertain political situation in Honduras and the intractable problems of third-world poverty in creating an adequate corporate response. Many companies, including H.B. Fuller, have corporate mission statements that express a concern for the welfare of the community, but what do such commitments entail when the "community" is a distant and very different place?

Finally, "Campbell Soup Company" is a richly detailed case study that covers a difficult period in the history of a corporation with a reputation for active social involvement. The company was forced to reassess the meaning of corporate social responsibility by the demands of a farm labor group for improvements in working and living conditions on the farms that supply tomatoes to Campbell. In developing a corporate response, Campbell had to manage relations with diverse constituencies that included not only traditional stakeholders, such as employees and stockholders, but also farm workers who were not directly employed by Campbell. In addition to the legitimate demands of the farm labor group, Campbell also had to cope with boycotts and pressure by church organizations and other third parties. The case provides an opportunity to view the development of corporate strategy in a complex situation where the social responsibility of a company is not immediately evident.

NOTES

1. Saul W. Gellerman, "Why 'Good' Managers Make Bad Ethical Choices," *Harvard Business Review*, July-August 1986, p. 85.

THE ENVIRONMENT OF THE CORPORATION

INTO THE MOUTHS OF BABES

James Traub

It is well within the reach of most white-collar criminals to assume an air of irreproachable virtue, especially when they're about to be sentenced. But there was something unusually compelling about the hearing of Niels L. Hoyvald and John F. Lavery as they stood before Judge Thomas C. Platt of the United States District Court in Brooklyn last month—especially in light of what they were being sentenced for. As president and vice president of the Beech-Nut Nutrition Corporation, Hoyvald and Lavery had sold millions of bottles of "apple juice" that they knew to contain little or no apple juice at all—only sugars, water, flavoring and coloring. The consumers of this bogus product were babies.

One prosecutor of the case, Thomas H. Roche, had summed up Beech-Nut's behavior as "a classic picture of corporate greed and irresponsibility." The company itself had pleaded guilty the previous fall to 215 counts of violating Federal food and drug laws, and had agreed to pay a $2 million fine, by far the largest ever imposed in the 50-year history of the Food, Drug and Cosmetic Act. Beech-Nut had confessed in a press release that it had broken a "sacred trust."

Yet there was Niels Hoyvald, 54 years old, tall, silver-haired, immaculately dressed, standing before Judge Platt with head bowed, as his attorney, Brendan V. Sullivan Jr., described him as "a person we would be proud to have in our family." When it was Hoyvald's turn to address the judge, he spoke firmly, but then his voice cracked as he spoke of his wife and mother: "I can hardly bear to look at them or speak to them," he said. "I ask for them and myself, please don't send me to jail."

Judge Platt was clearly troubled. He spoke in a semiaudible mutter that had the crowd in the courtroom craning forward. Though it was "unusual for a corporate executive to do time for consumer fraud," he said, he had "no alternative" but to sentence Hoyvald to a prison term of a year and a day, plus fines totaling $100,000. He then meted out the same punishment to the 56-year-old Lavery, who declined to speak on his own behalf. He received his sentence with no show of emotion.

The combination of babies, apple juice and a well-known name like Beech-Nut makes for a potent symbol. In fact, apple juice is not especially nutritious (bottlers often fortify it with extra Vitamin C), but babies love it

From *The New York Times Magazine*, July 24, 1988. Copyright © 1988 by The New York Times Company. Reprinted by permission.

and find it easy to digest. Parents are pleased to buy a product that says "no sugar added"—as Beech-Nut advertised—and seem to regard it as almost as pure and natural as mother's milk. That, of course, was the sacred trust Beech-Nut broke, and is now struggling to repair. The company's share of the $760 million United States baby-food market has dropped from a high of 20 percent in 1986, when Beech-Nut and the two executives were indicted, to 17 percent this year. Its losses in the fruit-juice market have been even more dramatic. Richard C. Theuer, the company's president since 1986, still gets a stream of letters from outraged parents "who don't realize that it was a long time ago." Some of them, he says are "almost obscene."

If parents are outraged by Beech-Nut's actions, many people are also baffled. Even after the trial and verdict, the question of motive lingers: why would two men with impeccable records carry out so cynical and reckless a fraud? Except for Theuer, no current Beech-Nut employee who was involved in the events of the trial agreed to be interviewed for this article, nor did Hoyvald or Lavery. But a vivid picture of the economic and psychological concerns that impelled the company along its ruinous course emerges from court documents and a wide range of interviews. The Beech-Nut baby-food scandal is a case study in the warping effects of blind corporate loyalty.

For three-quarters of the century after its founding in 1891 as a meat-packing company, Beech-Nut expanded steadily into a large, diversified food concern, eventually including Life Savers, Table Talk pies, Tetley tea, Martinson's coffee, chewing gum and, of course, baby food. The company had an image straight from Norman Rockwell—pure, simple, healthful. In 1969, Beech-Nut was taken over by the Squibb Corporation. Only four years later, a remnant of the old company was spun off and taken private by a group led by a lawyer, Frank C. Nicholas. The company that emerged from the Squibb umbrella sold only baby food, and, as in earlier years, regularly divided with Heinz the third or so of the market not controlled by Gerber. It was a completely new world for Beech-Nut's newly independent owners, and an extremely precarious one. Beech-Nut was in a continuous financial bind.

After an expensive and unsuccessful effort in the mid-1970s to market Beech-Nut as the "natural" baby food, the imperative to reduce costs became overwhelming. In 1977, when a Bronx-based supplier, who would later take the name Universal Juice, offered Beech-Nut a less-expensive apple-juice concentrate, the company abandoned its longtime supplier for the new source. The savings would never amount to much more than $250,000 a year, out of a $50 million-plus manufacturing budget, but Beech-Nut was under the gun.

At the time, the decision may have seemed insignificant. Ira Knickerbocker, head of agricultural purchasing at the main Beech-Nut plant in Canajoharie, N.Y., who has since retired, says that in 1977 the new concentrate was only slightly less expensive than the competition's. "There was never a question about the quality or anything else," he insists. Yet no other baby-food company, and no large apple-juice manufacturer, ever bought significant quantities of concentrate from Universal. In early 1981, Heinz would return the product to Universal after samples had failed to pass conventional laboratory tests and the supplier refused to let company officials visit the plant.

Another Federal prosecutor, John R. Fleder, contends that the low price of the Universal concentrate, which eventually reached 25 percent below the market, "should have been enough in itself to tip off anybody" that the concentrate was diluted or adulterated. Jack B. Hartog, a supplier who had sold Beech-Nut much of its apple concentrate until 1977, agrees with Fleder: "There was no question about it in the trade."

John Lavery, Beech-Nut's vice president of operations and manager of the plant in Canajoharie, did not question the authenticity of the concentrate. After spending his entire career at Beech-Nut, Lavery had risen to a position in which he managed almost 1,000 employees. In the small hamlets around Canajoharie, a company town in rural Montgomery County, northwest of Albany, Lavery was known as a figure of propriety and rectitude. "He was as straight and narrow as anything you could come up with," says Ed Gros, an engineer who worked with Lavery at Beech-Nut. Lavery was a fixture in the Methodist church, on the school board and in community organizations.

In 1978, after initial testing indicated the presence of impurities in the new concentrate, Lavery agreed to send two employees to inspect the "blending facility" that Universal's owner, Zeev Kaplansky, claimed to operate in New Jersey. The two reported that all they could find was a warehouse containing a few 55-gallon drums. The bizarre field trip aroused further suspicions among executives at the Canajoharie plant, but only one, Jerome J. LiCari, head of research and development, chose to act on them.

LiCari sent samples of the concentrate to an outside laboratory. The tests, he reported to Lavery, indicated that the juice was adulterated, probably with corn syrup. Rather than return the concentrate, or demand proof of its authenticity, as Heinz would do three years later, Lavery sent down the order that Kaplansky sign a "hold-harmless agreement," indemnifying Beech-Nut against damages arising from consumer and other complaints. (Ironically, in May 1987 Beech-Nut settled a class-action suit against it totaling $7.5 million.)

LiCari, however, was scarcely satisfied by Lavery's legalistic approach. Like Lavery, LiCari was also every bit the local boy. Born and raised in neighboring Herkimer County, he had worked in the Beech-Nut plant during summers home from college, and, after 14 years with Beech-Nut, he had achieved his greatest ambitions. Yet it was LiCari who accepted the solitary role of institutional conscience. In April 1979, and again in July, he sent samples of the concentrate to a second laboratory, in California. The April test again found signs of adulteration, but the July test did not. LiCari concluded that Kaplansky had switched from corn syrup to beet sugar, an adulterant that current technology could not detect. Once again he approached Lavery, suggesting that Beech-Nut require Kaplansky to repurchase the concentrate. This time, Lavery instructed that the concentrate be blended into mixed juices, where adulteration is far harder to detect. Lavery's attorney, Steven Kimelman, says that his client does not recall his rationale for the decision, but argues that on this matter, as on others, he acted in concert with other executives, including LiCari.

Lavery and LiCari were locked in a hopeless conflict of roles, values, and personality. Steven Kimelman characterizes Lavery as "more like a general. He's the kind of guy who gives orders, and he has no trouble making up his mind; LiCari was too much of a scientist type to him, and not practical enough." LiCari had become consumed by the issue of the concentrate. By the spring of 1981 he was working almost full time on tests to determine its purity. Finally, on Aug. 5, LiCari circulated a memo to executives, including Lavery. "A tremendous amount of circumstantial evidence," he wrote, makes for "a grave case against the current supplier" of apple concentrate. No matter what the cost, LiCari concluded, a new supplier should be found.

Several days later, LiCari was summoned to Lavery's office, where, as he told the jury, "I was threatened that I wasn't a team player, I wasn't working for the company, threatened to be fired." The choice could not have been more stark: capitulate, or leave.

Many of those who know Lavery find this picture of him simply unbelievable. The Canajoharie view is that Lavery was victimized. Ed Gros, Lavery's former colleague, speculates that LiCari "had a personal vendetta" against Lavery. Ira Knickerbocker blames the Government. Yet even Lavery's friends admit to a kind of moral bafflement. "I've lost a lot of sleep over this," says a former company vice president, Bill Johnsey.

Steven Kimelman denies that Lavery threatened LiCari, but concedes that his client made a "mistake in judgment." The mistake was in not kicking the matter up to Hoyvald when he received the Aug. 5 memo. Kimelman insists that Lavery "thought that LiCari tended to overreact," and in any case felt that there was no other concentrate whose purity he could entirely trust. In fact, LiCari's tests showed no signs of adulteration in several other, more expensive, concentrates. A harsher view is that Lavery acted quite consciously. "He just didn't care," says Thomas Roche, one of the prosecutors. "He showed an extraordinary amount of arrogance. I think his sole objective was to show Beech-Nut and Nestlé [since 1979, the corporate parent] that he could do well."

Or perhaps Lavery had simply blinded himself to the consequences of his acts. The apple juice had become merely a commodity and the babies merely customers. One exchange between another prosecutor, Kenneth L. Jost, and an executive at the Canajoharie plant, Robert J. Belvin, seemed to sum up Lavery's state of mind:

"Mr. Belvin, what did you do when you found that Beech-Nut had been using a product in what it called apple juice that was not in fact apple juice?"

"I—I became very upset."

"Why were you very upset?"

"Because we feed babies. . . ."

"Did you ever hear Mr. Lavery express a sentiment similar to that you have just described to the jury?"

"No."

By 1979, Beech-Nut's financial condition had become so parlous that Frank Nicholas admitted failure and sold the company to Nestlé S.A., the Swiss food giant. Nestlé arrived with $60 million in working capital and a commitment to restore a hallowed brand name to health. The view in the food industry was that Beech-Nut had been rescued from the brink. Yet evidence presented at the trial gives the exact opposite impression—of a Procrustean bed being prepared for nervous managers. Hoyvald, who chose to testify on his own behalf, admitted that in 1981, his first year as chief executive, he had grandiosely promised Nestlé that Beech-Nut would earn $700,000 the following year, though there would be a negative cash flow of $1.7 million. Hoyvald had arrived at Nestlé only a year before, but he was a seasoned executive in the food business. The answer nevertheless shot back from Switzerland: the cash flow for Beech-Nut, as for all other Nestlé subsidiaries, would have to be zero or better. "The pressure," as he conceded, "was on."

Hoyvald testified that he knew nothing about adulterated concentrate until the summer of 1982. In January 1981, however, LiCari had sent to both Lavery and Hoyvald a copy of an article in a trade magazine discussing signs of adulteration in apple juice, and had written and attached a memo noting, among other things, that "Beech-Nut has been concerned over the authenticity of fruit juice products." LiCari also told the jury that in August of that same year, several weeks after his disastrous confrontation with Lavery, he went to Beech-Nut's corporate headquarters in Fort Washington, Pa., to appeal to Hoyvald—an uncharacteristic suspension of his faith in the chain of command. Hoyvald had been appointed president only four months earlier, and LiCari testified that he liked and trusted his new boss, who he felt had a mandate from Nestlé to restore Beech-Nut's prestige. The meeting in Fort Washington persuaded LiCari that he had finally found an ally. Hoyvald, LiCari testified, "appeared shocked and surprised" at LiCari's report, and left him feeling "that something was going to be done and they would stop using it."

Then, month after month, nothing happened. Finally, at a late-fall company retreat at a ski resort in Vermont, LiCari raised the issue with Hoyvald one last time. Hoyvald told him, he testified, that he was unwilling to fire Lavery. (In his own testimony, Hoyvald denied that either meeting had taken place.)

LiCari was now convinced that the company was bent on lawbreaking, as he later testified, and rather than acquiesce, he quit, in January 1982. His allies concerned with quality control remained behind, but evidently none was stubborn or reckless enough to press his point.

Hoyvald, like Lavery, was a man with an exemplary background, though one that was a good deal more varied and sophisticated than his subordinate's. Born and raised in a provincial town in Denmark, he had relocated to the United States and received his Master of Business Administration degree from the University of Wisconsin in 1960. An ambitious man, Hoyvald had hopscotched across five companies before joining Beech-Nut as head of marketing in 1980, with the promise that he would be promoted to president within a year. Throughout his career, Hoyvald's watchword had been "aggressively marketing top quality products," as he wrote in a three-page "Career Path" addendum to a 1979 résumé. He had turned around the faltering Plumrose Inc., a large food company, by emphasizing quality, and he viewed the job at Beech-Nut as a chance to do just that.

In June 1982, Hoyvald's principles were abruptly tested when the quality of his own product was decisively challenged. A trade association, the Processed Apples Institute, had initiated an investigation into long-standing charges of adulteration throughout the apple-concentrate business. By April 1982, an investigator working for the institute, a former New York City narcotics detective named Andrew Rosenzweig (who is now chief investigator for the Manhattan District Attorney's office), was prowling around the Woodside, Queens, warehouse of a company called Food Complex, which was Universal's manufacturing arm. By diligent questioning, and searching by flashlight through a dumpster in the middle of many nights, Rosenzweig discovered that Food Complex omitted apples from its recipe altogether, and that its biggest customer was Beech-Nut. On June 25, Rosenzweig tracked a tanker truck full of sugar water out of the Food Complex loading dock and up the New York State Thruway to Canajoharie, where he planned to confront management with his findings. He was hoping to persuade the company to join a civil suit being prepared against Universal and Food Complex; but, expecting the worst, he secretly tape-recorded the ensuing conversation.

At the trial, the tape proved to be a damning piece of evidence. In the course of the discussion, Lavery and two other executives, instead of disputing Rosenzweig's claim that Beech-Nut was making juice from suspect concentrate, unleashed a cascade of tortuous rationalizations. When Rosenzweig explained that the trade association had made new strides in lab testing, Lavery, obviously panicking, suddenly announced: "At this point, we've made our last order from" Universal. But despite considerable pressure, Lavery refused to give Rosenzweig samples of the concentrate, and declined to join the suit. The one anxiety he expressed was the possibility of bad publicity.

On June 28, Paul E. Hillabush, the head of quality assurance at Canajoharie, called Hoyvald to tell him of Rosenzweig's visit. Hillabush testified that he suggested Beech-Nut recall the product. But Beech-Nut would not only have had to switch to a new and more expensive concentrate, it would have had to admit publicly that the product it had been selling since 1978 was bogus. The cover-up, which Lavery had begun three years earlier with the order to blend the concentrate in mixed juices, was attaining an irresistible momentum.

Hoyvald made the fateful decision to reject Hillabush's advice, and to devote the next eight weeks to moving the tainted products as fast as possible. It would be aggressive marketing, though not of a quality product.

The Apple Institute's suit, as it turned out, was only the first wave to hit the beach. Federal and state authorities had been investigating suppliers of adulterated concentrate since the spring, and the trail led them, too, to Canajoharie. On July 29, an inspector from the United States Food and Drug Administration arrived at the plant, announced that samples taken from supermarket shelves had proved to be adulterated, and took away cases of apple juice ready to be shipped. On Aug. 11, Paul Hillabush received a call from an old friend, Maurice Guerrette, an assistant director with the New York State Department of Agriculture and Markets, who reported much the same conclusion. Guerrette recalls receiving one of the great shocks of his life when Hillabush tried to laugh the whole thing off. It was only then that he realized—as would each investigator in his turn—that Beech-Nut was not the victim of a crime, but its conscious perpetrator.

Guerrette's phone call persuaded Lavery and others—incorrectly, as it turned out—that a seizure action was imminent. After consulting with Hoyvald, executives in Canajoharie decided to move the entire inventory of tainted juice out of the state's jurisdiction. And so, on the night of Aug. 12, nine tractor-trailers from Beech-Nut's trucking company were loaded with 26,000 cases of juice and taken in a ghostly caravan to a warehouse in Secaucus, N.J. One of America's most venerable food companies was fleeing the law like a bootlegger.

By the late summer of 1982, Beech-Nut was racing to unload its stock before regulators initiated a seizure action. On Sept. 1, Hoyvald managed to unload thousands of cases of juice from the Secaucus warehouse to Puerto Rico, despite the fact that the Puerto Rican distributor was already overstocked. Two weeks later, Hoyvald overruled his own lawyers and colleagues, who again suggested a recall, and ordered a feverish "foreign promotion"; under certain circumstances, American law does not prohibit the selling abroad of products banned at home. Within days, 23,000 cases were trucked at great expense from the company's San Jose, Calif., plant to Galveston, Tex., where they were off-loaded for the Dominican Republic, where they were sold at a 50 percent discount.

While Beech-Nut's sales staff shipped the evidence out to sea, its lawyers were holding the Federal and state agencies at bay. On Sept. 24, lawyers scheduled a meeting with F.D.A. officials that was designed to placate their adversaries. It worked. Three more weeks passed before the

F.D.A. Administrator, Taylor M. Quinn, threatened to seize the juice, and thus finally wrung from the company a pledge to begin a nationwide recall. New York State authorities, less patient, threatened a seizure before Beech-Nut hurriedly agreed to a state recall. But the delay allowed Niels Hoyvald to virtually complete his master plan.

By the middle of November Hoyvald could boast, in a report to his superior at Nestlé: "The recall has now been completed, and due to our many delays, we were only faced with having to destroy approximately 20,000 cases. We received adverse publicity in only one magazine." As it turned out, of course, Hoyvald's self-congratulation was premature.

Further Federal and state investigations exposed details of the cover-up, as well as the fact that Beech-Nut had continued to sell the juice in its mixed-juice product for six months after the recall. New York State sued Beech-Nut for selling an adulterated and misbranded product, and imposed a $250,000 fine, by far the largest such penalty ever assessed in the state for consumer violations. In November 1986, the United States Attorney obtained indictments of Hoyvald, Lavery, Beech-Nut, Zeev Kaplansky and Kaplansky's colleague Raymond H. Wells, the owner of Food Complex. Beech-Nut eventually settled by agreeing to pay a $2 million fine. Kaplansky and Wells, who had earlier settled the apple-institute suit with a financial agreement and by ceasing production of their concentrate, also pleaded guilty, and await sentencing. The F.D.A. referred the case to the Justice Department for criminal prosecution.

The case against Hoyvald and Lavery seemed overwhelming—so overwhelming that Lavery's first attorney suggested he plead guilty. Why did Lavery and Hoyvald insist on standing trial? Because both men, by most reports, are still convinced that they committed nothing graver than a mistake in judgment.

Hoyvald and Lavery seem to think of themselves as corporate patriots. Asked by one of the prosecutors why the entire inventory of concentrate was not destroyed once it came under suspicion, Hoyvald shot back testily: "And I could have called up Switzerland and told them I had just closed the company down. Because that is what would have been the result of it."

The questions of what Nestlé would have said, or did say, was not resolved by the trial. Jerome LiCari testified that in 1980 and 1981 he had expressed his concerns to six different Nestlé officials, including Richard Theuer, who was then a vice president of Nestlé and would become Beech-Nut's president in 1986. In an extraordinary effort to clear its reputation, Nestlé brought all six officials to court, mostly from Switzerland, and each one either contradicted LiCari's account or stated he had no memory of the alleged conversation. Nestlé is acutely sensitive to its public image, which was tarnished in the 1970s and early 80s when it aggressively promoted infant formula in third-world countries despite public health concerns, sparking international controversy and boycott campaigns.

Nestlé has defended its subsidiary's acts as vigorously as it defended its own in the past. The company has spent what sources close to the case estimate as several million dollars in defending the two executives, and has agreed to keep both men on the payroll—at annual salaries of $120,000 and $70,000—until their current appeals are exhausted.

In a memo sent to Canajoharie employees after the verdict, James M. Biggar, president of Nestlé's American operations, claimed that LiCari had confused "what he wished he had said" with "what he actually said or did," and faulted management only for failing to keep an "open door."

Richard Theuer, the man Nestlé chose to replace Hoyvald, promises to keep that door open. He hopes to convince the public that at "the new Beech-Nut" decisions will be taken, as he says, "on behalf of the babies."

WHEN E.F. HUTTON SPEAKS. . .

Joanne B. Ciulla

On May 2, 1985, E.F. Hutton pleaded guilty to mail and wire fraud. The brokerage house had been charged with fraudulently obtaining the use of more than $1 billion in interest-free funds by systematically overdrawing checking accounts at some 400 banks. Hutton's attorneys bargained with the Justice Department and agreed on a $2 million fine plus $750,000 to cover the cost of the investigation. Because the fine for mail fraud was $1,000 per case, Hutton's attorneys pleaded guilty to 2,000 counts of fraud. (Ironically, about the time of Hutton's settlement the fine for mail fraud was raised to $500,000 per count.)

Robert Fomon, CEO of E.F. Hutton, hoped that the guilty plea would minimize public scrutiny and put an end to the scandal—but it didn't. Investigations of the firm continued and were closely monitored by the press. E.F. Hutton, one of the most respected brokerage houses on Wall Street, became "the company that pleaded guilty to 2,000 counts of fraud."

COMPANY BACKGROUND

E.F. Hutton was founded by Edward F. Hutton and George Ellis, Jr., in 1904. The Hutton partnership aimed at maintaining a strong financial base and providing complete service to elite investors. It was the first New York Stock Exchange firm to open an office on the West Coast. As Western Union had no telegraph service across the Rocky Mountains, Hutton advanced it $50,000 to complete its first coast-to-coast telegraph system, which was opened in 1905. This established Hutton as a firm dedicated to speedy service.

This case was written by Joanne B. Ciulla. Reprinted by permission of the author.

Because of the importance of the telegraph wire to their business, brokerage firms were called "wire houses." This ability to move funds and to buy and sell quickly benefited Hutton's West Coast clients. For example, during the 1906 San Francisco earthquake, Hutton office managers retrieved their records from the destroyed office, and knowing that clients would need cash but could not be reached, liquidated their positions before news of the quake hit the East Coast.

While sharing in the prosperity of the 1920s, Hutton pursued a conservative course in keeping within margin requirements. Thus, when the market crashed in 1929, it lost less than $50,000 on its unsecured accounts. Even during the Great Depression that followed, Hutton continued to expand and improve its communications networks. By 1962 the firm had grown so much that it dissolved the partnership and became a corporation.[1]

ROBERT FOMON AND THE HUTTON ORGANIZATION

After graduating from the University of Southern California with a degree in English, Robert Fomon was hired by Hutton as a sales trainee in 1951. He told one interviewer that his first impression of the securities industry was an unrealistic one which came from reading F. Scott Fitzgerald novels.[2] Nonetheless, Fomon learned the business and worked his way up to become head of the company's West Coast corporate finance, syndicate, and institutional sales. He then was named CEO in 1970. The choice of Fomon was controversial. Some people in the firm had wanted John Shad, who was then head of corporate finance, to be CEO. (Shad left Hutton in 1981 to become chairman of the SEC.)

When Fomon became CEO, Hutton was losing money because the market was depressed and the firm's staff had grown too large—commissions accounted for almost 68 percent of Hutton's revenues (by 1979 commissions would shrink to 38 percent). Fomon began his term of office by firing 600 employees and trimming losses that had reached $1 million a month. This aggressive move, combined with the healthy market of 1972, got Hutton out of the red.

In 1972 Hutton became a publicly owned company, but Fomon continued to run the firm in the loose style of a partnership. The managing partners all sat on the board of directors. There were no outsiders on the board until 1974 when Harvard Business School Professor Warren Law became a member. Ten years later Edward F. Hutton's daughter, actress Dina Merrill, and California attorney Edward Cazier, Jr., joined the board. Baseball commissioner Peter Ueberroth became a member in 1984.

Disliking tight organizational systems, Fomon believed that "charts and boxes do not solve your problems." He said, "It's much more important to select the right people and I think that I'm pretty good at that."[3] But Fomon, who was described as moody and aloof, took little interest in the details of management. He did, however, pay close attention to business deals and was known to veto certain projects for ethical reasons or because of his personal tastes. For example, he refused to let Hutton underwrite a casino project and once vetoed a deal because it included a fast-food business.[4] Under Fomon's leadership, Hutton went from 95 branch offices and 1,250 account executives in 1972 to 400 offices worldwide and 6,600 account executives in 1985.

Hutton's strength was its retail sales force and distribution system. Hutton's rewards system plus its decentralized management system engendered a strong independent entrepreneurial spirit among employees in its branch offices. While the large and bureaucratic Merrill Lynch was symbolized by the herd, Hutton was best symbolized by the lone cowboy. At Hutton it was said that the client belonged to the account executive, whereas at other places like Merrill Lynch, the client belonged to the company.

INTEREST INCOME IN THE SECURITIES INDUSTRY

Interest income is very important to a brokerage firm. Basically, said one industry specialist, "Wire houses are giant factories designed to collect money from customers and lend it out." In order to do business with a brokerage house, both retail and institutional customers must either have money on hand to buy shares, or they can buy shares on credit (or margin). To buy on margin, they must borrow from the broker and deposit the shares as collateral. If clients want to sell short (sell stocks that they do not own so as to profit from a falling market), they must deposit the cash value of those shares in their brokerage account. This system boosts profits whenever interest rates rise—especially since customers often hold their profits in their brokerage account until another investment opportunity comes along.

Brokerage firms are allowed by the SEC to use the credit balances left by customers to lend out to other clients. For example, in 1981 the Bache Group described its policy this way:

> A portion of the funds loaned to customers by the company is derived from sources which are largely interest free to the company. [As a result of this] the company earns income in some cases equal to the entire interest rate charged to its customers. A primary source of such funds are the excess funds left with the company by its customers.[5]

With interest rates at 17 percent in 1981, Shearson Loeb Rhoades was able to cover all of its overhead with "Saturday and Sunday money," which is interest income derived from waiting until Monday to move customers' money into their private accounts.

Motivation in the brokerage business was based primarily on monetary rewards. The main source of account executives' income was the 1/2 to 2 percent commission they made on each trade—the more they traded, the higher the commission. High producers were treated like prima donnas. Firms regularly tried to steal good sales people from each other by offering them bonuses—which were sometimes as much as $300,000—to defect. The top producers at Hutton tended to gravitate to managerial positions. Branch managers received 10 percent of the net profit of their office; however, some successful sales people preferred to stay in sales, where they could earn more money.

GEORGE BALL

In 1977 Fomon named 38-year-old George Ball as Hutton president and head of retail operations. Ball was an aggressive salesman who had quickly worked his way up through the branch system. He began as an account executive trainee in 1962, became the Newark branch manager in 1967, and then regional sales manager in 1969. A charismatic public person, Ball was always out talking to employees—making sure that new sales ideas were in the pipeline. As one ex-Hutton employee said: "It wasn't a surprise to see him [Ball] anywhere. But when Fomon went anyplace other than the twelfth floor [the site of the executive offices], people would say, 'What the hell is he up to?'"[6] Ball's managerial abilities complemented those of the moody and sometimes reclusive Fomon, who was described as a "backroom deal maker" and talented investment banker.

All of the regional offices reported to Ball. The chain of command was short and loose—account executives reported to branch managers, who reported to their regional VPs, who reported to Ball. Ball and the executive VPs reported directly to Fomon. But in actual practice Ball was the dominant figure in the company, and other senior officers reported to him ex-officio. Hutton was described as a "comfortable" organization without a fixed hierarchy. The benefit of this arrangement, according to Ball, was that without a formal organizational chart, management could make fast decisions.[7]

CASH MANAGEMENT AT HUTTON

In 1980, with interest rates hovering near 18 percent, Hutton began to explore ways to maximize its interest earnings. Hutton managers recognized that if they could receive one-day credit on checks deposited with local banks, while checks written by Hutton required two days to clear, they could capture some of the "float" inherent in the banking system. By drawing checks on Monday, e.g., based on anticipated deposits on Tuesday, sufficient funds would be available in the bank to cover Hutton's checks when presented for payment on Wednesday. This required an estimate of the next day's deposits. A formula was derived that used past experience to produce a reasonable estimate. Since checks were written when funds were not on deposit, Hutton was technically overdrafting its account. If next-day deposits were overestimated, the account would be overdrawn and in reality have a negative balance. This could cause the bank either to demand immediate reimbursement by wire transfer of funds or refuse payment of Hutton's checks—although sometimes, for various reasons, the banks did nothing.

William Sullivan, designated as Hutton's "money mobilizer," had designed Hutton's cash management system in the late 1970s. The system moved money from branch office accounts to regional office bank accounts and then to national concentration accounts where the funds could be used by the company. Often delays in the processing of Hutton's checks between banks denied the company same-day availability of funds. To remedy this delay, funds were transferred as soon as possible. The objective of this system was to leave enough money in the bank account to compensate the bank for its services and withdraw the rest. From Hutton's point of view, it was compensating itself by overdrafting for the day in which the bank was holding its money.

When these alterations had been made in the cash management system, Sullivan and other Hutton officials met with its auditors, Arthur Andersen & Co. (AA&Co), to discuss the legality of the new procedures. A memorandum dated March 7, 1980, described that meeting:

> After the discussion of the procedure employed and its legality, Joel Miller, AA&Co engagement partner, requested that Tom Rae (Hutton's general counsel and former SEC lawyer) render a written legal opinion stating that Hutton's activities in this area don't present any legal problems. Mr. Rae declined to render such an opinion, stating that the banks are fully cognizant of Hutton's procedures, that this is an accepted banking practice, and that there is no question as to the propriety of such a transaction, again making reference to the "means of payment" principles. [The legal concept of check writing requires that you have the intent and the ability to cover the check on time.] After Tom Rae declined to issue an opinion on this matter, Bill Sullivan offered to call one of the banks that Hutton uses, Morgan Guaranty, and ask them what the banks would do if a company were to issue checks with no book balances. Joel Miller then stated that he would discuss the matter with other partners at AA&Co, whose clients include major money center banks, to ascertain what the banks' "point of view" is regarding these transactions.[8]

THE BANKS

Banks are compensated for their services to corporate customers by either requiring a minimum balance in the account or by charging set fees, or a combination of both. Most of the banks Hutton used required the firm to leave an average amount of money in the account so that the bank could produce a yield that would compensate it for its services. The bank and the customer agreed on the sum of the average balance and the time period over which the adequacy of compensation would be measured. If this arrangement did not yield enough compensation for a particular bank, it would inform the customer. Bank of America charged Hutton set fees for its services and only required Hutton to have sufficient funds in its account to cover a check when it was presented for payment—the rest of the time the account could have a zero balance.

Commercial banks, however, normally required corporate customers to maintain average account balances at negotiated target levels, and did not expect corporate customers to overdraft their accounts without prior consent. Nevertheless, bank managers expected occasional overdrafts to occur because of errors or inadvertence, such as the failure of an incoming wire to arrive on time. Most bank managers tolerated overdrafting by creditworthy customers as long as the amounts of money were relatively small and the overdrafts were infrequent.

The time that it takes for a check to clear, called "collection float," is based on the inefficiency of the payments system in this country. A check that is not cashed in person must be physically taken from the bank to a clearing house before its funds can become available. Electronic banking systems would eliminate this time lag by moving funds instantly. However, according to one Federal Reserve Board representative, an electronic payments system is not likely to displace checks during the remainder of this century.[9]

THE CAMPAIGN FOR INTEREST PROFITS BEGINS

On October 21, 1980, a memo written by Tom Morley (who had replaced William Sullivan as the money mobilizer) was sent to all Hutton branch managers. The memo emphasized the importance of interest income and suggested ways to increase interest profits. The memo pointed out that "net interest income accounted for approximately 50 percent of the average branch's profits. And by paying insufficient attention to net interest profits, a branch may be ignoring potential revenue." Four major areas generated interest profits: margin accounts, short positions, free credit balances, and interest on general-ledger balances. Morley pointed out that the last category had the greatest potential for profit. The memo said:

> The branch earns interest on all credit balances in its general ledger and is charged for all debit balances, both at the call rate. The lion's share of the interest profit generated in this category is due to the float earned on Bank of America checks and overdrafting the branch's account.[10]

At the time, interest from overdrafting was reported as part of a single line item on profit-and-loss statements. This item included interest generated by the overdrafting of branch bank accounts as well as interest generated by other bank transactions. Morley's memo broke down the components of interest in the Southeast Region. He noted that the first three categories accounted for approximately 55 percent of the interest earned, whereas the general-ledger interest accounted for 45 percent of the net interest profits.

In November 1980 Morley gave a speech to the regional operations managers and noted that it was a good idea for branch managers to inform local banks of Hutton's cash management system. However, one of Morley's staff members later sent a memo in June 1981 to Regional Operations managers, advising: "If an office is overdrafting its ledger balance consistently, it is probably best not to request an account analysis."[11]

EXPLAINING THE CASH MANAGEMENT POLICY

Tom Morley told branch managers how to use Hutton's money management system in a memo dated March 10, 1981:

> In collecting our branch receipts, we usually assign one-day availability to our local deposit. In doing this we anticipate our drawdown check clearing the bank the next business day, which will be when our local deposit becomes available. If the drawdown check fails to clear the bank the next business day, we attempt to capture the excess balances by increasing subsequent drawdowns. In handling our collections in this manner, we give the same clearing value to our drawdown check as we expect to receive on our branch deposit. This system is the standard cash management collection process used in the industry. What the system fails to address and cultivate is the situation where we can receive one day availability on our drawdown check, but it actually takes two days for the check to clear our bank.[12]

With the emphasis on interest income, the branch office cashier's job became more important because the cashier was the one who moved the money in and out of a branch office's account. In a memo to Tom Morley dated May 12, 1981, Tom Lillis, the vice president of accounting services, emphasized the importance of a good branch cashier, giving the following example:

> One branch had earned a consistent $30,000 per month in interest "just from overdrafting of the bank account." When the branch manager changed cashiers, the office only earned $10,000 from overdrafting.[13]

The overdrafting principle was implemented through a formula that incorporated a multiplier, which took weekends into account. Many cashiers found the formula difficult to understand and use. In July 1980 and in May 1981, Morley's assistant, Kevin Mahoney, suggested automating the procedure at the branch-office level. Using a computer software program, offices could only overdraft as much as would allow Hutton to maintain a zero balance.[14] Hutton did not, at either time, purchase this software.

The Mountain Region offices received instructions on how to use the formula in a memorandum. The Pacific Region was given instructions by telephone. Some branch offices did not get any instructions on how to use the formula. Traditionally, branch office practices were determined by the instructions that the branch manager gave to the office cashier.

Branch operations personnel in the Atlantic Region learned how to use the formula in a seminar. A memo from that seminar titled "Reminders from Seminar," dated June 2, 1981, contains this tip: "Drawdown as discussed. You may drawdown more than formula but not less! This will depend on individual branch/bank circumstances."[15]

Interest profits became a frequent topic of conversation at meetings of branch and regional personnel. Branch managers were concerned with interest profits because their compensation and job evaluation were based on their office's net profit. However, because of the sharp division in the Hutton organization between sales and operations, branch managers were mainly responsible for sales and reported to the regional vice president of sales, whereas their cashiers were answerable to the regional operations managers. Under this arrangement it was possible for a branch manager to assume that if the drawdown worksheets were being used incorrectly, he or she would be notified by operations.

GEORGE BALL'S ENCOURAGEMENT

Throughout 1981, George Ball wrote memos encouraging greater interest profits. A memo dated April 27, 1981, named New England as "The Region of the Month." In it, Ball recommended that managers get in touch with Tom Morley to find out how to maximize interest income and said, "Interest is an excellent way to legitimately optimize a branch's or region's results."[16] On June 25, 1981, Tom Lillis wrote in a memo

> I noticed that George Ball suggested to a number of RVPs [regional vice presidents] that they get in touch with Tom Morley to see if they can improve their interest profits. Tom Morley is only concerned with overdrafting at the branch level and I believe that there is far more to be done to improve interest profits.

Lillis went on to say:

> I would like to spearhead a retail system campaign to make branch managers aware of interest profit opportunities, but without a means of monitoring branch performance the program would be at best hit or miss. I need a priority for the proposed interest program so that we can improve the profitability of this $100,000,000 product.[17]

Ball continued to encourage interest earnings. In his memo dated August 5, 1981, he wrote: "High fences make good neighbors and high interest profits create good margins."[18] His December 18, 1981, memo states, "We have certainly had the luxury of high interest profits, profits which may be importantly lower in the year ahead. Our corporate goal is to earn in excess of $100,000,000 [in interest]. Together we can do it, but it will take a mighty push."[19]

THE BRANCHES PUSH

Branch managers became very conscious of how their interest income stacked up against other branch offices. Baltimore branch manager, Anthony Read, worried about his branch's poor interest earnings. His cashier informed him that the way in which managers increased interest was to arbitrarily increase drawdowns. Read began to do so periodically, adding $500,000 to $3 million to his account. The bank complained to Morley, and Hutton deposited a large sum of money and left it there for several days. Read was charged with the interest on that money and stopped overdrafting his account.

Alexandria, Va., branch manager Perry Bacon was known as a bright young manager. After someone in the Alexandria branch inadvertently added an extra zero to an overdraft, making the figure 9 million instead of 900,000, Bacon noticed that the bank did nothing. So he began aggressively to overdraft his account. Letters from Bacon's local bank indicated that Bacon maintained excellent relations with it.

In November 1981 Bacon's office was ranked as the number one profit center in the Central Region. George Ball sent a memo to the Central Regional vice president asking why the Alexandria office's interest earnings were so high. Ball queried, "Were these accounting adjustments?" The response was, "No, but the office does a superb job of money management."[20] Ball, Morley, and others later suggested that branch managers get advice from Bacon on how to increase their interest income.

Ernest Dipple, a VP for the Central Region, told the Louisville, Ky., branch manager, William Wilcox, to contact Bacon about how to improve his branch's interest earnings. Wilcox increased the multiplier used in connection with the drawdown formula and arbitrarily increased the amount of the branch drawdown. However, unlike Bacon and Read, Wilcox had negotiated a minimum service fee with his bank, The First National Bank of Louisville, in the fall of 1981. In order to assess the fees owed to it, the bank closely analyzed Wilcox's account and was fully aware of its status from day to day.

THE BIG OVERDRAFT

In December 1981 the Genesee County Bank in Batavia, N.Y., was presented with a large check that had been deposited in a New York City bank. Genesee had received Hutton checks drawn on the United Penn bank in Wilkes-Barre, Pa. The Genesee branch manager called United Penn to see whether Hutton had $8 million available in its account. United Penn said Hutton only had uncollected funds in the form of checks that were deposited the day before. Genesee and United Penn then refused to honor Hutton checks and closed the firm's account. Hutton immediately wired $18.8 million to United Penn and $20 million to Genesee.

This movement of money between the Genesee Bank and United Penn was called "chaining." The system had been developed by the Atlantic Region's operations manager, Arthur Jensen, and similar systems were used in other regions. These chains served the purpose of generating clearing delays in order to ease the region's task of concentrating funds from branches within the region. Clearing delays increased interest profits by giving Hutton one-day availability of checks written *to* Hutton and two-day clearance of checks written *by* Hutton. It was generally considered convenient and it improved the availability of funds. Unlike overdrafting, which was used to compensate Hutton for the float that was built into the banking system, chaining created additional float.

HUTTON'S AUDITORS ASK QUESTIONS

Hutton's AA&Co auditors called a meeting in early 1982 with Hutton CFO Tom Lynch, Hutton General Counsel Tom Rae and his assistants, and an attorney from Hutton's outside law firm, Cahill, Gordon & Reindel. They discussed Hutton's overdraft policy, the $8 million overdraft at the Genesee County Bank, and inquiries by banking regulators into excessive overdrafting of accounts at Manufacturers' Hanover Bank and Chemical Bank. A memo describing the meeting said the Federal Reserve Board had expressed concern that Hutton might be "creating float" as opposed to taking advantage of the float inherent in the banking system. The memo reported that "We were assured of the fact that no action has been brought against Hutton and that Hutton officials believed that banking regulators had no jurisdiction over their firm." The memo further stated that "the major concern of management was the potential negative publicity if the media were informed."[21]

Many other questions began to surface at Hutton. George Ball, in a March 19, 1982, memo again questioned the interest profits of the Alexandria office. Commenting on the contents of a memorandum on interest earnings, Ball said: "Note—commentary seems very aggressive. Who is calling the shots, and were the shots well called?"[22]

Four months later, in July 1982, to the surprise of some and the disappointment of many, George Ball left Hutton to become the president and chief executive of Prudential-Bache Securities. His departure was based on the desire for professional advancement and did not, according to Ball, have anything to do with problems at Hutton.[23] Ball's departure left a huge managerial gap in the Hutton organization. Fomon was without his public "hands-on manager."

HUTTON ATTRACTS ATTENTION

The Genesee incident attracted the attention of a young Assistant U.S. Attorney from the Middle District of Pennsylvania named Albert Murray. Murray doggedly traced the movement of Hutton's checks between banks and initiated a Justice Department investigation of Hutton's activities. On May 10, 1982, the U.S. Justice Department subpoenaed CEO Robert Fomon and Controller Michael Castellano, asking for virtually every document in E.F. Hutton's files.

At that time Attorney General Edwin Meese III had just taken office. Meese's appointment had been opposed by some in Congress who questioned the propriety of some low-interest loans that Meese obtained while working in the White House. The Democrats in particular not only questioned Meese's moral character but also worried that he would be soft on white-collar crime.

The Justice Department's investigation covered the firm's overdrafting from mid-1980 to February 1982. Hutton was charged with overdrafting its accounts and intentionally delaying check collection. Altogether, the Justice Department estimated that by shuffling $10 billion in uncollected funds from one account to another, Hutton obtained the interest-free use of $1 billion in uncollected funds from July 1980 through February 1982 (which was when short-term interest rates were 18 percent to 20 percent).[24]

HUTTON'S RESPONSE

The investigation dragged on from February 1982 until May 1985. When it was completed in the spring of 1985, the audit committee of Hutton's board of directors met. The committee, which consisted of the outside members of the board of directors, did not believe that the case against Hutton was very strong (a representative of the Justice Department later testified that, in the department's opinion, chances of convicting Hutton were fifty-fifty).[25] However, a guilty plea would avoid a long jury trial with the attendant publicity, and the risk that Hutton employees would be found guilty of fraud (in which case they could be barred from the securities industry). It was tentatively agreed to enter a guilty plea, if a satisfactory settlement could be worked out with the Justice Department.

One factor contributing to this decision was a memo that surfaced in February 1985. It was written on April 23, 1982, by Perry Bacon in response to a memo by Washington, D.C., branch manager Steve Bralove. Bralove had complained to Bacon about causing problems with the bank by overdrafting excessively. Bacon replied in reference to overdrafting:

> I believe those activities are encouraged by the firm and are in fact identical to what the firm practices on a national basis. Specifically we will from time to time draw down not only deposits plus anticipated deposits, but also bogus deposits. (See Exhibit 1.)

Some Hutton insiders said that this memo was "the nail in the coffin" that forced Hutton to plead guilty.[26] But the most compelling reason why Fomon chose to plead guilty was the hope that it would end the affair quickly.[27]

Hutton's board of directors later approved the settlement and the firm pleaded guilty to the agreed-upon 2,000 counts of fraud. Attorney General Meese said that the government had foregone prosecution of Hutton employees in order to avoid lengthy litigation. Meese believed that the overdrafting was a "corporate scheme" and "no one personally benefited from defrauding the banks."[28] The Justice Department had also agreed to send a letter to the SEC stating that, "the interests of the U.S. government have been served."

But many constituencies were not satisfied with the Justice

Department's investigation. The Chairman of the House Judiciary Crime Subcommittee, N.J. Democrat William J. Hughes, believed that individuals in the corporate hierarchy should be charged. Stephen Trott, the Justice Department Criminal Division chief, was unhappy with the way that Hutton delivered subpoenaed documents and thought the case should be reopened.[29] And the SEC wanted its own investigation. On top of all this, some banks considered filing a class-action suit under the Racketeer Influenced & Corrupt Organizations (RICO) statute.

Thus, it did not look like Hutton's guilty plea was going to put the scandal to rest. The press was keeping a watchful eye on Hutton and its publicity-shy CEO. After two years of investigations, even Robert Fomon was not sure what had gone wrong. One thing that the 34-year Hutton veteran did know was that he would have to do something to keep his prized employees from defecting, and to regain Hutton's credibility as a sound financial institution.[30]

EXHIBIT 1

E.F. HUTTON

INTEROFFICE MEMORANDUM
TO: Steve Bralove
FROM: Perry H. Bacon
DATE: April 23, 1982
SUBJECT: Your Memo—Banking Activities

Our banking activities during the last six months have been no different than our banking activities off and on for the last five years. Additionally, I believe those activities are encouraged by the firm and are in fact identical to what the firm practices on a national basis. Specifically, we will from time to time draw down not only deposits plus anticipated deposits, but also bogus deposits. One day prior to that incremental drawdown arriving at our bank, we may need to cover with a New York [Chemical, U.S. Trust] check. As long as the local bank honors that check with same-day availability, the firm profits at both the branch and the national level. We profit at the branch level by creating a surplus in general ledger revenues, which are credited at the broker call rate. We profit at the national level for two reasons: (1) Because New York is doing the same thing with the U.S. Trust check by reacting to our bank wire and floating checks based on those deposits which deposits may not really exist [and] (2) Because those bogus deposits create a reduction in our net capital ratio requirement, which allows the firm to deploy capital elsewhere. Furthermore, we (as a firm) learned to use the float because it is exactly what the banks do to us (see enclosed article). I know of at least a dozen managers at E.F. Hutton—managers who along with Bill Sullivan and Tom Morley taught me the system—who do precisely the same thing. Presumably, any manager who was willing to take the time to learn the system would want to use the system.

The obvious drawback to the system is that it can cost the bank money. If the bank honors a New York deposit check with same-day availability and subsequently have those funds withdrawn by a New York drawdown check before they get FED usage of the funds, they have a net debit. On the other hand, the bank is not quite the defenseless amoeba that your memo suggests. FIRST, the system only exists because, peculiarly, our mammoth federal banking system is more hand processed than automated—NB—a system which the banks well know how to use as the enclosed article discusses. SECOND, the system we use does not happen the day we open an account. We spend months working up to larger drawdowns leaving the bank surplus deposits, and I do not recall any bank offering to send us their earnings on those deposits.

NB—There is not much difference between what we do and when a bank tells you not to write checks on your out-of-state deposit for 10 days, clears that check through the FED in 2 days, and enjoys the float for 8 days. Essentially, the bank has created a net debit against you in the form of 8-day nonusable funds. By the way, Tom Morley believes that within 2–3 years the entire system will be automated and all domestic checks will clear in one day. Therefore, as Tom stated in our New York BOM meeting, the time to take advantage of the system is now. (See second enclosed article.)

THIRD, all banks either know or eventually figure out our system. When they do, they simply cease giving same-day availability, and often will not count regular checks as collected funds. In fact, contrary to your implication that all banks are *now* holding your checks, NBW (a bank with whom we have never dealt) had been doing that to you months *before* this issue arose. FOURTH, if a bank is slow to move on #3 above, documents a net loss and asks us for same, we will probably give it to them. Our objective is not to steal money from the banks. Whatever the bank may have lost, we have enjoyed a greater profit due to the spread float.* I am aware of four branches that have had to write checks within the last six months for just the reasons listed above. On the other hand, many banks accept their losses as a cost of doing business and never ask for the money.

This last point leads to some of the specific remarks in your memo. FIRST, when you called a few months ago and asked if I was aware that due to our overdrafts, 1st American was giving you trouble with your secondary account there, you will recall that I replied that I was not aware, and I replied that I would not do any more overdrafting at that bank. If I sounded unconcerned, it was because your terse interrogatory was limited to your secondary bank account. The first time I heard about an institutional problem was from Ernie [Ernest Dipple] some weeks ago. Your conclusion that my attitude to Hutton's reputation in the city is "indifferent" is ridiculous. I confess to an emotion somewhere between indifference and astonishment at your suggestion that the solution to your secondary account problem was to call and offer money to a bank that had not, and to this date has not called me to complain, ask for money or request to discuss the issue—in fact has never called me at all. SECOND, your remark that since 1st American has contacted all of the area banks and now all banks are holding checks is not only contradicted by your knowledge that NBW had already been doing that, but would further suggest violation of any number of federal and banking statutes regarding collusion and anti-trust. THIRD, and what really troubles me, is that your constant use of terminology such as "excessive," "blatant disregard," "casually damaged" and "indifferent" is way out of line—and I think you know it. I plead guilty to simply never having considered that an institutional relationship could be jeopardized. Importantly, if our zeal with the bank has in any way impaired your ability to do business with that bank, I am genuinely sorry and would like to apologize to you and anyone else adversely effected. However, your sweeping implication that such an isolated incident immeasurably damages our reputation and ability to transact. . . .

* Ex.—The average balance that we earned on during the months to which you refer was significantly greater than the 2 million figure that the bank stated.

Source: "The Hutton Report," Appendix Exhibit 17.

NOTES

1. "The Story of E.F. Hutton's Founding and Growth," published by E.F. Hutton.
2. James Steingold, "The Undoing of Robert Fomon," *The New York Times,* September 29, 1985, sec. 3, p. 10.
3. Ibid., p. 11.
4. Gregory Miller, "Bob Fomon: Is Being Tough Still Enough?," *Institutional Investor,* April 1985, p. 62.
5. Ibid., p. 60.
6. Nigel Adam, "The Productivity Game at E.F. Hutton," *Euromoney,* December 1981, p. 79.
7. Appendix to "The Hutton Report," by Griffin Bell, September 4, 1985, Exhibit 45.
8. "The Hutton Report," by Griffin Bell, September 4, 1985, p. 21.
9. Appendix to "The Hutton Report," Exhibit 35.
10. Ibid., Exhibit 6.
11. Ibid., Exhibit 31.
12. Ibid., Exhibit 13.
13. Ibid., Exhibits 26, 27, 28.
14. Ibid., Exhibit 20.
15. Ibid., Exhibit 40.
16. Ibid., Exhibit 39.
17. Ibid., Exhibit 13.
18. Ibid., Exhibit 13.

19. Ibid., Exhibit 19.
20. Nathaniel Nash, "Hutton Auditor Defends Role," *The New York Times,* October 4, 1985, sec. D, p. 3.
21. Appendix, Exhibit 40.
22. Scott McMurray, "E.F. Hutton Appears Headed for a Long Siege," *The Wall Street Journal*, May 4, 1985, p. 1.
23. Anthony Bianco, David Wallace, and Daniel Moskowitz, "What Did Hutton Managers Know—and When Did They Know It?," *Business Week*, May 20, 1985, p. 110.
24. Chris Wells, "Why the E.F. Hutton Scandal May Be Far from Over," *Business Week*, February 24, 1986, p. 98.
25. Steingold, "The Undoing of Robert Fomon," sec. 3, p. 1.
26. Bianco, Wallace, and Moskowitz, "What Did Hutton Managers Know—And When Did They Know It?," p. 111.
27. Wells, "Why the Hutton Scandal May Be Far from Over," p. 101.
28. Bianco, Wallace, and Moskowitz, "What Did Hutton Managers Know—And When Did They Know It?," p. 111.
29. Wells, "Why the Hutton Scandal May Be Far from Over," p. 99.
30. Special thanks to Professor Raymond Corey for his helpful advice on this case.

ETHICS IN INTERNATIONAL BUSINESS

WAIT INTERNATIONAL AND QUESTIONABLE PAYMENTS

Charles R. Kennedy, Jr.

In January 1990, Bill Glade, Director of Internal Audit for Wait International, Inc., had been asked to review the company's code of conduct and to make recommendations concerning questionable payments to government officials, suppliers, and contractors. Because Bill had been recently promoted to this new position, this was his first major assignment. The previous director of internal audit had been promoted to corporate controller.

The company's Board of Directors thought this review was necessary for two reasons: The U.S. Foreign Corrupt Practices Act (FCPA) had been significantly amended last year, and some of the countries where international expansion was planned had a history of demanding payments from foreign companies. In particular, a senior member of Indonesia's Capital Investment Coordinating Board (BKPM) had recently suggested that Wait International could receive "special consideration" under the Foreign Capital Investment Law (FCIL) if certain payments were made. Under FCIL, the following concessions were available to qualified applicants in "priority industries": exemption from import duties on capital equipment, construction materials, and raw materials for three years; exemption from corporate income taxes and dividend withholding for five years; and the

This case was prepared by Charles R. Kennedy, Jr., Babcock School of Management, Wake Forest University. Reprinted by permission of the author.

right to use accelerated depreciation and loss carryforward in determining income tax liabilities.

Besides these "entry" costs, government officials in Indonesia were also known to routinely demand payment from companies with ongoing operations in the country on such matters as work permits for expatriates, import licenses, brand-name approval, and price increases. To help expedite such matters, one American country manager, with several years' experience in Indonesia, told Bill that his U.S. company had routinely held an annual party for key government officials. These lavish parties included "willing" females. Another country manager for a Japanese firm informed Bill that everything in Indonesia had a fee attached to the approval process. For example, the Japanese manager recently paid an Indonesian official within the Patent and Trademark Office $1,000 to get his company's product's brand name approved for local sales. In another case, a manager for a German company suggested that Wait International should hire the brother of the director of the BKPM, who was a local lawyer with a successful track record in getting concessions under the FCIL. Bill understood that Wait International had planned to hire another local law firm, which had two American-trained partners that in-house counsel had gone to school with. Bill wondered if his company should go with the director's brother instead, even though he charged a 200 percent premium over the American-trained lawyers. In addition, Bill was not sure how the company's current code of conduct applied to these different kinds of payment demands, particularly in light of the amended FCPA, and he knew the company's Board of Directors had similar questions. Besides the legality of the company's position and of its employees, Bill felt the ethical dimension had to be clearly and explicitly addressed as well.

WAIT INTERNATIONAL, INC.

Wait International, Inc., is a billion-dollar-plus company that is a diversified manufacturer of consumer and light-industrial products. The company is incorporated and headquartered in the United States, but half of its sales and profits are from outside the United States. The company's normal international operation is a self-contained manufacturing and sales operation in each nation. Thus, subsidiaries in foreign countries are separate profit centers, headed by a country president who reports to a group officer in charge of a single product in a geographic area (e.g., the vice president of Far East operations for a product). At present, Wait International, Inc., has operations in England, Italy, Spain, France, Germany, Argentina, Brazil, Mexico, Japan, South Korea, Taiwan, South Africa, and the Philippines.

Wait International was a fast-growing, profitable company. Sales had climbed nearly 12 percent between 1988 and 1989, which exceeded a 10 percent average for the entire 1980s. Net income to sales was also over 8 percent in the last two years. Much of this growth and profitability was due to international operations, where sales had grown nearly 20 percent in the last ten years on net profit margins of over 12 percent. Because of this success, Wait International planned to expand into countries where it currently did not have operations. As a general rule, such an expansion would require capital investments of at least $5 million in each country in which it opened a new operation.

QUESTIONABLE PAYMENTS AT WAIT INTERNATIONAL

Unlike some other U.S. multinationals, Wait International had avoided major legal problems with questionable payments abroad. To some degree this was explained by the nature of the businesses that the company was in. For example, bribery and illegal payments to foreign officials have been most common in oligopolistic industries handling large, capital-intensive products; these would include aerospace, construction, and energy companies. In fact, the bulk of more than 400 U.S. corporations who voluntarily admitted over $300 million worth of questionable payments to U.S. government investigators in 1976 came from such industries. Exxon disclosed payments of $59.4 million; Lockheed, $55 million; Boeing, $50.4 million; and Northrop, $34.3 million. Wait International, being primarily a manufacturer of consumer and light-industrial products, was not subject to the same kind of pressures and temptations as were other companies.

Another factor helping to explain Wait International's relatively clean record on questionable payments is that the company before 1977, when the original FCPA was passed, did not operate in countries where demands for questionable payments were typically high. Investments in the developing countries of Argentina, Brazil, Mexico, South Korea, Taiwan, and the Philippines were not made until the late 1970s and early 1980s. By that time, the company had established a code of conduct that was vigorously enforced (see Exhibit 1).

Several country presidents of overseas subsidiaries were often frustrated and confused by the company's code of conduct statement. For one thing, the statement was very general and hard to interpret. In terms of the "payments and gifts" section, what did "significant value" actually mean? When did customary business entertainment become improper? Was impropriety mainly an issue of perception? Country presidents in Latin America and Asia found the issues to be particularly important because of how business in those areas was normally conducted. Facilitating or "grease" payments were expected by many government workers for the most routine decisions, including such a mundane task as when a telephone would be installed or serviced. Did the code-of-conduct statement forbid these kinds of payments? Certainly, the document was not very specific on such matters. Informally, the company allowed each country president a great deal of leeway in deciding what an acceptable gift or entertainment

---

EXHIBIT 1

CODES OF ETHICAL AND LEGAL CONDUCT

Code of Conduct: The highest standard of individual conduct is expected at all times from each employee and any of its subsidiaries, not only in matters of financial integrity, but in every aspect of business relationships.

Compliance with the Law: First and foremost, pertinent laws of every jurisdiction in which the company operates must be followed. Each employee is charged with the responsibility of sufficient knowledge of the law in order to recognize potential dangers and to know when to seek legal advice.

Competition: Competition based on quality, service, and price is the heart of the free enterprise system, and the company enthusiastically accepts this challenge and competes on a positive basis.

Conflicts of Interest: Employees are required periodically to read and verify their compliance with a policy that is intended to avoid actual or apparent impropriety. Favoritism, preferential treatment, and unethical business practices are to be avoided at all costs.

Payments and Gifts: Payment or receipt of kickbacks, bribes, or undisclosed commissions is contrary to company policy. Giving and receiving business gifts of nominal value, while discouraged, is permissible where customary. Giving or receiving gifts of significant value is prohibited. Customary business entertainment is proper; impropriety results when the value or cost is such that it could be interpreted as affecting an otherwise objective business decision.

The company will comply with the U.S. Foreign Corrupt Practices Act. This Act generally prohibits payments or gifts to any official of any government entity, or department, agency, or instrumentality thereof, illegally or corruptly to influence the act or decision of the government or official in order that the company can obtain or retain business or have business directed to it.

Company Assets and Transactions: Compliance with prescribed accounting procedures is required at all times. In all instances, employees having control in any manner over company assets and transactions are expected to handle them with the strictest integrity and to accurately and fairly record them in reasonable detail on the company's books.

---

expense was and how to interpret the FCPA. Nearly all country presidents reacted by being very wary of questionable practices. If there was any doubt at all in their minds about the impropriety of a particular payment or gift, it was not made. Consequently, business was at times adversely affected because either deals were not made or operations were disrupted owing to a slowdown in bureaucratic decision making.

FCPA

Before making a recommendation, Bill needed to understand fully the FCPA, as amended in the Omnibus Trade and Competitiveness Act of 1988. The FCPA attacks the problem of corporate bribery abroad in a twofold approach: first by banning certain types of foreign payments and second by requiring U.S. firms to keep accurate records and to maintain adequate internal accounting controls. The antibribery provisions of the act prohibit firms from paying foreign officials in order to obtain or retain business. The accounting provisions deter bribery by imposing an affirmative requirement on firms and managers to keep books and records that accurately reflect an entity's transactions (including any questionable payments) and to maintain an adequate system of internal controls to assure that the entity's assets are used for proper corporate purposes. Individuals violating the antibribery or the accounting provisions can be fined up to $100,000, imprisoned for up to five years, or both for each offense. Corporations, on the other hand, can be fined up to $2 million for criminal violations of the act.

The antibribery provisions of the Foreign Corrupt Practices Act thus criminalize certain questionable payments. The provisions apply to all corporations with reporting obligations to the SEC or whose securities are registered with the SEC *and* to all "domestic concerns." The FCPA defines "domestic concerns" as all citizens, nationals, or residents of the United States and all business entities organized under the laws of any state, territory, or possession, *or* having its principal place of business in the United States.

This definition would appear to exclude from the jurisdiction of the FCPA foreign subsidiaries of American corporations that are organized under the laws of a foreign country and that have their principal place of business outside the United States. However, the FCPA as amended in 1988 makes it unlawful to make, offer, or authorize payments to "any person while knowing that all or a portion of such money or thing will be offered or given or promised, directly or indirectly, to any foreign official. . . for purposes of. . . influencing any act or decision of such foreign official." Because *knowing* is defined as specific awareness or "willful blindness," U.S. corporations will typically be held responsible for illegal payments made by their foreign subsidiaries, particularly those that are wholly or majority-owned. For minority-owned subsidiaries, on the other hand, the corporation must act in good faith to use its influence on the subsidiary to comply with the law.

Besides defining the scope of the law in terms of the party making the payment, the FCPA also addresses the issue of who is being paid and why. If payments are made to foreign officials in order to expedite routine government action, such a payment is legal under the FCPA. Routine government action is defined as an action which is ordinarily and commonly performed by a foreign official in—

   (i)   obtaining permits, licenses or other official documents to qualify a person to do business in a foreign country;
  (ii)   processing government papers such as visas and work orders;
 (iii)   providing police protection, mail pick-up and delivery or scheduling inspections associated with contract performance or inspections related to transit of goods across country;
  (iv)   providing phone service, power and water supply, loading and unloading cargo or protecting perishable products or commodities from deterioration; or
   (v)   actions of similar nature.

Congress's interpretation of the law, as expressed by the Senate-House Conference Report, however, specifically excluded from routine action any decision that had the functional equivalent of "obtaining or retaining business for or with or directing business to any person." For example, payments to a ministry official responsible for authorizing price increases for a product would still be illegal under the FCPA because that would constitute an attempt to influence the discretionary power of a foreign official in order to gain or retain business.

Thus the intent of the law is that payments must be made "corruptly" in order to be considered a violation; an individual or entity making a payment would be held liable under the act only if he or she were found to possess "an evil motive or purpose [or] an intent to wrongfully influence the recipient." For example, the legislative history behind the act indicates that "true extortion situations" would not be illegal since "a payment to keep an oil rig from being dynamited should not be held to be made with the requisite corrupt purpose."

The FCPA identifies three classes of foreign individuals or entities to whom payments are prohibited, unless they are for expediting routine government action; these individuals are:

   (1)   any foreign official;
   (2)   any foreign political party or official thereof or any candidate for foreign political office;
   (3)   *any* person, when a company knows that person will give, promise or offer all or part of the company's payment to a third party who is a foreign official, political party or candidate for political office. The FCPA defines a "foreign official as any officer or employee of a foreign government or any department, agency, or instrumentality thereof, or any person acting in an official capacity for or on behalf of any such government or department, agency, or instrumentality. Such term does not include any employee of a foreign government or any department, agency, or instrumentality thereof whose duties are essentially ministerial or clerical.

By excluding from its definition of "foreign officials" those persons "whose duties are essentially ministerial or clerical," Congress apparently intended to allow under the FCPA so-called facilitating or grease payments made to minor functionaries to persuade them to carry out their customary tasks—such as allowing shipments through customs, issuing construction permits, or giving police protection.

The FCPA thus would not bar large payments to minor officials—as long as their duties are "ministerial or clerical." In addition, the 1988 amendments provide areas of affirmative defense against charges of FCPA violations. For example, a firm could defend itself on the basis that "the payment of a gift, offer or promise of anything of value that was made was lawful under the written laws and regulations of the foreign official's, political party's, party official's or candidate's country." In addition, the 1988 amendments provide an affirmative defense that

> the payment, gift, offer or promise of value that was made was a reasonable bona fide expenditure, such as travel and lodging expenses. . . directly related to—
> (A) the promotion, demonstration or explanation of products or services; or
> (B) the execution or performance of a contract with a foreign government or agency thereof.

The Conference Report, however, explicitly stated that if a gift or payment is corruptly made to obtain or retain business then such a defense would not be acceptable.

Whereas the antibribery provisions apply to all "domestic concerns," whether or not these are businesses registered with the SEC, the accounting provisions cover only companies subject to securities laws—that is, only public companies. In a sense, however, the accounting provisions have a wider scope than the antibribery statutes. Bribery is a rare event, compared to record-keeping and control, which are day-to-day activities.

The accounting provisions as amended in 1988 have the following features. First, the law limits criminal liability for violating the accounting provisions to those who "knowingly circumvent" the system of internal accounting controls or who "knowingly falsify" accounting records or transactions. This legal standard conforms to the earlier SEC announcement that "if a violation was committed by a low level employee, without the knowledge of top management, with an adequate system of internal controls, and with appropriate corrective action taken by the issuer, we do not believe that any action against the company would be called for." Second, the 1988 amendments explicitly define both the "reasonable detail" in which firms must keep their books and the "reasonable assurance" that management has control over corporate assets. The definition employed is "such a level of detail and degree of assurance as would satisfy prudent officials in the conduct of their own affairs having in mind a comparison between benefits to be obtained and costs to be incurred in obtaining such benefits." Again, this definition mirrors earlier SEC statements or interpretations that guided enforcement under the FCPA.

TOWARD A NEW CODE OF CONDUCT

After reviewing and studying the amended FCPA, Bill Glade decided to seek the advice of a lawyer outside the company on legal responsibilities and actions that Wait International should take. The lawyer was asked to address two key issues: what the firm should do if FCPA violation by employees were discovered and what preventative measures should be taken to reduce the likelihood of violations occurring in the first place. The lawyer's report is contained in Exhibit 2.

EXHIBIT 2

MEMO
TO: Bill Glade, Director of Internal Audit
           Wait International, Inc.
FROM: Chedrick R. Kellington
RE: FCPA Compliance
DATE: 1/7/90

You have asked me to address the fundamental issues regarding FCPA compliance by your firm. I understand that you are familiar with the details of the law as amended in 1988, so my comments will be made under that assumption. In particular, you wanted to know your firm's legal responsibilities if violations of the FCPA occur and how to best reduce the chances of such violations occurring. I will address these two interrelated issues in turn.

What should your firm do if suspected violations of the FCPA have occurred? Probably the least painful course for any company discovering its own violations is the SEC's voluntary disclosure program, which started in 1975. If you find yourself in such a situation, the firm can conduct internal investigations, publicly file the material facts (usually on Form 8–K, filed with the SEC), and adopt preventative measures. The SEC requires that the internal investigation be conducted by independent members of the board of directors, with help from the firm's regular external auditing firm. Preventative measures include strengthened internal controls and a corporate policy statement from the board of directors. The policy statement is intended to prevent illegal foreign and domestic political payments as well as false or incomplete books and records.

I also offer the following advice. If managers or auditors of public companies discover possible violations, they should inform inside counsel and the audit committee (or the board itself, if the company has no audit committee) and seek advice from outside counsel. If the lawyers believe that the violations may be significant, the audit committee or the board should authorize an internal inquiry. Investigators should include outside counsel and outside auditors, and they should report directly to the board or to the audit committee. When the inquiry is complete, the audit committee can determine whether or not a corrective Form 8–K must be filed with the SEC. At this point, the company will be able to negotiate with the SEC. The manner of resolution acceptable to the SEC will depend on the seriousness of the violation and the degree of participation by senior managers. A. Clarence Sampson, the SEC's former Chief Accountant, has stated that the SEC would look more kindly on companies that make timely disclosures and take preventative actions on their own. Privately held companies should follow similar internal procedures, conferring instead with the Justice Department on the best means of resolution.

What sorts of preventative measures are possible? Most lawyers urge that a company's first step should be to set up an audit committee of independent and energetic outside directors. Secondly, managers should review existing controls—to avoid violating either the record-keeping or the controls provision. Such a review could begin with the external auditor's criticisms and suggestions. Thus, senior managers, internal counsel, and internal auditors should carefully examine the auditor's suggestions. If managers choose not to make any of the proposed changes, they should record the reasons for that decision.

Controls of certain sensitive transactions should be carefully reviewed whether or not external auditors are critical of them. Such transactions include the following: political contributions; transfers of funds outside of the country; use of tangible corporate assets, such as aircraft, boats, apartments and estates; and possible insider-dealings, such as sales to firms owned in part by corporate officials. In all these instances it is particularly important that the records show not only the amounts but also the circumstances and true purposes of all transactions.

Allowable facilitating payments must also be carefully documented and controlled, to comply with the accounting provisions as well as to ensure that employees do not escalate purported grease payments into bribes. Castle and Cook, Inc., a Honolulu-based diversified food company, has described its methods of controlling facilitating payments. Robert Moore, vice president and general counsel, has told me that the firm draws up careful budgets for all "specially regulated costs." No grease payments may be made unless they have been budgeted. The total budget for facilitating payments is usually over $200,000 per year; the money is used to get local army and police personnel to guard warehouses, to move shipments through customs, and to get ships out of port. Each division's budget for such payments is screened by internal and external legal counsel in the host countries to determine that the payments are legal under local laws. The division's treasurer must certify that the payments are used for the purposes specified. Then the budgets pass up through the ranks to be approved by group managers, internal auditors, general counsel, and the vice president of finance.

Auditors also recommend that certain types of accounts and assets are particularly vulnerable to misappropriation and therefore require stringent controls. For example, political payments have often been made from accounts without tangible assets—such as accounts for consulting expenses, for sales expenses (advertising, commissions, discounts), or for employee remuneration (bonuses, travel, entertainment). Accounts payable have also been drained. Other endangered assets are those that are unrecorded and readily converted to cash—such as scrap, vending machine revenue, sales samples, marketing plans and data lists (lists of stockholders, employees, or customers). Lastly, all payments to third-party intermediaries (sales agents, outside counsel, consultants) need to be carefully controlled and monitored.

In addition to reviewing existing controls and strengthening them if necessary, your firm will want to consider whether the firm's organization fosters compliance. For example, internal auditors are less likely to be influenced if they report directly to the audit committee or to the board than if they report to senior financial managers. Similarly, internal auditors of divisions and subsidiaries are less susceptible if they report to central auditors rather than to divisional or subsidiary managers—although the latter procedure is more often the case. In general, the more decentralized the company and the greater a unit's distance from headquarters, the greater the chances that the unit will disregard corporate controls if they seem to be a nuisance. Because corporations can be held liable for subsidiaries' actions, some companies are now requiring from their subsidiaries quarterly reports documenting and explaining financial conditions, sensitive payments, and irregularities in internal controls.

Your firm should also consider whether or not the climate in the company subtly persuades employees to override controls and resort to creative accounting or bribes. Sometimes overly optimistic forecasts motivate executives to manipulate accounts and falsify reports. Other pressures might include excess capacity, obsolete product lines, unrealistic demands for more profits, and sales dependent on a few customers or transactions.

Finally, written corporate conduct codes will help employees to understand the law and to resist temptation. Although you cannot completely eliminate the actions of dishonest employees, it is crucial that top management record its disapproval of such activity in writing and communicate that policy periodically to all employees. One should also stress that the resulting code of conduct is not only a document of legal compliance but one that sets the tone of ethical business practices as well. It is within that context that compliance with the law and the company's code of conduct is most assured. Employees should know in no uncertain terms that the document is as much a moral as it is a legal statement and that violations of the code will result in immediate dismissal.

I hope this advice has been helpful. If you ever require any additional assistance, please let me know.

After receiving and reading the lawyer's report, Bill was convinced, more than ever, that an amended code of conduct was required. Bill's proposal is contained in Exhibit 3. In particular, the "Payments and Gifts" section of the earlier statement was completely rewritten. This section in the old code of conduct was too vague in Bill's opinion, and if compliance was left up to the interpretation of each country president, the probability of FCPA violations would increase. Bill was concerned this would happen because the amended law seemed to allow many more payments than in the past, and if their country presidents engaged in more questionable payments as a result, then the chances were high that missteps would be made. To counter potential legal problems, the company must be more specific and stringent in what was allowed in the area of questionable payments. Moreover, for Bill this was the ethical approach to take. To pay government officials or workers anything but insignificant sums of money seemed wrong to him. Such payments only encouraged or reinforced unethical behavior.

EXHIBIT 3

CODE OF CONDUCT COMPLIANCE PROCEDURES RELATING TO QUESTIONABLE PAYMENTS

1. The following Code of Conduct applies to Wait International, Inc., and its subsidiaries and advises employees in management responsibilities throughout the world of the Company's responsibility to comply with the U.S. Foreign Corrupt Practices Act and foreign law; it generally prohibits bribes, kickbacks, or undisclosed commissions. The Code is redistributed annually and recipients are required to acknowledge their receipt, understanding, and agreement to comply therewith.
2. The Wait International Corporate accounting Manual has replicated the content of the Code of Conduct insofar as this subject is concerned.
3. Management advises operating personnel that, while payments to government officials may be legal under U.S. and foreign law ("Facilitating Payments"), the Company's policy is that such Facilitating Payments should not be made. However, Facilitating Payments will be tolerated if necessary to prevent substantial disruption to the business, and then *only* if (i) such payments receive prior approval by the managing director, (ii) any individual payment does not exceed $100 (or its foreign currency equivalent), and (iii) each such payment is reported to the Internal Audit Department.
4. The entry into new countries, or the commencement of large projects in

foreign countries, is preceded by researching the local laws as to any pro-
hibitions or permission for the payment of money or giving of gifts to government officials.

5. Any third-party intermediaries whom an operating unit proposes to retain
   are chosen from those candidates who are highly recommended by reputable sources in the country and who have demonstrated a history of successful efforts with an unblemished reputation for integrity and compliance with the law.

6. Such third-party intermediaries are required to sign contracts containing
   acknowledgments of the existence of U.S. and foreign laws relating to illegal payments and of the Company's policies regarding compliance with
   law and the conduct of business, and the intermediary's agreement to
   comply therewith.

7. Prior to engagement by an operating unit, the proposed compensation for
   an intermediary is compared to other reasonable and customary charges
   of known reputable parties in similar circumstances. Actual charges once
   third parties are retained are audited by local management on a 100%
   basis, and on a periodic sampling basis by the Internal Audit Department.

8. An intermediary is required to supply detailed written support for each
   payment to be made by the intermediary to any third party in the course
   of the contract.

9. Payments deemed questionable under foreign or U.S. law are referred to
   the Corporate or Operating Unit Law Department for determination as to
   legality.

10. Matters referred to the Law Department for determination may be further
    referred to local counsel, as to foreign law matters, or to the U.S. Justice
    Department for an advisory opinion, as to questions involving the Foreign
    Corrupt Practices Act.

Bill circulated his proposed changes prior to the upcoming meeting of
the Board of Directors. His cover memo for the proposed changes can be
seen in Exhibit 4. One member of the board, the executive vice president for
international affairs, had a very negative reaction. He was so opposed to
Bill's recommendation that a stinging memo was written and distributed to
other board members before the meeting (see Exhibit 5). Bill wondered
whether he had made a political mistake in making his own recommendation and how he should defend himself in the meeting.

EXHIBIT 4

MEMO
TO: Board of Directors, Wait International, Inc.
FROM: Bill Glade, Director of Internal Audit
RE: Proposed Changes in Company's Code of Conduct
DATE: 1/15/90

I've attached my recommended changes to the code-of-conduct statement given my review of the amended FCPA. I should stress that the

proposal is meant to replace the "Payments and Gifts" section of the old statement only. I think the new wording has the advantage of being more specific and detailed. Our country presidents certainly need more guidance, especially given the recent changes in the law. Without clearer and stricter guidelines, the probability grows that mistakes will be made, and the company will then face the legal consequences. If adopted, the revised code-of-conduct statement would not only be in full and complete compliance with the law but would also place the company on a high ethical plane. As a general rule, the company should not make payments to government officials or workers who are violating the public trust. I will be glad to explain these recommendations more fully at the upcoming meeting of the board next week.

EXHIBIT 5

MEMO

TO: Board of Directors, Wait International, Inc.
FROM: Bryan C. Wade, Executive Vice President for International Affairs
RE: Bill Glade's Proposed Changes in the Company's Code-of-Conduct Statement
DATE: 1/18/90

Before our meeting next week, I want to express my strong opposition to Bill Glade's proposed changes in the company's code-of-conduct statement. I have several problems with his proposal. First, why would we want to impose a much stricter set of standards than we had earlier when the government has decided to loosen its restrictions? The amended FCPA was in response to the adverse competitive consequences the original law had on American firms abroad. Our firm certainly suffered some negative consequences, as our country presidents avoided any and all payments that might have been even remotely perceived as improper. Now when the amended law clearly says that "facilitating payments" to any government official or worker are legal, irrespective of amount, Bill Glade recommends that such payments not be made a general rule, and even when such payments are "necessary to prevent substantial disruption to the business," they are limited to $100. Why such an arbitrary limit? If the demand is for $101, do we allow our business to be seriously disrupted? If the managing director is getting involved in any case, why can't he decide if the amount is proper and justified? I could imagine many situations where a facilitating payment of several hundred dollars would not only be good business but also clearly within the law.

On another level, I question Bill Glade's imposition of his ethical standards on others. In fact, I'm personally offended by his implication that individuals who support facilitating payments when they are legal and make good business sense are engaged in questionable or unethical behavior. Moreover, if I were a government official or worker in a foreign country, I would find Bill Glade's self-righteous attitude offensive as well. Who are we to tell them that they are engaged in unethical behavior when they ask for customary facilitating payments? In many countries, such payments are accepted as part of the job and have been going on for decades, if not centuries. As long as payments are not used for corrupting purposes, which are true violations of their public trust, money spent to facilitate their normal duties, such as providing import licenses, telephone service, expatriate permits, etc., are completely ethical. Thus I oppose Bill Glade's recommendations on both moral and practical business grounds.

H.B. FULLER IN HONDURAS: STREET CHILDREN AND SUBSTANCE ABUSE

Norman E. Bowie and Stefanie Ann Lenway

In the summer of 1985 the following news story was brought to the attention of an official of the H.B. Fuller Company in St. Paul, Minnesota.

GLUE SNIFFING AMONG HONDURAN STREET CHILDREN IN HONDURAS:
CHILDREN SNIFFING THEIR LIVES AWAY
An Inter-Press Service Feature
by Peter Ford

Tegucigalpa July 16, 1985 (IPS)—They lie senseless on doorsteps and pavements, grimy and loose limbed, like discarded rag dolls.

Some are just five or six years old. Others are already young adults, and all are addicted to sniffing a commonly sold glue that is doing them irreversible brain damage.

Roger, 21, has been sniffing "Resistol" for eight years. Today, even when he is not high, Roger walks with a stagger, his motor control wrecked. His scarred face puckers with concentration, his right foot taps nervously, incessantly, as he talks.

Since he was 11, when he ran away from the aunt who raised him, Roger's

Norman E. Bowie and Stefanie Ann Lenway, University of Minnesota. All rights reserved by Graduate School of Business, Columbia University. The authors express their deep appreciation to the H.B. Fuller Company for providing access to company documents and personnel relevant to this case.

home has been the streets of the capital of Honduras, the second poorest nation in the Western Hemisphere after Haiti.

Roger spends his time begging, shining shoes, washing car windows, scratching together a few pesos a day, and sleeping in doorways at night.

Sniffing glue, he says, "makes me feel happy, makes me feel big. What do I care if my family does not love me? I know it's doing me damage, but it's a habit I have got, and a habit's a habit. I cannot give it up, even though I want to."

No one knows how many of Tegucigalpa's street urchins seek escape from the squalor and misery of their daily existence through the hallucinogenic fumes of Resistol. No one has spent the time and money needed to study the question.

But one thing is clear, according to Dr. Rosalio Zavala, head of the Health Ministry's Mental Health Department, "these children come from the poorest slums of the big cities. They have grown up as illegal squatters in very disturbed states of mental health, tense, depressed, aggressive."

"Some turn that aggression on society, and start stealing. Others turn it on themselves, and adopt self-destructive behavior. . . ."

But, he understands the attraction of the glue, whose solvent, toluene, produces feelings of elation. "It gives you delusions of grandeur, you feel powerful, and that compensates these kids for reality, where they feel completely worthless, like nobodies."

From the sketchy research he has conducted, Dr. Zavala believes that most boys discover Resistol for the first time when they are about 11, though some children as young as five are on their way to becoming addicts.

Of a small sample group of children interviewed in reform schools here, 56 percent told Zavala that friends introduced them to the glue, but it is easy to find on the streets for oneself.

Resistol is a contact cement glue, widely used by shoe repairers, and available at household goods stores everywhere.

In some states of the United States, glue containing addictive narcotics such as toluene must also contain oil of mustard—the chemical used to produce poisonous mustard gas—which makes sniffing the glue so painful it is impossible to tolerate. There is no federal U.S. law on the use of oil of mustard, however. . . .

But even for Dr. Zavala, change is far more than a matter of just including a chemical compound, such as oil of mustard, in a contact cement.

"This is a social problem," he acknowledges. "What we need is a change in philosophy, a change in social organization."

Resistol is manufactured by H.B. Fuller S. A., a subsidiary of Kativo Chemical Industries, S. A., which in turn is a wholly owned subsidiary of the H.B. Fuller Company of St. Paul, Minnesota.[1] Kativo sells more than a dozen different adhesives under the Resistol brand name in several countries in Latin America for a variety of industrial and commercial applications. In Honduras the Resistol products have a strong market position.

Three of the Resistol products are solvent-based adhesives designed with certain properties that are not possible to attain with a water-based formula. These properties include rapid set, strong adhesion, and water resistance. These products are similar to airplane glue or rubber cement and are primarily intended for use in shoe manufacturing and repair, leatherwork, and carpentry.

Even though the street children of each Central American country may have a different choice of a drug for substance abuse, and even though Resistol is not the only glue that Honduran street children use as an inhalant, the term *Resistolero* stuck and has become synonymous with all street children, whether they use inhalants or not. In Honduras Resistol is identified as the abused substance.

Edward Sheehan writes in the *Agony in the Garden*:

> Resistol. I had heard about Resistol. It was a glue, the angel dust of Honduran orphans. . . . In Tegucigalpa, their addiction had become so common they were known as los Resistoleros.

HONDURAS

The social problems that contribute to widespread inhalant abuse among street children can be attributed to the depth of poverty in Honduras.[2] In 1989, 65 percent of all households and 40 percent of urban households in Honduras were living in poverty, making it one of the poorest countries in Latin America. Between 1950 and 1988, the increase in the Honduran gross domestic product (GDP) was 3.8 percent, only slightly greater than the average yearly increase in population growth. In 1986, the Honduran GDP was about U.S. $740 per capita and has only grown slightly since. Infant and child mortality rates are high, life expectancy for adults is 64 years, and the adult literacy rate is estimated to be about 60 percent.

Honduras has faced several economic obstacles in its efforts to industrialize. First, it lacks abundant natural resources. The mountainous terrain has restricted agricultural productivity and growth. In addition, the small domestic market and competition from more industrially advanced countries has prevented the manufacturing sector from progressing much beyond textiles, food processing, and assembly operations.

The key to the growth of the Honduran economy has been the production and export of two commodities—bananas and coffee. Both the vagaries in the weather and the volatility of commodity markets had made the foreign exchange earned from these products very unstable. Without consistently strong export sales, Honduras has not been able to buy sufficient fuel and other productive input to allow the growth of its manufacturing sector. It also had to import basic grains (corn and rice) because the country's traditional staples are produced inefficiently by small farmers using traditional technologies with poor soil.

In the 1970s the Honduran government relied on external financing to invest in physical and social infrastructures and to implement development programs intended to diversify the economy. Government spending increased 10.4 percent a year from 1973. By 1981, the failure of many of these development projects led the government to stop financing state-owned industrial projects. The public-sector failures were attributed to wasteful administration, mismanagement, and corruption. Left with little increase in productivity to show for these investments, Honduras continues to face massive budgetary deficits and unprecedented levels of external borrowing.

The government deficit was further exacerbated in the early 1980s by increasing levels of unemployment. By 1983, unemployment reached 20–30 percent of the economically active population, with an additional 40 percent of the population underemployed, primarily in agriculture. The rising unemployment, falling real wages, and low level of existing social infrastructure in education and health care contributed to the low level of labor productivity. Unemployment benefits were very limited and only about 7.3 percent of the population was covered by social security.

Rural-to-urban migration has been a major contributor to urban growth in Honduras. In the 1970s the urban population grew at more than twice as fast a rate as did the rural population. This migration has increased in part as a result of a high birth rate among the rural population, along with a move by large landholders to convert forest and fallow land, driving off subsistence farmers to use the land for big-scale cotton and beef farming. As more and more land was enclosed, an increasing number of landless sought the cities for a better life.

Tegucigalpa, the capital, has had one of the fastest population increases among Central American cities, growing by 178,000 between 1970 and 1980, with a projected population of 975,000 by the year 2000. Honduras's second largest city, San Pedro Sula, is projected to have a population of 650,000 by 2000.

The slow growth in the industrial and commercial sectors has not been adequate to provide jobs for those moving to the city. The migrants to the urban areas typically move first to *cuarterias* (rows) of connected rooms. The rooms are generally constructed of wood with dirt floors, and they are usually windowless. The average household contains about seven persons, who live together in a single room. For those living in the rooms facing an alley, the narrow passageway between buildings serves both as sewage and waste disposal area and as a courtyard for as many as 150 persons.

Although more than 70 percent of the families living in these *cuarterias* had one member with a permanent salaried job, few could survive on that income alone. For stable extended families, salaried income is supplemented by entrepreneurial activities, such as selling tortillas. Given migratory labor, high unemployment, and income insecurity, many family relationships are unstable. Often the support of children is left to mothers. Children are frequently forced to leave school, helping support the family by shining shoes, selling newspapers, or guarding cars. Such help often is essential income. If a lone mother has become sick or dies, her children may be abandoned to the streets.

KATIVO CHEMICAL INDUSTRIES S.A.

Kativo celebrated its 40th anniversary in 1989.[3] It is now one of the 500 largest private corporations in Latin America. In 1989, improved sales in most of Central American were partially offset by a reduction of its sales in Honduras.

Walter Kissling, chairman of Kativo's board and senior vice president for H.B. Fuller's international operations, has the reputation of giving the company's local managers a high degree of autonomy. Local managers often have to respond quickly because of unexpected currency fluctuations. He comments that, "In Latin America, if you know what you are doing, you can make more money managing your balance sheet than by selling products." The emphasis on managing the balance sheet in countries with high rates of inflation has led Kativo managers to develop a distinctive competence in finance.

In spite of the competitive challenge of operating under unstable political and economic conditions, Kativo managers emphasized in the annual report the importance of going beyond the bottom line:

> Kativo is an organization with a profound philosophy and ethical conduct, worthy of the most advanced firms. It carries out business with the utmost respect for ethical and legal principles and its orientation is not solely directed to the customer, who has the highest priority, but also to the shareholders, and communities where it operates.

In the early 1980s the managers of Kativo, which was primarily a paint company, decided to enter the adhesive market in Latin America. Their strategy was to combine their marketing experience with H.B. Fuller's products. Kativo found the adhesive market potentially profitable in Latin America because it lacked strong competitors. Kativo's initial concern was to win market share. Resistol was the brand name for all adhesive products including the water-based school glue.

KATIVO AND THE STREET CHILDREN

In 1983, Honduran newspapers carried articles about police arrests of *Resistoleros*—street children drugging themselves by sniffing glue. In response to these newspaper articles, Kativo's Honduras advertising agency, Calderon Publicidad, informed the newspapers that Resistol was not the only substance abused by street children and that the image of the manufacturer was being damaged by using a prestigious trademark as a synonym for drug abusers. Moreover, glue sniffing was not caused by something inherent in the product but was a social problem. For example, on one occasion the company complained to the editor, requesting that he "make the necessary effort to recommend to the editorial staff that they abstain from using the brand-name Resistol as a synonym for the drug, and the adjective *Resistolero*, as a synonym for the drug addict."

The man on the spot was Kativo's vice president, Humberto Larach ("Beto"), a Honduran who headed Kativo's North Adhesives Division. Managers in nine countries including all of Central America, Mexico, the Caribbean, and two South American countries, Ecuador and Columbia, reported to him. He had became manager of the adhesive division after demonstrating his entrepreneurial talents managing Kativo's paint business in Honduras.

Beto had proven his courage and his business creativity when he was among 105 people taken hostage in the Chamber of Commerce building in downtown San Pedro Sula by guerrillas from the Communist Popular Liberation Front. Despite fire fights between the guerrillas and government troops, threats of execution, and being used as a human shield, Beto had sold his product to two clients (fellow hostages) who had previously been buying products from Kativo's chief competitor! Beto also has a reputation for emphasizing the importance of "Making the bottom line," as a part of Kativo corporate culture.

By summer 1985, more than corporate image was at stake. As a solution to the glue-sniffing problem, social activists working with street children suggested that oil of mustard, allyl isothiocyanate, could be added to the product to prevent its abuse. They argued that a person attempting to sniff glue with oil of mustard added would find it too powerful to tolerate. Sniffing it has been described like getting an "overdose of horseradish. " An attempt to legislate the addition of oil of mustard received a boost when Honduran Peace Corps volunteer, Timothy Bicknell, convinced a local group called the "Committee for the Prevention of Drugs at the National Level" of the necessity of adding oil of mustard to Resistol. All members of the committee were prominent members of Honduran society.

Beto, in response to the growing publicity about the *Resistoleros*, requested staff members of H.B. Fuller's U.S. headquarters to look into the viability of oil of mustard as a solution with special attention to side effects and whether it was required or used in the U.S. H.B. Fuller's corporate industrial hygiene staff found toxicology reports from 1983 that oil of mustard was a cancer-causing agent in tests conducted on rats. A 1986 toxicology report from the Aldrich Chemical Company described the health hazard data of allyl isothiocyanate:

Acute Effects:
    May be fatal if inhaled, swallowed, or absorbed through skin.
    Carcinogen.
    Causes burns.
    Material is extremely destructive to tissue of the mucous membranes and
    upper respiratory tract, eyes and skin.
Prolonged Contact Can Cause:
    Nausea, dizziness and headache.

Severe irritation or burns.
Lung irritation, chest pain, and edema, which may be fatal.
Repeated exposure may cause asthma.
In addition, the product had a maximum shelf-life of six months.
To the best of our knowledge, the chemical, physical, and toxicological properties have not been thoroughly investigated.

In 1986, Beto contacted Hugh Young, president of Solvent Abuse Foundation for Education (SAFE), and gathered information on programs SAFE had developed in Mexico. Young, who believed that there was no effective deterrent, took the position that the only viable approach to substance abuse was education, not product modification. He argued that reformulating the product was an exercise in futility because "nothing is available in the solvent area that is not abusable." With these reports in hand, Beto attempted to persuade Resistol's critics, relief agencies, and government officials that adding oil of mustard to Resistol was not the solution to the glue-sniffing problem.

During the summer of 1986 Beto had his first success in changing the mind of one journalist. Earlier in the year Mary Kawas, an independent writer, wrote an article sympathetic to the position of Timothy Bicknell and the Committee for the Prevention of Drugs in Honduras. In June, Beto met with her and explained how both SAFE and Kativo sought a solution that was not product-oriented but that was directed at changing human behavior. She was also informed of the research on the dangers of oil of mustard (about which additional information had been obtained). Kawas then wrote the following article:

EDUCATION IS THE SOLUTION FOR DRUG ADDICTION
La Ceiba. (By Marie J. Kawas)

A lot of people have been interested in combating drug addiction among youths and children, but few have sought solutions, and almost no one looks into the feasibility of the alternatives that are so desperately proposed. . . .

Oil of mustard (allyl isothiocyanate) may well have been an irresponsible solution in the United States of America during the sixties and seventies, and the Hondurans want to adopt this as a panacea without realizing that their information sources are out of date. Through scientific progress, it has been found that the inclusion of oil of mustard in products which contain solvents, in order to prevent their perversion into use as an addictive drug, only causes greater harm to the consumers and workers involved in their manufacture . . . .

Education is a primordial instrument for destroying a social cancer. An effort of this magnitude requires the cooperation of different individuals and organizations . . . .

Future generations of Hondurans will be in danger of turning into human parasites, without a clear awareness of what is harmful to them. But if drugs and ignorance are to blame, it is even more harmful to sin by indifference before those very beings who are growing up in an environment without the basic advantages for a healthy physical and mental existence. Who will be the standard-bearer in the philanthropic activities which will provide Honduras with the education necessary to combat drug addiction? Who will be remiss in their duty in the face of the nation's altruism?

At first, Beto did not have much success at the governmental level. In September 1986, Dr. Rosalio Zavala, head of the Mental Health Division of the Honduran Ministry of Health, wrote an article attacking the improper use of Resistol by youth. Beto was unsuccessful in his attempt to contact Dr. Zavala. He had better luck with Mrs. Norma Castro, Governor of the State of Cortes, who after a conversation with Beto became convinced that oil of mustard had serious dangers and that glue sniffing was a social problem.

Beto's efforts continued into the new year. Early in 1987, Kativo began to establish Community Affairs Councils, as a planned expansion of the worldwide company's philosophy of community involvement. These employee committees had already been in place in the U.S. since 1978.

A company document gave the purpose of Community Affairs Councils:

- To educate employees about community issues.
- To develop understanding of, and be responsive to the communities near our facilities.
- To contribute to Kativo/H.B. Fuller's corporate presence in the neighborhoods and communities we are a part of.
- To encourage and support employee involvement in the community.
- To spark a true interest in the concerns of the communities in which we live and work.

The document goes on to state, "We want to be more than just bricks, mortar, machines and people. We want to be a company with recognized values, demonstrating involvement, and commitment to the betterment of the communities we are a part of." Later that year, the Honduran community affairs committees went on to make contributions to several organizations working with street children.

In March 1987, Beto visited Jose Oqueli, Vice-Minister of Public Health, to explain the philosophy behind H.B. Fuller's community affairs program. He also informed him of the health hazards with oil of mustard; they discussed the cultural, family, and economic roots of the problem of glue-sniffing among street children.

In June 1987, Parents Resource Institute for Drug Education (PRIDE) set up an office in San Pedro Sula. PRIDE's philosophy was that through adequate *parental* education on the drug problem, it would be possible to deal with the problems of inhalant use. PRIDE was a North American organization that had taken international Nancy Reagan's "just say no" approach to inhalant abuse. Like SAFE, PRIDE took the position that oil of mustard was not the solution to glue-sniffing.

Through PRIDE, Beto was introduced to Wilfredo Alvarado, the new head of the Mental Health Division in the Ministry of Health. Dr. Alvarado, an advisor to the Congressional Committee on Health, was in charge of preparing draft legislation and evaluating legislation received by the Honduran Congress. Together with Dr. Alvarado, the Kativo staff worked to prepare draft legislation addressing the problem of inhalant-addicted children. At the same time, five congressmen drafted a proposed law that required the use of oil of mustard in locally produced or imported solvent-based adhesives.

In June 1988, Dr. Alvarado asked the Congressional Committee on Health to reject the legislation proposed by the five congressmen. Alvarado was given 60 days to present a complete draft of legislation. In August 1988, however, he retired from his position and Kativo lost its primary communication channel with the committee. This was critical because Beto was relying on Alvarado to help ensure that the legislation reflected the technical information that he had collected.

The company did not have an active lobbying or government monitoring function in Tegucigalpa, the Honduran capital, which tends to be isolated from the rest of the country. (In fact, the company's philosophy has generally been not to lobby on behalf of its own narrow self-interest.) Beto, located in San Pedro Sula, had no staff support to help him monitor political developments. Monitoring, unfortunately, was an addition to his regular, daily responsibilities. His ability to keep track of political developments was made more difficult by the fact that he traveled about 45 percent of the time outside of Honduras. It took over two months for Beto to learn of Alvarado's departure from government. When the legislation was passed in March, he was completely absorbed in reviewing strategic plans for the nine-country divisions which report to him.

On March 30, 1989, the Honduran Congress approved the legislation drafted by the five congressmen. After the law's passage Beto spoke to the press about the problems with the legislation. He argued:

> This type of cement is utilized in industry, in crafts, in the home, schools, and other places where it has become indispensable; thus by altering the product, he said, not only will the drug addiction problem not be solved, but rather, the country's development would be slowed.
>
> In order to put an end to the inhalation of Resistol by dozens of people, various products which are daily necessities would have to be eliminated from the marketplace. This is impossible, since it would mean a serious setback to industry at several levels. . . .
>
> There are studies that show that the problem is not the glue itself, but rather the individual. The mere removal of this substance would immediately be substituted by some other, to play the same hallucinogenic trip for the person who was sniffing it.

H.B. FULLER: THE CORPORATE RESPONSE

In late April 1986, Elmer Andersen, chairman of the board of H.B. Fuller, received the following letter:

4/21/86
Elmer L. Andersen
H.B. Fuller Co.

Dear Mr. Andersen:

I heard part of your talk on public radio recently, and was favorably impressed with your philosophy that business should not be primarily for profit. This was consistent with my previous impression of H.B. Fuller Co. since I am a public health nurse and have been aware of your benevolence to the nursing profession.

However, on a recent trip to Honduras, I spent some time at a new home for chemically dependent "street boys" who are addicted to glue sniffing. It was estimated that there are 600 of these children still on the streets in San Pedro Sula alone. The glue is sold for repairing *tennis shoes* and I am told it is made by H.B. Fuller in *Costa Rica*. These children also suffer toxic effects of liver and brain damage from the glue.

Hearing you on the radio, I immediately wondered how this condemnation of H.B. Fuller Company could be consistent with the company as I knew it before and with your business philosophy.

Are you aware of this problem in Honduras, and, if so, how are you dealing with it?

That a stockholder should write the 76-year-old chairman of the board directly is significant. Elmer Andersen is a legendary figure in Minnesota. He was responsible for the financial success of H.B. Fuller from 1941 to 1971, and the values reflected in his actions as CEO are embodied in H.B. Fuller's corporate mission statement.

H.B. FULLER MISSION STATEMENT

The H.B. Fuller corporate mission is to be a leading and profitable worldwide formulator, manufacturer, and marketer of quality specialty chemicals, emphasizing service to customers and managed in accordance with a strategic plan.

H.B. Fuller Company is committed to its responsibilities, in order of priority, to its customers, employees and shareholders. H.B. Fuller will conduct business legally and ethically, support the activities of its employees in their communities, and be a responsible corporate citizen.

It was also Elmer Andersen, who as president and CEO, made the decision that foreign acquisitions should be managed by locals. Concerning the 1967 acquisition of Kativo Chemical Industries Ltd., Elmer Andersen said:

We had two objectives in mind. One was directly business related and one was altruistic. Just as we had expanded in America, our international business strategy was to pursue markets where our competitors were not active. We were convinced that we had something to offer Latin America that the region did not have locally. In our own small way, we also wanted to be of help to that part of the world. We believed that by producing adhesives in Latin America and by employing only local people, we would create new jobs and help elevate the standard of living. We were convinced that the way to aid world peace was to help Latin America become more prosperous.

Three years later a stockholder dramatically raised the Resistol issue for a second time. On June 7, 1989, Vice President for Corporate Relations, Dick Johnson, received a call from a stockholder whose daughter was in the Peace Corps in Honduras. She asked, "How can a company like H.B. Fuller claim to have a social conscience and continue to sell Resistol, which is 'literally burning out the brains' of children in Latin America?"

Dick Johnson was galvanized into action. This complaint was of special concern because he was about to meet with a national group of socially responsible investors who were considering including H.B. Fuller's stock in their portfolio. Fortunately, Karen Muller, Director of Community Affairs, had been keeping a file on the glue sniffing problem. Within 24 hours of receiving the call, Dick Johnson had written a memo to Tony Andersen, who had succeeded his father, Elmer Andersen, as CEO.

In that memo he set forth the basic values to be considered as H.B. Fuller wrestled with the problem. Among them were the following:

1. H.B. Fuller's explicitly stated public concern about substance abuse.
2. H.B. Fuller's "Concern for Youth" focus in its community affairs projects.
3. H.B. Fuller's reputation as a socially responsible company.
4. H.B. Fuller's history of ethical conduct.
5. H.B. Fuller's commitment to the intrinsic value of each individual.

Whatever "solution" was ultimately adopted would have to be consistent with these values. In addition, Dick Johnson suggested a number of options including the company's withdrawal from the market or perhaps altering the formula to make Resistol a water-based product, eliminating sniffing as an issue.

Tony Andersen responded by suggesting that Dick Johnson create a task force to find a solution and a plan to implement it. Dick decided to accept Beto's invitation to travel to Honduras to view the situation firsthand. He understood that the problem crossed functional and divisional responsibilities. Given H.B. Fuller's high visibility as a socially responsible corporation, the glue-sniffing problem had the potential for becoming a public relations nightmare. The brand name of one of H.B. Fuller's products had become synonymous with a serious social problem. Additionally, Dick Johnson understood that there was an issue larger than product misuse involved, and it had social and community ramifications. The issue was substance abuse by children, whether the substance was an H.B. Fuller product or not. As a part of the solution, a community relations response was required. Therefore, Dick invited Karen Muller to join him on his trip to Honduras.

Karen recalled a memo she had written about a year earlier directed to Beto. In it she had suggested a community relations approach rather than Beto's government relations approach. In that memo Karen wrote:

> This community relations process involves developing a communitywide coalition from all those with a vested interest in solving the community issue—those providing services in dealing with the street children and drug

users, other businesses, and the government. It does require leadership over the long-term both with a clear set of objectives and a commitment on the part of each group represented to share in the solution. . . .

In support of the community relations approach, Karen argued that:

1. It takes the focus and pressure off H.B. Fuller as one individual company.
2. It can educate the broader community and focus on the best solution, not just the easiest ones.
3. It holds everyone responsible, the government, educators, H.B. Fuller's customers, legitimate consumers of our products, and social service workers and agencies.
4. It provides H.B. Fuller with an expanded good image as a company that cares and will stay with the problem—that we are willing to go the second mile.
5. It can de-politicize the issue.
6. It offers the opportunity to counterbalance the negative impact of the use of our product name Resistol by re-identifying the problem.

Karen and Dick left on a four-day trip to Honduras on September 18, 1989. Upon arriving they were joined by Beto; by Oscar Sahuri, general manager of Kativo's adhesives business in Honduras; and Jorge Walter Bolanos, Vice-President Director of Finance, Kativo. Karen had also asked Mark Connelly, a health consultant from an international agency working with street children, to join the group. They began the process of looking at all aspects of the situation. Visits to two different small shoe-manufacturing shops and a shoe-supply distributor helped to clarify the issues around pricing, sales, distribution, and the packaging of the product.

A visit to a well-run shelter for street children provided them with some insight into the dynamics of substance abuse among this vulnerable population in the streets of Tegucigalpa and San Pedro Sula. At a meeting with the officials at the Ministry of Health, they reviewed the issue of implementing the oil-of-mustard law, and the Kativo managers offered to assist the committee as it reviewed the details of the law. In both Tegucigalpa and San Pedro Sula, the National Commission for Technical Assistance to Children in Irregular Situations (CONATNSI), a countywide association of private and public agencies working with street children, organized meetings of its members at which the Kativo managers offered an explanation of the company's philosophy and the hazards involved in the use of oil of mustard.

As they returned from their trip to Honduras, Karen and Dick had the opportunity to reflect on what they had learned. They agreed that removing Resistol from the market would not resolve the problem. However, the problem was extremely complex. The use of inhalants by street children was a symptom of Honduras's underlying economic problems—problems with social, cultural, and political aspects as well as economic dimensions.

Honduran street children come from many different circumstances.

Some are true orphans while others are abandoned. Some are runaways, while others are working the streets to help support their parents. Children working at street jobs or begging usually earn more than the minimum wage. Nevertheless, they are often punished if they bring home too little. This creates a vicious circle; they would rather be on the street than take punishment at home—a situation that increases the likelihood they will fall victim to drug addiction. The street children's problems are exacerbated by the general lack of opportunities and a lack of enforcement of school attendance laws. In addition, the police sometimes abuse street children.

Karen and Dick realized that Resistol appeared to be the drug of choice for young street children, who were able to obtain it in a number of different ways. There was no clear pattern, and hence the solution could not be found in simply changing some features of the distribution system. Children might obtain the glue from legitimate customers, from small shoe-repair stalls, by theft, from "illegal" dealers, or from third parties who purchased it from legitimate stores and then sold it to children. For some, selling Resistol to children could be profitable. The glue was available in small packages, which made it more affordable, not only to children, but to the typical legitimate customer.

The Honduran government had long been unstable. As a result there was a tendency for people working with the government to hope that new policy initiatives would fade away within a few months. Moreover, there was a large continuing turnover of government officials, so that any knowledge of H.B. Fuller and its corporate philosophy soon disappeared. Government officials usually had to settle for a quick fix, for they were seldom around long enough to manage any other kind of policy. Although it was on the books for six months by the time of Karen and Dick's trip, the oil-of-mustard law had not yet been implemented, and national elections were to be held in three months. During meetings with government officials, it appeared to Karen and Dick that no further actions would be taken as current officials waited for the election outcome.

Kativo company officers, Jorge Walter Bolanos and Humberto (Beto) Larach, discussed continuing the government relations strategy, hoping that the law might be repealed or modified. They were also concerned with the damage done to H.B. Fuller's image. Karen and Dick thought the focus should be on community relations. From their perspective, efforts directed toward changing the law seemed important but would do nothing to help with the long-term solution to the problems of the street children who abused glue.

Much of the concern for street children was found in private agencies. The chief coordinating association was CONATNSI, created as a result of a seminar sponsored by UNICEF in 1987. CONATNSI was under the direction of a general assembly and a board of directors elected by the general assembly. It began its work in 1988; its objectives included (1) improving the quality of services, (2) promoting interchange of experiences, (3) coordinating human and material resources, (4) offering technical support, and (5) promoting research. Karen and others believed that CONATNSI had a shortage of both financial and human resources, but it appeared to be well organized and was a potential intermediary for the company.

As a result of their trip, Karen and Dick knew that a community relations strategy would be complex and risky. H.B. Fuller was committed to a community relations approach, but what would a community relations solution look like in Honduras? The mission statement did not provide a complete answer. It indicated the company had responsibilities to its Honduran customers and employees, but exactly what kind? Were there other responsibilities beyond that directly involving its product? What effect can a single company have in solving an intractable social problem? How should the differing emphases in perspective of Kativo and its parent, H.B. Fuller, be handled? What does corporate citizenship require in a situation like this?

NOTES

1. The subsidiaries of the North Adhesives Division of Kativo Chemical Industries, S.A., go by the name "H.B. Fuller (Country of Operation)," e.g., H.B. Fuller S.A. Honduras. To prevent confusion with the parent company we will refer to H.B. Fuller S. A. Honduras by the name of its parent, "Kativo."
2. The following discussion is based on *Honduras: A Country Study* (2nd ed.), James D. Rudolph, ed. (Washington, D.C.: Department of the Army, 1984).
3. Unless otherwise indicated, all references and quotations regarding H.B. Fuller and its subsidiary Kativo Chemical Industries S.A. are from company documents.

CORPORATE SOCIAL RESPONSIBILITY

CAMPBELL SOUP COMPANY

S. David Model

R. Gordon McGovern, president and CEO of Campbell Soup Company, listened to the radio as he drove toward the company's Camden, N.J., headquarters early one morning in the fall of 1985. A brief news item snapped him out of his reverie: The Ohio-based Farm Labor Organizing Committee had just announced its intentions to picket Campbell headquarters during the annual shareholders' meeting two weeks hence.

This case was developed by S. David Model, Wharton M.B.A. 1986, under the supervision of Assistant Professor Paul Tiffany and Professor Thomas W. Dunfee. The case is intended as a basis for class discussion. Copyright © 1986 by the Trustees of the University of Pennsylvania. Reprinted with permission.

The Farm Labor Organizing Committee, (or FLOC, as it is commonly known), had recently presented McGovern with one of the most frustrating issues he had encountered during his five years at the helm of the $4 billion food-processing company. Despite Campbell's past efforts to address FLOC's concern for the plight of migrant farmworkers, the group continued to attack Campbell through publicity, boycott activity, and public demonstrations similar to the one now being planned.

It was not that these actions immediately damaged the company in any material or financial way, McGovern thought, but that they served stubbornly to undermine one of the facets of the company of which he was most proud—Campbell's principles of social involvement. (See Exhibit 1 for a statement of those principles.) But there was more at stake than simply corporate pride. The issue had the potential to directly affect Campbell's profitability, yet FLOC's position on farm worker rights was difficult to reconcile with standard industry practice. McGovern believed Campbell had taken reasonable steps within its power to deal with the underlying problem, and yet it seemed that just as negotiations showed the promise of resolution, events had once again conspired to cast Campbell as the villain.

EXHIBIT 1

CAMPBELL STATEMENT OF SOCIAL INVOLVEMENT (EXCERPTED)

CAMPBELL SOUP COMPANY'S SOCIAL INVOLVEMENT

Campbell Soup Company has a responsibility to its employees, shareholders, and the public at large to operate profitably. But Campbell is also dedicated to the fulfillment of broader, social involvement within the scope of a successful corporate financial statement.

Simply stated, Campbell believes it has an obligation to help where it can in bringing about solutions to some of the problems that face our society today.

Without profits, which are valid and necessary for the creation of new facilities and new jobs, Campbell's social involvement would be limited. Profits serve not only as an incentive to the basic investment which makes the existence of the Company possible; they also make possible Campbell's continued service to society.

Campbell is a good corporate citizen. The Company is an equal opportunity employer, assists minority enterprises, fosters a clean environment, supports urban and community betterment projects, and contributes to education, medical and scientific research. The company is engaged in a number of ongoing efforts aimed at the promotion of sound nutritional practices including classroom projects and messages presented before the general public and specialized professional groups.

Its products are often made available for distribution to the needy, and to victims of natural disasters throughout the world.

The Company's resources of people, products, time and money have benefited a broad range of worldwide programs and projects where Campbell employees work and live.

BACKGROUND ON CAMPBELL

In 1899, John T. Dorrance, a 24-year-old whiz kid with a Ph.D. in chemistry from Cornell, discovered a way to can soup in a condensed form. The company he worked for, the Jos. Campbell Preserve Company, had been started in 1869 when fruit merchant Joseph Campbell formed a partnership with an ice-box manufacturer to can tomatoes, vegetables, jellies, and condiments. Under the direction of Dr. J.T. Dorrance and his uncle, Arthur Dorrance (who had succeeded Joseph Campbell as company president in 1894), Campbell's soups, in red and white labels inspired by the football uniforms of the younger Dorrance's alma mater, became the company's most successful product. In 1904, Philadelphia artist Grace Gebbie Drayton created the Campbell Kids, two wholesomely overfed characters who became a symbol for American plenty in the years ahead. Although more recent generations were just as likely to associate the Campbell label with pop culturist Andy Warhol than with Mom's kitchen, in the 1980s the Dorrance family still controlled over 60 percent of the company's stock, and the Campbell Soup Company (the name was changed in 1922) accounted for an overwhelming 85 percent of the domestic canned soup market.

By 1980, although Campbell was a two-and-one-half-billion-dollar operation with subsidiaries in all corners of the globe, its growth and profitability had begun to stagnate. Changing demographics had altered the buying habits of American consumers, and Campbell's staple products— soup and frozen dinners—just weren't staples any longer. One bright spot, however, was the success of its Pepperidge Farm subsidiary, which had grown from $60 million to $300 million in annual sales under the guidance of R. Gordon McGovern, who headed the division from 1968 to 1980. In the summer of that year, the 54-year-old McGovern was chosen to succeed Harold Shaub as chief executive officer of Campbell Soup.

Immediately upon assuming his new position, McGovern began initiating broad changes in the century-old company. Marketing expenditures tripled between 1981 and 1984. Campbell's four divisions were reorganized into fifty business groups. Many products, such as Prego spaghetti sauce and Le Menu frozen dinners, were launched to appeal to the changing American life-style and palate. Under McGovern's leadership, Campbell would no longer rely on soup for its future.

By 1985, however, the phenomenal success of McGovern's early tenure had slowed. For the first nine months of that fiscal year, net income grew by less than 6 percent, and pretax income actually dropped in comparison with the previous year. Meanwhile, marketing expenditures continued to expand, now comprising over 12 percent of total sales. The performance of new product entrants, such as JuiceWorks (a children's fruit juice drink), and Pepperidge Farm's "Starwars Cookies" didn't live up to expectations. Even canned soup, the company's flagship product line, was encountering a stiff challenge from dry-soup products, which now accounted for 22 percent of domestic soup sales. Finally, although McGovern had been slated to ascend to the chairmanship of Campbell's Board of Directors when interim Chairman William S. Cashel, Jr., retired, it was rumored that Julia McGovern had recently asked her husband to step down from the presidency of the company.

McGovern himself felt mixed emotions about his future at Campbell. On one hand, he would welcome release from the relentless pressures of the chief executive's job; on the other, there was much he still wanted to accomplish in that position. He was clearly unhappy with the recent financial performance of the firm. Moreover, he did not relish the thought that, despite his sincere attention to community relations both within the city of Camden and elsewhere around the Campbell empire, he might ultimately step down without having been able to reconcile Campbell policy with the concerns of FLOC.

ORIGINS OF FLOC

In 1967, Baldemar Velasquez, the 20-year-old son of a migrant farmworker, began organizing agricultural laborers in the tomato-growing region of northwestern Ohio and southeastern Michigan. Like other migrant families, the Velasquez family had traveled north each summer from their home in Texas to pick crops primarily in Ohio, Michigan, and Indiana. Instead of making the return trip south at the end of the harvesting season, the Velasquez family eventually settled in the region as did other migrant families. Velasquez had finished high school and started college, first in Texas and later in Ohio, when his desire to help his "people" overtook his interest in breaking free from migrant harvesting.

Although farmworkers are often paid on a piece-rate basis, they are generally considered employees of the farmer on whose land they work. Nevertheless, Congress excluded farmworkers from the National Labor Relations Act (NLRA) of 1935, which governs the rights of employees to engage in collective bargaining, partly in response to farmers' concerns that a strike during the harvesting season would be financially ruinous.

Against this background, Velasquez spent ten years with midwestern tomato growers negotiating contracts to provide some protection for the migrant labor they employed. It was difficult work, because Velasquez was fighting not only the farmers' natural aversion toward organized labor, but also the fixed-price structure of the tomato crop.

BACKGROUND ON THE TOMATO CROP

Each winter, the large tomato-processing companies active in the Ohio-Michigan region, such as H.J. Heinz, Hunt, and Campbell Soup, determine their tomato requirements for the coming year. The companies negotiate with growers individually, but generally only one price per grade of tomato per processor results for the entire season's crop. The farmers have virtually no bargaining power, because the buyers' market is limited to a few large processors. On the other hand, the processors offer a price attractive enough to ensure that the farmers will continue to provide an adequate supply. Campbell is unique in the industry in that the company contracts by acreage, but pays by the ton. This provides an incentive for the farmers, who can sell more to Campbell if they have a particularly productive year. The consistency of the product from farm to farm and from year to year is critical to processors. Campbell needs fresh tomatoes to send to its nearby large juice-processing plant in Napoleon, Ohio, yet consumer demands dictate that a can of Campbell's tomato juice made from tomatoes harvested in southeastern Michigan this year must taste the same as a can of juice made from last year's California crop. To accomplish this, Campbell retains the seeds from each year's crop to germinate seedlings on its own farm in Georgia. The seedlings are shipped to the growers with whom Campbell has contracted. In every case, the farmers are "dedicated" to Campbell in the sense that their entire season's tomato production will derive from plants Campbell has provided. Only Campbell will purchase the harvested tomatoes from those farms.[1] The grower, in turn, has responsibility for hiring whatever permanent and seasonal labor is required to harvest the crop.

1978: THE STRIKE

Baldemar Velasquez concluded early on that the growers were not in a position to improve drastically the farmworkers' wages and working conditions, because the growers' operating margins were controlled by the price offered to them each year by the processing companies. Velasquez knew that he would never gain any long-term concessions from the growers without some guarantee from the processors that the additional costs incurred through improved wages and conditions would be reflected in higher contract prices. The processors, however, were reluctant to recognize the Farm Labor Organizing Committee, as Velasquez began calling his group in the mid-1970s, because it would imply that the processors were directly responsible for the welfare of employees of the farms from which they bought produce. Velasquez knew he would have to escalate the battle if he was to entertain any hope of success.

In 1978, FLOC convinced over 2,000 workers to walk off the tomato fields contracted for by Campbell and Libby McNeil Libby. In addition,

Velasquez told the processors that if they did not negotiate with FLOC soon, he would make every effort to urge the migrant workers to avoid all farms contracted for by Campbell and Libby during the next growing season.

In early 1979, several factors, including the threat of a continued strike, motivated Campbell to order the ninety farms with which it had contracted for tomatoes to use mechanical harvesters exclusively from then on. This had the effect of drastically reducing the number of farmworkers required for the harvest and thereby substantially lessening the threat of the planned strike.[2]

1979: THE BOYCOTT

In response to this challenge, and because Campbell, more than the other tomato processors in the region, had a strong public image that identified the company with its products, FLOC began concentrating its activity on Campbell. In 1979, FLOC initiated a nationwide consumer boycott of all Campbell products.

By the time Gordon McGovern became CEO in 1980, Campbell was being targeted by FLOC as a violator of human rights. That year, Campbell approached the Protestant Ohio Council of Churches (OCC) to offer funds for retraining programs for tomato workers who had been displaced by mechanization. The company contends that it received verbal support over the telephone for the programs Campbell outlined. However, the OCC ultimately refused, stating that Campbell should disburse the funds themselves. Campbell chose not to pursue this option.

1982: FLOC SUPPORT GROWS

In May 1982, however, the OCC did intervene in the conflict between Campbell and FLOC by endorsing the FLOC boycott "in the hope that such economic and social pressure will help convince the Campbell Soup Company to enter a dialogue with both the farmworkers about wages and representation, and with growers about negotiation for price."[3] Later that same year, some individual Catholic churches in Ohio also voiced support for the boycott.[4]

Support for FLOC by religious organizations began to spread outside the state of Ohio when John Moynihan, director of the Justice and Peace Commission of the Roman Catholic Archdiocese of Boston, called for representatives of both Campbell and FLOC to meet and produce a list of issues to be resolved between the two groups. Over a two-month period in 1982, Ray Page, vice president of corporate relations for Campbell, met with Fr. Moynihan and Baldemar Velasquez on three separate occasions. Campbell maintained that Page proposed to fund various welfare projects under FLOC's administration, but that Velasquez refused to cooperate. FLOC replied that Campbell offered the social programs in an attempt to induce the group to give up its quest for union recognition. Velasquez did not wish to exchange short-term gains for long-term goals.

1983: CAMPBELL INITIATES REFORMS

In 1983, several important developments in the FLOC controversy occurred. In January, a federal district judge in Grand Rapids, Michigan, ruled in favor of a pickle farmer over allegations by the U.S. Department of Labor that he violated child labor laws by permitting children to work alongside their parents on his farm. The judge decided that although the children most likely did work in the fields, their parents were independent, self-employed contractors, who had sufficient control over their own work and who shared in the profits of the harvest. Thus, the judge concluded, the farmer was not directly employing the children, and he had no obligation to prevent them from working.[5]

For groups that had long advocated that farmworkers receive the same employment protection as other workers, the decision was an angry shock. FLOC seized the child labor issue as a centerpiece in its continuing campaign against Campbell, charging that Campbell knowingly endorsed the use of children in its contracts for fields.[6]

On July 7, 1983, one hundred FLOC members and their supporters left their Toledo, Ohio, headquarters for a 560-mile protest march, arriving at Campbell headquarters in Camden on August 8. They were joined there by several hundred other supporters, including Cesar Chavez, who had successfully organized the United Farm Workers union in California after a consumer boycott of nonunion produce in the late 1960s. When FLOC members reached Campbell headquarters, they demanded to see McGovern, who was out of town. Instead, Campbell representatives agreed to a meeting between Page and Velasquez at a later date. This took place two months later, at which time Campbell again maintained that it had agreed to support the collective bargaining process, as well as fund social service programs for migrants under FLOC's direction. Velasquez, said Campbell sources, refused, charging the company with taking a "paternalistic" attitude toward the problem, which Campbell officials interpreted as meaning Velasquez was concerned that he might be edged out of the negotiation process.

Nevertheless, certain issues were resolved that year, although not necessarily as a result of either the protest march or the Page-Velasquez meeting. The Ohio State Legislature, which had been investigating migrant worker conditions for several years, passed a bill that upgraded the minimum standards for migrant worker housing. At the time, Campbell was contracting with nineteen tomato farmers on whose farms migrants were housed. Nine months in advance of the passage of the bill, the company had given these farmers a choice: If the farmers wished to continue housing workers, they would have to build new housing, designed by Campbell, which would exceed the new state standards. Campbell would pay for half the cost of construction and finance the rest with low-interest loans. Alternatively, the farmers could discontinue selling to Campbell, or stop housing the migrants. Only seven of the nineteen accepted Campbell's proposal.[7] There are two important reasons for this. First, cucumber pickles are a commodity item, without the high "value added" of tomatoes. The growers' margins are therefore quite low and could most likely not support the additional cost of new housing. Second, pickle harvesting is much more labor-intensive than tomatoes. Many more workers are needed, and thus more housing facilities. Campbell was reluctant to subsidize and supervise construction of new farmworker housing until it could evaluate the success of the tomato housing program. The Campbell ombudsman (see below), who was charged with the duty of addressing workers' complaints against their employers, did inspect the housing on all farms each winter, and Vlasic, Campbell's pickle division, asked the grading stations not to purchase pickles from farms with poor facilities. In addition, Campbell began a pilot health insurance program to cover basic health and major medical insurance for migrant families for the duration of the tomato harvest.

Partly in response to FLOC's allegations of child labor practices, Campbell hired a company ombudsman for migrant affairs in 1983. Alfredo Carrizales, an Hispanic and a long-time resident of the tomato-growing region, had spent the previous ten years working with migrant farmworkers for the Ohio Department of Labor. His new job was principally to make regular inspections of the farms contracting with Campbell to ensure that they met state, federal, and company requirements for wages and for living and working conditions.

One of Carrizales's first duties as ombudsman was to promote the availability of three day-care centers in the region, which Campbell funded for the specific use of the migrant children. Carrizales was also charged with the duty of ensuring that older children attended Ohio schools during the school year.

1984: THE CORPORATE CAMPAIGN

In April 1984, FLOC was offered the support of two well-known New York labor consultants, Ed Allen and Ray Rogers. Their company, Corporate Campaign, Inc., had been instrumental in engineering the 1980 victory of the Amalgamated Clothing and Textile Workers' Union (ACTWU) over the J.P. Stevens Company. In the Stevens case, Allen and Rogers had researched the network of financial backers and boardroom directors involved with the company. By publicizing these links, they were able to attract negative publicity to such organizations as the Seamen's Bank for Savings, Sperry Corporation, and Metropolitan Life Insurance Company, each of which responded to the internal and external pressures by influencing J.P. Stevens to negotiate with the ACTWU.

When Allen and Rogers began to conduct similar research into the Campbell network, they immediately found an obvious candidate for their campaign: the Philadelphia National Bank (PNB) and its parent, CoreStates Financial. PNB had a threefold tie with Campbell. Its chairman, G.M. Dorrance, was a member of the family that still controlled the majority of Campbell stock. Second, some of those shares were held in trust for the family by PNB. Finally, Campbell's president, Gordon McGovern, sat on the CoreStates board. Realizing that family ties and trust accounts were beyond the reach of the firm's usual strategy of external pressure, Corporate Campaign, Inc., went for the weakest link: to pressure CoreStates not to reelect McGovern at the bank's shareholders' meeting in April 1985.

1984: THE NCC INTERVENES

At the same time that Corporate Campaign, Inc., was beginning to investigate Campbell's financial links to other firms, the National Council of Churches (NCC) was considering a request from FLOC to support its continuing boycott effort. At the council's semiannual Governing Board meeting in May 1984, the NCC instead opted to appoint a mediation committee to help the two sides resolve their dispute. William Thompson, the former leader of the Presbyterian Church of America, was chosen to head the committee. It was Thompson's support for the boycott of Nestlé products in 1977 that had led to negotiations between Nestlé and the NCC and convinced the company to endorse a world health code that required Nestlé to modify its baby formula marketing strategy in third-world countries.

Thompson listened to Campbell, FLOC, and the growers before preparing a report for the next NCC Governing Board meeting in November 1984. At that meeting, the board decided to give Thompson's committee until the following meeting in May 1985 to mediate the conflict and come up with some sort of resolution before voting on economic sanctions against Campbell.

Thompson called for a series of meetings between Campbell and FLOC, with Ray Page and Baldemar Velasquez once again representing their respective sides. This time, however, a real deadline hung over the processing company: The large and relatively powerful NCC's support for the boycott would bring a considerable amount of adverse publicity to the company in addition to financial effects.

JANUARY TO MAY 1985: NEGOTIATIONS

The meetings began in January 1985. They were kept secret, not only from the media, but within the two organizations themselves. Campbell's Ray Page kept senior corporate management informed, but not even the president of the Vlasic Foods Division knew the details of the negotiations. At FLOC, Velasquez maintains that he informed only his closest associates.

The main reason for the secrecy was that FLOC was particularly vulnerable to media misinterpretation. Baldemar Velasquez felt that disclosure of the negotiation proceedings would confuse the public into interpreting them as a signal that the boycott was over. Velasquez made it clear that FLOC would not call off the boycott until the group had realized its goal of a farmworker labor contract with Campbell.

Ray Page agreed to Velasquez's request with one restriction: Neither he nor his staff would evade a direct question if raised by the media. For example, if a reporter was merely "fishing" for a story, Page would not comment; but if it was clear that the reporter had heard the story elsewhere and was seeking confirmation, Page would not deny what he knew to be true.

The negotiations centered largely around process rather than substance. Both FLOC and Campbell were quite clear about the issues. Campbell had never opposed the rights of workers to organize, but had rather objected to company intervention on the farms. Its argument consisted of two points: First, that the grower, not Campbell, was the employer, and was therefore responsible for wages and working conditions on the farm; and second, that Campbell did not want to dictate to the growers whether the farm should or should not be unionized. FLOC's position, on the other hand, was that the company had always dictated everything to the growers about the cultivation of produce before (as it had in 1979 by requiring mechanical harvesters), so it would not be unreasonable for Campbell to take responsibility for the work force as well.

Once Campbell began to negotiate with FLOC, however, the company had in effect conceded that it would now assist FLOC in its efforts to organize the farmworkers.[8] The difficulty lay in the method by which this might be accomplished. Campbell could not dictate whether the farmers would or would not negotiate with the workers; nor could it legally negotiate on behalf of the farmers without their approval. Either the farmers would have to confront FLOC directly, as they had in the early 1970s, or designate Campbell as their agent. Both of these options required some form of organization by the growers themselves.

MAY 1985: THE AGREEMENT

Campbell and FLOC ultimately agreed on two critical points: First, a commission would be formed to establish the rules and regulations for the "representation proceedings," in which the farmworkers would determine whether they wanted to be represented by FLOC, by some other agent, or not represented at all. The commission would consist of a chairman and eight independent representatives, four to be nominated by the farmworkers and four by the growers. Campbell would neither participate in nor nominate representatives for the commission. Second, Campbell would help to organize the farmers into one or more "growers associations" for the purpose of collective bargaining with the farmworkers once they had elected a representative.

Dr. John T. Dunlop, former U.S. Secretary of Labor and subsequently Lamont Professor of Business Administration at Harvard, agreed to head the commission. Dunlop had extensive experience in labor issues and was highly regarded by both labor leaders and corporate executives. Other representatives chosen were Douglas Fraser, former president of the United Auto Workers, and Don Paarlberg, former Assistant Secretary of Agriculture.

The agreement was formalized into a "document of understanding" and signed by both Velasquez and Page on May 13, 1985, in time for William Thompson to report to the NCC at the semiannual board meeting on May 16. Both Page and Velasquez had agreed to keep the existence of the document a secret, but neither could control its confidentiality once Thompson had reported to the NCC. (See Exhibit 2 for a copy of a Campbell-prepared outline of the understanding.)

EXHIBIT 2

CAMPBELL-PRODUCED OUTLINE
OF THE CAMPBELL-FLOC UNDERSTANDING

UNDERSTANDING BETWEEN CAMPBELL SOUP COMPANY AND FLOC (OUTLINE)

Under the auspices of the National Council of Churches, Campbell Soup Company and the Farm Labor Organizing Committee (FLOC) have reached an understanding as follows:

A. Commission
  1. A Commission will be formed to find a basis for resolving the controversy. It will:
  (a) Include four representatives of the farmworkers, four representatives of the growers, and an impartial Chairman. Dr. John T. Dunlop, former Secretary of the U.S. Department of Labor and now Lamont University Professor at Harvard University has agree to serve as Chairman;
  (b) Be funded by third-party sources;
  (c) Expire on July 1, 1989, unless its life is extended.
  2. The Commission's responsibilities are to:
  (a) Short range
      —Set rules and regulations for the conduct of representation proceedings among agricultural farmworkers on Ohio and Michigan farms selling tomatoes and cucumbers to Campbell. The representation proceedings could be either a card count or secret ballot elections;
      —Set rules and regulations for the subsequent conduct of collective bargaining between FLOC and growers' associations.
      —Mediate or arbitrate differences that might arise.
  (b) Long range
      —Hold hearings on the purported differences among Campbell, FLOC, and the growers, and make appropriate recommendations;
      —Draft proposed agricultural collective bargaining legislation for Ohio with the cooperation of Campbell, FLOC, and growers' associations, taking into consideration their 1985 experience.
  3. Campbell and FLOC have agreed to cooperate with the Commission.

B. Growers Associations
1. Subject to applicable federal and state law, Campbell will cooperate in the formation of one or more voluntary associations of tomato and cucumber growers in Ohio and in Michigan.
2. Each association will:
   (a) Include more than one but not necessarily all of the growers selling tomatoes to Campbell or cucumbers to Vlasic.
   (b) Accept the Commission's rules and regulations covering representation proceedings and collective bargaining.
3. Campbell will consider the effect of collective bargaining agreements on growers' costs when proposing tomato and cucumber prices.
C. Boycott
1. All boycott and anti-boycott activities will be suspended by FLOC and Campbell from the date of the first representation proceeding through July 1, 1988.
D. Other
1. FLOC will be consulted on Campbell's Ohio programs, e.g., day-care centers, now in place.
2. Both parties waive the statute of limitations as a defense for any actions taken during the term of this understanding.
3. The understanding extends from July 1, 1985, to July 1, 1989.

The NCC adopted a recommendation to assist the commission in its mediation efforts. However, the group also set a timetable: If Campbell and FLOC could not reach a collective bargaining agreement by September 1, 1985, the NCC would once again consider endorsing the FLOC boycott.

JUNE 1985: THE STORY BREAKS

The Ohio Catholic Conference of Bishops did not abide by the NCC timetable. On Monday, June 17, 1985, the bishops, representing Ohio's 2.3 million Catholics, announced its support for the boycott of Campbell products.

On the Friday prior to the bishops' announcement, Scott Rombach, a Campbell spokesman in Ray Page's Corporate Affairs Department, received a call from an Associated Press reporter who said she had received a copy of the "Understanding" from John Nichols, a reporter from the Toledo *Blade*. The AP reporter, Sue Cross, then read portions of the "Understanding" to Rombach, and asked him to comment on the document's official status.

Rombach knew that Nichols had been accompanying Velasquez in the tomato fields as preparation for a feature article on FLOC. He had also heard that a Campbell employee in Ohio had received two copies of the "secret" agreement from farmers in the region, who had said that they were given the documents by Velasquez. Rombach admitted that it was an official document, and both the AP and the Toledo *Blade* ran stories of the confirmation on Sunday, June 16, the day before the Ohio Catholic Conference of Bishops announced their support for the FLOC boycott.

FLOC immediately charged that Campbell had deliberately leaked the story to the press to undermine the effectiveness of the boycott, which appeared to be gaining momentum as a result of the bishops' endorsement. Indeed, Velasquez's earlier fears seemed to be coming true. Two days after the AP story, the Philadelphia *Inquirer* ran a story on the front page of its business section entitled "Campbell boycott will end." The article did, however, contain a statement from FLOC indicating that the boycott would continue until FLOC was recognized as an official bargaining agent for the farmworkers, which would be determined at the representation proceedings later in the summer.

The *Inquirer* ran what amounted to a retraction ("Farm union and Campbell still far apart") later that week, but the damage had been done. FLOC was forced to distribute statements to its membership assuring them that the boycott would continue until a collective bargaining agreement was reached. "The story [in the *Inquirer*] hurt us," conceded Mike Casey, a FLOC spokesman, "but it just means that we have to play hardball with Campbell."[9]

In fact, FLOC had already engaged in "hardball" of a sort two months earlier, when it organized a grass-roots protest of Philadelphia National Bank, which culminated in a demonstration during the bank's annual shareholders' meeting on April 16, 1985. FLOC members picketed the meeting and distributed copies of a "FLOC Annual Report," which dramatized the plight of migrant workers in the Midwest. Although Gordon McGovern was reelected to the CoreStates board, the demonstration successfully drew media attention away from the meeting itself and toward FLOC. Corporate Campaign, Inc., had been instrumental in choreographing this particular play by FLOC.

JULY-AUGUST 1985: PROCEDURES ESTABLISHED

Under the direction of John Dunlop and his commission, the mechanics of conducting representation proceedings were slowly being resolved. Campbell representatives began a series of meetings with tomato and pickle farmers to set up growers associations. The establishment of such associations marked the first formal organization of the farmers for any purpose. Campbell knew that this in itself presented some risk to the company because, once organized, the growers might insist that Campbell negotiate with them for produce contracts. In the highly competitive, low margin food processing industry, this disadvantage could impact sales volume in the long run. Even as things stood, Campbell had assured the growers who joined the association that any additional costs incurred by them as a result of bargaining agreements with the farmworkers would be covered by the company. Still, many tomato farmers were reluctant to join the association, and the pickle growers were unable to form an association at all.[10]

Part of the growers' reluctance stemmed from the politicization of what had started out, in FLOC's early days, as an issue between farmers and the farmworkers they employed. In *The Great Lakes Vegetable Growers News*, Pat Cohill wrote: "While FLOC and Campbell may claim their 'Understanding' was made to try to resolve differences between growers and workers, the truth of the matter is this: THE ISSUE IS *NOT* BETWEEN FARMERS AND FARMWORKERS. It is between certain church leadership, FLOC and Campbell Soup Company."[11]

Many growers felt that by negotiating with FLOC, Campbell strengthened the farmworkers' group and made life more difficult for the majority of growers who employed local labor. Yet because Campbell enjoyed a position of power as a large purchaser of tomatoes, farmers who did not join a growers association did not protest out of fear of reprisal from Campbell.

There were other difficulties as well. A key question facing the commission involved the exact procedure for determining whether the farmworkers wanted to be represented by FLOC in the first place. FLOC, which had spent the summer canvassing the fields to enlist farmworker support, favored a "card check" ballot of all eligible workers to determine whether a majority favored the organizing group. This procedure essentially involved comparing a FLOC-produced membership list against each employer's record of those workers on his farm on a given date. The growers, on the other hand, favored a secret ballot, in which each farmworker would answer "yes" or "no" to the question "Do you wish to be represented by FLOC in collective bargaining negotiations with the growers?"

The growers contended that a card check would be meaningless because they did not believe that the farmworkers understood the FLOC ballot question. FLOC countered that Campbell was trying to control the election because each farmer would be solely responsible for producing a list of his employees, hence for determining voter eligibility, and FLOC viewed the growers as puppets for the company. In addition, many farmers used both migrant and local labor during the harvest season and felt that all of their workers should be eligible to vote. This was not a trivial issue, both because the farmers did not want a "two-tiered" employment structure on their farms and because FLOC, which had naturally concentrated its recruiting efforts on migrant workers, was likely to lose an election in which the majority of the workers were local help.

The commission voted in favor of a secret ballot, to be conducted on a farm-by-farm basis during the upcoming tomato season. FLOC protested the decision, charging that both the farmers and Campbell's ombudsman, Alfredo Carrizales, had used intimidation to prevent farmworkers from registering with FLOC. Campbell advised the farmers and ordered Carrizales to avoid discussing union issues with the farmworkers until the representation proceedings were concluded, but conceded that because of the language barrier and the complexity of the voting procedure, the farmworkers would naturally direct questions to the company's bilingual ombudsman.

SEPTEMBER 1985: THE REPRESENTATION ELECTION

The voting procedure was conducted during the first month of the tomato harvest.[12] During the elections, which took place on thirteen farms, FLOC filed over forty complaints of "unfair labor practices" with the commission, including charges that farmers brought in locals to work the fields on the day of the election and permitted only machine operators, and not hand workers, to vote.

Because of these allegations, the commission did not release the results of the election, calling instead for the growers and FLOC to meet once again on October 14, 1985, to formalize representation procedures for the 1986 season. Privately, it appeared that if all workers were eligible to vote, FLOC would lose the election; if only migrant workers were counted, then FLOC would win by a narrow margin.

Although FLOC was disappointed in the recent turn of events, the group remained committed to its cause. FLOC's Mike Casey, responsible for organizing activities in the Camden-Philadelphia area, said: "Campbell is waiting to see what kind of stuff we're made of. They know we won't go away, and they'll eventually have to get out of the boycott; the only question is how much it will cost them."[13] On August 3, 1985, FLOC had held its annual Constitutional Convention in Toledo, Ohio. Cesar Chavez, the president of the California-based United Farm Workers union, was the keynote speaker. Chavez encouraged FLOC to continue to press for workers' rights, and a resolution was passed to pursue affiliation between FLOC and the UFW. By October, Casey and other FLOC members were making plans to begin a grass-roots organizing campaign in California where Campbell buys much of its produce. FLOC also planned a demonstration at Campbell's upcoming shareholders' meeting on November 22.

NOVEMBER 1985: BACK TO THE FUTURE

R. Gordon McGovern turned his automobile into Campbell Place and parked in his reserved space in the executive parking garage. He walked through the main reception area, past the exhibit displaying a century of Campbell memorabilia—the original soup label, the first Campbell kids, pictures of generations of mothers ladling out soup on a wintry day, and so forth. As McGovern entered his office, he thought about John T. Dorrance, the young chemist who first canned condensed tomato soup in 1899. McGovern could not help wondering whether the tomato, which had been a symbol of strength for the company for a hundred years, had somehow been turned into a symbol of weakness. Nonetheless, he contemplated the company's next move in its ongoing dispute with FLOC.

NOTES

1. Generally speaking, farmers in the region devote only about 10 percent of their arable land to the tomato crop.
2. Campbell and FLOC dispute the impact of mechanization. Campbell maintains that the actual impact of their mandate was not as drastic as it might seem. In 1978, 40 percent of the crop was already being harvested mechanically; even before the strike, Campbell had been urging its growers to switch, both because it was more economical in the long run and because Campbell was currently supplying a different type of seedling for hand and mechanical harvesting, which made crop consistency more difficult. FLOC also contends that the mechanization is not as critical as it might seem, but for different reasons. The group says that the harvesters are ineffective in rain and mud, that the machines miss the corners of the fields, and that, under the time pressure of the harvest, farmers resort to the reliability of hand labor, often only keeping the machines to satisfy Campbell.
3. James Wall, quoting the OCC in "Campbell Boycott Decision Nears," *Christian Century* (November 7, 1984), p. 1027.
4. Neither group directly endorsed FLOC as the legal representatives of the farmworkers, but merely supported the cause for which FLOC was fighting. In fact, the OCC never even mentioned FLOC by name in its 1982 boycott resolution.
5. *Brandel v. United States*, U.S. District Court, Western District of Michigan, Southern Division, 83-1228. The decision was upheld on appeal, to the Sixth Circuit Court of Appeals.
6. FLOC's main contention on this issue is that if the wage structure were not so depressed, the migrant families would not have to press their children into service in order to survive. Campbell's view, on the other hand, is that the *Brandel* decision refers specifically to pickles, which are harvested differently from tomatoes. First, pickles grow very rapidly; one acre can add a ton of weight overnight. Because consumers prefer a smaller pickle (although size does not affect the taste), this means that pickles must be harvested quickly. Second, pickles are more difficult to harvest than tomatoes, and they must be picked by hand. Both of these factors favor a piece-rate over an hourly wage, which was central to the judge's reasoning in *Brandel*.
7. An eighth farm has since built the housing; eight other farms continue to employ migrants without housing them. No similar program has been instituted for pickle farms, although state standards must still be met. Enforcement of state standards, however, remains difficult. According to FLOC spokesman Mike Casey, pickle farms contracted by Vlasic still have the same "subhuman, ramshackle conditions that workers have endured for the last 100 years." Campbell concedes that housing on pickle farms is still a problem, but has not directly intervened as it did on the tomato farms.
8. FLOC, as its full name makes clear, is an "organizing committee." It is not a union, but is merely trying to create one.
9. Campbell stands by its story that it was Velasquez who originally and deliberately leaked the document to *Blade* reporter Nichols and local farmers; the company only operated under the ground rules that Ray Page had spelled out when negotiations first began.
10. Because most pickle farmers also raise other crops, many of which are equally or more lucrative, many farmers would rather abandon pickles entirely than face the risk of an organized labor force. Nevertheless, Campbell intended to continue its efforts to organize the pickle growers in 1986.

11. Pat Cohill, writing a guest editorial for *The Great Lakes Vegetable Growers News*, December 1985.
12. Because the pickle farmers had refused to form a growers association, a non-binding "straw vote" was conducted on thirteen of the sixty pickle farms. FLOC won convincingly, but real representation proceedings were not scheduled until 1986. Even so, FLOC contends that Campbell "denied over 600 workers" on nineteen pickle farms from participating in the election process.
13. Although the Understanding signed in May called for FLOC to cease boycott activity once representation proceedings began, the clause was void if FLOC charged Campbell with unfair labor practices, which is exactly what FLOC did.